Y0-CDQ-790

Parks and Protected Areas in Canada

Planning and Management

Rob Davis
Senior Ecologist
Ontario Parks

 Ontario

Ministry of Natural Resources
300 Water Street
Peterborough ON K9J 8M5
Tel: 705 755-1731
Fax: 705 755-1701
E-mail: Rob.Davis@mnr.gov.on.ca
Website: www.ontarioparks.com

Edited by

Philip Dearden and Rick Rollins

OXFORD
UNIVERSITY PRESS

OXFORD
UNIVERSITY PRESS

70 Wynford Drive, Don Mills, Ontario M3C 1J9
www.oup.com/ca

Oxford University Press is a department of the University of Oxford.
It furthers the University's objective of excellence in research, scholarship,
and education by publishing worldwide in

Oxford New York

Auckland Bangkok Buenos Aires Cape Town Chennai

Dar es Salaam Delhi Hong Kong Istanbul Karachi Kolkata

Kuala Lumpur Madrid Melbourne Mexico City Mumbai Nairobi

São Paulo Shanghai Singapore Taipei Tokyo Toronto

with an associated company in Berlin

Oxford is a trade mark of Oxford University Press
in the UK and in certain other countries

Published in Canada by Oxford University Press

Copyright © Oxford University Press Canada 2002

The moral rights of the author have been asserted

Database right Oxford University Press (maker)

First published 2002

All rights reserved. No part of this publication may be reproduced,
stored in a retrieval system, or transmitted, in any form or by any means,
without the prior permission in writing of Oxford University Press,
or as expressly permitted by law, or under terms agreed with the appropriate
reprographics rights organization. Enquiries concerning reproduction
outside the scope of the above should be sent to the Rights Department,
Oxford University Press, at the address above.

You must not circulate this book in any other binding or cover
and you must impose this same condition on any acquirer.

National Library of Canada Cataloguing in Publication Data

Main entry under title:
Parks and protected areas in Canada : planning and management

2nd ed.

Includes bibliography references and index.
ISBN 0-19-541601-5

1. National parks and reserves–Canada–Management.
2. Natural areas–Canada–Management.
3. Wilderness areas–Canada–Management. I.Dearden, Philip II. Rollins, Rick

QH77.C3P37 2002   333.78'3'0971   C2002-900637-6

Cover design: Brett Miller
Text design: Valentino Sanna, Ignition Design and Communications

1 2 3 4 - 05 04 03 02
This book is printed on permanent (acid-free) paper ∞.
Printed in Canada

Contents

List of Figures

List of Tables

List of Boxes

Contributors

Jim Butler is Professor of Parks, Wildlife, and Conservation Biology in the Renewable Resources Department of the University of Alberta. As a conservation scientist active in the management and protection of threatened parks, nature reserves, and wildlife species throughout the world, he works with the World Wildlife Fund, the IUCN (World Conservation Union) and the International Council on Bird Preservation (ICBP). His work has taken him on projects to Europe, Indonesia, China, Australia, Thailand, New Zealand, Central and South America, the Caribbean, Africa, and the Soviet Union.

Philip Dearden is Professor of Geography at the University of Victoria. He is a member of the World Commission on Protected Areas of IUCN and has been active in the planning and management of protected areas in many different countries. He is the co-author of *Environmental Change and Challenge: A Canadian Perspective*, also published by Oxford.
E-MAIL: pdearden@office.geog.uvic.ca

Jessica Dempsey is a Geography student at the University of Victoria.
E-MAIL: dempsey@uvic.ca

Paul Eagles is Professor in the Department of Recreation and Leisure Studies at the University of Waterloo. He has extensive experience in many aspects of parks' planning and management gained through work in more than 20 countries. Currently he is Chair of the Tourism Task Force for the World Commission in Protected Areas, a commission of the World Conservation Union (IUCN).
E-MAIL: eagles@healthy.uwaterloo.ca

Glen Hvenegaard is Associate Professor in the Department of Geography at Augustana University College in Camrose, Alberta where he teaches environmental studies, physical geography, and parks and wilderness. His research interests include ecotourism, park management, and environmental education. He is a member of the World Commission on Protected Areas of IUCN and is active with Leadership for Environment and Development (LEAD) International.
E-MAIL: hveng@marcello.augustana.ab.ca

Kevin McNamee was one of the 21 original signatories of the Canadian Wilderness Charter in 1989, served as the federal endangered spaces co-ordinator with the Canadian Nature Federation from 1989 to 2000 with a focus on completing Canada's national park system, and is now on leave to Parks Canada as its Director for Park Establishment. E-MAIL: kevin_mcnamee@pch.gc.ca

J. Gordon Nelson is Professor Emeritus in the Department of Geography at the University of Waterloo with particular interests in landscape planning and human ecology.

Per Nilsen as Head, Human Use Management and Public Safety for Parks Canada, integrates social science research into planning, management, and decision-making for national parks, historic sites, and marine conservation areas. E-MAIL: Per_Nilsen@pch.gc.ca

Bob Payne is a Professor in the Department of Outdoor Recreation and Tourism at Lakehead University, with special interests in human use management in protected areas. E-MAIL: rjpayne@flash.lakeheadu.ca

Juri Peepre is the Executive Director of the Yukon Chapter of the Canadian Parks and Wilderness Society and regional co-ordinator for World Wildlife Fund Canada. He has been consulted on protected areas, wilderness, recreation, and conservation issues in western and northern Canada since 1981. In 1998, Mr. Peepre was appointed to the Minister's Panel on the Ecological Integrity of Canada's National Parks. E-MAIL: peepre@yknet.yk.ca

Dave Robinson is a faculty member in the Department of Recreation and Tourism at Malaspina University College. His teaching and research interests involve sustainable tourism and the social dimensions of forest management in Canada.

Rick Rollins is both a faculty member in the Department of Recreation and Tourism at Malaspina University College and an adjunct faculty member in the Department of Geography at the University of Victoria. His teaching and research deals with recreation behaviour and management in natural settings. E-MAIL: rollins@mala.bc.ca

Scott Slocombe is Professor of Geography and Environmental Studies at Wilfrid Laurier University. His research and teaching focus is on regional environmental planning, and sustainability, including protected areas, regional planning, environmental assessment, and systems approaches.

Guy Swinnerton is Professor of Parks and Protected Areas in the Faculty of Physical Education and Recreation at the University of Alberta, Edmonton. His research interests focus on parks and protected areas policy, planning, and management; the stewardship of heritage resources within working landscapes; and countryside planning and outdoor recreation environments. He served as a member of the Scientific Review Committee for the Banff-Bow Valley Study and was the academic representative on the Provincial Co-ordinating Committee for the Alberta Special Places Program. E-MAIL: guy.swinnerton@ualberta.ca

Jeanette Theberge is a wildlife ecologist studying grizzly bears in pursuit of her Ph.D. at the University of Calgary.

John Theberge is a wildlife ecologist specializing in wolves and predator-prey relationships. He taught at the University of Waterloo for 30 years and has been active in the establishment and ecologically-based management of wilderness parks in Canada. He received the Harkin Award from the Canadian Parks and Wilderness Society for his contribution to protected areas in Canada.
E-MAIL: johnmarythe@telus.net

Stephen Woodley is an ecologist, and is currently Chief Ecosystem Scientist with Parks Canada. He works on a number of issues related to protected areas, including developing techniques for the monitoring and assessing of ecological integrity, ecological restoration, and sustainable forestry.
E-MAIL: Stephen_Woodley@pch.gc.ca

Pamela Wright is a resource and environmental management specialist in both the social and ecological sciences with undergraduate degrees from Lakehead University in northern Ontario and graduate degrees (M.Sc. and Ph.D.) from the School of Natural Resources at Ohio State University. She has been vice-chair of the Panel on the Ecological Integrity of Canada's National Parks and is currently working with the US Forest Service on a research exchange program where she co-ordinates the USFS initiatives for forest-level sustainability monitoring in the US and internationally. She serves as a national trustee to the Canadian Parks and Wilderness Society. E-MAIL: pwright@island.net

Foreword

Ten years ago, when I wrote the foreword to the first edition of this book, I felt a real sense of urgency about protecting wilderness in Canada. I still do.

In the late 1980's Canada's signature forest, the boreal, was the subject of an astounding onslaught. From British Columbia to Newfoundland, hundreds of thousands of square kilometres of this landscape of lakes and rivers, caribou and lichens, songbirds and forests were allocated to logging companies for the production of toilet paper, newsprint, chopsticks, and particle board. Soon after the assault on boreal wilderness, the discovery of diamonds extended this trend out onto the tundra. Lust for diamonds led to the staking of the entire Slave geological province of the Canadian Shield—from Great Slave Lake to the Beaufort Sea. Oil and gas exploration pushed deeper into northern Alberta and British Columbia. Cod stocks collapsed along the east coast, and many west coast salmon stocks went into precipitous decline. The Great Whale hydroelectric megaproject was on track to destroy thousands of kilometres of northern Quebec. An open pit copper mine and road threatened the pristine Tatshenshini Valley in northwestern British Columbia. The discovery of nickel at Voisey's Bay set off a staking frenzy in Labrador. Had it continued, this feverish pace of destruction would have largely eliminated unprotected wilderness from Canada by now.

Even our protected areas were not safe 10 years ago. In national parks, clear-cut logging marred forests in Wood Buffalo and a commercial development boom underway in Banff threatened to spread to other parks. Logging continued in Ontario's Algonquin Provincial Park and in Manitoba's wilderness parks. Alberta's Willmore Wilderness Park lay open to oil and gas development.

But some things have changed for the better. The pace of development of wild areas has abated somewhat. Megaprojects and subsidized resource extraction have fallen out of favour. Commodity prices, especially for mineral products, have collapsed. The Endangered Spaces campaign placed wilderness protection on the agenda of every government in Canada as the public voiced its concern for protecting wildlands. Market pressure stopped the Great Whale hydro-electric project. An international campaign protected the Tatshenshini. A public campaign to stop commercial development in Banff largely succeeded. Litigation stopped logging in Wood Buffalo. Efforts to protect areas resulted in many new parks in British Columbia, Manitoba, Ontario, and Nova Scotia and a few gains in other provinces. Canada's National Parks Act has been amended to ensure the primacy of ecological integrity in park management and to allow caps to be placed on commercial development. Recognition of First Nations land claims has also improved conservation in some areas.

So things are not quite as bleak today as I feared 10 years ago they would be. We have had a bit of a breather. But I do not mean to imply that all is well. Logging continues in Algonquin and some Manitoba parks, development pressures still simmer in Banff and Jasper, and climate change and airborne pollutants menace the country, especially the high Arctic. The Atlantic salmon is in trouble and the number of endangered species continues to rise. Oil and gas roads and wells continue to spread northward from Alberta, where over 10,000 wells per year are drilled. But on the positive side, vast swaths of the boreal forest still stand intact, temperate old-growth forests can still be protected on the west coast and much of the Arctic is still wild. The remaining wild pockets of southern Canada can be protected, restored, expanded, and woven back together.

Parks and protected areas remain our best tool for saving wildlife and wilderness. Yet recent findings of conservation biologists have taught us they alone will not suffice to save Nature. Large, core, protected, wilderness areas must be linked together and buffered by non-intensive land uses across the landscape. Our highways and railways must be designed to enable wildlife, as well as people, to move safely on their travels. The Yellowstone to Yukon Conservation Initiative, begun in 1993, has shown that a bold vision of protected areas, woven together through wildlife movement corridors across a vast landscape, can excite the public imagination, meet human needs, and achieve such tangible conservation results as the six-million-hectare Muskwa-Kechika Management Area in northern British Columbia. The idea has spread to inspire the Algonquin-to-Adirondacks and Baja-to-Bering-Sea Initiatives.

The best hope for the future of wilderness and wildlife in Canada is the Canadian people. However, we also pose the biggest threat to them if our past actions continue into the future. But they need not. Canada has changed. We are no longer primarily hewers of wood and drawers of water. Canada is a sophisticated, multi-cultural, knowledge-based society. While vast amounts of the country have already been dedicated to resource extraction, much wilderness remains. The question before us at the dawn of the twenty-first century is whether we continue down the path of environmental destruction that characterizes all nations of the industrialized world, or we develop a new vision and chart a different course for our future.

It is time for a new national dream, one that embraces wilderness and wildlife as a central part of Canadian civilization. Our artists, from Emily Carr and the Group of Seven to modern Haida and Inuit sculptors and printmakers, have intuitively honoured wilderness values, but we must do more as a nation. We need to invest some of our vast creativity and financial resources in a national effort for wildness. Such a course would distinguish us globally, satisfy us ethically, and enrich us spiritually. Canadians will not be a truly great people worthy of this great land if we squander the opportunity to lead the world in this most fulfilling and altogether fitting way.

Harvey Locke
Vice President, Conservation
Canadian Parks and Wilderness Society and
President, The Wildlands Project
Cambridge, Massachusetts
February 2001

Overview

These good people to whom the park is also dedicated were the tourists there down in the sunlit valley, driving by the little box of my cabin and the toy horses in their corral. Clouds of smoke billowed up to the cabin, as lines of cars and tour buses drove past the sign that says NO THROUGH ROAD, to the campground where they stopped, each in turn, to stare blankly at the end of the conquered world—a place where you actually cannot drive a motor vehicle.

Sid Marty, *Men for the Mountains*

Part I, overview, sets the stage for specific issues pursued in subsequent chapters. We begin by asking, 'Why have parks and protected areas? What scientific, ethical, aesthetic, spiritual, or other reasons have been used to rationalize our passionate feeling about these special places? Chapter 1 reveals many reasons for protecting natural areas and the many benefits realized from existing parks.

From a historical perspective the Canadian vision for parks has changed over time (Chapter 2). In the early days parks were viewed mainly as playgrounds or tourist attractions set in exotic natural surroundings. Over the past century this view has changed, to a large extent because the amount of wilderness or undeveloped landscape in Canada has been drastically reduced. As a consequence of this historical evolution of thinking about why we need parks, the style or approach to management has varied considerably. Hence, in the past 20 years we have seen revisions to parks legislation, park policies, and park regulations. In short, we have been agonizing over, 'How should parks be managed?' The present view places a much higher emphasis on ecological integrity. However, the legacy of past thinking remains. We still have town sites in Banff, Jasper, and Riding Mountain National Parks. We condone alpine skiing, golfing, hunting, and other questionable recreation activities in some parks. Logging occurs in the heart of Algonquin Provincial Park in Ontario, as does mining in the heart of Strathcona Provincial Park in BC. These park management decisions were made in the past when we viewed parks differently. To make sense of these apparent contradictions in the context of thinking about parks, one needs an appreciation for the history of parks as provided in Chapter 2.

The importance of parks to Canadians raises other questions: 'How many parks are needed?' and 'Where should they be located?' These issues are taken up in Chapter 3, which describes the Endangered Spaces Campaign in Canada. This campaign asserted that a major purpose of parks is to protect the variety of natural phenomena—biodiversity—characteristic of the Canadian landscape. In order to achieve this objective, it was determined that cores of parks and protected areas were needed in the various natural regions of the country. The academic base of the campaign was not hard to establish; what was truly remarkable was the development of political strategies to make this process a reality.

CHAPTER 1

The Times They Are Still A-Changin'

Philip Dearden & Rick Rollins

INTRODUCTION

Come senators, congressmen
Please heed the call
Don't stand in the doorway
Don't block up the hall
For he that gets hurt
Will be he who has stalled
There's a battle
Outside and it's ragin'
It'll soon shake your windows
And rattle your walls
For the times they are a-changin'.

Bob Dylan, 1963
The Times They Are A-Changin'

This book encapsulates Canadian practices in protected area designation and management. It is intended to provide a background for students undertaking courses in the area, or any others seeking an overview. When the first edition of this book appeared in 1993, major new initiatives were afoot with the federal government's Green Plan, agreement between the federal and provincial governments to establish 12 per cent of the country as protected area, commitment to complete the national park system and establish five marine parks by 2000, and a new national parks policy (about to be released). In retrospect, perhaps it was inevitable that such an ambitious list could not be completed. However, some progress has been made.

CHANGING PARKS

At the beginning of the 1990s much of the concern and emphasis regarding protected areas in Canada was on system expansion. The federal and most provincial systems appeared to be making little progress in designating additional protected areas. Canada was well short of the 12 per cent figure recommended by the World Commission on

Environment and Development (WCED, 1987) as an international target for the amount of land to be included in protected areas as part of the overall quest for 'sustainable development'. Major environmental protests were generated across the country from Gwaii Hanaas to Temagami in an effort to persuade decision-makers to establish more protected areas. Politicians responded and the promises came thick and fast. Unfortunately, few of those promises were kept, although system expansion has occurred at unprecedented rates. Since 1992, approximately 25 million hectares have been added to the Canadian parks system (Federal Provincial Parks Council, 2000), protecting more than twice as much landscape—yielding a total protected area about the size of the UK. From 1989, the percentage of protected terrestrial lands went from 2.95 per cent to 6.84 per cent, an increase of 3.89 per cent.

Only one jurisdiction in the country has achieved the 12 per cent (BC, in November 2000), although several provinces are to be congratulated on the dramatic increases in their provincial park systems (Chapter 3). We are also a long way from completing the national park system, a goal that was supposed to have been achieved by the end of the last century. Of Parks Canada's 39 natural regions, 14 still are not represented by a national park. The current system of 39 parks covers about 2.5 per cent of the total landscape. Nonetheless, some new parks have been created and several more are in advanced planning stages (Chapter 9). Even less progress has been made on the marine front. Bill C10, the Act to create a system of National Marine Conservation Areas (NMCAs) was before Parliament again in 2001. At the moment there is only one bona fide national marine protected area, the Saguenay, and the Fathom Five dive site on Lake Huron (Chapter 14). There are other national parks with a marine component, but often they are small, not fully representative of the marine biodiversity in the area, and even if we count them, 24 of the 29 National Marine Conservation Areas still lack representation.

Of perhaps more significance than system expansion over this last decade has been the widespread environmental degradation occurring in existing protected areas. The 1988 amendments to the National Parks Act stated that 'maintenance of ecological integrity through the protection of natural resources shall be the first priority when considering Park zoning and visitor use in a management plan'. Parks Canada brought out their new policy in 1994 that unequivocally expounded 'Protecting ecological integrity and ensuring commemorative integrity take precedence in acquiring, managing and administering heritage places and programs. In every application of policy, this guiding principle is paramount' (Ministry of Supply and Services, 1994: 16). However, at both the park (Wipond and Dearden, 1998) and system level (Auditor General, 1996), it was abundantly clear this was not happening. The 1997 State of the Parks Report (Parks Canada, 1998) found only one of 39 national parks, Vuntut, that was judged to have its ecology intact. Others had suffered greatly through environmental changes largely external to the park, such as forestry, mining, and agriculture on adjacent lands, and from practices within the parks, such as excessive tourism development (Figure 1.1). Thirty-one parks reported ecological stresses from significant to severe, and in 13 parks these stresses had increased in intensity since 1992.

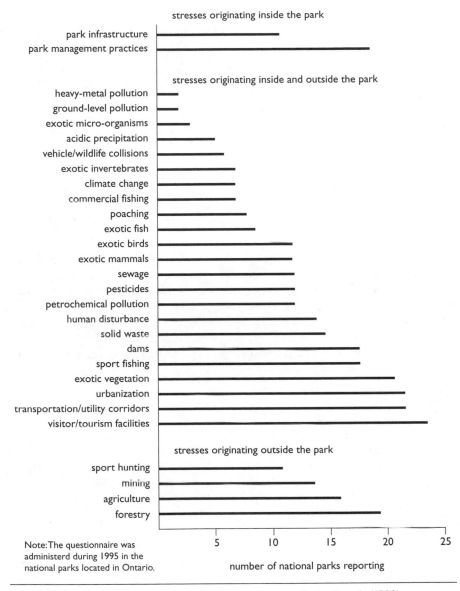

stresses originating inside the park

park infrastructure
park management practices

stresses originating inside and outside the park

heavy-metal pollution
ground-level pollution
exotic micro-organisms
acidic precipitation
vehicle/wildlife collisions
exotic invertebrates
climate change
commercial fishing
poaching
exotic fish
exotic birds
exotic mammals
sewage
pesticides
petrochemical pollution
human disturbance
solid waste
dams
sport fishing
exotic vegetation
urbanization
transportation/utility corridors
visitor/tourism facilities

stresses originating outside the park

sport hunting
mining
agriculture
forestry

Note: The questionnaire was
administerd during 1995 in the
national parks located in Ontario.

5   10   15   20   25

number of national parks reporting

FIGURE 1.1 Sources of stress on national parks. SOURCE: Parks Canada (1998).

In 1994, the Minister, concerned about the decline in environmental quality of Banff, Canada's first national park, struck a Task Force to examine the problem and report not only on Banff, but on the regional context of the entire Banff-Bow Valley corridor. The Task Force held extensive consultations involving 14 different interests

> ## BOX 1.1 Summary of Key Findings of the Panel on Ecological Integrity
>
> - The biggest single challenge facing Parks Canada in the protection of ecological integrity is the internal restructuring that is required to ensure that all aspects of the organization support this mandate.
> - The entire planning process needs revising to place ecological integrity at its core.
> - Parks Canada lacks capacity in both the natural and social sciences to effectively manage for ecological integrity.
> - Greater attention to active management is required to restore ecological processes and species to many parks.
> - Inventory, research, and monitoring are essential tools for assessing and understanding ecological integrity.
> - A process of healing is required to develop trust and respect between Aboriginal peoples and Parks Canada.
> - There is need to develop a comprehensive national protected area strategy that folds the various conservation initiatives into an integrated system.
>   Protected area systems need to be managed on a greater ecosystem basis.
>   Interpretation is a vital role of parks and needs reviving.
> - Human use is a valid component of park use, but has not been managed effectively.
> - The built environment of the parks must reflect sound environmental principles.
> - Parks Canada needs greater management and financial support to be able to achieve its mandate.
>
> SOURCE: Parks Canada Agency (2000).

sectors, conducted public meetings in many cities across the country, and received 261 written submissions. The Minister, the Honourable Sheila Copps, accepted all the recommendations from the stakeholder group (Banff-Bow Valley Study, 1996) and took immediate measures to implement them (Chapter 10). However, the fact that such informed opinion had found Banff to be so seriously at risk, acted as a canary in a mine. In response to the inevitable questions regarding the ecological integrity of all the other parks in the system, the Minister struck a blue-ribbon panel to advise her on the topic and to make recommendations regarding remedial measures (Chapter 9). The panel made many recommendations with far-reaching implications for Parks Canada and the way in which the parks are managed. Their report (Parks Canada Agency, 2000) is essential reading for anyone interested in park management. Some of its more important recommendations are outlined in Box 1.1.

Although the Minister was quick to accept the recommendations of the panel, it remains to be seen how well they will be implemented. Some require fundamental changes in the way that Parks Canada functions as a culture and as an Agency, others require substantial funding. Whether the bureaucratic and political will exists to effectively answer the challenge will not be apparent for some years. However, one main recommendation, for a new Canada National Parks Act (Bill C27), has already been enacted. This Act makes it clear that ecological integrity is the prime factor underlying all aspects of Parks Canada's operations. Management plans, for example, must contain a 'long-term ecological vision for the park, a set of ecological integrity objectives and indicators and provisions for resource protection and restoration, zoning, visitor use, public awareness and performance evaluation.' The new Act formally established seven new parks, raised poaching fines, and established a legislative framework for park communities. The Act should also assist in the designation of new parks through simplified establishment and enlargement procedures.

In addition to passing the Act, the Minister also released several other decisions that auger well for protecting park environments in the future. The released management plans for Jasper, Waterton Lakes, Yoho, and Kootenay display strong adherence to the principles outlined by the Panel on Ecological Integrity. The plans enacted regulations made possible by the 1988 amendments to the National Parks Act that allowed for the formal designation of wilderness areas within parks, but that had never been implemented. Over 90 per cent of the Rocky Mountain National Parks area was protected as wilderness, and in future, as management plans are revised for other parks, wilderness zones also will be legislated. Another decision was made relating to the long-standing challenge of planning and managing the ski areas in national parks. Again, the thrust of the recommendations (Box 1.2) should convey a higher level of environmental protection.

Amidst all these shifts, the senior park agency in the country, Parks Canada, has also seen significant changes. One of the most devastating has been the decline in government support. Agency funding fell by 25 per cent between 1994/5 and 1998/9 at the same time as the system was increasing in size and management problems were becoming more acute. This pressure no doubt contributed to the greater emphasis placed on cost recovery and income generation in the parks, along with pronounced reductions in manpower and other resources available. Many other park agencies in Canada have felt similar pressures. In BC, the number of parks has doubled since 1991, yet since 1994 the Ministry of Environment, Lands and Parks has seen a 50 per cent cut in its operating budget. In 1985 the parks budget represented 0.5 per cent of the provincial budget. By 1998, this funding had shrunk to 0.15 per cent.

Considering the sensitivity of politicians to re-election, the funding figures suggest that public support for parks in Canada is languishing. Nothing could be further from the truth. An Environics poll in September 2000 found that 79 per cent of Canadians agree that they are 'currently very upset about threats to nature and natural ecosystems in Canada' and 40 per cent remain dissatisfied with the shortage of park and wilderness areas in the country (Environics International, 2000). Nature is also big business in Canada. A survey of the importance of nature to Canadians (Federal-Provincial-Territorial Task Force on the Importance of Nature to Canadians, 1999) showed that in 1996 20 million Canadians took part in one or more nature-related activities and spent $11 billion on trip-related items, increased from $6 billion

BOX 1.2 Planning and Management of National Park Ski Areas

In the four mountain national parks—

- Capacity limits will be permanently capped through updated long range plans finalized with ski area operators within two years. Any consideration of capacity increases will be limited by industry standards and the principle of no net negative environmental impact;
- There will be no new ski runs or expansion of existing runs, and no significant terrain modification, including glading. Replacement or upgrading of ski lifts will be considered provided capacity limits are not exceeded and tree removal is minimized;
- No expansion beyond existing parking lot foothills will be considered. Offsetting parking pressures through public transit for skiers will be required;
- No new facilities will be considered. The commercial areas will be permanently capped through updated long-range plans, to be finalized within two years. Prior to finalizing new long-range plans, consideration for replacement or upgrading of existing facilities will be limited to existing footprints.

In addition, the following conditions will apply to all ski area proposals:

- Ski area policy will be regulated under the *National Parks Act* and the management of ski areas will continue to be screened through the principle of no net negative environmental impact,
- Any expansion of existing facilities considered through a long-range plan will be restricted to previously disturbed areas, permit no tree cutting, uphold the highest environmental management systems standards and basic design standards appropriate for the approved ski area capacity limit.

in 1991. Almost 44 per cent of Canadians surveyed participated in one or more of 17 specified outdoor activities in natural areas. Over half of these participants visited national or provincial parks or other protected areas for these activities.

One response to the declining government support was for Parks Canada to become a separate Agency with its own Act (Parks Canada Agency Act) and to be given more autonomy and flexibility than accorded departments within government ministries. Changes include the ability to hold over funds from year to year to enable a more efficient long-term financial strategy, revenue retention and reinvestment, more flexible employer status designations, and a non-lapsing account to finance the establishment of new parks. Section 8.1 of the Act also provides for greater accountability by requiring that the Minister convene a round table, at least every two years, of persons interested in matters for which the Agency is responsible to advise the Minister on the performance by the Agency.

TABLE 1.1 Protected Area Values with Suggested Allegories

Value	Allegory
aesthetic	art gallery
wildlife viewing	zoo
historical	museum
spiritual	cathedral
recreation	playground
tourism	factory
education	schoolroom
science	laboratory
the 'extra'ordinary	movie theatre
ecological capital	bank
ecological processes	hospital
ecological benchmarks	museum

SOURCE: P. Dearden (1995).

CHANGING PARADIGMS

Parks are not an end in and of themselves but rather a means towards an end. That end is to retain certain values in the landscape that otherwise might not survive due to the dominance of market evaluations in resource allocation. Some of these values are depicted in Table 1.1 as different buildings in a city and illustrates that protected areas are not 'single use' areas any more than all the building functions could be united into one.

- *Art gallery*: Many parks were so designated for their scenic beauty, which is still a major attraction for people who visit parks.
- *Zoo*: As one component of the art gallery, parks are usually places to more easily watch wildlife in relatively natural surroundings. Most park wildlife is protected from hunting and is not as shy of humans as wildlife outside of parks.
- *Playground*: Parks provide excellent recreational settings for many outdoor pursuits.
- *Theatre*: Like a movie or play, parks are able to transport us into a different setting from our everyday existence. An excellent treatise on this topic is *Mountains Without Handrails* by Sax (1980).
- *Cathedral*: Many people derive spiritual fulfillment from nature, just as others go to human-built structures, such as churches, temples, and mosques. Such sites help us, irrespective of denomination, to appreciate, the existence of forces more powerful than ourselves and remind us that humility is a virtue.
- *Factory*: The first national parks in Canada were designated with the idea of generating income through tourism. Since these early beginnings, the economic role of parks has been recognized, although it has become controversial due to the potential for conflict with most of the parks' other roles. A study by Eagles et al. (2000) on national parks, wildlife areas, and provincial parks in Canada calculated an economic impact of between $120.47 to $187.69 per person per day of park use.

Over the year the economic impact was between $13.9 and $21.6 billion dollars.

- *Museum*: Parks protect the landscape to appear as it might have when European colonists first arrived in North America, thus acting as museums to remind us of their pristine state. Nash (1967), in his well-known history of the wilderness movement, attests this to be a main reason behind the early growth of the parks movement in the US, although it is certainly a less prominent motivation now. These museums also provide areas against which to measure ecological change in the rest of the landscape.
- *Bank*: Parks are places in which we store and protect our ecological capital, including threatened and endangered species (see Dearden, 2000 for a review of the role of Canadian National Parks in this regard). From these 'accounts' we can withdraw the 'interest' to repopulate other areas with species that have disappeared. For example, the musk oxen from the Thelon Game Sanctuary have recolonized terrain outside the Sanctuary, and the elk and bison from Elk Island National Park outside Edmonton have been used to start herds elsewhere.
- *Hospital*: Ecosystems are not static and isolated phenomena but are linked throughout the planet. Protected areas constitute some of the few places where natural processes still operate in a relatively unimpeded manner. As such, they may be considered 'hospitals' that help maintain ecosystem processes. To illustrate: much attention, is now focused on the carbon cycle as imbalances among components caused by rapid mobilization of fossil fuels by human activity helps contribute to global warming. Forests are major carbon 'sinks' where carbon dioxide is taken in from the atmosphere and stored in organic form. Thus, forests that are protected play a major role in maintaining some balance in the carbon cycle.
- *Laboratory*: As relatively natural landscapes, parks provide outdoor 'laboratories' for scientists to unravel the mysteries of nature. For example, Killarney Provincial Park in Ontario provided important opportunities for early research on acid precipitation in Canada.
- *Schoolroom*: Parks can play a major role in education as outdoor classrooms. Direct physical contact with the complexities of the natural environment help teach facts as well as inspire awe, humility, and respect.

Many of the values that we seek from parks do not compete effectively in the market place. We call them 'market failures', despite the fact that they relate to values that we hold most dear in life, such as spirituality, beauty, learning, freedom, recreation, and stimulation. If these values are protected by market allocation it is usually by coincidence rather than by design. Markets give scant attention to the outcomes affecting tomorrow, compared with the material gains of today, and even less attention to the good of society overall compared with the returns to individuals.

Realization of these fundamental human weaknesses was one of the mainsprings of the move to set aside protected areas over a hundred years ago, beginning with Yellowstone National Park in the US. As time has passed, so has the wisdom of the initiative appreciated. Environmental degradation outside these systems has continued apace and now spills over into the parks. On a global scale, humans have appropriated

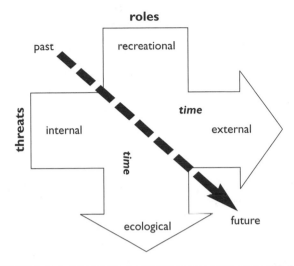

FIGURE 1.2 The changing emphasis in park roles over time.

over 40 per cent of the planet's net primary productivity for support of just their own species (Vitousaek et al., 1997). The other 15 million or so species must either struggle to exist in ecosystems that are manipulated to support human resource extraction, or be confined to the ever-decreasing amount of natural ecosystem remaining. If this is the case now, what will be the situation by the end of this century when it is predicted that the human population will have doubled?

The World Conservation Union (IUCN, 2000) reports that an increasing number of species are in danger of extinction. A total of 11,046 species of plants and animals are threatened, facing a high risk of extinction in the near future, in almost all cases as a result of human activities. This includes 24 per cent (one in four) of mammal species and 12 per cent (one in eight) of bird species. The total number of threatened animal species has increased from 5,205 to 5,435 since 1996. Given this situation it is little surprise that although protected areas are set aside to protect many values that both globally and nationally ecological values now are being given high priority in management (Figure 1.2).

The World Commission on Protected Areas (WCPA) of IUCN defines a protected area as 'an area of land and/or sea especially dedicated to the protection and maintenance of biological diversity,[1] and of natural and associated cultural resources, and managed through legal or other effective means.' (IUCN, 1996). However, just as pro-

---

[1] Biological diversity is often shortened to 'biodiversity', meaning the variety of life forms that inhabit the earth. Biodiversity includes the genetic diversity among members of a population or species as well as the diversity of species and ecosystems.

TABLE 1.2 IUCN Categories of Protected Areas

Category	Description
I Strict protection	Strict Nature Reserve(a)/ Wilderness Area(b)
II Ecosystem conservation and recreation	National Park
III Conservation of natural features	Natural Monument
IV Conservation through active management	Habitat/Species Management Area
V Landscape/seascape conservation and recreation	Protected Landscape/Seascape
VI Sustainable use of natural ecosystems	Managed Resource Protected Area

SOURCE: IUCN (1994).

TABLE 1.3 Matrix of Management Objectives and IUCN Protected Area Management Categories

Management Objective	Ia	Ib	II	III	IV	V	VI
Scientific research	I	3	2	2	2	2	3
Wilderness protection	2	I	2	3	3	—	2
Preservation of species and genetic diversity	I	2	I	I	I	2	I
Maintenance of environmental services	2	I	I	—	I	2	I
Protection of specific natural/cultural features	—	—	2	I	3	I	3
Tourism and recreation	—	2	I	I	3	I	3
Education	—	—	2	2	2	2	3
Sustainable use of resources from natural ecosystems	—	3	3	—	2	2	I
Maintenance of cultural/traditional attributes	—	—	—	—	—	I	2

KEY: I, Primary objective; 2, Secondary objective; 3, Potentially applicable objective; —, Not applicable
SOURCE: IUCN (1994).

tected area values (Table 1.2), are diverse, so also are members of the protected area family diverse. Different types of protected areas give priority to different values (Table 1.3). Thus, Category I protected areas exhibit the strongest restrictions on use to accomplish their primary function of biodiversity protection. Category II lands, usually administered as national parks, have somewhat less stringent protective regulations and a mandate for human use and enjoyment, along with biodiversity protection. The relaxation of protective standards continues through the categories to Category VI, which allows sustainable use although still managed primarily for biodiversity protection.

We can think of landscape as a continuum of values bounded on one side by market values and on the other by protected area values (Figure 1.3). How much of the landscape should be devoted to providing these different kinds of values for society? The target of 12 per cent has been adopted by many jurisdictions both in Canada and abroad, however, there is a danger that the landscape will become divided into two dichotomous types, protected or non-protected, and people will assume that for the

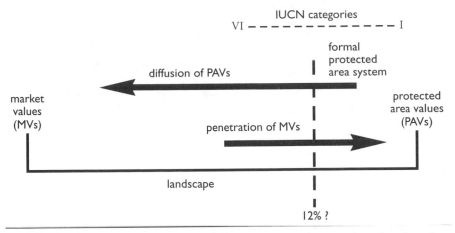

FIGURE 1.3 The landscape as 'valuescape', showing unwanted penetration of market values into protected areas and the use of IUCN protected area categories and an ecosystem-based approach to diffuse protected area values throughout the landscape. A major question is how much land should fall under protective designations, with 12 per cent providing an average international guideline.

latter we do not need to pay any attention to non-market values. This produces not only every-day landscapes of destruction, but will lead to the eventual choking of the protected areas also, as they become islands of extinction cut off from other protected areas (Chapter 4). An ecosystem-based approach to incorporation of Protected Area Values (PAVs) needs to be taken (Chapter 12). This involves making greater use of the less restrictive categories of protected area (Categories IV–VI) to diffuse PAVs into a higher proportion of the landscape, as shown in Figure 1.3. It also involves a greater emphasis being placed on a broader range of stewardship approaches to landscape planning that complement, but are not substitutes for, more centralized, government initiatives, such as park systems (see Chapter 15).

These more expansive approaches to protected areas are finding expression in large scale, bio-regional conservation landscape models. Such approaches have evolved from a preoccupation with nodes of conservation, such as national parks, to ways of connecting networks of different types of protected areas throughout the landscape. One of the best known initiatives is the Yellowstone to Yukon (Y to Y) initiative started by The Wildlands Project, the Canadian Parks and Wilderness Society (CPAWS) and others in 1993 (Locke, 1993, Willcox and Aengst, 1999). Prompted by scientific investigations that showed certain species migrated all along the Rockies from the southern US states up to Alaska, the initiative links together different protected areas along the way (Figure 1.4). Two recent designations by the BC Government have been central to realizing the vision. The Muskwa-Kechika Management Area (MKMA) covers some 4.4 million ha and since 1997 has been managed primarily for conservation,

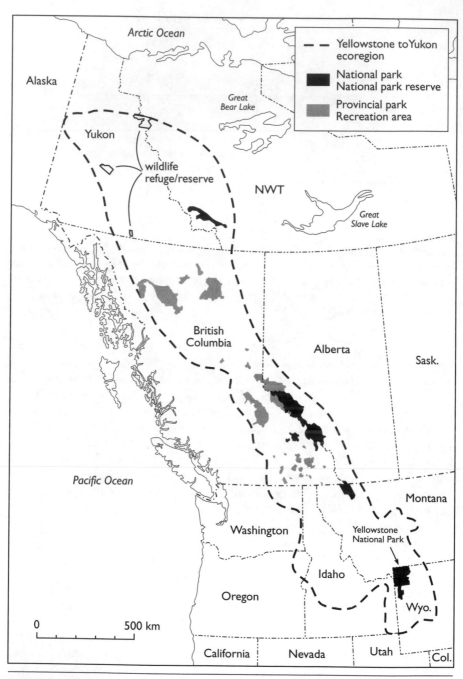

FIGURE 1.4 Map showing some of the main protected areas linked through the Yellowstone to Yukon initiative.

including 1.1 million ha in parks. Any development in the areas outside of the parks must, by law, allow for environment as a primary consideration. The MKMA is adjacent to the latest conservation designation, where, after 7 years of roundtable discussions, 475,000 ha of new parks have been added to the existing 116,000 ha, with an additional 410,000 ha of special management zones and 900,000 ha of no-logging zones. Together with the MKMA these new areas create a conservation matrix of 6.3 million ha connecting the ecosystems of the Rocky and Cassiar Mountains with those of the Pacific coast. This area provides a home to the greatest combined abundance and diversity of large mammals in North America, among them thousands of moose, elk, caribou, and the continent's largest concentration of Stone sheep, all accompanied by a healthy population of predators. In fact wolves from this area and Alberta were re-introduced to Yellowstone. As emphasized by Rivard et al. (2000), large size is still one of the most important criteria for an effective protected area.

THEMES

The themes addressed in this volume were selected as a result of consultation with authors and users of the previous edition. Some chapters have been dropped, others added, and most have been substantially rewritten since the last edition. However, the focus has remained on large, natural area parks, rather than smaller regional and local systems. Even at this scale, however, it should be noted that the emphasis is on formally-designated park systems, rather than on other forms of protective designation of natural areas, such as national wildlife areas. The insights provided by many of the management-oriented chapters still apply to those other kinds of designation, but extending the scope beyond formally designated systems is too expansive a task for this volume. However, one chapter (Chapter 15) is devoted to the increasing role that different forms of conservation covenant play in natural area protection in Canada, particularly in areas under private stewardship.

Six sections provide the framework for the book. Following this Introduction, the first section, the Overview, continues with a historical overview of the development of the protected area system in Canada. Attending mainly to the national park system, Kevin McNamee traces the growth of the system, the main management issues, and the critical role that politicians and conservationists have played as the system has evolved. McNamee is also the author of Chapter 3, a perspective on the status of protected areas in different parts of the country. Great strides have been made since the World Wildlife Fund initiated the Endangered Spaces campaign a decade ago to generate public support for increasing the protected area system in Canada; however, much remains to be done at both the federal and the provincial levels.

The second section, Conservation Theory and Application, recognizes the key roles that the understanding and the application of ecological principles plays in park planning. Chapter 4 by Jeannette and John Theberge is an ecological primer on concepts underlying the designation and management of protected areas. Next, a new chapter by Stephen Woodley of Parks Canada conveys some of the ways the agency is managing for ecological integrity. Several examples ground the theories of the previous chapter in actual management practices.

The third section reviews the main social science concepts fundamental to park planning. In Chapter 6 Rick Rollins and Dave Robinson discuss social science approaches to protected area management. Most park management is people management, yet, as emphasized by the Panel on Ecological Integrity (Parks Canada Agency, 2000), this is often overlooked and understaffed. Rollins and Robinson outline various approaches that give insight into why and how people use protected areas, into crowding, into conflict management and into some of the social and economic impacts of parks. The contribution by Bob Payne and Per Nilsen further develops these concepts and relates them to specific approaches towards visitor management frameworks, such as the Visitor Activity Management Process (VAMP) of Parks Canada. Again, they provide many examples to relate the theory to actual management approaches in particular parks.

The section is rounded out by by Jim Butler and Glen Hvenegaard who look at one critical aspect of human use management in parks: interpretation. Perhaps no aspect of park services suffered so badly during the economic climate of the last decade. Interpretation infrastructure was allowed to fall into disrepair, new initiatives were put on hold, and many existing services were either cut completely as 'uneconomic' or made into 'pay-for-service' features with costs that discouraged all but the most ardent of park-lovers. These were definitely retrograde steps for park agencies in raising environmental awareness in the public and in easing their management problems. However, the pendulum has swung back a little, at the impetus of the Panel on Ecological Integrity (Parks Canada Agency, 2000),with support emerging for the interpretation function within the national parks.

In the fourth section we have four chapters that consider park management from a more holistic perspective. First, Pam Wright, the Deputy Chair of the Panel on Ecological Integrity, and Rick Rollins, book co-editor, provide a comprehensive overview of national park management outlining the main changes in legislation and policy, park management planning and administration and the current status of the system plan. Guy Swinnerton in the next chapter concentrates on just one park, but along many different dimensions. The site is Canada's oldest and best-known park, Banff, and the case study embodies many of the challenges that are being felt or soon will be felt at many different parks in the system as visitor pressures and the surrounding land-use intensity continue to increase.

Chapter 11 by Paul Eagles looks more specifically at different aspects of site management within park systems. Using examples ranging from endangered species to paleontology he looks at the values that influence management decisions. The final chapter in this section, by Scott Slocombe and Phil Dearden, broadens this perspective by looking at the need to place protected areas within an ecosystem context for their planning and management. A synthesis of different approaches, tools, and examples, is suggested, but the authors have to conclude that there are still few working examples of ecosystem-based approaches to protected area management.

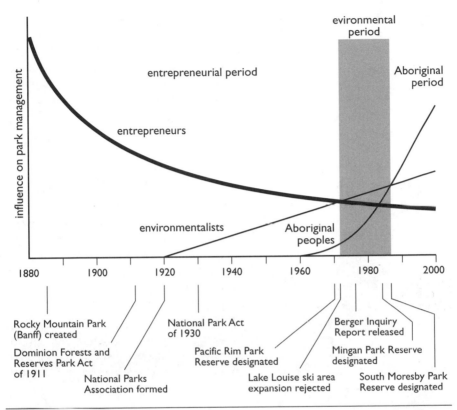

FIGURE 1.5 Suggested influences of various external groups on park management over time. SOURCE: Dearden and Berg (1993).

Part V examines particular thematic issues. In 1993, Dearden and Berg suggested that over the years parks have been designated and managed according to the interests of different parties (Figure 1.5). Although entrepreneurs were dominant for many years, the power of environmental interests steadily grew to become in the 1970s and 1980s a dominant force until it too was eclipsed by the rising influence of the First Nations. In much of Canada treaties were not entered into with the people already living on the land when white people colonized—they simply took the land. As this has now been recognized as not only unethical, but also illegal, treaty negotiations are underway across the country. In many instances First Nations have made conservation one of their top priorities in treaty negotiations, however, there are also challenges. Peepre and Dearden provide in Chapter 13 some historical perspective on this situation before discussing its implications for parks across the country.

Although the politicians did not meet their promise to complete the national park system and extend protected area status to 12 per cent of the country by the end of the

BOX 1.3 Liberal commitments: politics counts, or does it?

'Preventative environmental care is…a wise public investment like preventative social policies and preventative health care. A Liberal government will lead in protecting Canada's environment. We will maintain the commitment to complete the National Parks System by 2000' *Creating Opportunity: The Liberal Plan for Canada, 1993*.

'Canada's National Parks…hold special value for Canadians. Parks Canada will, in line with government priorities, pursue completion of the system of National Parks.' *Budget Plan 1996*. Honourable Paul Martin, Minister of Finance.

'Creating new National Parks and protecting our existing park system remains a high priority for me personally.' Prime Minister Jean Chrétien, United Nations General Assembly, New York, June 24, 1997.

'The creation of new national parks will continue under a new Liberal government as we work towards the completion of the national park system by the year 2000. A new Liberal government will continue to establish new marine conservation areas and develop legislation and policies for a marine conservation system.' *Securing Our Future Together: The Liberal Plan*, 1997.

'The Panel heard consistently that the financial resources currently devoted to Parks Canada are insufficient for Parks Canada to meet its objective for protecting ecological integrity…it will not be sustainable to continue to fund new parks from within Parks Canada's current budget, and new resources will be required to develop and operate these new parks and conservation areas.' *Panel on Ecological Integrity, Parks Canada Agency*, 2000.

century, at least some progress was made. Little, if any progress, however, has emerged for marine parks. Declarations have been made, agreements have been signed, but there is still no Act in the closing months of 2001 to permit the establishment of National Marine Conservation Areas (NMCAs). Still only Fathom Five in Lake Huron and the Saguenay-St Lawrence in Quebec, established under separate legislation, remain as national marine parks, although there are marine adjuncts to some existing parks. In Chapter 14 Philip Dearden discusses the current status of marine protected areas and outlines the main challenges being faced.

This book examines the establishment and management of large, natural parks established by governments. However, other approaches in conservation are also growing that protect smaller pieces of land and do not rely solely on government coffers, if at all. Yet, these smaller parcels of land can be critically important in linking larger protected areas together as well as conserving important features in their own right. In Chapter 15 Jessica Dempsey, Philip Dearden, and J. Gordon Nelson describe some of the initiatives being made outside the main park systems, with special emphasis on private land stewardships and the emerging role of nature conservancies in the acquisition and protection of conservation lands.

In the Conclusion the editors summarize the work of their contributors and point to issues that will be significant in the future.

As should be evident from the foregoing, there have been many changes in protected area designation and management over the last decade. Pressures on the landscape have grown and it is becoming increasingly evident that only big-picture thinking will lead to the overall survival of many of the protected area values that we look to our parks to provide into the future. Unfortunately, the political response to this challenge has been slow and opportunities for conservation continue to decline. Emergence of a landscape that celebrates the splendour of Canada and the values of her people will happen only with concerted public pressure on our politicians (Box 1.3). Although we can all help apply such pressure, there are strengths to be gained from banding together. This is one good reason to get involved with a non-government organization (NGO) that is dedicated to the protection of the wild.

REFERENCES

Auditor General of Canada. 1996. 'Canadian-Heritage-Parks Canada: Preserving Canada's Natural Heritage', *Report of the Auditor General of Canada to the House of Commons. Ottawa.*

Banff-Bow Valley Study. 1996. 'Banff-Bow Valley: At the Crossroads', *Summary Report of the Banff-Bow Valley Task Force.* Ottawa: Auditor General of Canada.

Dearden P. 1995. 'Park Literacy and Conservation', *Conservation Biology* 9: 1–3.

———. 2000. 'Endangered Species and Terrestrial Protected Areas', in K. Beazley and R. Boardman, eds, *Politics of the Wild: Canada and Endangered Species.* Toronto: Oxford University Press, 75–93.

——— and L. Berg. 1993. 'Canada's National Park: A Model of Administrative Penetration', *The Canadian Geographer* 37: 194–211.

Eagles, P.F.J., D. McLean, and M.J. Stabler. 2000. 'Estimating the Tourism Volume and Value in Parks and Protected Areas in Canada and the USA', *George Wright Forum.*

Environics International. 2000. *Canadian Public Opinion on Nature and Biodiversity.* Toronto: Environics International.

Federal Provincial Parks Council. 2000. *Working Together: Parks and Protected Areas in Canada.*

Federal-Provincial-Territorial Task Force on the Importance of Nature to Canadians. 1999. *The Importance of Nature to Canadians: Survey Highlights.* Ottawa: Minister of Public Works and Government Services.

International Union for the Conservation of Nature (IUCN). 1994. *Guidelines for Protected Area Management Categories.* Gland: CNPPA/IUCN.

———. 1996. *CNPPA in Action.* Gland: CNPPA/IUCN.

———. 2000. *IUCN Red List of Threatened Species.* Gland: IUCN.

Locke, H. 1993. 'Yellowstone to Yukon', *Wild Earth Winter:* 68.

Nash, R. 1967. *Wilderness and the American Mind.* New Haven: Yale University Press.

Parks Canada. 1994. *Guiding Principles and Operational Policies.* Ottawa: Ministry of Supply and Services.

Parks Canada. 1998. *State of the Parks, 1997.* Ottawa: Minister of Public Works and Government Services Canada.

Parks Canada Agency. 2000. 'Unimpaired for Future Generations? Protecting Ecological Integrity with Canada's National Parks', in *Setting a New Direction for Canada's National Parks. Report of the Panel on the Ecological Integrity of Canada's National Parks*, vol. 2. Ottawa.

Rivard, D.H., J. Poitevin, D. Plasse, M. Carleton, and D.J. Currie. 2000. 'Changing Species Richness and Composition in Canadian National Parks', *Conservation Biology* 14: 1099–109.

Sax, J. 1980. *Mountains Without Handrails*. Ann Arbor: University of Michigan Press.

Vitousaek, P.M., H.A. Mooney, J. Lubchenco, and J.M. Melello. 1997. 'Human Domination of Earth's Ecosystems', *Science* (25 July): 494–9.

Willcox, L., and P. Aengst. 1999. 'Yellowstone to Yukon: Romantic Dream or Realistic Vision of the Future?', *Parks* 9: 17–24.

Wipond, K., and P. Dearden. 1998. 'Obstacles to Maintaining Ecological Integrity in Pacific Rim National Park Reserve', in N.W.P. Munro and J.H.M. Willison, eds, *Linking Protected Areas with Working Landscapes Conserving Biodiversity*. Proceedings of the Third International Conference on Science and Management of Protected Areas, Wolfville, NS: 901–10.

World Commission on Environment and Development. 1987. *Our Common Future*. Oxford: Oxford University Press.

KEY WORDS/CONCEPTS

National Parks Act (Bill C27)

ecological integrity

ecological degradation

protected area values

IUCN

Y to Y

protected area categories

bioregional approaches

political will

STUDY QUESTIONS

1. Are parks and protected areas important to Canadians? Discuss the results of national polls on this issue.
2. Why are parks important to Canadians? Provide a list of benefits or reasons for having parks.
3. What forces in society seem to be opposed to parks? What individuals, organizations, or sectors of the economy can you identify that are opposed to parks or would benefit if parks were reduced or eliminated? Develop a list of disadvantages or reasons that could be advanced to reject the idea of parks.
4. Discuss and evaluate the validity of each list (advantages and disadvantages of parks).
5. What is 'sustainable development?' What is the connection between parks and sustainable development?
6. Six types of protected areas have been identified by the IUCN. Briefly describe each of these types of parks, and identify examples of protected areas in Canada that approximate each of these IUCN designations.
7. Outline the main changes that have occurred relating to protected areas in Canada over the last decade. What do you think are the main forces behind these changes?

CHAPTER 2

From Wild Places to Endangered Spaces: A History of Canada's National Parks

Kevin McNamee

INTRODUCTION

Canada's national parks system plays a critical role in conserving biological diversity and wilderness landscapes. At the beginning of the twenty-first century, almost 250,000 sq. km, or 2.5 per cent of Canada, is protected from industrial development in 39 national parks and reserves. These parks constitute over 30 per cent of all lands conserved from industrial development within Canada's network of protected areas, making the federal government the largest custodian of protected areas within the nation. Figure 2.1 shows the current distribution of national parks.

The evolution of the national parks system since its inception in 1885 has been influenced more by the nation's focus on economic development and prevailing social values, and less on the need to preserve wilderness. Historically, government, industry, and local communities placed an emphasis on the economic value of national parks as places of recreation and as tourism destinations. However, as Canada's wilderness dwindles and efforts to implement regional conservation strategies increase, the essential role of national parks and protected areas in preserving important natural ecosystems is being more broadly acknowledged. Parks are now viewed as agents of conservation rather than of recreation, particularly in that the preservation of natural areas from industrial development is increasingly acknowledged as a critical step in conserving the world's biological diversity.

This chapter explores the evolution of the national parks system and some of the landmark events that have shaped it over the last century—particularly the expansion of the national parks system—and the range of management issues that have preoccupied governments and conservation groups for most of its history. Also featured is the critical role that politicians, Aboriginal people, and conservationists have played in shaping the parks system.

FIGURE 2.1 National Parks in Canada.

1 Pacific Rim
2 Gwaii Haanas
3 Kluane
4 Ivvavik
5 Vuntut
6 Glacier
7 Mt Revelstoke
8 Yoho
9 Kootenay
10 Waterton Lakes
11 Banff
12 Jasper
13 Elk Island
14 Wood Buffalo
15 Nahanni

16 Tuktut Nogait
17 Aulavik
18 Quttinirpaaq
19 Prince Albert
20 Grasslands
21 Riding Mountain
22 Wapusk
23 Sirmilik
24 Auyuittuq
25 Pukaskwa
26 Bruce Peninsula
27 Georgian Bay Islands
28 Point Pelee

29 St Lawrence Islands
30 La Maurice
31 Kouchibouguac
32 Forillon
33 Mingan Archipelago
34 Gros Morne
35 Fundy
36 Kejimkujik
37 Prince Edward Island
38 Cape Breton Highlands
39 Terra Nova

BIRTH OF THE CANADIAN PARKS NETWORK (1885–1911)

Canada's national parks system began somewhat inauspiciously. The impetus for Canada's first national park, Banff, was the discovery of the Cave and Basin mineral hot springs by three employees of the Canadian Pacific Railway (CPR). They sought to establish a claim over the hot springs so that they personally could profit from their commercial development.

BOX 2.1 Key Dates in the Evolution of National Park Management

1885   Canada's first national park (Banff) established

1911   Dominion Parks Branch—World's first national park service

1911   Dominion Forest Reserves and Parks Act

1930   Canada's first National Parks Act

1930   Transfer of resources agreement

1937   First federal-provincial agreement to establish a park (Cape Breton Highlands NP)

1964   First comprehensive statement of national parks policy

1971   First National Park System plan approved

1976   Canada signs World Heritage Convention; Nahanni designated the world's first natural World Heritage Site by UNESCO

1976   First northern national park reserves established

1979   Revised National Parks Policy gives first priority to ecological integrity

1984   Canadian Rocky Mountain Parks World Heritage Site established

1984   Ivvavik National Park : first park established under a land claim agreement

1986   Approval of first national policy and system plan for National Marine Conservation Areas

1988   Amendment to the National Parks Act legally formalizes the principle of ecological integrity

1989   Endangered Spaces Campaign launched

1990   Canada's Green Plan commits to complete the National Park system by the year 2000.

1992   Canada signs the UN Convention on Biological Diversity

1993   Gwaii Haanas Agreement establishes terms of unprecedented co-management agreement between the federal government and the Haida Nation

1991   Tabling of first State of the Parks Report in Parliament

1994   The revised Guiding Principles and Operational Policies released

1996   Banff-Bow Valley Study sets a new benchmark for ecological management in Canada

1997   Government commits to 'maintain the long-term ecological integrity of our national parks in Securing our Future Together (Liberal Party Platform— "Red Book II")

1998   Tabling of 1997 State of Parks Report

1998   Moratorium announced on commercial development outside of park communities within national parks

1998   Parks Canada becomes an operating agency through the proclamation of the Parks Canada Agency Act and government declares the parks will not be commercialized or privatized

1998   Parliament votes to establish Tuktut Nogait National Park and to reject proposals to carve from it land for mining

BOX 2.1 Key Dates in the Evolution of National Park Management

1999   Three Arctic national parks are established through the first Inuit Impact and Benefits Agreement under the Nunavut Land Claim Agreement.

1999   Series of decisions and guidelines on commercial development in the Rocky Mountain Parks are released

2000   Panel on the Ecological Integrity of Canada's National Parks releases report

2000   Revised Canada National Parks Bill (Bill C-27) passed in Parliament

2000   Government proposes to increase funding to establish new national parks and maintain ecological integrity (Red Book III)

The federal government denied the claim. Instead, in November 1885, it established a 26-sq.-km (10-sq.-mi.) reservation around the Banff hot springs on the slopes of Sulphur Mountain. The hot springs were now protected in the public interest and no longer available for 'sale, or settlement, or squatting'. The government, in partnership with the CPR, sought to exploit the economic benefits of the hot springs (Figure 2.2). The wording of the Order in Council that established the reserve reflected the value of the hot springs to the government: 'there have been discovered several hot mineral springs which promise to be of great sanitary advantage to the public' (Lothian, 1976: 20).

Wilderness preservation had little to do with the establishment of the Banff Hot Springs reserve and other national parks around the turn of the century. The Banff hot springs were to become, as the Deputy Minister of the Interior stated in 1886, 'the greatest and most successful health resort on the continent'(ibid.: 23). To achieve this, he called for a plan 'to commence the construction of roads and bridges and other operations necessary to make of the reserve a creditable national park' (ibid.). The hot springs, the clean air, and the mountain scenery would attract tourists to Banff on the newly constructed railway. They would stay at new hotels, such as the Banff Springs Hotel, that were constructed within the new parks. Thus, both the government and the CPR, which constructed the hotels, would profit.

The First National Parks

The federal government moved quickly both to expand the Banff Hot Springs reserve and to establish other parks. A Dominion Land Surveyor hired to complete a legal survey of the Banff reserve drew the government's attention to 'a large tract of country lying outside of the original reservation'with 'features of the greatest beauty'. The surveyor noted that these lands 'were admirably adapted for a national park' (ibid.).

Acting on the surveyor's find, Parliament passed the Rocky Mountain Park Act in June 1887 to establish the boundaries for a more extensive park of 673 sq. km (260 sq.

FIGURE 2.2 The first bathing establishment constructed at the Cave and Basin in Rocky Mountain Park (c.1887–8). The architecture for the two bath houses is fashioned after Swiss-style buildings. In 1887, 3,000 availed themselves of the park's mineral hot springs. Cascade Mountain rises in the background. *Photo: Canadian Parks Service.*

FIGURE 2.3 The sleepy frontier town of Banff is pictured here in 1887, with Cascade Mountain rising over what is now Banff Avenue. Regulations passed under the National Parks Act in 1890, prohibited 'furious riding and driving on public roads' in the town. Cows, however, were permitted to graze on the main street.

mi.), which would later be called Banff National Park. The area was to be 'a public park and pleasure ground for the benefit, advantage and enjoyment of the people of Canada'. Under the legislation, the government could make rules for 'the protection and preservation of game, fish (and) wild birds', and to preserve some of the park's natural features and to control the cutting of timber (ibid.: 11). This was one of the first times the need to conserve park resources was acknowledged.

The creation of Rocky Mountain Park was partly modelled on earlier actions in the United States. Prime Minister Sir John A. Macdonald was advised to protect the commercial value of the Banff hot springs by establishing a reserve similar to the Arkansas Hot Springs Reserve in Arkansas, which was created by Congress in 1832. The Rocky Mountain Park Act used similar language to that contained in the legislation establishing in 1872 Yellowstone in Wyoming as the world's first national park. The Yellowstone Park Act set land aside 'as a public park or pleasuring ground for the benefit and enjoyment of the people' (ibid.: 24).

Here the similarity to Yellowstone ends. While Yellowstone sat unattended for almost two decades, the Canadian federal government made sure that Rocky Mountain Park was made useful and contributed to the national economy (Figure 2.3). The Prime Minister confirmed this policy: 'the Government thought it was of great importance that all this section of country should be brought at once into usefulness' (Craig Brown, 1969: 49). Timber cutting, mineral development, and grazing were allowed. Mineral claims were worked in Banff for almost half a century.

There was virtually no opposition to resource development activities within the park. The National Policy of the Macdonald government in the 1880s stressed the need to develop and exploit natural resources as the means for developing a national economy. National parks that produced profits from tourism and resource development were viewed simply as an extension of that policy. The underlying assumption of the National Policy was that there were plenty of natural resources to exploit, and that government and industry had a shared responsibility to develop those resources. The first parks were manifestations of that policy (ibid.).

During the Parliamentary debate, there was at least one MP who gave voice to the more contemporary view of national parks. Samuel Burdette, a Liberal MP, warned the House of Commons: 'Allow coal miners and hunters and lumberers to frequent and work it and it ceases to be a national park and they would certainly destroy the game, and the fish, and the scenery, and all the beauties we have heard so much about.' (Foster, 1978, 25). Even Prime Minister Macdonald acknowledged that 'as much attention as possible should be paid to the protection of the timber in the general line of the park.' (MacEachern, 2001; 18). Nevertheless, the extent to which the government developed and manipulated park resources in the decades that followed suggest that while some noble words were spoken, the park was made 'useful'.

In addition to Rocky Mountain Park, several other parks were created under the National Policy. In 1886, A.W. Ross, a Member of Parliament from Manitoba, suggested the federal government examine the potential for more parks along the railway. As a result, Glacier and Yoho parks were established in 1888 to make the British Columbia and the mountain sections of the CPR as 'popular as possible'. And to ensure their popularity, the CPR constructed the Glacier Park Lodge and Mount Stephen House hotels within the two parks. The parks were also created 'to preserve the timber and natural beauty of the district' (Foster, 1978: 31). Policies promoting both the exploitation and conservation of park resources were consistent, because preserving natural scenery was central to retaining the first parks as tourist attractions.

Other parks were established outside the Banff area. F.W. Godsal, a local rancher from Cowley, Alberta, spearheaded efforts to establish the Waterton Lakes National Park despite the opposition of the federal bureaucracy. Godsal urged the government to protect the Crowsnest Pass and Waterton Lakes in a national park, 'otherwise a comparatively small number of settlers can control and spoil these public resorts' (Rodney, 1969: 172). The bureaucracy, however, felt the government should focus on the three existing parks, and manage them properly. One civil servant warned the Deputy Minister of Interior: 'Don't you think it possible to overdo this park reservation business?' The comment was ignored. The Hon. T. Mayne Daly, Minister of the Interior, established the Waterton Lakes Forest Park in 1895 (Figure 2.4), observing that 'Posterity will bless us' (Lothian, 1976: 32). His observation was quite prescient given that a century later, the United Nations jointly declared Waterton Lakes National Park, along with its neighbour to the south, Montana's

FIGURE 2.4 Visitors to Waterton Lakes Park pause beside their car at the park entrance west of Pincher Creek, Alberta, c.1930. The Pincher Creek Automobile Club began construction on the Pincher Creek–Waterton Road in 1911. Only 64 visitors arrived in Waterton that year. In 1938, Ottawa imposed fees on motor vehicles entering the Waterton Lakes parks: 25 cents for a single trip and one dollar for the season.

Glacier National Park, a World Heritage Site, ranking it with some of the planet's most astonishing natural wonders.

By 1911, the federal government had protected a number of areas for posterity: Rocky Mountain Park, the Yoho and Glacier Park Reserves, and the Waterton Lakes and Jasper Forest Parks. These areas were multiple-use parks, inspired by a profit motive and were not founded in any environmental ethic. Yet, their creation was prompted by a need to protect the spectacular scenery for its tourism value, and proved critical to today's legacy of wilderness reserves. Through the first federal parks, the federal government acknowledged its responsibility to hold lands in trust for the public benefit, that there was a need to conserve natural resources, and that the creation and maintenance of parks was a government responsibility. Canadians continue to benefit from the far-sighted decisions of Canada's early political leaders, no matter what the early rationale for creating the nation's first national parks.

This period of park development, from 1885 to 1911, requires more research. As MacEachern (2001) points out in his history of national parks in Atlantic Canada, the 'doctrine of usefulness thesis has been accepted rather uncritically as the perspective from which to view Canadian park history' (ibid., 16). He cites several 'preservation impulses' in the early political debates and actions of civil servants, suggesting that some also saw these early national parks as places of preservation.

BRINGING THE PARKS TO CANADIANS (1911–1957)

This period is characterized by government actions to expand the national parks system beyond its initial Rocky Mountain focus to include natural areas in central and eastern Canada. In order to secure the political support for an enlarged network of national parks, federal civil servants promoted the recreational and tourism benefits of the parks. During this period, also, some of the first examples of public advocacy for park values were exhibited.

In 1911, there was no system of national parks: instead, there was one legislated park and four created by order in council; there were parks, park reserves, and forest reserves. Each was run with no real policy direction by a superintendent under the Minister of the Interior. It became clear to the government that there was a need for a separate branch of government to administer the parks.

The parks were growing in popularity and proving to be a national asset. The success of the first parks convinced the government of the need to protect their scenery. The Hon. Frank Oliver, Minister of Interior, introduced legislation into the House of Commons in 1911 that shifted parks policy from promoting parks as 'primarily places of business' to places where 'there will be no business except such as is absolutely necessary for the recreation of the people' (Foster, 1978: 75).

To this end, Parliament passed the Dominion Forest Reserves and Parks Act in 1911 to accomplish several things: it created two categories of conservation lands—forest reserves and dominion parks; it reduced the level of development permitted in the parks; and it placed the dominion parks under the administration of the world's first national parks branch, known variously over the years as the Dominion Parks Branch, the National Parks Branch, Parks Canada, and Canadian Parks Service, and now the Parks Canada Agency. The legislation was a disappointment to the new parks branch because it dramatically reduced the size of the Rocky Mountain, Jasper, and Waterton Lakes Dominion Parks. Rocky Mountain, for example, was reduced by more than half. The reductions occurred because the government concluded that large parks were not required for recreation and for providing people access to natural areas. Thus, land was withdrawn from the parks system and placed into the forest reserves, which concentrated on protecting wildlife.

The government's action to reduce the parks was not a popular decision with James B. Harkin, the first commissioner of the Dominion Parks Branch. The chief civil servant in charge of the dominion parks from 1911 to 1936, Harkin left an indelible mark on Canada's national parks system. He brought a philosophy to the position that was a mixture of reverence for the power of nature, and a pragmatic view of the economic value of nature and the parks to society.

FIGURE 2.5 The bath house at the Upper Hot Springs in Banff National Park, c. 1935. William McCardell claims to have discovered these springs on New Year's Day in 1884. The first road for carriages to the spring, which was then privately operated, was completed in 1886. The bath house pictured here was constructed in 1932 by unemployed local men. *Photo: Canadian Parks Service.*

Harkin was heavily influenced by the writings of John Muir, one of America's foremost naturalists and national park advocates. Harkin believed that the national parks 'exist in order that every citizen of Canada may satisfy his soul-craving for Nature' (ibid.: 81). He believed the parks provided people with a chance for 'wholesome recreation that would physically and spiritually rejuvenate them' (ibid.). In parks, people could experience nature and beauty, and absorb the peace of the forests.

To that end, Harkin believed that Canadians had a responsibility to safeguard Canada's wildlands by establishing more parks. Harkin also believed that anything that impaired the natural beauty of the park, or its peaceful tranquillity, had to be excluded. Small wonder that under Harkin the national parks system expanded from its western base to eastern Canada, the number of parks increased from 5 to 16, and resource extraction activities were prohibited.

However, to obtain the political support and government finances to accomplish this, Harkin promoted very strongly the economic value of the national parks. He was

FIGURE 2.6 Mountain guide Rudolph Aemmer is pictured here on the summit of Mount Victoria near Lake Louise in Banff National Park in 1931. In July 1954 four Mexican women and their male guide were killed after falling 600m in Abbot Pass. Three other women were rescued by a Swiss guide and Canadian Pacific Railway staff. *Photo:W.J. Oliver.*

particularly impressed by the tourism value of the parks (Figures 2.5, 2.6). In one annual report Harkin wrote that the 'National Parks provide the chief means of bringing to Canada a stream of tourists and a stream of tourist gold' (Marty, 1984: 98). The CPR agreed with Harkin, because their calculations demonstrated that the Rocky Mountains generated $50 million a year in tourism revenue (Foster, 1978). Harkin calculated the value of scenic lands to be $13.88 an acre, while wheatland was worth $4.91 (ibid.). Armed with Harkin's statistics, politicians rose in the House of Commons time and again to defend government expenditures on the dominion parks.

Harkin's promotion of the tourism value of parks produced improved visitor accommodation, the provision of minor attractions to supplement natural features, and the construction of first-class roads, such as the Banff-Jasper Highway, and trails so that natural attractions could be reached in safety and comfort. The national park regulations were changed in 1911 to allow the first automobiles into the parks. Several decades later, Harkin's work in developing the recreational potential of national parks would begin to cause their deterioration.

The Birth of a Public Constituency for Parks

Public protests against the reduction in size of some of the dominion parks in 1911 provide some of the first examples of how public pressure shaped the national parks system. Organizations such as the Alberta Game and Fish Protective Association, the Camp Fire Club of America, and the Canadian Northern and Grand Trunk Pacific Railway lobbied for a return of the parks to their larger sizes. Backed by the Camp Fire Club of America and other civil servants, Harkin was able to get the government to expand the Waterton Lakes park from 34 to 1095 sq. km (13 to 423 sq. mi.) so that it would form a natural continuation of the U.S. Glacier National Park in Montana. While the park was again reduced by half in 1921, a core wilderness area had been protected because of public pressure. Harkin was also successful in using public pressure to expand Rocky Mountain Park to protect park wildlife.

The first Canadian organization to promote the value of national parks was formed in 1923 to oppose the Calgary Power Corporation's plan to dam the Spray River near Canmore, inside Rocky Mountain Park. The National Parks Association of Canada was formed to promote the conservation of national parks for 'scientific, recreational and scenic purposes, and their protection from exploitation for commercial purposes' (Bella, 1987: 51). Arthur Wheeler, who led the fight against the dam, encouraged the Association to 'protest against any actions that will create a precedent for commercial encroachment upon the integrity of the Canadian National Parks' (Johnston, 1985: 9). Thus ensued a debate over the need to protect national park lands versus the desire to develop their natural resources.

The Spray Lakes debate resembled a similar issue in the United States. A 1913 decision to flood the Hetch Hetchy Valley in Yosemite National Park was preceded by a tremendous national debate on the value of national parks and the need to preserve wilderness. While the valley eventually was lost, the fight promoted a broad swell of public support for the concept of national parks and wilderness. In Canada, where the Spray River cause also was lost, no large base of public support for the Canadian National Parks emerged and the National Parks Association faded from view.

The Spray Lakes fight and other issues reinforced Harkin's efforts to further protect the dominion parks. Harkin was especially concerned that a 1926 agreement between Canada and Alberta to transfer control of natural resources to the province would impact on the parks. In 1927 he convinced the Hon. Charles Stewart, Minister of the Interior, to introduce legislation in the House of Commons in 1927 that would establish the principle of the absolute sanctity of the national parks.

Premier Rowntree of Alberta opposed the legislation because he did not want to lose control over the natural resources contained in the parks, citing the water power resources of the Upper Spray Lakes, and the coal deposits in Rocky Mountain and Jasper parks as examples. Rowntree's opposition prompted a survey of the parks to identify and remove areas that had important industrial potential. This was an extension of the 'parks must be useful' philosophy. If resource development is to be prohibited in parks, then useful resources should not be included within their boundaries. In 1928, the survey recommended that the Kananaskis and Spray Lakes watersheds with their potential for hydro power, as well as other areas suitable for grazing, or for coal and timber extraction, be withdrawn from the parks.

In 1930, Parliament passed legislation transferring control over natural resources to the governments of Alberta, Saskatchewan, and Manitoba. As part of the deal, the boundaries of the Rocky Mountain Park were changed to delete the Kananaskis and Spray Lakes and areas now known as Canmore and Exshaw. However, in the process, it was agreed that the control of the national parks, such as the Rocky Mountain parks, Prince Albert National Park in Saskatchewan, and Riding Mountain National Park in Manitoba, would rest solely with the federal government.

The National Parks Act

Parliament also passed the National Parks Act in 1930, providing a sweeping statement on parks that reflected Harkin's philosophy. Neither could new parks be established nor existing parks be eliminated, nor their boundaries changed, without Parliament's approval. Mineral exploration and development was prohibited and only limited use of green timber for essential park management purposes was allowed. The parks also were confirmed as absolute sanctuaries for game. And the dominion parks were renamed national parks, and Rocky Mountain Park became Banff National Park.

Parliament did exercise its right to eliminate several national parks that were wildlife sanctuaries for species threatened with extinction. For example, Buffalo National Park at Wainwright, Alberta, was eliminated in 1947 because the buffalo had been saved with the establishment of Wood Buffalo and Elk Island National Parks in the 1920s. The Nemiskan National Park in Saskatchewan, established to protect the pronghorn antelope, also was abolished in 1947 because of the growth in antelope populations and because farmers and ranchers wanted to use the land for cattle grazing.

Harkin's efforts to promote the value of national parks resulted in more parks being established under the new National Parks Act. For example, Nova Scotia was the first province to agree to transfer provincial land to the federal Crown to create Cape Breton Highlands National Park in 1936. Prior to that, the national parks were established from lands administered by the federal government or from lands that were purchased.

During Harkin's period, political support for national parks was high: Cape Breton Highlands was established through the support of the Yarmouth Fish and Game Protective Association and the Premier of Nova Scotia; a Member of Parliament and the mayor of Dauphin, Manitoba lobbied for Riding Mountain Park; and another Member of Parliament wanted a park in PEI. And while there was a decidedly commercial basis to this support, it clearly resulted in the preservation of large tracts of wilderness.

Sometimes national parks were the product of more intricate political dealing. The Prince Albert Liberal Riding Association presented a list of demands to Mackenzie King in 1926 before agreeing to nominate him as their candidate to the House of

Commons. The list included a request for a national park. King defeated a young lawyer named John Diefenbaker in 1926, and as Prime Minister presided over the opening of Prince Albert National Park in 1928. Diefenbaker, a future prime minister, later referred to Prince Albert National Park as 'that mosquito park offered to Prince Albert as a reward for the election of Mackenzie King' (Waiser, 1989: 43).

In expanding the national park system into eastern Canada, the federal government had to deal with local populations that made a living from the lands that they sought to protect in new national parks. As MacEachern (2001: 19) noted, the process was simple—the 'Parks Branch chose land it thought appropriate for a park, the provinces expropriated the land, and the landowners settled' (ibid.). Families were expropriated to create Cape Breton Highlands (1936), Prince Edward Island (1937), Fundy (1948), and Terra Nova (1957) national parks. Feeling they had no choice, landowners accepted the government's offer and moved into communities next to the parks. As MacEachern details in his history, the bad feelings generated by these actions lingered for years. While this period—1911 to 1957—was characterized by a tremendous growth in the number of national parks, in eastern Canada it was at the expense of local landowners. It would not be until the 1980s that the federal government would deal with communities and landowners as part of the process, and not as an impediement, to the creation of national parks.

One year before he died at the age of 80 in 1958, Harkin lamented the lack of a public constituency in Canada for the protection of wilderness (Nash, 1969). Perhaps, if Harkin had lived into the next decade, he would have been pleased at the sudden growth in citizens' organizations that were dedicated to promoting the value of national parks to all Canadians.

GROWING SUPPORT, DWINDLING WILDERNESS, NEW PARKS (1958–1984)

The 1960s saw dramatic growth in public concern for the environment. Rapid industrial and urban development, air and water pollution, threats to northern wilderness areas in Alaska and Canada, and the publication of Rachel Carson's *Silent Spring* energized citizens to demand government action to protect the environment. Part of their agenda included a demand for more parks, and less industrial and recreational development within the boundaries of existing parks.

The minister in charge of national parks generally has to make decisions on the establishment of new national parks, and on the commercial uses to be permitted within them. Such decisions usually were ad hoc, and while the parks were managed under the National Parks Act for the 'benefit, education and enjoyment' of Canadians, the public had little or no influence on those decisions.

Several parks' ministers decried the lack of an organized constituency for national parks. In 1960, the minister in charge of national parks, the Hon. Alvin Hamilton, made an impassioned plea in the House of Commons for help in defending national park values: 'How can a minister stand up against the pressures of commercial interests who want to use the parks for mining, forestry, for every kind of honky-tonk device known to man, unless the people who love these parks are prepared to band together and support the minister by getting the facts out across the country' (Henderson, 1969: 331).

Participants at the 1961 Resources for Tomorrow Conference in Montreal agreed with Hamilton. They concluded that there was a need for a non-government organization 'to perform a watchdog role over those areas now reserved for park purpose' (ibid.: 332). The National and Provincial Parks Association of Canada (now the Canadian Parks and Wilderness Society) was formed in 1963 to perform this watchdog role by promoting the value of parks and advocating the expansion of park networks.

The National and Provincial Parks Association of Canada (NPPAC) subsequently lobbied successfully for the creation of Kluane and Nahanni National Park Reserves. It helped defeat proposals to hold the 1972 Winter Olympics in Banff National Park and to construct a multi-million dollar resort complex in Lake Louise. These were major battles that focused public and political attention on the ecological value of national parks. It also marked the beginning of a policy shift away from the recreational value of national park lands to their ecological value. The NPPAC, along with other organizations such as the Alberta Wilderness Association and the Canadian Nature Federation, were instrumental in developing environmental standards for national parks to ensure that they were 'maintained and made use of so as to leave them unimpaired' as required by the National Parks Act.

National Parks Policy

Among the NPPAC's most important achievements was its successful advocacy for the first comprehensive national parks policy. In 1958 the government completed a broad policy statement to guide the use, development, and protection of the national parks. However, it sat on the shelf for years. In response to the NPPAC's lobbying, the federal cabinet adopted and implemented the policy in September 1964.

Until the adoption of the 1964 policy, the national parks were administered piecemeal. The National Parks Act, with its dual mandate for use and protection, left ample room for varying opinions as to what Parliamentarians meant exactly when they passed the legislation in 1930. Parliament dedicated the national parks 'to the people of Canada for their benefit, education and enjoyment,' and they were to be 'maintained and made use of so as to leave them unimpaired'. What kind of benefits were the parks to provide to Canadians? What did 'unimpaired' mean? Where do the limits to recreational development end, and requirements for conservation begin?

Each successive government, and the ministers in charge of the national parks, had different interpretations of these requirements. The National Parks Branch wanted a policy statement that would provide continuity for the management of the parks that would extend beyond the terms of office for any particular government, and that was not in danger of being changed on a political whim (Canada, 1969).

The 1964 policy established the preservation of significant natural features in National Parks as its 'most fundamental and important obligation'. Other provisions were to guard against private exploitation, overuse, improper use, and inappropriate development of parklands. It drew a distinction between urban types of recreation, which were to be discouraged, and recreation that involved the use and conservation of natural areas within the parks.

Since then, the federal government has approved two substantive revisions to the policy, placing a progressively stronger emphasis on the preservation of ecological values over public use. In 1979, Cabinet put to rest the debate over the dual mandate contained in the National Parks Act by establishing the maintenance of the ecological integrity of parklands as a prerequisite to use. It committed the government to setting legislative limits to the size of downhill ski areas and the towns Banff and Jasper. Tourism facilities and overnight accommodation were to be located outside the parks wherever possible. The public was to be consulted on the development of park management plans, changes to the park zoning systems, and revisions to the policy. Reflecting strong public concerns over the loss of parklands to development, the policy revision stated that the 'majority of National Park lands and their living resources are protected in a wilderness state with a minimum of man-made facilities' (Canada, 1982: 40).

In 1995, further revisions to the Parks Canada's policy defined how the national parks would be managed to maintain their ecological integrity. There is now a strong emphasis on working with other jurisdictions to co-ordinate the management of lands both inside and outside the national parks so that the greater ecosystems, of which the national parks are part, sustain the overall ecological processes and components that the parks are trying to represent and protect. While the 1979 policy also stressed the need for co-operation between Parks Canada and its neighbours, it was couched in the context of economic development rather than the current ecological context.

A Systematic Approach to Park Expansion

Progress in expanding the national parks system came to a halt after Harkin's resignation in 1936. Only two national parks were created between 1936 and 1968—Fundy in 1948 and Terra Nova in 1957. The federal government's 1930 policy of establishing a national park in each province had not been attained because still there were no parks in Quebec. And there were no plans to expand the system.

In 1962, the Canadian Audubon Society, now the Canadian Nature Federation, sought to reverse this situation by challenging the federal and provincial governments to expand the national park system to mark the nation's 1967 Centennial year. Observing that Canada lacked 'a representative west coast national park . . . , no true example of the once-vast prairie grassland, and no truly good example of Great Lakes shoreline' (Anon., 1962: 74) the Society recommended the creation of at least 12 new national parks that are 'representative of the tremendously varied scenic, topographic and cover features of the nation' (ibid.). The idea, well received by such leading conservationists as Sigurd Olsen, did not spur much initial action because of the lack of co-operation of the provinces, who owned most of the land suitable for the new parks.

However, political impetus was given to expanding the national parks system into Quebec and other areas when the Hon. Jean Chrétien took charge of the national parks portfolio in 1968, just after the Centennial year. Chrétien immediately declared that to achieve an adequate representation of Canada's heritage, 40 to 60 new national parks would be required to complete the national park system by 1985. He saw a need for urgent action: costs for new parkland were reaching 'prohibitive' levels; and potential national park lands could be quickly spoiled 'by different forms of economic and social development' (Chrétien, 1969: 10).

Chrétien's statement was significant for acknowledging the need for some criteria to guide the location of new national parks. The park establishment process was still largely ad hoc, with parks being created wherever there was political support or interest. In 1971, Parks Canada adopted a natural regions system plan to guide park expansion activities. The government's goal is to represent the characteristic physical, biological, and geographic features of each of 39 natural regions within the national parks system. While Chrétien had suggested completing the national parks system by 1985, the centennial year of Banff's establishment, no target date would be confirmed until two decades later.

Chrétien did meet one target. The president of the NPPAC wagered the minister five dollars he could not establish nine parks over a five-year period (Anon., 1972). Chrétien won the bet handily, establishing 10 new national parks totalling 52,870 sq. km (18,500 sq. mi.). His successes included: the first national parks in Quebec, including La Mauricie, located in Chrétien's riding of Shawinigan; the first new national park in British Columbia in almost four decades, Pacific Rim; and the first national parks in northern Canada—Kluane, Nahanni, and Auyuittuq.

In the 1960s political and local response to new national parks was different from what it had been during Harkin's era, particularly because the federal government, and not local communities and politicians, was initiating many of the new park proposals. Chrétien encountered strong opposition from local communities and Aboriginal people to new park proposals. The Association for the Preservation of the Eastern Shore successfully opposed the creation of the proposed Ship Harbour National Park in Nova Scotia. Intense opposition from the Inuit and Innu in Labrador forced the postponement in 1979 of federal-provincial negotiations for two new national parks in Labrador (Bill 1982).

While this opposition stopped the creation of several national parks, it resulted in a park establishment process vastly more sensitive to the social and economic concerns of local residents. This new approach helped revive the two Labrador proposals. The Labrador Inuit have agreed through their land claim agreement-in-principle to Torngat Mountains National Park Reserve as well as to the interim protection of the park lands from any future commercial leasing or development. Furthermore, in March 2001, both the Labrador Inuit and the Innu Nation joined with Parks Canada and the Government of Newfoundland and Labrador in launching a study to determine the feasibility of a national park in the Mealy Mountains of southern Labrador. Progress on either project would have been out of the question had Parks Canada not adopted a more co-operative approach to working with local communities and with Aboriginal people.

FIGURE 2.7 Old fishing village along the Bay of Gaspé in Forillon National Park, Quebec east of Grande-Grave, c. 1968–70. Park visitors can now bike or hike along the old road to the most easterly point in the park, Cap Gaspé. Most of the houses pictured here were removed after the Quebec government expropriated local residents to make way for the new federal park. In an ironic twist, the central theme of the park's interpretive program is 'Harmony between man, the land, and the sea.' *Photo: Canadian Parks Service.*

Local Communities Force Changes to Parks Policy

Government policy until the 1970s was to expropriate and remove local communities located within the boundaries of proposed national parks. More than 200 families were expropriated to create Forillon National Park in Quebec (Figure 2.7). Some 1200 residents in 228 households were also removed from their land and communities to complete the land acquisition process for Kouchibouguac National Park in New Brunswick.

Prior to the 1960s, there was little civic resistance to expropriations for national parks. However, society began to reassess its relationship with authority (La Forest and Roy, 1981). Residents affected by government plans to establish Kouchibouguac and Gros Morne national parks demonstrated their opposition in a massive resistance.

This resistance resulted in a number of actions. In 1980, Canada and New Brunswick commissioned a special inquiry into the violence and public controversy that surrounded the establishment of Kouchibouguac National Park. The inquiry condemned the government's policy of requiring mass expropriations of lands required for national park purposes. And while it urged the government to proceed with developing the park, it recommended that affected residents be allowed to continue commercial fishing and clam-digging activities within the park, that Parks Canada emphasize bilingual staffing because the park lay in a predominantly French-speaking area, and that the history of the Acadian community be stressed in the park's communication programs.

The government began to change its approach to dealing with local people starting in Gros Morne National Park, Newfoundland. Under the Family Homes Expropriation Act, passed by the Newfoundland legislature in 1970, the 125 families affected by the park were not forced to move. Few accepted the offer to leave their outport communities. Today, there are seven communities located within several park enclaves where the park boundary simply is drawn around them. The National Parks Act also was amended in 1988 to allow local residents to continue cutting firewood and snaring rabbits within the national park, thereby redressing two of their main grievances against the park.

The government amended its policy in 1979 and again in the Canada National Parks Act in 2000, to prohibit the expropriation of private landowners in areas where it wants to establish or enlarge national parks. Private land can now be acquired for parks purposes only if the owner is willing to sell the land to the government. Cases in point are the current land acquisition programs for the Grasslands and Bruce Peninsula National Parks. Land is being acquired only from those landowners willing to sell their land.

Finally, the government now must ensure that there is local support for new national parks before proceeding with park establishment. While this has lengthened the time it takes to successfully negotiate a national park, it involves local communities in the negotiations for new parks. The government is trying to ensure that new national parks are supported by local communities and that they make a positive contribution to the community's way of life.

Aboriginal Land Claims

In 1962 the federal government began to examine potential national park sites in the Yukon and Northwest Territories. Plans to mine the Kluane Game Sanctuary in the Yukon and to dam the Nahanni River in the Northwest Territories prompted public campaigns for their protection. The government of Prime Minister Pierre Elliot Trudeau announced plans to turn both areas into national parks in 1972.

Jean Chrétien, Trudeau's parks minister, wrote that 'when I saw the Nahanni River in the Northwest Territories and the Kluane Range in the Yukon, I wanted to protect them forever and eventually did' (Chrétien, 1985: 68). He was similarly moved to create Auyuittuq National Park after flying over Baffin Island. 'I was so excited that I said to my wife, "Aline, I will make this a national park for you"' (Chrétien, 1985: 68).

Legislation to create the three parks was opposed, however, by several Native organizations representing Aboriginal people who lived in the territories. For example, the Inuit Taparisat of Canada, who represented the Inuit of the eastern Arctic, contended that the government was acting unilaterally and taking Inuit land to establish the parks. The Inuit charged that the government was, in effect, expropriating land from the Aboriginal people in contravention of the Canadian Bill of Rights (Fenge, 1978). The issue was resolved through amendments to the National Parks Act that designated the three parks as national park reserves pending the resolution of Aboriginal land claims. The Act also enshrined the rights of Aboriginal people to hunt, trap, and fish in northern national parks. In essence, the Native people were not giving up their claim to lands to which they asserted Aboriginal title; they simply agreed to allow the federal government to administer a park on their land until such time as their land claim agreement was ratified by both Parliament and Aboriginal people. The claim itself would establish final park boundaries and management conditions.

The amendments to the National Parks Act established the precedent for all other national parks that are subject to Aboriginal land claim agreements. To establish new national parks, the government must now negotiate agreements both with the provincial or territorial governments, and with Aboriginal people. Hence, parks such as South Moresby, Pacific Rim, and the Mingan Archipelago in southern Canada are designated national park reserves pending the settlement of land claims. In October 2000, Auyuittuq was legally changed from a national park reserve to a national park with the conclusion of a formal agreement between federal government and Inuit and the passage of legislation only days before the 2000 federal election.

Northern Canada and New Parks

Justice Tom Berger's Mackenzie Valley Pipeline Inquiry of 1974–5 set the tone for the founding of new national parks for the next two decades. Among other things, Berger drew attention to the need to protect the northern wilderness and to 'do so now'. Berger argued that in northern Canada 'Withdrawal of land from any industrial use will be necessary in some instances to preserve wilderness, wildlife species and critical habitat' (Berger, 1977: 31). To that end, Berger recommended the north slope of the Yukon as a national park to protect the calving grounds of the Porcupine caribou herd from industrial development.

When the Hon. J. Hugh Faulkner became the minister in charge of parks in 1978, he acted on Berger's recommendations. In 1978, he withdrew the north slope of the Yukon from industrial development and announced plans to establish a national park in the area. He also announced the '6 North of 60' program to initiate public consultation on a plan to establish five new national parks in the territories, and a Canadian Landmark to protect the Pingos of Tuktoyaktuk. Twenty-two years later, three of the proposed areas are now protected in national parks (Northern Yukon, Ellesemere Island, and Banks Island) with a fourth area, Wager Bay, scheduled to become a national park in 2001. The fifth area, Bathurst Inlet, was dropped because of extensive mineral staking and a lack of local support. Tuktut Nogait National Park was established instead, to represent its natural region. While it took some time to achieve these parks, Faulkner's announcement clearly gave the park establishment program some concrete areas to focus on, and remained a preoccupation of Parks Canada for several decades.

As the 1985 centennial year drew close, announcements on new national parks were reduced to a trickle because of budget cuts, the onset of a recession, and an overall decline in public and political interest both in the environment and in wilderness protection. The lack of local, Aboriginal, and provincial support for many of the planned parks was also an important factor. New monies for park expansion were in short supply partly because of the need to spend money developing facilities in the new parks. Many of the new park agreements signed by Chrétien called for a large investment of federal dollars in the development of recreational and tourism infrastructure. For example, $22 million was spent to build a 62-km stretch of road in La Maurice National Park (Lothian, 1987). But there was some progress. Two park agreements were signed between 1974 and 1984: Pukaskwa in 1974 and Grasslands in 1981, although the latter agreement failed to produce a park until a new agreement between Canada and Saskatchewan was approved in 1988. And in the dying days of the Liberal government of Prime Minister John Turner, two additional parks were established: the Mingan Archipelago National Park Reserve in Quebec and the Northern Yukon National Park.

The establishment of the Northern Yukon National Park (now called Ivvavik) was the first park established as part of the comprehensive land claims settlement process, setting a precedent for future northern national parks (Sadler, 1989). Both the Government of Canada and the Committee for Original People's Entitlement, representing the Inuvialuit of the Western Arctic, agreed to the park because it met their respective objectives: it represents several natural regions of the national parks system; and it prohibits any industrial development within the calving grounds of the Porcupine caribou herd, which supports the traditional way of life of Aboriginal people.

Between 1968 and 1984, the Liberal governments of Prime Minister Trudeau and his short-term successor, John Turner, made a substantial contribution to the preservation of Canadian wilderness, particularly in the creation of 13 new national parks and the protection of more than 64,000 sq. km of wilderness lands: a land mass greater than the combined size of Nova Scotia and Prince Edward Island. But with the election of Brian Mulroney's Conservative government in September 1984, park advocates wondered if the Mulroney government would work to finish and expand on the many Liberal park initiatives that were left uncompleted.

PARKS ON THE POLITICAL AGENDA (1984–PRESENT)

The centennial year of the national parks should have been a chance to celebrate the achievements of the past century, and to plan for their future. Instead, it proved to be a low point in their history. The new Conservative parks minister, the Hon. Suzanne Blais-Grenier, quickly angered Canadians when she cancelled all guided walks in national parks, and suggested she would not rule out logging and mining in them. The public outcry that followed was tangible proof that Canadians rejected the industrial exploitation of park resources, and was cited as a major reason for her loss of the portfolio in August 1985 (Bercuson, 1986).

In the centennial year no new national parks were established, nor was any plan to complete the system adopted, but it was not for lack of trying. In the dying months of the Liberal government, Parks Canada had been developing plans to expand the national parks system as its centrepiece for the 1985 centennial year. It was seeking cabinet approval to complete the national parks system by the year 2000 and for an allocation of $495 million to fund 20 new terrestrial and 10 new marine parks.

Blais-Grenier gutted the plan and it never saw the light of day (McNamee, 1992).

The public clearly demonstrated in 1985 the extent to which government action to protect wilderness was an urgency. Participants in the Canadian Assembly Project, a citizen's celebration of 100 years of heritage conservation, identified over 500 natural areas in need of protection. At the top of the list was a wilderness area on the far western shores of Canada that would increasingly dominate Ottawa's parks agenda—South Moresby.

Post Centennial Action on New Parks

The Hon. Tom McMillan took over the parks portfolio in late 1985 and made it a high priority. Under McMillan, five new national parks were created, Parliament approved the first comprehensive amendments to the National Parks Act since 1930, the National Marine Parks policy finally was adopted, the first National Marine Park was established at Fathom Five in Ontario, and the federal Task Force on Park Establishment was appointed to examine new strategies to facilitate the creation of new national parks.

Reporting in June 1987, the Task Force concluded that Canada must take decisive action to protect its disappearing wilderness. It called on McMillan and Parks Canada to develop a strategic plan to ensure substantial progress by the year 2000 in completing the national parks system. Substantial progress was required, because, in 1985, the national parks system was less than half complete (Dearden and Gardner, 1987). However, McMillan was not interested in developing a blueprint to complete the system (McNamee, 1986). His priorities were the preservation of the South Moresby wilderness archipelago in BC as a national park, and the completion of several unfinished park initiatives. Political negotiations were finally completed by McMillan to establish Ellesmere Island, Pacific Rim, Grasslands, and the Bruce Peninsula as National Parks.

The success of McMillan with the support of thousands of Canadians in preserving South Moresby may have been a turning point in the wilderness preservation movement (Dearden, 1988). John Broadhead (1989: 51), a leader of the South Moresby lobby, observed that:

> South Moresby had shaken the national tree. A profound moral dilemma had crystallized in the Canadian conscience, and it could no longer be ignored. It was this: which is more important—the integrity of the earth and the spiritual recreation of future generations, or short-term legal responsibilities to corporations and their shareholders? More to the point, what kind of system is this that renders the two mutually exclusive?

In 1988, both McMillan and the Canadian Parliament came down on the side of the integrity of Canada's national parks. Responding to requests from several conservation groups to make the protection of natural resources in parks the priority, McMillan approved and Parliament amended the National Parks Act to state: 'Maintenance of ecological integrity through the protection of natural resources shall be the first priority when considering park zoning and visitor use in a management plan' (Canada, 1988).

This amendment was significant for two reasons. First, it clearly established the chief purpose of national parks to be the protection of natural resources. Second, in order to maintain the ecological integrity of the national parks, the government must now take action to define and eliminate the range of internal and external threats to park resources. Thus, the act compels the government to act against threats to park resources that emanate from areas outside the parks. This amendment prompted Parks Canada during the 1990s to define and implement programs that emphasized the protection of park resources over the traditional emphasis on developing and using parklands for tourism and recreation.

In the political arena, the exploitation of wilderness areas was clearly the dominant ideology. While resource development was accelerating, there was no corresponding effort by governments to preserve special natural areas. The federal government's lack of interest in developing a plan to complete the job of representing each of its 39 natural regions spurred the conservation community to lobby for the political commitment necessary to achieve this goal.

The Endangered Spaces Wilderness Campaign

The launching of the Endangered Spaces campaign by World Wildlife Fund Canada and the Canadian Parks and Wilderness Society in 1989 stimulated public advocacy efforts to expand the national parks system. The campaign goal was to persuade the federal, provincial, and territorial governments to complete their parks and protected areas systems by the year 2000 in order to represent each of the nation's approximately 350 natural regions.

In 1989, the Hon. Lucien Bouchard, then minister in charge of national parks, announced that the federal government would complete the national parks system by the year 2000 because 'the very fragility of the planet compels the expansion of the national parks system' (McNamee, 1992). The federal cabinet confirmed this as a government-wide commitment when it released Canada's Green Plan, a federal environmental strategy, in December 1990. The Green Plan established targets to meet this commitment: at least five new terrestrial national parks were to be established by 1996, and agreements on an additional 13 parks that were required to complete the system would be achieved by 2000. It also allocated over $40 million to help plan and found new parks.

The campaign played a key role in prompting significant achievements by the federal government (see Chapter 2). Between 1989 and 2000, Parks Canada established five new national parks, adding over 66,700 sq. km to the system. Unfortunately, at the end of the campaign, 14 of Parks Canada's 39 natural regions still lacked a national park. However, significant progress was made in five of the 14 unrepresented natural regions. For example:

- In 1996, Prime Minister Chrétien announced the interim-protection of 32,300 sq. km, land that may be permanently protected in two new national parks around Wager Bay and on northern Bathurst Island, Nunavut.

- In northern Labrador, an additional 6,600 sq. km was given permanent protection by the government of Newfoundland and Labrador and is soon to be designated the Torngat Mountains National Park Reserve.
- A land acquisition program to establish a national park in the Gulf Islands, one of the most threatened Canadian landscapes, was launched in 1995. In 2001, the federal and British Columbia governments negotiated a final agreement to establish a national park reserve that will protect all or a portion of 13 islands and total approximately 2,500 ha.
- A study on the proposed Manitoba Lowlands National Park concluded in 1998 that the proposed park was feasible.

National Parks as Endangered Spaces

While the loss of unprotected wilderness lands has captured public attention, there is growing concern over the degradation of existing parklands and their natural resources. In the 1960s and 1970s, the prevailing concern was the impact of too many visitors, and the inappropriate development of tourism facilities on park resources. In the 1980s, there was growing evidence that developments in and around national parks were isolating them, and causing a decrease in the environmental quality of the parks. The 1990s saw a growing effort to identify actions to protect the ecological integrity of National Parks, and to develop the greater national park ecosystem concept as a way to co-ordinate the management of parklands and adjacent areas.

The first indication that many of Canada's national parks were at risk came in a 1987 report by Parks Canada that concluded 'that the magnitude and frequency of transboundary concerns will increasingly become a problem because of continuing development and pollution' (Irvine, 1987: vii). Three years later, the first State of the National Parks Report confirmed that none of the parks was immune to internal and external threats, citing water pollution, poaching, and logging on lands adjacent to park boundaries as some of the major threats to the integrity of parklands.

A decade later, Parks Canada confirmed that 13 of 36 national parks reported that the significant impact of human activities on park ecosystems was increasing relative to a similar analysis in a 1992 report. In essence, there was a measured decline in the health of natural ecosystems in one-third of our national parks over a five-year period. Only three national parks reported that the impact is decreasing, and only one— Vuntut— could report its ecosystems in a pristine state. National parks that were part of efforts to manage the broader landscape for sustainability, such as biosphere reserves, fared no better. None of the three Biosphere Reserves could report a decrease in the cumulative impact of human activities. Three of five model forests reported that activities on external land were having a 'severe' and increasing impact on ecological integrity (the worst rating).

For most of their history, national parks were wild spaces located within larger expanses of wilderness. More recently, industrial and agricultural development on adjacent lands has moved right up to national park borders. The boundaries of Riding Mountain National Park are clearly visible from space because agricultural development has removed the boreal forest right up to the straight-line boundaries of the park. The 1990 State of the Parks Report described Fundy national park as 'an ecological island in [an] area of intensively managed forest land' (Canadian Parks Service, 1991: 49). It also reported that Pacific Rim National Park Reserve is a narrow strip of wilderness and predicted that 'logging adjacent to [the] park could adversely affect [park] resources [and] watershed' (ibid.: 223). In effect, human activities outside parks are reducing them to 'endangered spaces'.

The growing consensus that Canada's national parks were under increasing assault led to two landmark studies, one on the future of Banff National Park and another on the future of the national park system. The motivation for both studies was similar— a need to secure independent substantiation that Banff and the rest of the national parks were under threat, and to develop an action plan to save these natural areas.

In 1994, the federal minister for national parks appointed the Banff-Bow Valley Task Force to provide direction on the management of human use and development within the Bow Valley watershed of Banff National Park. After two years, the Task Force concluded that if the current trends continue 'it will lead to the destruction of the conditions in the Banff-Bow Valley that are required for a National Park ' (Banff-Bow Valley Study, 1996: 18) Furthermore, the independent Task Force stated that Banff 'is clearly at a crossroads and changes must come quickly if the Park is to survive' (ibid.). Its 400-page report, released in October 1996 and backed by a consensus statement from a multi-stakeholder round table set up to support the review, produced a number of immediate actions. A new management plan for the park was released, legally protected wilderness areas were designated by the federal Cabinet, and a number of park developments were removed. And the report continues to influence the direction of the park as it works to restore its ecological integrity (see Chapter 10).

Several years later, the federal government appointed the Panel on the Ecological Integrity of Canada's National Parks to review the health of the entire national park system and to recommend directions on how best to protect it (see Chapter 9). Its conclusions were dramatic: 'Ecological integrity in Canada's national parks is under threat from many sources and for many reasons. These threats to Canada's sacred places present a crisis of national importance' (Parks Canada Agency, 2000: 1–9).

In releasing the Panel's report, national parks minister Sheila Copps informed Canadians that the Panel's report 'will not be gathering dust' and that she was 'asking Parks Canada to find ways of implementing all of the Panel's recommendations, if humanly and legally possible . . .' (Lopoukhine, 2000). At the same time, Parks Canada released an Action Plan concentrating on four major targets: making ecological integrity central in legislation and policy; building partnerships for ecological integrity; planning for ecological integrity; and renewing Parks Canada to support the ecological integrity mandate. A year later, a progress report on Parks Canada's actions on all 127 recommendations was released to the first meeting of the Round Table that is required to meet every two years pursuant to the *Parks Canada Agency Act* (Parks Canada Agency, 2001).

Some political action was taken by Parliament to implement the Panel's report. Shortly before the 2000 Federal Election, a new *Canada's National Parks Act* was passed with a revised mandate that now states: 'Maintenance or restoration of ecological integrity, through the protection of natural resources and natural processes, shall be the first priority of the Minister when considering all aspects of the management of parks' (Parliament, 2000). The new section broadens the direction to Parks Canada both to maintain ecological integrity and to restore it in degraded parks. It also directs the Minister to consider ecological integrity in all aspects of park management, as recommended by the Panel.

In the fight to protect Canada's national parks, environmental groups have broadened their tool kit by turning increasingly to the Federal Court. The first example of success came when the Canadian Parks and Wilderness Society took the government to court in 1992, alleging that logging in Wood Buffalo National Park was in contravention of the National Parks Act. Several months later, the Federal Court of Canada declared a 1983 contract that allowed logging in the park, and the order in council approving the contract, to be 'invalid and unauthorized by the provisions of the National Parks Act' (Federal Court of Canada, 1992). The Society was back in court in 2001 when it launched another legal action against the government, this time for Parks Canada's decision to allow the clearing and opening of an abandoned road through Wood Buffalo National Park. (In October 2001, the Federal Court of Canada ruled against the Society, stating, in part, that the new ecological integrity clause afforded no higher level of protection to the national parks.)

Environmental groups have also used the courts to protect national parks from external threats. In 1998, the Federal Court ordered the federal and Alberta governments to redo their environmental assessment of a proposed open-pit coal mine on lands immediately adjacent to Jasper National Park. The Court found that the environmental assessment failed to consider the cumulative impact of the coal mine along with a series of other approved and proposed mineral and timber projects in the larger region. Shortly after the second series of hearings were concluded, the proponent announced that for financial reasons the Cheviot project was on hold. Once again, public advocacy groups proved a potent force in shaping the government's national parks policy and preserving the Canadian wilderness.

CONCLUSION

When Parliament passed the National Parks Act in 1930, it declared that the national parks are 'dedicated to the people of Canada for their benefit, education and enjoyment and such parks shall be maintained and made use of so as to leave them unimpaired for the benefit of future generations'. Administrators of the parks have, for many years, interpreted this as being support for a recreational mandate. Today, however, national parks benefit Canadians by providing environmental protection for shrinking wilderness and wildlife habitat, opportunities for them to experience wild places, and benchmarks against which to measure the impact of society's activities on the landscape. And with the report of the Ecological Integrity Panel, much more emphasis is being placed on the notion of maintaining and passing on the national parks to future generations in an unimpaired state.

History has shown that governments do not act in a benevolent fashion when it comes to wilderness protection. Politics and public pressure are what drive the park establishment process, and will continue to do so, because there is no law requiring the establishment of parks, or the preservation of wilderness areas. Therefore, we must understand more fully the political process, and seek to influence it with better information on the full range of national park and wilderness values so that politicians will act more decisively to preserve wilderness.

History has also demonstrated that wilderness preservation is a non-partisan political issue, and one that requires the commitment of the minister in charge of the national parks portfolio. Jean Chrétien, from the Liberal party, and Tom McMillan, from the Conservative party, shared a common determination to achieve political deals that, together, resulted in the creation of 15 national parks and the preservation of almost 100,000 sq. km of wilderness. It will require other politicians with the determination of Chrétien and McMillan to establish the remaining national parks. And public advocacy groups will have to ensure that each successive parks minister takes action to create new national parks, and to stop the incremental loss of national park lands to commercial development.

Perhaps Chrétien said it best when he opened Kejimkujik National Park in 1969: 'Our national parks are part of the original face of Canada, inviolable spots which provide sanctuaries for man as well as nature. But it is man who must extend and preserve them. This is the task that lies ahead' (Lothian, 1976: 122).

ACKNOWLEDGEMENTS

The author kindly acknowledges Jacinthe Seguin for her insight, comments, and help in revising this chapter.

REFERENCES

Anon. 1962. 'A Plan for Canada's Centennial', *Canadian Audubon* 24, 3: 72–5.

Anon. 1972. 'Well Done, Mr. Chrétien!', *Park News* 8, 3: 2.

Banff-Bow Valley Study. 1996. 'Banff-Bow Valley: At the Crossroads', *Summary Report of the Banff-Bow Valley Task Force*. Ottawa: Auditor General of Canada.

Bella, L. 1987. *Parks for Profit*. Montreal: Harvest House.

Bercuson, D., J.L. Granatstein, and W.R. Young. 1986. *Sacred Trust? Brian Mulroney and the Conservative Party in Power*. Toronto: Doubleday Canada.

Berger, T. 1977. *Northern Frontier, Northern Homeland: The Report of the Mackenzie Valley Pipeline Inquiry*. Ottawa: Minister of Supply and Services.

Bill, R. 1982. 'Attempts to Establish National Parks in Canada: A Case History in Labrador from 1969 to 1979', MA thesis, Carleton University.

Broadhead, J. 1989. 'The All Alone Stone Manifesto', in M. Hummel, ed., *Endangered Spaces: The Future for Canada's Wilderness*. Toronto: Key Porter Books, 50–62.

Canada. 1969. *National Parks Policy*. Ottawa: Queen's Printer.

———. 1982. *Parks Canada Policy*. Ottawa: Minister of Supply and Services.

———.1988. *An Act to Amend the National Parks Act Bill C-30*. Ottawa: Minister of Supply and Services Canada.

———. Canadian Environmental Advisory Council. 1991. *A Protected Areas Vision for Canada*. Ottawa: Minister of Supply and Services.

Canadian Parks and Wilderness Society. 1988. *Park News*, 25th Anniversary Issue and Park News Final Edition, 23.

Canadian Parks Service. 1991. *State of the Parks 1990 Report*. Ottawa: Minister of Supply and Services.

Chrétien, J. 1969. 'Our Evolving National Parks System', in J.G. Nelson and R.C. Scace, eds, *The Canadian National Parks: Today and Tomorrow*. Calgary: University of Calgary Press, 7–14.

———.1985. Straight from the Heart. Toronto: Key Porter.

Craig-Brown, R. 1969. 'The Doctrine of Usefulness: Natural Resource and National Parks Policy in Canada, 1887–1914', in J.G. Nelson, ed., *Canada Parks and Perspective*. Montreal: Harvest House, 46–62.

Dearden, P. 1988. 'Mobilising Public Support for Environment: The Case of South Moresby Island, British Columbia', in *Need-to Know: Effective Communication for Environmental Groups*. Proceedings of the 1987 Annual Joint Meeting of the Public Advisory Committees to the Environment, Council of Alberta, 62–75

——— and J. Gardner. 1987. 'Systems Planning for Protected Areas in Canada: A Review of Caucus Candidate Areas and Concepts, Issues and Prospects for Further Investigation', in R.C. Scace and J.G. Nelson, eds, *Heritage for Tomorrow: Canadian Assembly on National Parks and Protected Areas*. Ottawa: Environment Canada Parks, 2: 9–48.

Federal Court of Canada. 1992. *Canadian Parks and Wilderness Society v. Her Majesty the Queen in Right of Canada*. Trial Division, Vancouver.

Fenge, T. 1978. 'Decision Making for National Parks in Canada North of 60', Working Paper #3, President's Committee on Northern Studies, University of Waterloo.

Foster, J. 1978. *Working for Wildlife: The Beginning of Preservation in Canada*. Toronto: University of Toronto Press..

Henderson, G. 1969. 'The Role of the Public in National Park Planning and Decision Making', in G. Nelson, ed., *Canadian Parks in Perspective*. Montreal: Harvest House, 329–43.

Irvine, M.H. 1987. 'Natural Resource Management Problems, Issues and/or Concerns in Canadian National Parks', Natural Resources Branch, Environment Canada Parks, (unpublished).

Johnston, M.E. 1985. 'A Club with Vision: The Alpine Club of Canada and Conservation 1906–1930', *Park News* 21: 6–10.

La Forest, G.V., and M.K. Roy. 1991. *The Kouchibouguac Affair: The Report of the Special Inquiry on Kouchibouguac National Park*. Fredericton.

Lohnes, D.M. 1992 'A Land Manager's Perspective on Science and Parks Management', in J.H.M. Willison et al., eds, *Science and the Management of Protected Areas*. Proceedings of an international conference held at Acadia University, Nova Scotia, 14–19 May 1991. Amsterdam: Elsevier Science Publishing Company, 19–24.

Lopoukhine, Nik. 2000. Presentation to the IVth meeting of SAMPA, University of Waterloo, 19 May.

Lothian, W.F. 1976. *History of Canada's National Parks*, vols. 1 and 2. Ottawa: Parks Canada, Minister of Indian and Northern Affairs.

———. 1987. *A Brief History of Canada's National Parks*. Ottawa: Minister of Supply and Services Canada.

Marty, S. 1984. *A Grand and Fabulous Notion: The First Century of Canada's Parks*. Ottawa: Minister of Supply and Services Canada.

MacEachern, Alan. 2001. *Natural Selections: National Parks in Atlantic Canada, 1935–1970*. Montreal: McGill-Queen's University Press.

McNamee, K. 1986. 'Tom McMillan: Our Friend in Court', *Park News* 21: 40–1.

———.1992. 'Overcoming Decades of Indifference—The Painful Process of Preserving Wilderness', *Borealis* 3: 55.

Nash, R. 1969. 'Wilderness and Man in North America', in G. Nelson and R.C. Scace, eds, *The Canadian National Parks: Today and Tomorrow*. Calgary: University of Calgary Press, 35–52.

Parks Canada Agency. 2000. *Unimpaired for Future Generations? Protecting Ecological Integrity with Canada's National Parks, Vol. 2: Setting a New Direction for Canada's National Parks*. Report of the Panel on the Ecological Integrity of Canada's National Parks. Ottawa.

Parks Canada Agency. 2001. *Parks Canada First Priority: Progress Report on Implementation of the Recommendations of the Panel on the Ecological Integrity of Canada's National Parks*. Ottawa: Minister of Public Works and Government Services Canada.

Parliament of Canada. 2000. An act respecting the national parks of Canada. Statutes of Canada 2000. Chapter 32, Second Session, Thirty-sixth Parliament, 48–9 Elizabeth II, 1999–2000.

Rodney, W. 1969. *Kootenai Brown: His Life and Times*. Sidney, B.C.: Gray's Publishing.

Sadler, B. 1989. 'National Parks, Wilderness Preservation and Native Peoples in Northern Canada', *Natural Resources Journal*: 185–204.

Waiser, W. 1989. *Saskatchewan's Playground: A History of Prince Albert National Park*. Saskatoon: Fifth House.

KEY WORDS/CONCEPTS

CPR

National Policy

multiple use

tourism

Rocky Mountain Park Act (1887)

Dominion Forest Reserves and Parks
 Act (1911)

National Parks Act (1930)

John Muir

James Harkin

Spray Lake controversy

Silent Spring

National Park Policy (1964)

National Park Policy (1979)

dual mandate

National Parks System Plan

Endangered Spaces campaign

Amendment to the National Parks
 Act (1988)

Banff–Bow Valley Task Force

Revised National Parks Act (Bill C-27)

STUDY QUESTIONS

1. Discuss the connection between the construction of the Canadian Pacific Railway (CPR) and the early development of national parks in Canada.
2. Comment on the 'National Policy' of John A MacDonald, and how this influenced the management of Canada's first national parks.
3. Compare the Canadian view of national parks in the late 1800's (e.g., Banff) with the American view (e.g., Yellowstone).
4. Compare the Spray Lakes debate (Banff) with the Hetch Hetchy debate (Yosemite).
5. Discuss the role of James Harkin on the evolution of national parks in Canada.
6. What was the significance of the public response to the creation of a new national park at Kouchibouguac, New Brunswick? Discuss the role of local communities in the establishment and management of national parks.
7. Discuss the role of the National and Provincial Parks Association of Canada (now the Canadian Parks and Wilderness Society—CPAWS) on the development of national parks in Canada.
8. Comment on the role of provincial governments in the development of new national parks over the past 50 years.
9. What was the purpose of the Endangered Spaces Campaign?
10. Why study the history of parks? Of what relevance is this history to the management of parks today?

CHAPTER 3

Protected Areas in Canada:
The Endangered Spaces Campaign

Kevin McNamee

INTRODUCTION

In just over 10 years, an environmental campaign succeeded in more than doubling the amount of protected wilderness in Canada. The Endangered Spaces Campaign, launched in 1989 by World Wildlife Fund Canada (WWF), came to an end on Canada Day 2000 after helping to protect 390,000 sq. km or 3.9 per cent of the Canadian landscape. Entering the twenty-first century, Canada has now protected almost 7 per cent of its natural heritage from logging, wilderness, hydroelectric development, and oil and gas activities.

An additional 5 per cent is conserved in protected areas that do not legally prohibit industrial development. For example, the Canadian Wildlife Service administers several hundred national wildlife areas and migratory bird sanctuaries across Canada. These were not counted by World Wildlife Fund because under legislation, the Minister of Environment can permit logging, mining, oil and gas extraction, and other activities. However, Polar Bear Pass National Wildlife Area was counted because it is protected from industrial development through a land withdrawal order under federal legislation.

This Campaign succeeded in protecting more land in a decade than had been protected over the previous century. During those 104 years between 1885 when Canada's first national park was established in Banff, and 1989 when the Campaign was launched, just under 3 per cent of Canada was protected. Between the fall of 1989 when WWF unveiled the Endangered Spaces Campaign, and its conclusion in 2000, the amount of protected land in Canada more than doubled. The purpose of this chapter is to examine the goals and accomplishments of the Campaign, some of the reasons behind its success and some of its failures, and to reflect on its legacy and on the challenge ahead.

Background to the Campaign

In launching the Endangered Spaces Campaign, WWF challenged Canada's federal, provincial, and territorial governments to protect a representative sample of each of Canada's 486 terrestrial natural regions by the year 2000, and each of its marine regions by the year 2010. It sought to turn the growing level of public support for environmental and wilderness protection during the 1980s into political actions that would protect the nation's disappearing natural diversity.

The notion for such a Campaign was prompted by several factors that emerged during the 1980s, all coalescing to suggest that a co-ordinated national campaign was needed to push governments to place wilderness protection on the political agenda. With 90 per cent of Canada being Crown land, it falls largely to governments to set aside sufficient wilderness designations. Such an effort as the Endangered Spaces Campaign was required because, at the time, there were no laws in Canada forcing governments to set aside wilderness areas.

First, in 1985, Parks Canada celebrated its Centennial year (Chapter 2). Amidst all the hoopla accompanying the festivities, it formed regional caucuses to evaluate the current status of park establishment across the country (Scace and Nelson, 1987) and a national committee to evaluate and synthesize this work. The committee observed that Parks Canada's national park system was less than half complete. Furthermore, most provinces did not even have a system's plan to guide future growth. The Committee posed two questions:

1. Are agencies responsible for protected area systems making systems completion one of their top priorities and allocating resources accordingly, or are they merely seeking to maintain what they have?
2. Is there the political will at all levels to recognize the importance and urgency of systems completion and land acquisition in an increasingly competitive environment?

They concluded that negative answers to either of these two questions would be sufficient to stall any further growth. They called for a national campaign to raise public awareness to generate agency and political response (Dearden and Gardner, 1987: 37).

Second, in 1987, the federal Task Force on Park Establishment (Environment Canada, 1987) warned that if Canada did not act to preserve its wilderness areas with some urgency, opportunities to do so would have all but disappeared by the year 2000. Reporting to the minister in charge of Parks Canada, the Task Force's warning served as a clarion call, prompting the launch of a national campaign to try to identify and protect such wilderness areas. Following on the Task Force's report, Dianne Pachal of the Alberta Wilderness Association organized a meeting in Calgary of non-government organizations from every province and territory to begin to articulate a national wilderness strategy. While this particular effort was sporadic, it helped plant the seeds for a national campaign.

Third, in 1987, the landmark report of the World Commission on Environment and Development (United Nations, 1987) called on all nations to complete a network of strictly protected areas. Building on the work of several global protected area meetings, the Commission recommended that this network represent each of the earth's major ecosystems as part of its overall commitment to protecting diversity of species and ecosystems and implementing sustainable development. Once this was achieved, the land protected should total approximately 12 per cent. Thus, a high-profile world commission placed the need to complete a protected areas network as a central component in the fight to save the planet from destructive human practices that are imperilling the web of life.

Fourth, after a 13-year battle, the federal and BC governments signed an agreement to establish the South Moresby/Gwaii Haanas National Park Reserve to protect a wilderness archipelago that was home to an impressive temperate rain forest and the traditional homelands of the Haida Nation (Broadhead, 1989). This issue demonstrated that the cost to governments and conservation groups of fighting for the protection of wilderness areas on an issue-by-issue basis was prohibitive. Instead, a national campaign was required that would firmly establish the need to preserve wilderness on the political agenda. It also prompted Arlin Hackman, a major architect of the Endangered Spaces Campaign, to ask: 'Can we sustain the momentum of the campaign to protect South Moresby? . . . Or is the cause of wilderness inevitably reactive, advanced only through case-by-case confrontation' (Hackman, 1988).

Finally, the experience of conservation groups in Ontario in the early 1980s demonstrated that a large number of protected areas could be established within the context of one land use decision. In 1983, the Ontario government established 155 new provincial parks as part of its provincial Strategic Land Use Plan. The groups lobbied the government to identify and establish the protected areas required to represent each of the province's 66 natural regions and to meet the government's own protected area goals. This approach served as the blueprint for the Endangered Spaces Campaign.

The Endangered Spaces Campaign was launched at a very timely period in Canadian history. First, in the late 1980s, Canadians were very concerned about the state of the planet's environment, with a number of disasters, including the Exxon Valdez oil spill in Alaskan waters, the hole in the ozone layer, and the advent of the twentieth anniversary of Earth Day prompting a collective anxiety and mood for action. Next, a number of regional wilderness issues began to shatter the great Canadian myth that our nation is made up of endless tracts of wilderness that will never suffer the axe. Third, a number of global, national, and provincial initiatives, such as the focus on sustainable development, national conservation strategies, conserving biodiversity, and the fate of rain forests, all created a context in which to push for new protected areas.

The Elements of the Campaign

One of the immediate decisions of the Campaign, and one that was never revisited over the 10 years of its effort, was the question of protection. Just declaring an area as a park or ecological reserve was not enough. The Campaign set the following standard: 'an area had to be permanently protected (usually through legislation) and prohibit industrial uses, including logging, mining, hydro-electric and oil and gas development. For a marine area, a qualifying protected area must prohibit oil and gas drilling, dumping, dredging, bottom trawling and dragging, along with other non-renewable resource exploration and extractive activities' (World Wildlife Fund, 2000).

When the Campaign was launched in the fall of 1989, there were two foundation documents: a book entitled *Endangered Spaces: The Future for Canada's Wilderness*; and the Canadian Wilderness Charter. According to the book's general editor (Hummel, 1989), the book placed a fundamental question before all Canadians: 'How important is wilderness to the future of our country?' (ibid.: 9). *Endangered Spaces* described the natural environment of each jurisdiction, and provided an overview of the challenge that each jurisdiction faced. The book was delivered to each and every federal, provincial, and territorial politician of every political party across Canada. Campaign patrons, such as Glen Davis of the N.M. Davis Corporation in Toronto, personally delivered books to the House of Commons in Ottawa.

The more enduring piece was the Canadian Wilderness Charter. It called on governments, industries, environmental groups, and individual Canadians to commit themselves 'to a national effort to establish at least one representative protected area in each of the natural regions of Canada by the year 2000'. By the end of the Campaign, over 600,000 individual Canadians and an impressive list of institutions, such as the Canadian Chamber of Commerce, had endorsed the Charter. Some of these individuals participated in annual climbs of the CN Tower, the Calgary Tower, and Signal Hill in St. John's, or walked along the Rideau Canal to Parliament, or paddled or biked across Canada to raise money and support for wilderness preservation.

Backed by several key philanthropists, foundations, and corporations, World Wildlife Fund Canada was able to fund and keep in place a network of endangered spaces co-ordinators in each political jurisdiction to advance the Campaign's goal. Thus, while there was a centrally directed Campaign based in Toronto, there was clearly a very strong regional approach for each jurisdiction, taking into account their differing political, economic, and social circumstances. The constant day-to-day presence of co-ordinators was an essential element of the Campaign. Organizations such as the Canadian Nature Federation (CNF) and the Canadian Parks and Wilderness Society (CPAWS) provided some of the co-ordinators. For example, the federal co-ordinator was the CNF's Wildlands Campaign Director.

Perhaps one of the most difficult and early questions that the Campaign faced was —What constitutes representation? Each jurisdiction had a different idea. Some felt that the simple presence of a protected area within a natural region meant that that region was fully represented. Others argued that, based on conservation biology principles, a natural region could only be adequately represented if each of its defining features was protected within a park or ecological reserve large enough to maintain natural processes. And some jurisdictions, such as New Brunswick and the Northwest Territories, had not even defined natural regions within their jurisdictions, so for them the question was moot.

Despite the fact that all of Canada's senior governments endorsed the Campaign goal, a consensus among governments never emerged on how to measure progress. So it fell to WWF, working with the Canadian Council on Ecological Areas (CCEA), to develop a national approach to measuring progress. Together they developed the 'enduring features approach'. The CCEA recommended defining natural regions based upon 'enduring features of the environment . . . relatively stable landforms and seaforms and their accompanying plant and animal communities' (World Wildlife Fund, 2000: 5).

Judging the ability of protected areas to represent the enduring features within each of the natural regions was the next task. WWF (ibid.) describes the approach taken:

> The approach developed . . . was to first measure the extent to which each endur-
> ing feature in a natural region was protected, and, second, to measure how well all
> the enduring features of the region were protected, as a whole. Finally, an assess-
> ment of the suitability of the protected area for such things as wide-ranging
> species, or the area's ability to withstand large natural disturbances such as
> wildfires, was also factored in.

All of this led to the ultimate goal—the ability to map out natural regions, and to indicate for each the level of ecological representation by protected areas—'adequate',
'moderate', 'partial', or 'little or none'. WWF could now show decision-makers and
Canadians at large where the holes in the representation were and could help design
new protected areas to fill them.

The final element of the Campaign was an annual national report card released virtually every spring, reporting on the progress of all senior governments towards the
goal of completing their protected area networks. Grades were awarded to each of the
federal, provincial, and territorial governments based on their adoption of a natural
regions framework, annual progress towards protecting areas and completing their
networks, adoption of incentives to promote conservation of private lands, and use of
interim protection measures to keep candidate sites from being lost to development.

The grades were effective throughout most of the Campaign in generating either
political action or public attention. Numerous national and provincial editorials supportive of the Campaign's goal, and chiding lagging governments, were published in
newspapers across Canada. The threat of getting a failing grade, or the opportunity
to improve a grade at the last minute, provoked some progress by several governments over the course of the Campaign. It was reported that one Premier's mother,
upon learning about her son's 'F', took him to task.

PUBLIC SUPPORT FOR THE SPACES CAMPAIGN

No Campaign can succeed in doubling the amount of protected wilderness lands
without enjoying a significant level of public and institutional support. The
Endangered Spaces Campaign enjoyed both throughout most of its decade-long run.

Political Support

Foremost among the Campaign's achievements was soliciting the support of all senior levels of government. In November 1992, the Canadian Parks Minister's Council,
along with the Canadian Council of Ministers of the Environment and the Wildlife

Minister's Council of Canada, all endorsed *A Statement of Commitment to Complete Canada's Networks of Protected Areas*. The key commitment in this Tri-Council statement was to 'make every effort to complete Canada's networks of protected areas representative of Canada's land-based natural regions by the year 2000 and accelerate the protection of areas representative of Canada's marine natural regions.'

This was the first time that all levels of government in Canada reached agreement on a consistent national goal for the nation's parks and protected areas. And over the course of the Campaign, other statements of similar support emerged. For example, in 1991, the Canadian Parliament passed a motion in support of the federal government working co-operatively with other jurisdictions to complete Canada's network of protected areas.

Industry Support

Important statements of support also emerged from both the forestry and mining sectors. The National Forest Sector Strategy and the Leadership Accord of the Whitehorse Mining Initiative, both multi-stakeholder processes, produced consensus statements that include support for the idea of completing a representative network of protected areas. In the case of the mining industry, they were seeking the support of environmental groups for a series of reforms to the mining industry. In turn, the environmentalists were only willing to grant their support in return for the mining industry's support for a network of protected areas free of mineral exploration and development, as well as other key environmental initiatives. That support was achieved in the fall of 1994.

The support of timber and mineral interests did not guarantee that such networks would be easily completed. But they were important statements to government that some important elements of the industry supported the goal put forward in their Tri-Council Statement of Commitment. And they created an opening for discussions.

Another important source of support was from the Canadian Association of Petroleum Producers. While the oil and gas sector did not produce a similar industry-wide statement of support, it did greatly assist in the protection of several important natural areas, including the Northern Rockies in British Columbia, Gwaii Haanas national marine conservation area reserve, and the Whaleback area in Alberta.

Industry was motivated to support the protected areas' goal for several reasons. First, some industrial companies wanted to project a green image and to communicate to the public that protecting the environment was part of their corporate ethic. Second, some companies and associations accepted the argument that early action on identifying, establishing, and ultimately completing protected area networks would remove a great deal of uncertainty around which lands were open or closed to development. Such industries were seeking 'certainty' as to the matrix of land uses that would characterize the Canadian landscape.

Finally, in some cases, they simply acknowledged that certain areas had to be protected. Forestry companies such as Tembec were active proponents of new protected areas in Ontario, and West Fraser Timber voluntarily relinquished logging rights to the Kitlope Valley, enabling the creation of the world's largest temperate rain forest protected area. The Manitoba Mining Association continues to be an active proponent of new protected areas in that province, while several mining companies voluntarily relinquished mineral rights for the creation of Vuntut and Grasslands National Parks. While industry is the first to be criticized for opposing new protected areas, it is seldom the first to be applauded when it makes such decisions possible.

During the Campaign, World Wildlife Fund Canada worked to introduce the concept of protected areas into attempts to certify forest companies and practices as environmentally sustainable. Almost half of Canada is forested. As Hackman observed: 'The Endangered Spaces goal will be difficult if not impossible to attain if the vice-grip of industrial demand on forest land, as expressed in approved harvest levels, is not relaxed . . . it is the volume of timber extraction permitted from the forest, as well as rights and expectations about future volumes, which fundamentally constrain options for new protected areas in Canada's forest today' (Hackman n.d.).

Working through the Forest Stewardship Council, the WWF and other conservation groups, such as Ontario's Wildlands League, sought to ensure that establishment of representative protected areas was part of the criteria that would allow corporations and others to achieve the 'stamp'of their timber operations being declared ecologically sustainable. One of the principles that must be addressed in order to achieve FSC approval is that 'representative samples of existing ecosystems within the landscape shall be proteced in their natural state and recorded on maps' (Elliott and Hackman, 1996: 47).

Aboriginal Support

The involvement of First Nations was a critical factor in the success of many protected area proposals (Chapter 13). A number of land claim agreements, such as the 1993 Nunavut Land Claim Agreement, included sections that outlined a process for establishing new national parks and other forms of protected areas. As a result, the Nunavut claim has paved the way for the creation of three new national parks, and may soon see the establishment of at least two more national parks, one around Wager Bay and another on Bathurst Island.

In summarizing the progress of the Campaign, WWF (World Wildlife Fund, 2000: 8, 13) cited some impressive examples:

> The Vuntut Gwich'in . . . negotiated the establishment of a national park on the Old Crow Flats, an area of outstanding ecological, cultural and economic importance to the Vuntut Gwich'in people. Similarly, the Nisga'a Nation in BC and the Inuit community of Clyde River in Nunavut took the lead in seeking protection for important lands and waters in their traditional territories.
>
> In Manitoba, a precedent-setting agreement between the provincial government and First Nations opened the door to wilderness protection in many significant

areas. In 1998 the Government of Manitoba, the Assembly of Manitoba Chiefs, and Keewatinowi Okimakanak Inc. signed a Memorandum of Understanding for First Nations participation in the selection, establishment, and management of new protected areas. In 1999, this led to protection of two park reserves nominated by First Nations—Polar River (800,000 hectares) and the Chitek Lake Park Reserve.

In the far north, the leadership of First Nations ensured the protection of some magnificent natural areas. Support by the Tr'on dek Hwech'in was critical to the creation of Tombstone Territorial Park, while the involvement of the Vuntut Gwich'in was critical to the establishment of the 430,000-hectare Vuntut National Park.

Aboriginal people were prepared to support the establishment of new protected areas on their traditional territory for several reasons. First, in some cases, the parks were established as part of, or pursuant to, land claim agreements reached with governments. The claims set down the rules regarding establishment and management. In many cases, Aboriginal people maintained their rights to maintain their traditional ways of life within new parks, secured co-management arrangements, and negotiated an economic and social benefits package.

Second, the spaces Campaign placed much less emphasis on discussing the 'wilderness' values of such places, with more emphasis on the ecological and cultural values of specific natural areas. The wilderness concept is fraught with all kinds of cultural baggage, different meanings, and past practices whereby Aboriginal people were forcibly removed from areas that were designated as national or provincial parks for wilderness reasons. The discussion of landscape and wildlife conservation was one that was more applicable to their understanding of the value of land and wildlife. The science of spaces enabled a more informed and common basis for discussion.

Conservation Group Support

Conservation groups played a pivotal role in securing the successes of the Endangered Spaces Campaign. A host of tactics was employed, including lobbying government and industry to establish new protected areas, running public education and outreach programs to promote the benefits of protected areas, undertaking field trips into candidate areas, supporting scientific studies, threatening legal action, working with industry, and conferring with Aboriginal people. Here are some specific examples.

World Wildlife Fund Canada provided sustained and strong leadership throughout the 10-year campaign. Many conservation groups launch campaigns, only to see them dissipate as time passes, little progress is made, areas are lost to development, volunteers come and go, and financial backing is never secured or is lost. WWF's campaign avoided these pitfalls and worked hard with its partners to chart and maintain a diversified but sustained campaign.

Such national conservation groups as the Canadian Parks and Wilderness Society and Canadian Nature Federation openly supported and worked on delivery of the campaign. Both organizations were prepared to allow WWF to reap most of the 'glory' for the campaign, but clearly benefited from it in terms of raising the national consciousness through the campaign. Also, both organizations dedicated members of their own staff to work on the campaign, thus ensuring a diversified approach. CPAWS delivered protection of such large new protected areas as the Northern Rockies in BC and the Tombstone Mountains in the Tuktut Nogait National Park, preventing a last-minute amendment to reduce the size of the park to permit mineral development in the core calving grounds of the Bluenose caribou herd.

New organizations, such as the Protected Areas Association of Newfoundland and Labrador, BC Spaces for Nature, and the New Brunswick Protected Natural Areas Coalition, were formed to help deliver the spaces agenda. Hiring local people from Newfoundland, New Brunswick, and BC, these organizations helped to deliver a campaign that was not Toronto-oriented, but evolved in the regions. The New Brunswick coalition was successful in mounting and maintaining a campaign that produced a government decision to create 10 new wilderness areas totalling almost 150,000 ha.

Through WWF's Local Action Fund a large number of grants made available to national, regional, and local organizations helped them publicize and advocate the protection of specific natural areas that, if protected, would help advance the Campaign objective. In this fashion, WWF helped to empower existing groups rather than trying to either deliver the campaign entirely on its own or entirely through a new network of protected area advocates.

A range of conservation groups worked to secure commitments from the forestry and mining sectors through their multi-sector strategies. Multi-stakeholder processes typically required a large amount of volunteer and precious staff time, time that could have been better spent on campaigns. However, a number of groups and individuals devoted time to ensuring broadly based support from industry for the Campaign's goal.

ACCOMPLISHMENTS

When all is said and done, was more said than done? Just what was accomplished? At the beginning of this chapter, we mentioned that the Endangered Spaces Campaign succeeded in raising Canada's protected lands network from 2.95 per cent to 6.84 per cent, an increase of 3.89 per cent between 1989 and 2000. This means that 389,025 sq. km of the Canadian landscape was legally protected from industrial development during the decade-long Campaign. For its part, governments state that from the time they signed the Tri-Council Statement of Commitment in 1992, until 2000, they protected an additional 2.4 per cent of Canada (World Wildlife Fund, 2000; Federal Provincial Parks Council, 2000).

While the focus on the percentage of land protected is simple and compelling, it ignores the actual focus of the Campaign—representing natural regions. The focus on percentage was a persistent problem during the Campaign. The Canadian Wilderness Charter stated that once the goal of representing all of Canada's natural regions was achieved, it would 'comprise at least 12 per cent of the lands and waters of Canada'. Unfortunately, many skipped past the goal of representation, focusing instead on the

12 per cent figure. Monte Hummel and Arlin Hackman (1995), the major architects of the campaign, wrote about the 12 per cent fixation:

> To set the record straight, Endangered Spaces is not a campaign to protect 12 per cent of Canada. The 12 per cent guideline was derived from Our Common Future, the 1987 report of the World Commission on Environment and Development . . . It suggested that 'nearly 4 per cent of the Earth's land area is managed explicitly to conserve species and ecosystems', and 'that the total expanse of protected areas needs to be at least tripled if it is to constitute a representative sample of Earth's ecosystems.'

> We never said that 12 per cent was a specific target or ceiling. In fact, it has been carefully used from the start, as it was in the Brundtland Report, as a bare minimum. We never suggested that 12 per cent was a science-based figure, although the important goal of adequately representing all of our natural regions certainly is. Furthermore, we never stated that our goal was to protect 12 per cent of Canada, and therefore 12 per cent of every province, and therefore 12 per cent of every natural region—the interpretation adopted by some jurisdictions and expressed as their official policy!

> The goal, we repeat, is to establish a network of protected areas representing all of the natural regions of Canada.

So, after establishing over 1000 new protected areas, and protecting almost 390,000 sq. km of wilderness and natural areas from industrial development, just how did Canada do in representing its natural regions?

When the Campaign started, 66 of 486 natural regions were adequately or moderately represented; by the end, this number was doubled to 132. Thus, just over 27 per cent of the nation's 486 natural regions are adequately or moderately represented. This also suggests just how much work is left to do; just under three-quarters of the nation's natural regions are partially or not represented at all. So while much progress was made—doubling the amount of protected land and the number of represented natural regions—much remains to be done.

Progress by governments on their protected area agendas was promoted through a number of provincial protected area strategies. The following documents were adopted to help translate the broad policy direction established by the Tri-Council Statement into specific, on-the-ground actions by each jurisdiction:

- British Columbia: *Protected Areas Strategy (1992)*
- Alberta: *Special Places Program*
- Saskatchewan: *Representative Areas Network (1997)*
- Manitoba: *An Action Plan for Manitoba's Network of Protected Areas*
- Ontario: *Living Legacy Land Use Strategy*
- Quebec: *Plan d'action sur les parcs: La nature en heritage (1992)*

- New Brunwick: *Protected Areas Strategy*
- Prince Edward Island: *Significant Areas Plan*
- Nova Scotia: *Protected Areas Strategy and Interim Management Guidelines: Candidate Protected Areas*
- Yukon: *Wild Spaces and Protected Places: A Protected Areas Strategy*
- NWT: *Protected Areas Strategy: A Balanced Approach to Establishing Protected Areas in the Northwest Territories*
- The Government of Newfoundland and Labrador released its *Natural Areas Plan* after the Endangered Spaces Campaign ended, and only hours before the minister in charge of the province's protected areas program resigned. And the Government of Nunavut is committed to creating *Parks and Conservation Areas System Plan* and a *Protected Areas Strategy*.

There are two documents that best summarize what Canada accomplished during the 1990s in the race to preserve Canada's wilderness landscapes. In October 2000, World Wildlife Fund Canada published *Endangered Spaces: The Wilderness Campaign that Changed the Canadian Landscape (1989–2000)*. It summarizes the highlights and accomplishments of the campaign, with the centrepiece being two maps that contrast the the level of representation of Canada's natural regions in 1989 and in 2000. The figures on which these maps are based are shown in Tables 3.1 and 3.2.

For its part, the Canadian Parks Ministers' Council published *Working Together: Parks and Protected Areas in Canada* in August 2000. This document provides a more

TABLE 3.1 Amounts of land protected in each jurisdiction at the beginning and end of the Endangered Spaces Campaign.

	Area protected at Campaign start Hectares	%	Area protected Campaign end Hectares	%	Increase in % protection
Federal	18,205,000	1.82	24,961,500	2.50	0.68
Yukon	3,218,300	6.67	5,008,000	10.38	3.71
NWT/ Nunavut	6,978,550	2.03	17,941,954	5.22	3.19
British Columbia	4,958,300	5.25	10,770,100	11.40	6.15
Alberta	5,642,000	8.52	6,612,303	8.99	1.47
Saskatchewan	1,936,000	2.97	3,912,800	6.01	3.04
Manitoba	315,400	0.49	5,579,883	8.61	8.13
Ontario	5,152,900	4.79	9,405,300	8.74	3.95
Quebec	622,800	0.40	6,646,278	4.31	3.91
New Brunswick	88,800	1.22	232,500	3.19	1.97
Nova Scotia	138,700	2.51	458,615	8.30	5.79
PEI	6,000	1.06	23,709	4.19	3.13
Nfld/Labrador	367,500	0.91	1,736,300	4.28	3.38
Total	29,425,250	2.95	68,327,742	6.84	3.90

TABLE 3.2 Level of protection of natural regions in all jurisdictions at beginning and end of the Endangered Spaces Campaign.

	Total number of natural regions	Natural regions adequately or moderately represented at Campaign start	Natural regions adequately or moderately represented at Campaign end	% of regions adequately or moderately represented at Campaign start	% of regions adequately or moderately represented at Campaign end
Yukon	23	4	6	17.4	26.1
NWT/ Nunavut	69	10	12	14.5	17.2
British Columbia	100	25	36	25.0	36.0
Alberta	20	4	5	20.0	25.0
Sask.	11	2	2	18.2	18.2
Manitoba	18	1	5	5.6	27.8
Ontario	66	11	24	16.7	36.4
Quebec	75	5	6	6.7	8.0
New Bruns.	7	0	0	0.0	0.0
Nova Scotia	77	4	34	5.2	44.2
PEI	1	0	0	0.0	0.0
Nfld/ Labrador	19	0	2	0.0	10.5
Total	486	66	132	13.58	27.16

detailed summary of the accomplishments of each jurisdiction, with a focus on specific natural areas protected. Unfortunately, it fails to provide a national perspective on how Canadian governments collectively addressed the 1992 Statement of Commitment, one of the major failings of governments. They never did develop a common approach to measuring their progress on representing Canada's natural regions; that task fell, by default, to WWF.

While virtually every jurisdiction made important contributions to the representation of the nation's natural regions, four stand out for their impressive accomplishments.

British Columbia

Since 1992, the province has created more than 325 new protected areas and additions to existing ones totalling approximately 47,200 sq. km. This means that almost 11.4 per cent of the province is now in protected status, an increase from the 6.3 per cent protected in 1992. A fair number of these new protected areas were established through regional land use plans, including one for Vancouver Island, the Cariboo-Chilcotin area in the province's interior, and the east and west Kootenay area of the province, that were unveiled by Premier Mike Harcourt.

Highlights of the 325 new protected areas include;

FIGURE 3.1 Alsek Lake lies between the confluence of Alsek and Tatshenshini Rivers in NW British Columbia and is part of the 9,740 sq.-km Tatshenshini-Alsek Provinical Park created in 1933. *Photo: P Dearden.*

- At 9,470 sq. km, the Tatshenshini-Alsek Park protects an area recognized internationally for its outstanding wildlife, biodiversity, and wilderness values. One of the wildest rivers in North America, the Tatshenshini, was the focus of a major international campaign, which included then Senator Al Gore calling on Canada to end a proposed open pit copper mine that threatened an Alaskan national park and fishery located downstream.
- Created in 1992, the 44,902-ha Khutzeymateen Park was established to protect the largest known concentration of grizzly bears along the coast of British Columbia. It is Canada's first grizzly bear sanctuary, and one of the first major protected areas established by the NDP when it came to power, signalling to the world the province was starting to change its approach to the conservation of old-growth forests and wildlife habitat.
- Over 4.4 million ha of wilderness was set aside in the Muskwa-Kechika Management Area through the establishment of a matrix of protected areas and special management areas (see Chapter 1).

No other jurisdiction maintained the pace and sustained level of commitment to representing its natural regions as did the province of British Columbia. All of this activity, however, only raised the level from 25 to 36 of the province's 100 natural regions that were judged to be adequately or moderately represented. The fact that BC is the only jurisdiction in Canada that has surpassed the 12 per cent mark, but still has so many regions that are not adequately represented, again illustrates the weaknesses of adopting a uniform ceiling as a target for protected area coverage.

Ontario

Throughout much of the Spaces campaign, Ontario was a major disappointment. Only in the last year did the provincial government pull off a stunning announcement. In 1999, Premier Mike Harris announced *Ontario's Living Legacy*, which created 378 new parks and protected areas totalling 2.4 million ha. The province contends that this is the biggest single expansion of parks and protected areas anywhere. For Ontario, this meant that their 66 natural regions ranked as adequately or moderately represented rose from 11 to 24, tying it with British Columbia for the second-largest percentage of natural regions judged to be adequately or moderately represented across Canada—at 36 per cent.

The announcement gave prominence to nine signature sites, each containing exceptional natural features that warranted special protection; they included:

- Over 52,000 ha of the Algoma Highlands in a new provincial park that includes the headwaters of three major rivers, and protects old-growth red and white pine forests.
- Over 247,230 ha of land in the Nipigon Basin, linking Wabakimi Provincial Park to the north with the Great Lakes Heritage Coast, which is more than 2,900 km of shoreline that includes 65 parks and protected areas. This initiative should help conserve Lake Nipigon, the world's tenth-largest freshwater lake.

This decision was illustrative for several reasons. The Conservative government of Premier Harris was so vilified by groups operating left of the political centre that the government got very little credit for a very important conservation decision. By association, World Wildlife Fund, and in particular, its President Monte Hummel, was attacked by editorials produced by the Toronto Star and such groups as Western Canada Wilderness Committee because it worked with the Conservatives and the forestry industry to deliver this decision. Criticism was generated, in part, because mineral exploration might be permitted in a portion of about a dozen of the new protected areas, should areas of high mineral potential be found.

Nova Scotia

Nova Scotia is the jurisdiction with the largest percentage of natural regions adequately or moderately represented at the end of the campaign's with 44 per cent of their natural regions well protected. When the Spaces campaign began, a scant 4 of 77 natural regions were adequately or moderately represented. However, in December 1995 the province agreed to designate 31 new protected wilderness areas, protecting 285,700 ha of land. As a result, 34 natural regions are now judged to be adequately or moderately represented.

What was most gratifying about Nova Scotia's decision is that it set aside almost 20 per cent of all of its Crown land in protective status. This is even more impressive when one considers the fact that less than 30 per cent of Nova Scotia is publicly owned. To assist in the conservation of private lands (see Chapter 15), the Nova Scotia Nature Trust was formed to encourage voluntary stewardship initiatives. Reforms to the province's tax systems and the development of other incentives were under consideration when the campaign came to an end.

Manitoba

In protecting over 5.2 million ha of provincial land, Manitoba, in its 18 natural regions, increased from one to five its number of regions that are adequately or moderately represented. What is even more significant about Manitoba is the extent to which it has worked with Aboriginal people and the mining industry.

Through the province's Protected Areas Initiative, the Mining Association of Manitoba worked with the provincial government and WWF's Endangered Spaces Co-ordinator for Manitoba to help establish new protected areas. This work has assisted in approving over 20 candidate areas covering about 2.2 million ha. In addition, the Mining Association has openly supported the creation of the proposed Manitoba Lowlands National Park. Here is how they have worked.

Essentially, the industry association and its representatives meet with the government's parks and mining branches and the WWF spaces co-ordinator to help identify areas of high mineral potential within proposed study areas. However, as part of the process, they examine the ability of a reduced protected area to represent a natural region, while respecting First Nations treaty and other land use obligations. If representation is lost or reduced, the industry works to find ways to achieve ecological representation. In essence, they use the science of mineral potential along with the science of ecological representation to design protected areas that are ecologically viable. The approach ensures that the candidate protected areas identified have good ecological values and industry support (McNamee, 1999).

This work makes Manitoba virtually the only jurisdiction that kept alive the vision of the Whitehorse Mining Initiative, which was to maintain the multi-stakeholder approach to resolving mining and land use issues.

CONCLUSION

The Endangered Spaces Campaign accomplished a lot. It resulted in a coalescing of conservation groups, governments, Aboriginal people, industry, funders, and individual Canadians around the need to preserve and pass on some of the wildest, biologically rich, and simply beautiful Canadian landscapes to future generations. In the end, 1000 new protected areas were created, over 390,000 sq. km of Canadian wilderness was protected, and 132 of our nation's 486 natural regions adequately or moderately protected. This is an outstanding natural legacy for those generations who will inherit our country and our planet in the twenty-first century.

The Endangered Spaces Campaign clearly demonstrated the need to place the preservation of the Canadian wilderness landscapes squarely on the political agenda. And many of the new protected areas were established precisely because there was strong political commitment. The jurisdictions that made progress, either systematically, or in protecting some difficult sites, such as Alberta's ecologically rich montane, Whaleback, or Newfoundland's Little Grand Lake, did so because the 'centre' of government demanded progress. Premiers wanted action to demonstrate to their constituency that they had acted on their election promises to complete their jurisdiction's protected areas network. The processes used varied, from the traditional 'submit a brief and show up at a public consultation meeting' used by Nova Scotia, to the round table approach of developing regional land use plans as used by Ontario and British Columbia, to the use of a representative group of interested stakeholders as in thecase of New Brunswick. What drove important decisions in some jurisdictions is the fact that their Premiers and the responsible ministers demanded progress.

The Endangered Spaces campaign also demonstrated that the myth of Canada as one limitless tract of wild space left forever untouched is clearly just that—a myth. Consider the following statistics released by WWF at the end of the campaign:

- one acre (just under 0.5 ha) of Canada's forests is logged every 13 seconds;
- new mineral claims were staked in 1997 at a rate of 12,412 acres (496 ha) per hour;
- 174 million acres (69.6 million ha) of land were staked by the mining industry in 1998 alone; and
- Canada ranks a mediocre 33rd among all nations in protecting wilderness in terms of the proportion of the land base protected.

During the course of the campaign, Canada has seen tremendous growth in the allocation of land to development. New oil and gas fields, coupled with new diamond mines, are opening up areas of the western and central Arctic that only a generation ago many thought would remain out of the hands of industrial society for ever. One ecosystem that came under increasing scrutiny, and that will remain a focus of protected area advocates' post-spaces is the boreal forest. Even the Canadian Senate called for concerted public and political actions to save large tracts of what remains of the boreal forest. And of course, the protection of marine ecosystems has seen virtually no progress over the last decade (Chapter 14).

During the 1990s, the Endangered Spaces Campaign wrapped itself in the Canadian flag. For all of its emphasis on a scientific approach to identifying and designing new protected areas, the campaign remained an emotional pitch to Canadians to save what few other countries on this planet still fleetingly possess— large tracts of undeveloped wildlands. Canada possesses 20 per cent of the world's remaining wilderness. Should another Endangered Spaces Campaign emerge in the coming decade, perhaps it will be founded not on national identity, but on the very survival of the human and wildlife species that call this planet home.

REFERENCES

Broadhead, J. 1989. 'The All Alone Stone Manifesto', in Hummel (1989: 50–62).

Dearden P., and J. Gardner. 1987. 'Systems Planning for Protected Areas in Canada: A Review of Caucus Candidate Areas and Concepts, Issues and Prospects for Further Investigation', in Scace and Nelson (1987: 9–48).

Eliot, Chris, and Arlin Hackman. 1996. *Current Issues on Forest Certification in Canada: A WWF Canada Discussion Paper.* Toronto: World Wildlife Fund Canada.

Environment Canada. 1987. 'Our Parks—Vision for the 21st Century', report of the Minister of Environment's Task Force on Parks Establishment, Heritage Resource Centre, University of Waterloo.

Federal Provincial Parks Council. 2000. *Working Together: Parks and Protected Areas in Canada.* Ottawa: Government of Canada.

Hackman, Arlin. 1988. 'Forging a National Wilderness Agenda', *Alternatives* 15, 3: 48–55

———. (no date). 'Preface', in *Timber Supply and Endangered Spaces: A World Wildlife Fund Canada Discussion Paper.* Toronto: World Wildlife Fund Canada.

———. 1995. *Protecting Canada's Endangered Spaces: An Owner's Manual.* Toronto: Key Porter Books.

——— and Arlin Hackman. 1995. 'Introduction', in Hummel (1995: xiii–xvi).

Hummel, M. 1989. *Endangered Spaces: The Future for Canada's Wilderness.* Toronto: Key Porter Books.

McNamee, Kevin. 1999. 'Undermining Wilderness', *Alternatives* 25, 4: 24–31.

Scace, R.C., and J.G. Nelson, eds. 1987. *Heritage for Tomorrow: Canadian Assembly on National Parks and Protected Areas*, vol. 2. Ottawa: Environment Canada Parks.

United Nations World Commission on Environment and Development. 1987. *Our Common Future.* Oxford: Oxford University Press.

World Wildlife Fund Canada. 2000. *Endangered Spaces: The Wilderness Campaign That Changed the Canadian Landscape (1989–2000).* Toronto: World Wildlife Fund Canada.

Web site

http://www.gov.bc.ca/elp/

KEY WORDS/CONCEPTS

Endangered Spaces Campaign
World Wildlife Fund
WCED Report (1987)
Canadian Wilderness Charter
Canadian Council on Ecological Areas
Crown land

STUDY QUESTIONS

1. Why was 'industry' generally supportive of the Endangered Spaces Campaign?
2. Why were Aboriginal groups generally supportive of the Endangered Spaces Campaign?
3. Describe the role of the 'conservation community', and list the strategies developed to pressure decision-makers to create more parks and protected areas.
4. Outline the reasons for identifying 12 per cent as a target for the Endangered Spaces Campaign. Discuss the advantages and disadvantages of this strategy.
5. Outline the successes and shortcomings of the Endangered Spaces Campaign.
6. Examine the network of parks and protected areas in your province in light of the Endangered Spaces Campaign and comment on the apparent successes and shortcomings. Interview a park official regarding this issue.

PART II

Conservation Theory and Practice

The one process on-going . . . that will take millions of years to correct is the loss of genetic and species diversity by the destruction of natural habitats. This is the folly that our descendants are least likely to forgive us.

E.O. Wilson, Harvard University

This section supplies the background for understanding the ecological basis for protected area planning and management. Understanding of these principles is necessary to answer questions such as, 'Where should parks be located? How many parks are needed? Where should boundaries be placed? What criteria should be used for determining the size and shape of parks, and the impacts of adjacent land management? If the protection of biodiversity is to be an important objective of parks, or the most important objective of parks, then we need to examine the basic principles of conservation biology, and determine how they can be applied to the management of parks and protected areas (Chapter 4).

Managing for ecological integrity represents a significant and controversial 'paradigm shift' from the thinking that parks should be managed always to allow for natural processes (i.e., minimal interference). A number of factors contribute to an active approach to management: the small size of many parks; previous management actions (such as fire suppression); considerations regarding the safety of communities and resources in adjacent communities; and the fluid nature of ecosystem functioning (rarely recognizing park boundaries). These factors create less than ideal conditions in most parks and require at least short-term measures. Since many park agencies are moving towards management policies that place a priority on ecological integrity, it is imperative to consider the issues around the implementation of such policies.

CHAPTER 4

Application of Ecological Concepts to the Management of Protected Areas

Jeannette C. Theberge & John B. Theberge

INTRODUCTION

Increasingly, a more environmentally conscious society views parks and other protected areas less as playgrounds and more as green spaces that perform vital ecological functions. Green spaces moderate water cycles, absorb pollutants, regulate
atmospheric gasses, buffer the spread of crop and livestock diseases, capture energy,
stabilize populations, act as gene pools, and provide habitat for wildlife. The primary goal of Canada's national parks is the maintenance of ecological integrity.
Similar goals related to ecosystem protection are expressed in other protected area
systems in Canada.

As a result, politicians and those people responsible for the management of parks,
forests, and wildlife look to ecologists for direction. The stakes for Canada are high,
because 22 per cent of the world's remaining wilderness lies within its borders (Parks
Canada Agency, 2000). The stakes are high, too, because we have lost so much already.
Gone are all virgin old-growth remnants of Acadian forests in the Maritime provinces.
Very few patches remain of northern or southern hardwood forests, oak savannah,
tall- or short-grass prairie, Osoyoos shrub-grassland desert in south central British
Columbia, or the temperate rain forest on the west coast. We have lost almost all unaltered examples of every Canadian biome except the boreal forest and tundra—a scan-
dalous litany. Add to that what we have done to the great auk, passenger pigeon, plains
bison, eastern cougar, black-tailed prairie dog. . . .

The focus of this chapter is the various ideas and theories that are useful in protecting park ecosystems. The science of ecology is rich in concepts, hypotheses, and
ways of understanding nature. Like most sciences, ecology has gone through trends
and phases as it progressed, each contributing to the body of thought and its appli-
cability today. Description and classification of ecosystems, an early focus, still form
the basis for understanding any natural environment—what is there and where is it?
Ecology advanced beyond that to the analysis of ecosystem functions—what processes
are taking place, what is happening? Much early ecological thinking came from traditional game and fish management as put forth by Aldo Leopold in his book *Game
Management* (1933) and taught, with modifications, in universities ever since. Its

focus was, and still is, setting appropriate harvest quotas based on an understanding of population demographics and habitat relationships. Early efforts matured in the 1960s and 1970s into a broader set of hypotheses about how animal populations are regulated, theory that is vital to resolving species management problems in parks, particularly related to endangered or threatened species.

Early community ecologists developed theories about species diversity, gradients, competition, and controlling factors that are relevant to understanding and maintaining biodiversity today. After a temporary eclipse, community ecology re-emerged in the 1980s, enriched in an applied way as 'conservation biology' with an emphasis on the development of eleventh-hour techniques to stem the tide of species extinctions. Today the guiding principles of conservation biology are that: (1) the ecological world is dynamic and non-equilibrial, and (2) human presence must be included in conservation planning (Meffe and Carroll, 1997), both being ideas that influence how park ecosystems are perceived.

While conservation biology was emerging, advances in the field of remote sensing and Geographical Information Systems (GIS) have allowed the processing of large data sets and facilitated ecosystem analyses across expansive landscapes. At the same time, the formal field of landscape ecology surfaced (Forman and Godron, 1986). Contributing to growing interest in analysis at the landscape level was the realization that our understanding of biotic evolution has been too reductionist. We have parsed life apart, studying it downward from species to cell and DNA structure, with limited upward synthesis. Eldredge (1985) postulated in his book *Unfinished Synthesis* that whole new dimensions of evolutionary understanding await discovery if we study upward as well as downward, exploring the origins, behaviours, and unique attributes of communities and regional landscapes. Accordingly, ecology has expanded from a traditional deductive emphasis on the study of single species in small homogeneous areas to include searches for systematic relationships at larger scales (Kerkhoff et al., 2000; Senft et al., 1987; Johnson, 1980).

GIS allows us to overlay resource maps such as those showing physiography, soils, hydrology, vegetation, wildlife, and land use, a flexibility that enhances the possibilities of discovering functional relationships. Often incorporating satellite imagery, GIS allows us to view protected areas in their regional setting and is a powerful tool for both park system planning and regional planning. GIS analysis is especially useful for ecological land classifications such as those used in national parks or for resource surveys to find environmentally significant areas. Most importantly, GIS is useful in communicating modelling options and future scenarios, especially to decision-makers and the public, thereby allowing the management of protected areas to be a more democratic process.

This history of progress and recent advances has endowed the science of ecology with a diversity of ways of thinking about the structure, function, and composition of ecosystems. Due to the incremental evolution of ecosystem thinking and associated technologies, the concepts and tools related to protected areas management need continuous updating. From this broad field of ecological understanding, aspects that have particular relevance today are grouped under the umbrella of 'environmental' or 'ecosystem management' (Agee and Johnson, 1988; Christensen et al., 1996). This umbrella has largely replaced the earlier term 'sustainable development' that came from the World Conservation Strategy (1980) and the Brundtland Commission report (World Commission on Environment and Development, 1987). Sustainable development was criticized for its anthropocentric bias—nature as stock and commodity for humans. Ecosystem management, in contrast, leaves room for a more biocentric philosophy that holds all species and ecosystems as having inherent worth, regardless of their usefulness to humans (Stanley, 1995; Grumbine, 1994).

Today, the generally accepted objectives for the management of protected areas include representation of native ecosystem types, maintenance of viable populations, maintenance of ecological and evolutionary processes, and continuance of ecosystem resilience in the face of human pressures, both in the short and long term (Noss, 1996). These objectives are derived from ecological theory. In this chapter, we frame several ways of thinking to aid in the application of ecological theory to the management of protected areas.

THINKING BIG

Any application of ecological thinking to parks today must extend beyond park boundaries to include the region in which the park is situated, and in ways related to life support systems, even beyond that. Neither air, soil, wildlife, nor plant propagules are bounded by parks (Box 4.1) While this fact is generally understood and accepted among park agencies, institutional and societal barriers present a daunting challenge to its application (Chapter 14). From a technical standpoint, because GIS allows ecological analysis across vast areas, it has spawned investigations of spatial patterns and analytical scales that change perceptions of nature. Scale is understood as a combination of grain (i.e., the resolution that one picks to view landscape components, vegetation types, human activities) and extent (i.e., the dimensions of the outer boundaries of the area under study). If you zoomed into a small extent (or area) with a fine grain (or resolution), patterns across the landscape would look different than would observations at a larger extent or coarser grain (Figure 4.1).

The management prescription for a particular ecological issue could vary depending on the scale at which the investigation takes place. This is because the mechanisms and constraints that produce ecological phenomena at one scale might be different at another scale (Levin, 1992). For example, Keddy (1991) concluded that tree species richness was strongly correlated with (1) evapotranspiration and energy availability at the continental scale, (2) biomass, stress, disturbance, and dominance at the regional scale (i.e., among vegetation types), and (3) species regeneration potential at the local scale (i.e., within vegetation types).

Changes in grain and extent can greatly influence the identification of candidate protected areas and help answer questions about how big they should be and where in the region they should be placed. Observing the landscape at a coarse scale would

BOX 4.1 Ecologically-Based Boundaries for Protected Areas

Many parks agencies hope to reduce transboundary ecological problems by applying a set of criteria to minimize the potential that problems may arise. While application of the following guidelines (Theberge, 1989) is rarely completely possible because of existing and conflicting land uses and resource rights, the criteria represent an objective to strive for.

Abiotic Guidelines

1. Boundaries should sever drainage areas as little as possible.

2. Boundaries should not leave out headwater areas.

3. Boundaries should consider subsurface trans-basin water flow.

4. Boundaries should not cross active permafrost terrain.

5. Boundaries should include and not threaten rare geomorphic and hydrological features and processes.

Biotic Guidelines

6. No rare or unique community in the candidate natural area should be severed with a boundary.

7. Boundaries should not sever highly diverse communities, especially wetlands, ecotones and riparian zones, or lakes or marine coastal zones to compensation depth.

8. Boundaries should not sever communities with a high proportion of dependent faunal species.

9. Boundaries should not jeopardize the ecological requirements of either numerically rare or distributionally rare (or uncommon) species.

10. Boundaries should not jeopardize the ecological requirements of niche specialists.

11. Boundaries should not jeopardize populations of spatially vulnerable species: those that migrate locally, are space demanding, seasonally concentrating, or limited in powers of dispersal.

12. Boundaries should not jeopardize populations of K-selected (low fecundity) species.

13. Boundaries should not jeopardize populations of range-edge or disjunct species.

14. Boundaries should take into special account pollution-susceptible species.

15. Boundary delineation should take into special account the ecological requirements of ungulate species (including their predators).

FIGURE 4.1 A heterogeneous landscape in Banff National Park, Alberta. In the foreground (at a fine degree of resolution) the environment is a complicated mix of grassland and open spruce/fir forest. At a coarser scale (the distant walls of the valley) the landscape is comprised of conifer forest, rock, and avalanche chutes.

be more useful for ensuring that protected areas maintain connectivity, whereas a finer scale might be more appropriate when the goal is to protect species with high levels of endemism (restriction to a certain area). Decision-makers do not necessarily have to wait for fine-scaled ecological surveys before candidate protected areas or linkages between them are identified. Coarse surveys of landscape-wide patterns and processes—such as aquifers, major streams, large rare habitats, high species diversity, concentrations of wide-ranging species, major centers of wildlife movement or flow)—have the potential to identify areas that would protect most aspects of biodiversity (Forman and Collinge, 1997).

When the establishment or management of protected areas includes a concern over the habitat requirements of certain individual species, it is useful to investigate how those species use a landscape. For example, one might find that a mobile species, such as a bear, might select feeding sites at a fine scale based on the abundance of berries on particular shrubs, or at a coarse scale on the diversity of vegetation types that contain edible foods on an entire mountain slope. Habitat selection, on a coarse scale, involves landscape 'complementation' and 'supplementation' (Dunning et al., 1992). Both are important concepts in habitat evaluation. Landscape complementation is the situation where an animal must move between two or more essential patch types that contain different and non-substitutable types of resources, such as for foraging and for roosting. To obtain these resources the animal must move to the patches through the matrix between them. A landscape that contains necessary patch types in close proximity to each other has the potential to support a larger population than landscapes where the habitat patches are far apart (Petit, 1989).

Landscape supplementation occurs where a single type of resource required by an organism can be augmented by accessing nearby patches that contain additional quantities of the same resources. A population within a patch might increase if that patch is near other patches of the same habitat type containing the same resource, or even other habitat types containing different, but useable, resources. Under these circumstances a population might persist in a patch that may otherwise be too small to sustain a population solely on the preferred available resources.

In applying landscape complementation and supplementation to the management of protected areas, analysis needs to be conducted at appropriate scales. For example, at a fine scale, within a park, a biologist might need to consider the movements of an endangered rodent between small patches of resources, and so consider the average size and distance between habitat patches. On a larger scale, it might be necessary to investigate the spatial arrangement of habitat types inside a park and the linkages that exist to other useable habitats outside the park. When managing for large-bodied mobile organisms, this large regional scale becomes important to species persistence. Because the management of protected areas requires a multi-species approach it must also include the simultaneous consideration of the multiple scales by which those species operate.

Various ways exist to investigate spatial patterns at multiple scales (O'Neill et al., 1988; Turner and Gardner, 1991; Peterson and Parker, 1998), but especially relevant to protected areas are methods to investigate the response of wildlife populations to the spatial pattern of human use. Habitat effectiveness modeling (Gibeau,1998) allows an estimate of the relative usability of various vegetation types for a single species by evaluating the impact of human presence on each type. Questions regarding the potential impacts of changes in human land use on wildlife habitat (for multiple species that operate at different scales) have been studied using spatially explicit habitat suitability modelling (Riitters et al., 1997). Percolation models have been used to investigate thresholds of fragmentation beyond which individuals of a species cannot move effectively across a landscape (With and Crist, 1995; With, 1997). These spatial models, and others, are useful in park management and human land use planning across broad regions.

The foregoing are examples of thinking big at an ecosystem level. Very important ideas have developed about thinking big at a population level, too—the metapopulation concept. This concept of population drastically alters the way management prescriptions can be applied, and forces park managers into multi-jurisdictional dialogue to protect park species. A metapopulation is a population of populations linked by dispersal (Levins, 1970). A single population of a species may, in reality, consist of many subpopulations, with flows between them, that live in sometimes vast, semi-discontinuous habitats. For example, one could view caribou as comprising one metapopulation living in northern British Columbia, the Yukon, and parts of Alaska. This herd ebbs and flows across the landscape, spawning seemingly discrete herds here and there for awhile that may persist or decline.

The key concepts related to metapopulation theory revolve around having populations that are spatially discrete and that have high probabilities of extinction in at least one of the population patches (McCullough, 1996). Most isolated small populations eventually go extinct, whereas connected populations, even ones that experience only periodic exchange of members, are more likely to persist. Original models of metapopulations were too simplistic to account for the complexity of variables that influence population distributions (Hastings and Harrison, 1994) such as variations in the distances between populations, in habitat quality of different patches, in rates of demographic change and population turnover, or in ecological processes affecting subpopulations, such as competition or predator-prey interactions. Consequently, more sophisticated metapopulation models have been developed (ibid.). Movements in and out of or between populations have been difficult to study, but emerge as important in population persistence. Although metapopulations occur naturally, populations are increasingly becoming disjunct due to the spatial arrangement of human activities. Single, discreet populations can become metapopulations from (1) habitat fragmentation, (2) habitat deterioration (without major land conversion), (3) overexploitation of a species, and (4) the establishment of isolated reserves to protect recovering species (McCullough, 1996). In recognition of this human influence, it is imperative that the management of protected areas goes beyond park boundaries to consider population welfare in this broad context.

THINKING CONNECTED

Park system planning once was primarily concerned about capturing representatives of all types of ecosystems that lie within a jurisdiction such as a province or territory, or in the case of Parks Canada, all of Canada. Little concern was directed to the location of parks in relationship to one another, or to the types of land uses that were being practiced between them. However, the eastern North American songbird decline, first recognized in the late 1980s (Terborgh, 1989), changed all that. Coincidentally, theory developed from empirical research undertaken largely from islands, and so the topics of island biogeography, patch dynamics, and fragmentation were born. Today, the objective of establishing connected parks with corridors between is seen as vital to maintaining not only parks but ecological functions across broader landscapes. Initiatives like the Yellowstone to Yukon project (Locke, 1998) are underway to establish and maintain a corridor of sufficient naturalness that subpopulations such as grizzly bears and wolves—two space-demanding species—retain intraspecific connections.

Island Biogeography

The possibilities of periodic immigration to a park or reserve have been explored through concepts of island biogeography. The concepts apply to ecological islands surrounded either by water or by urban or agriculture lands, although these situations may not be completely equivalent.

Several classic studies have shown that small islands are unable to support as many species as large islands of similar habitat (Diamond, 1975; Simberloff, 1974). As a rough guide, a tenfold increase in area results in a near doubling in the number of species (MacArthur and Wilson, 1967).

The number of species surviving on an island is not, however, merely a function of the island's size. It represents an equilibrium between species immigration and extinction, which depends not only on island size but on its distance from a colonizing source (ibid.). In theory, the number of species on an island will be greater if the island is large and sources of immigration are close. For example, the same number of species might persist on two islands, one large and far from sources of immigrants, one small but close to sources of immigrants.

Although the theory was criticized on statistical and ecological grounds (summarized in Doak and Mills, 1994), the analogy between islands and isolated terrestrial patches remains appealing because similarities between terrestrial habitat fragments and islands have sustained the analogy. For example, western North American parks have experienced more extinctions than colonizations since the parks were established, and the extinction rates are inversely related to park size (Newmark, 1995).

These variables of size and distance led to discussion on the optimum pattern for a system of reserves: the so-called SLOSS debate (Single Large or Several Small). Diamond (1975) proposed that one large reserve was better than a number of small ones; that a number of reserves close together was better than the same number spread out; that three reserves in a triangular pattern were better than three reserves strung

BOX 4.2 Principles for Species Conservation, Reserve Design, and Ecosystem Conservation

1. Species well distributed across their native range are less susceptible to extinction than species confined to small portions of their range.
2. Large blocks of habitat, containing large populations, are better than small blocks with small populations.
3. Blocks of habitat close together are better than blocks far apart.
4. Habitat in contiguous blocks is better than fragmented habitat.
5. Interconnected blocks of habitat are better than isolated blocks.
6. Blocks of habitat that are roadless or otherwise inaccessible to humans are better than accessible habitat blocks.
7. Populations that fluctuate widely are more vulnerable than populations that are more stable.
8. Disjunct or peripheral populations are likely to be more genetically impoverished and vulnerable to extinction, but also more genetically distinct than central populations.
9. Maintaining viable ecosystems is an effective approach to conservation planning. As well, some species need special attention (since species define ecosystems and the scale at which they should be managed). Conservation planning should integrate the needs of multiple species (such as ones with large area requirements, keystone effects, sensitivity to human activity) instead of addressing one species at a time in a piecemeal fashion.
10. Biodiversity is not distributed randomly or uniformly across the landscape. In establishing protection priorities, consider hotspots (i.e., areas of concentrated conservation value such as high habitat quality or presence of rare species).
11. Ecosystem boundaries ideally should be determined by reference to ecology, not politics.
12. Because conservation value varies across a landscape, zoning is a useful approach to land-use planning and reserve network design.
   SOURCE: Summarized in Noss et al. (1997)

out linearly; and that a circular reserve was better than one with an oval shape (having less edge). Soule (1983) proposed that three small reserves are better than one large one, and four reserves spaced out are better than four tightly grouped. From a study of Canadian national parks, Glenn (1990) found that several parks contained the same number, or more, mammalian species than a single large park of the same area. That same study indicated that as total area conserved increased, so did the number of species that require undisturbed landscapes. Benefits of various reserve designs obviously vary with the dispersal abilities, mobility, and habitat requirements of species (Box 4.2). Today the rules for optimum reserve design, although grounded in this academic theory, are less specific and target the maintaining of connectivity across landscapes while minimizing the effects of fragmentation. In particular, these targets are aimed at (1) protecting multiple large patches with a large core which permit the dispersal of species, and are aligned to aid recolonization, (2) maintaining corridors and networks between these patches across the landscape, and (3) accounting for the juxtaposition of other vegetation or land uses (Forman, 1997).

Patch Dynamics

Investigations into the theories of metapopulations and island biogeography have become more focused with the growing awareness of patch dynamics. Forman and Godron (1986) complained that ecology had not focused sufficiently on between-patch dynamics, except related to species migration in island biogeography. They introduced the paradigm that all landscapes are composed of patches, corridors, and a matrix. Landscapes are heterogeneous and differ structurally according to the distribution of species, energy, and materials among these patches, corridors, and matrices. For example, a vegetation patch might be surrounded by extensive agricultural land (i.e., the matrix) and be connected to other patches through a strip of natural vegetation (i.e., the corridor). Or, a protected area might be considered a patch surrounded by a matrix of other human land uses. If we consider parks and reserves as separate from the landscapes in which they are situated, then we fail to see the flow of species, energy, and materials that may confer long-term viability and persistence.

Relationships that involve the exchange of species, energy, and materials among patches depend on a whole range of factors: patch shape, isolation, pattern of dispersion across a landscape, ratio of edge to interior, species diversity, patch persistence, and, of course, linkages or corridors between patches. Corridors themselves have been classified by origin and structure (Forman and Godron, 1986; Forman, 1995).

Corridors maintain higher species diversity in refuges by allowing reciprocal immigration (Simberloff and Cox, 1987), lowering extinction rates, and minimizing the effects of demographic stochasticity (Simberloff et al., 1992). However, corridors have disadvantages, too; they can contribute to the spread of disease, disrupt local genetic adaptation by facilitating outbreeding, increase susceptibility to fire, and make poaching easier (Noss, 1987). Consequently, the types and extents of corridors in a network of protected areas should be decided on the basis of the purpose that the corridor would serve for the species expected to use them.

The relationships of patches to their matrix, or surrounding area, has provided a primary focus for the study of the effects of disturbance, whether natural or caused by humans. Pickett and White (1985) developed a theory of vulnerability to disturbance that includes a number of system structures: proportional biomass above and below ground; availability of nutrients and other resources; growth rates and resource demands of species; competition among species; landscape characteristics, such as the composition and configuration of patches; and natural disturbance regimes (fire, flood, etc.). Once again, the message that comes from patch dynamics is that species and ecological functions within parks may not be able to persist if the parks loose their connectivity to other natural areas.

Natural disturbance can influence the spatial arrangement of patches on the landscape, or its heterogeneity (Kolasa and Rollo, 1991). Heterogeneity is relevant to protected areas because of the need to conserve a cross-section of vegetation and wildlife habitat types. Managing to maintain natural levels of heterogeneity is not always easy because the relationship between disturbance and heterogeneity often is not linear, that is, as you increase disturbance, heterogeneity might not increase at the same rate. To illustrate: if a disturbance were to affect 50 per cent of an area of homogeneous vegetation type, then one might consider that area now to be heterogeneous. On the other hand, if that original area had many patch types (a heterogeneous environment), then the outcome of the disturbance might decrease the overall heterogeneity (Kolasa and Rollo, 1991). Similarly, if the disturbance were to affect 80 per cent of the area, then the result would be an environment that was relatively homogenous in the disturbed vegetation.

On balance, most severe human disturbances simplify, or homogenize environments. Park managers need to defend against this trend.

Fragmentation

The flip side of patch dynamics is fragmentation, the break-up of a natural matrix. Fragmentation is seen as a damaging process (Wilcox and Murphy, 1985). Some generalizations can be made about habitat fragmentation. For example, Wilcove et al. (1986) concluded that the effects of fragmentation are greater in tropical than in temperate regions. Temperate species occur in higher densities and have wider distributions and greater dispersal powers than do tropical species.

Species that are especially susceptible to the effects of fragmentation include deepforest species and long-distance migrants. Other vulnerable species are those with low dispersal, short life cycles, dependence upon patchy or unpredictable resources, large-patch or interior utilization (Noss and Csuti, 1997), large territories, specialized habitats, colonist habits, and low productivity. The latter two characteristics make species vulnerable to overhunting or poaching when fragmentation is caused by roads. The impact of roads upon wildlife populations is becoming of increasing concern for biologists (Forman, 1995, Mace et al., 1996), and there is growing emphasis on devising ways to mitigate the effects of these barriers through the experimental implementation of overpasses and underpasses (Rodriguez et al., 1996). There is also increasing demand for maintaining roadless areas in North America.

Much traditional literature on wildlife management emphasizes the importance of edge habitat to maintaining high species diversity. Habitat manipulations were, and still are, designed to fragment large blocks of uniform habitat by creating more openings, thereby improving conditions for the considerable number of edge species. However, conservation concern increasingly is shifting from obtaining maximum species diversity per se to providing for deep-forest species that may be jeopardized by fragmentation (Yahner, 1988). Soule (1986: 234) coined the term sedge for the ratio of edge to size, and observed that 'edge and sedge effects feed upon themselves autocatalytically. The result is a creeping edge that can eventually reach the core of even a relatively large reserve.'

Thinking About Species

Efforts have been made to classify the biological traits that make some species more vulnerable than others to human disturbance and the probability of local or widespread extinction. Species showing these traits are important candidates for protected areas.

1. K-strategists win the evolutionary game when environmental conditions are stable by producing few offspring, investing a great deal of parental care in their welfare, and being long-lived. Their low reproductive rate makes them vulnerable. Sometimes they are habitat specialists, as well, which limits their ability to switch habitat types if one habitat is destroyed (Shaw, 1985). Large mammals and large birds tend to be K-strategists. Many amphibians and reptiles, while fecund, show habitat specificity, which can be a threat to them.

2. Summit predators feed at the top of food chains and hence depend on all the lower links (Wootton, 1994; Morin and Lawler, 1995). Under specific conditions, the presence of populations of summit predators can have a profound impact on the structure and productivity of other trophic levels (McLaren and Peterson, 1994). As well, summit predators may suffer from the concentration of toxins in food chains. Most vertebrate summit predators, for example, birds of prey, are K-strategists, making them doubly vulnerable.

3. Species that concentrate spatially are vulnerable because large number or even significant portions of regional populations can be wiped out by local environmental events such as an oil spill or vandalism. Such species include seabirds, geese, swans, and other congregating waterfowl, as well as musk-oxen and caribou (Smith et al., 1986).

4. Migratory birds are vulnerable because of destruction of migratory or tropical wintering habitats and accumulation of toxins along migration routes.

5. Long-distance migratory mammals are vulnerable if they cross-jurisdictional boundaries and if no co-operative management is in place. For example, the George River caribou herd migrates across northern Labrador and Quebec on land managed by both provinces and by two groups of Native peoples. Big-game species migrating across park boundaries commonly are open to exploitation outside the park.

6. Large-bodied species are often vulnerable because of generally low reproductive rates (Vemreij, 1986) and extensive ranges. Large-bodied carnivores have large home ranges, ranging from 150 km^2 for black bears (including extreme excursions) to over 2000 km^2 for wolf packs (reviewed in Noss et al., 1996). Some species with large home ranges, particularly adult male grizzly bears, have such extensive movements that they will frequently or seasonally enter several management jurisdictions each year, such as grizzly bears in the Banff National Park region (Herrero, 1994) or wolves in Algonquin Provincial Park (Forbes and Theberge, 1996).

Considering habitats rather than biological traits, the species most in need of protected areas in Canada include those that live in montane, old-growth forest, tundra, prairie, cold desert, and wetlands. Montane ecosystems in the Rocky Mountains are threatened due to concentrated human activity in the valley bottoms that restrict the movements of species such as grizzly, black bear, and wolf. Old-growth forest species such as Roosevelt elk, black-tailed deer, many herds of woodland caribou, and some large raptors such as eagles and great grey owls need extensive reserves both to conserve their habitat and to free them from exploitation. Tundra species, while affected less by habitat alteration, need large wilderness preserves to protect their often large traditional areas for calving and rutting (caribou and musk-oxen) and to protect herds from exploitation. Prairie species need large protected areas for much the same reasons as do tundra wildlife, although the dominant wide-ranging herbivore, the plains bison, and its predator, the prairie subspecies of wolf, have vanished. The recovery of the swift fox and even possibly the black-footed ferret, however, will require extensive areas of habitat protection and freedom from exploitation. A narrow arm of western North America's cold desert extends into south central British Columbia with so many rare species that this Osoyoos biome itself is listed by COSEWIC as threatened. Wetland wildlife, living in the greatest pockets of species diversity, need protection from marsh drainage or over-enrichment from nutrients, as well as from overhunting. Wetland decline has contributed to a decline in amphibians such as leopard and pickerel frogs.

Protected areas are less significant for urban wildlife (grey squirrel, cottontail, cardinal and other backyard birds), farm wildlife (red fox, coyote), and wildlife of early successional forests (white-tailed deer, moose, beaver), although some species need preserves for critical denning, nesting, and rutting functions and for winter cover, especially in heavily lumbered regions. However, protected areas in regions containing intensive human use may play an important role in providing humans with a place to connect with nature.

The species-by-species approach to conservation has some limitations (Noss et al., 1997). Consequently it may be appropriate to take a dual approach of applying coarse (ecosystem) and fine (species) filters (Noss and Cooperrider, 1994) to place priority on conservation efforts. According to Lambeck (1997) and Noss et al. (1997), these fine filter species include: (1) resource-limited species that require specific resources that are often in critically short supply, (2) process-limited species that are sensitive to the frequency and level of ecological processes, (3) narrow-endemic species that are restricted to small geographic ranges and low population densities, (4) area-limited species that require large amounts of land to maintain a viable population (and maintain low population densities), (5) dispersal-limited species that have limited movement abilities, (6) keystone species that are ecologically pivotal because their impact upon an ecosystem is disproportionately large compared to their abundance, and (7) flagship species that promote public support. Coarse and fine filters may be used together in ecosystem analysis. For example, in applying a species filter to vertebrates in Algonquin Provincial Park, the second author identified two suites of species-at-risk that grouped into wetlands and old-growth habitats (Theberge, 1995) thereby targeting management to these ecosystem types.

Thinking about the welfare of selected species requires population-level consideration. How many individuals are necessary for population persistence? This topic has received attention since the early 1980s, through various calculations of 'minimum viable population', or MVP. Involved are attempts to calculate the smallest size of a park or reserve needed to support the minimum number of individuals for a viable and self-sustainable population. Often MVP is calculated for the most space-demanding species in an environment, with the hope that the space requirements of other species will be met within that area. Hence, calculations often focus on large carnivores such as the gray wolf (Theberge, 1983; Hummel, 1990) or the tiger (Tilson and Seal, 1987). As well, some have suggested that MVP analyses target critical or keystone species (Power et al., 1996), such as the major herbivore (Soule, 1987).

Two conceptual bases exist for calculating minimum viable population sizes: genetics and population demography. The genetics basis is founded upon the 1-per-cent rule: a population should not show more than 1 per cent inbreeding per generation. Inbreeding reduces genetic adaptability and the potential for responding to environmental change. Franklin (1980) and Soule (1980) explored this topic in depth. From mathematical formulations comes the conclusion that at least 50 free-breeding adults are necessary to prevent more than 1 per cent inbreeding per generation, a population size that must be adjusted upwards for non-breeding animals such as juveniles or those excluded from breeding by social behaviour. Minimum population size and space requirements per individual then determine the minimum size of a park or reserve.

For large carnivores these calculations show a need for very large reserves. In *A Conservation Strategy for Large Carnivores* (Hummel, 1990) are rough estimates for a minimum population size for wolves of about 150. With an approximate average density of 100 sq. km. per wolf in western parts of the species' range (based on a survey made by the second author of provincial and territorial wildlife management agencies in 1990), this results in a need for 15,000 sq. km. Few parks in Canada are that large. Even that calculation represents a minimal short-term value. For long-term genetic viability the minimum population size may be at least 10 times larger. Given no immigration, Franklin and Soule (1981) calculated that large carnivores (10–100 kg) can be expected to survive the next century in only 0–22 per cent of the world's parks and in none after 1,000 years.

The second basis for calculating minimum viable population size is through demography. Unlike the genetics-based calculation of minimum viable population size, these demographic calculations do not result in one single number, rather are expressed in probabilities of extinction, and are both species- and environment-specific (Gilpin and Soule, 1986). Mathematical formulations and computer programs (e.g., Belovsky, 1987) have been used to determine the probability of extinction over specified periods through varying such population parameters as birthrate, mortality, and reproductive age and output.

Minimum areas calculated in these ways tend to be even larger than those calculated through genetics. Especially at risk of extinction through demographic processes are large-bodied, long-lived species with low rates of turnover, such as elephants and redwood trees, compared with small-bodied, short-lived species such as shrews and annual plants. For example, elephants require a minimum area of 10,000 sq. km for a 99 per cent probability of persistence for 1,000 years, whereas shrews require 1,000 sq. km (Belovsky, 1987).

Today, MVP calculations are most often called PHVA—population and habitat viability analysis. Using a computer program called Vortex, a team of specialists from the Conservation Breeding Specialist Group of the World Conservation Union travels worldwide to host workshops on populations at risk. This program requires data not only from genetics and demographics, but from environmental variables such as frequency of catastrophe (meaning sudden change) and habitat alteration (Goodman, 1987; Boyce, 1992). Calculation of the size of a viable population is only one product of these workshops. More important are conservation plans developed from the analysis of vulnerable characteristics in the biology/ ecology of the population. PHVA workshops have been run in several Canadian parks—for grizzly bears in Banff (Herrero et al., 2000), and wolves in Algonquin (Box 4.3).

BOX 4.3 Ecological Effects on a Park Wolf Population of Killing by Humans Adjacent to the Park.

In Ontario's Algonquin Provincial Park wolf population, between 1988 and 1999, an average of 67 per cent of wolf deaths were caused by human killing. This mortality took place in lands adjacent to the park, affecting packs that held transboundary territories and that migrated annually to a white-tailed deer wintering area outside the park. Snaring and shooting were most common causes of death.

FIGURE 4.2 Algonquin Park wolf.

The ecological impact of this killing was to contribute to an average annual mortality of 35 per cent, which was beyond the productivity of the population, causing it to drop by 1/3 during the study. A 'Population and Habitat Viability Analysis' workshop was held by the World Conservation Union to address the conservation problem faced by this population, and using a predictive model called 'Vortex', the population failed to sustain itself more than a few decades (CSBG, 2000).

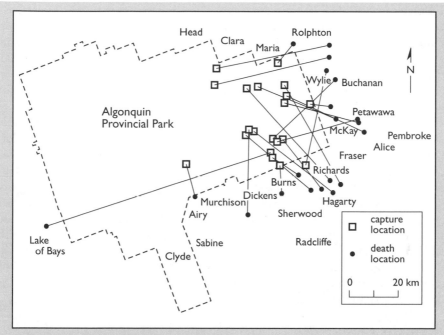

FIGURE 4.3 Map of wolf deaths surrounding Algonquin Park.

As serious as the human killing has been on the population demography of Algonquin Park wolves is the threat of accelerated hybridization with coyotes that live adjacent to the park and have at times invaded and interbred with park wolves. Just as hybridization with expanding coyotes doomed the exploited and fragmented red wolf populations in the southern United States by the late 1960s, hybridization has eliminated the wolf south of Algonquin Park and threatens the park population. Field data indicate that coyote-like animals tend to invade or show up in the park where wolf packs have been eliminated or fragmented.

Genetics analysis (Wilson et al., 2000) has shown that Algonquin wolves are red wolves, not gray wolves as formerly thought. The North American evolved red wolf has the capacity to interbreed with coyotes, which are believed to have diverged from each other in relatively recent times 150, 000 to 300,000 years ago. The gray wolf, with a different evolutionary history played out over a long time in Eurasia, does not appear to interbreed with coyotes.

Thus, human killing has contributed to both demographic and genetic deterioration of a supposedly protected park wolf population. Protective conservation measures are necessary to reduce or eliminate this near-park killing of transboundary packs, or the park will suffer the loss of the integrity that its summit mammalian predator provides. As well, as the least hybridized wild red wolves in the world, the integrity of a species is at risk.

Thinking About Health

Both patch dynamics and fragmentation address the impact of external factors on natural areas. So does stress ecology. Closely related to stress ecology is the concept of ecosystem health; that is, the presence of fully functional ecosystems with natural rates of energy capture and flow, nutrient uptake and cycling, with intact food webs and undisturbed mechanisms of population regulation.

Stresses from outside or within play an integral and ongoing role in the organization, evolution, and functions of ecosystems. Many natural stressors exist, differing in intensity, duration, and frequency of occurrence. They may act to influence ecosystems additively, in multiple ways, or by synergistic effects (Turner and Bratton, 1987). Lugo (1978) observed that without a periodic disruption, ecosystem growth processes stagnate as resources are immobilized by their structure. Bursts of growth and high net productivity usually follow disturbances, and rejuvenated systems replace senescent systems.

Widespread agreement exists that ecosystems exhibit common patterns of response when stressed by either natural or human causes (Freedman, 1989; Woodwell,1983). Indeed, natural stressors such as climate variation, succession, fire, disease, and changes in population sizes of predators may preadapt ecosystems to human-caused stresses. Among characteristics exhibited by stressed ecosystems, extracted from a list of 18 characteristics by Odum (1985) and by Rapport et al. (1985), are the following:

1. Changes in nutrient cycles, including increased leakiness.
2. Changes (normally an increase) in net primary productivity.
3. Changes in species composition, including loss of late successional stage species and a greater proportion of small-bodied, rapidly reproducing, hardy species.

Feedback allows ecosystems to cope with the effects of stress. For example, some ecosystems react to stress by replacing their more sensitive species with functionally similar but more resistant species. But just as in human systems, stress can go too far. Lovelock (1988) contends that 'from physiology, we know that the perturbations of a system that is close to instability can lead to oscillations, chaotic change, or failure.' For example, Rapport et al. (ibid.) observed that northern forested areas treated with herbicide stayed in shrubland even after the spraying program was stopped.

Protected areas are subjected to constant human-caused stress from both outside and within. A basis for ecosystem monitoring has emerged from the exploration of stress ecology and ecosystem health (Woodley and Theberge, 1992). Parks Canada's State of the Parks report (1998) requires that all parks monitor stresses and indicators. But monitoring for ecosystem stress only aids in identifying threats, the first step in ecosystem management. Bureaucratic and political will, budgets, and public concern all need to be in place or stress monitoring will be of little consequence.

Dealing With Uncertainty

Only the arrogant promote ecology as a fully predictive science. Like climate, ecosystems exhibit non-equilibrium and non-linearity. A high degree of interconnections create new relationships, make them dynamic. Succession never rebuilds exactly what was there before. Stochastic (unpredictable) events drive change.

Uncertainty arises from many different sources, such as indirect influences of an activity upon on an unintended target, synergistic effects of two or more stresses (e.g., interactions between toxins), cumulative space effects (e.g., activities in one jurisdiction automatically affect the health of the next ecosystem), and environmental stochasticity (i.e., random, unpredictable change such as a catastrophe) (Carroll and Meffe, 1997).

Catastrophe theory has significantly altered earlier concepts of stability in ecosystems. It has placed a greater premium on resilience in ecosystems; that is, on their capacity to bounce back (Holling, 1973). Catastrophe—sudden change such as a population crash or eruption or a wholesale change in the ecosystem through fire or flood—is natural in most ecosystems. It only carries a pejorative connotation if resource management demands a steady state. A steady system is not the objective in most protected areas, where natural ecological forces are supposed to prevail.

Population models before, during, and after a catastrophe were advanced by Jones (1975). Most frequently cited examples of catastrophe are fire (Bormann and Likens, 1979; Holling, 1973) and spruce budworm (Holling, 1973; May, 1977). In all the examples, predisposing environmental factors increase in intensity until a catastrophe becomes inevitable. Similar to this idea, Kaufman et al. (1998) postulated that there may be a critical level of biodiversity at which ecosystems are highly susceptible to mass extinction.

Sometimes it is possible to incorporate catastrophe and uncertainty in population models, thereby informing managers of protected areas of the potential outcomes of various management actions (Marshall et al., 1998). If we allow for catastrophes with some predictable periodicity (based upon probabilities) in models of minimum viable population sizes, the results again argue for very large reserves. They argue, too, for the protection of more than one example of ecosystems, and for multiple reserves to protect rare and endangered species.

Uncertainty in ecosystems forms a rationale for the application of 'adaptive management' as a general approach. Rather than taking a normative planning approach that, on the basis of best existing information, invokes management prescriptions for a fixed and usually lengthy period, adaptive management involves viewing management as a continuous experiment. As such, adaptive management embodies the capacity to change prescriptions as ongoing research—an essential component of the approach—dictates. The concept has been around for awhile (Holling, 1978). While often espoused by governments, it has been practiced less often because of increased costs of the research component and added complexity. Nonetheless, its incorporation into park management, despite its inherent admission of uncertainty, is an antidote to misjudgment and error.

Thinking Beyond the Obvious

Most ecologists believe that ecosystems are more than the sum of their parts. Properties emerge by virtue of the complex interconnections and interdependencies among species. The literature is small on this topic, but future advances in ecological thinking will undoubtedly occur.

TABLE 4.1. Ecosystem Stability

Stability (resistance to change) means:
• relatively constant set of species (low extinction rates, few colonizers).
• relatively constant abundance of those species (absence of fluctuations).
• resultant relatively constant energy capture and partitioning of flow through trophic levels.

Stability is an ever-adjusting state that reflects a number of conditions:

Condition	Effect
1) trophic web complexity	high = stable
2) species diversity	high = stable
3) stage of succession	climax = stable
4) structural complexity	complex = stable
5) cybernetic population mechanisms in dominant, keystone and summit species	presence = stable
6) size of area	large = stable
7) distance to re-colonizers (new species)	far = stable
8) extent of non-lethal interspecific relationships (symbiosis, mutualism, commensalism, parasitism)	more = stable
9) number and frequency of catastrophes	few and infrequent = stable
10) proportion of r–K strategists as influencing fecundity	K strategists = stable in terms of infrequent eruptions
11) proportion of generalists/specialists	more generalists = stable
12) geographic location	community central in its range = stable

TABLE 4.2. Ecosystem Resilience

Resilience is the ability to bounce back after disturbance. In any ecosystem, resilience is an ever-adjusting state that reflects a number of conditions:

Condition	Effect
1) succession	recurs frequently = resilient early successional stage = resilient
2) distance to re-colonizers (new species)	close = resilient
3) proportion of r - K strategists nearby	more r-strategists = resilient
4) residual soil fertility	high = resilient
5) proportion of asexually reproducing plant propagules	high = resilient
6) survival of bacteria, seeds, and spores in the soil	high = resilient
7) species diversity	low = resilient (replacement time)
8) population sizes of keystone species	above danger threshold = resilient

Some properties that emerge by virtue of the self-organized complexity in ecosystems include stability (ability to resist perturbations) and resilience (ability to bounce back from perturbations). A host of ecological processes contribute both positively and negatively to these properties so that various ecosystems may exhibit a natural level and a range around them that may be expressed at different stages of succession (Tables 4.1 and 4.2). For example, stability is conferred by trophic interconnections and reduced by the frequency of natural disturbance. Resilience is enhanced by a preponderance of r-selected (high reproductive rate) species in the ecosystem, and is reduced by erosional processes.

For all park ecosystems, it would be a constructive exercise to think through the processes, and human influences on them, that, in turn, influence ecosystem stability and resilience. The result would form a foundation for ecosystem monitoring based upon emergent ecological processes. More thinking on this topic could form the next wave of conceptual advances in the science.

CONCLUSIONS

Ecosystem management in parks involves consideration from all the angles we have described in the foregoing. Management programs based on broad ecological thinking will be most successful in identifying problems at early stages; as in human medicine, early detection results in a much enhanced probability of successful cures. Park budgets for ecosystem management often are so small that only crisis topics get attention. This needs to change.

Ecological theory has pointed out that protected areas everywhere in Canada, and worldwide, are too small and too few to withstand external and internal assaults indefinitely or to protect minimum viable population sizes, especially of the functionally dominant large predators and migratory species, over the long term. As a consequence, parks and reserves must be seen for what they are—only parts of regional landscapes—and so should be parts of regional conservation strategies. Because parks and reserves are not ecologically self-sufficient, regional environmental management is absolutely necessary. Incumbent upon park managers is to take the lead in the formation of such regional strategies. More than the parks are at stake.

REFERENCES

Agee, J.K., and D.R. Johnson. 1988. *Ecosystem Management for Parks and Wilderness*. Seattle: University of Washington Press.

Belovsky, G.E. 1987. 'Extinction Models and Mammalian Persistence', in M.E. Soule, ed., *Viable Populations for Conservation*. Cambridge: Cambridge University Press, 3–57.

Bormann, F., H. Likens, and G.E. Likens. 1979. 'Catastrophic Disturbance and the Steady State in Northern Hardwood Forests', *American Scientist* 67: 66–9.

Boyce, M.S. 1992. 'Population Viability Analysis', *Annual Review of Ecology and Systematics* 23: 481–506.

Carroll, C.R., and G.K. Meffe. 1997. 'Management to Meet Conservation Goals: General Principles', in Meffe and Carroll (1997a: 347–84).

Christensen, N.L., A.M. Bartuska, J.H. Brown, S. Carpenter, C. D'Antonio, R. Francis, J.F. Franklin, J.A. MacMahon, R.F. Noss, D.J. Parsons, C.H. Peterson, M.G. Turner, and R.G. Woodmansee. 1996. 'The Report of the Ecological Society of America Committee on the Scientific Basis for Ecosystem Management', *Ecological Applications* 6, 3: 665–91.

Conservation Breeding Specialist Group (CBSG). 2000. 'The Wolves of Algonquin Park', PHVA: *Final Report*. Apple Valley, Minn.: CBSG.

Diamond, J.M. 1975. 'The Island Dilemma: Lessons of Modern Biogeographic Studies for the Design of Nature Reserves', *Biological Conservation* 7: 129–46.

Doak, D.F., and L.S. Mills. 1994. 'A Useful Role for Theory in Conservation', *Ecology* 75, 3: 615–26.

Dunning, J.B., B.J. Danielson, and H.R. Pulliam. 1992. 'Ecological Processes That Affect Populations in Complex Landscapes', *Oikos* 65, 1: 169–75.

Eldredge, N. 1985. *Unfinished Synthesis: Biological Hierarchies and Modern Evolutionary Thought*. Oxford: Oxford University Press.

Forbes, G.J., and J.B. Theberge. 1996. 'Cross-boundary Management of Algonquin Park Wolves', *Conservation Biology* 10, 4: 1091–7.

Forman, R.T.T. 1995. *Land Mosaics: The Ecology of Landscapes and Regions*. Cambridge: Cambridge University Press.

Forman, R.T.T. 1997. 'Designing Landscapes and Regions to Conserve Nature', in Meffe and Carroll (1997a: 331–2).

———— and S.K. Collinge. 1997. 'Nature Conserved in Changing Landscapes With and Without Spatial Planning', *Landscape and Urban Planning* 37: 129–35.

———— and M. Godron. 1986. *Landscape Ecology*. New York: John Wiley and Sons.

Franklin, I.R. 1980. 'Evolutionary Change in Small Populations', in Soule and Wilcox (1980: 135–49).

Franklin, O.H., and M.E. Soule. 1981. *Conservation and Evolution*. Cambridge: Cambridge University Press.

Freedman, W. 1989. *Environmental Ecology: The Impacts of Pollution and Other Stresses on Ecosystem Structures and Functions*. San Francisco: Academic Press.

Gibeau, M.L. 1998. 'Grizzly Bear Habitat Effectiveness Model for Banff, Yoho, and Kootenay National Parks', *Ursus* 10: 235–41.

Gilpin, M.E., and M.E. Soule. 1986. 'Minimum Viable Populations: Processes of Species Extinction', in Soule (1986a: 19–34).

Glenn, S.M. 1990. 'Regional Analysis of Mammal Distributions among Canadian National Parks: Implications for Park Planning', *Canadian Journal of Zoology* 68: 2457–64.

Goodman, D. 1987. 'The Demography of Chance Extinction', in M.E. Soule, ed., *Viable Populations for Conservation*. Cambridge: Cambridge University Press, 11–34.

Grumbine, R.E. 1994. 'What is Ecosystem Management?', *Conservation Biology* 8, 1: 27–38.

Hastings, A., and S. Harrison. 1994. 'Metapopulation Dynamics and Genetics', *Annual Review of Ecology and Systematics* 25: 167–88.

Herrero, S. 1994. 'The Canadian National Parks and Grizzly Bear Ecosystems: The Need for Interagency Management', *International Conference on Bear Research and Management* 9, 1: 7–22.

————, P.S. Miller, and U.S. Seal, eds. 2000. 'Population and Habitat Viability Assessment for the Grizzly Bear of the Central Rockies Ecosystem (Ursus arctos)', *Eastern Slopes Grizzly Bear Project*, University of Calgary, Calgary, Alberta, and Conservation Breeding Specialist Group, Apple Valley, Minn.

Holling, C.S. 1973. 'Resilience and Stability of Ecological Systems', *Annual Review of Ecological Systems* 4: 1–23.

———. 1978. *Adaptive Management Assessment and Management*. London: John Wiley and Sons.

Hummel, M. 1990. *Conservation Strategy for Large Carnivores in Canada*. Toronto: World Wildlife Fund Canada.

Johnson, D.H. 1980. 'The Comparison of Usage and Availability Measurements for Evaluating Resource Preference', *Ecology* 61, 1: 65–71.

Jones, D.D. 1975. 'The Application of Catastrophe Theory to Ecological Systems', in G.S. Innis, ed., *New Directions to the Analysis of Ecological Systems*. Simulation Councils Proceedings Series, vol. 5, 133–48.

Kaufman, J.K., D. Brodbeck, and O.R. Melroy. 1998. 'Critical Biodiversity', *Conservation Biology* 12, 3: 521–32.

Keddy, P.A. 1991. 'Working with Heterogeneity: An Operator's Guide to Environmental Gradients', in J. Kolasa and S.T.A. Pickett, eds, *Ecological Heterogeneity*. New York: Springer-Verlag, 181–201.

Kerkhoff, A.J., B.T. Milne, and D.S. Maehr. 2000. 'Toward a Panther-centered View of the Forests of South Florida', *Conservation Ecology* 4, 1: 1. Available at: <http://www.consecol.org/vol4/iss1/art1>.

Kolosa, J., and C.D. Rollo. 1991. 'Introduction: The Heterogeneity of Heterogeneity—A Glossary', in Kolosa and S.T.A. Pickett, eds, *Ecological Heterogeneity*. New York: Springer-Verlag, 1–23.

Lambeck, R.J. 1997. 'Focal Species: A Multi-Species Umbrella for Nature Conservation', *Conservation Biology* 11: 849–56.

Leopold, A. 1933. *Game Management*. New York: Scribner.

Levin, S.A. 1992. 'The Problem of Pattern and Scale in Ecology', *Ecology* 73, 6: 1943–67.

Levins, R. 1970. 'Extinction', in M. Gerstenhaber, ed., *Some Mathematical Questions in Biology*. Providence, RI: American Mathematical Society.

Locke, H. 1998. 'Yellowstone to Yukon Conservation Initiative', in N.W.P. Munro and J.H.M. Willison, eds, *Linking Protected Areas with Working Landscapes Conserving Biodiversity*. Proceedings of the Third International Conference on Science and Management of Protected Areas, Wolfville, NS, 255–9.

Lovelock, J. 1988. *The Ages of Gaia*. New York: W.W. Norton.

Lugo, A.E. 1978. 'Stress in Ecosystems', in J.H. Thorpe and J.W. Gibbons, eds, *Energy and the Environment: Stress in Aquatic Ecosystems*. United States Department of Energy Symposium, series 78. Springfield, Ill.: National Technical Information Service, 61–101.

MacArthur, R.H., and E.O. Wilson. 1967. *The Theory of Island Biogeography*. Princeton, NJ: Princeton University Press.

Mace, R.D., J.S. Waller, T.L. Manley, L.J. Lyon, and H. Zuuring. 1996. 'Relationships among Grizzly Bears, Roads, and Habitat in the Swan Mountains, Montana', *Journal of Applied Ecology* 33: 1395–404.

Marshall, E., R. Haight, and F.R. Homans. 1998. 'Incorporating Environmental Uncertainty into Species Management Decisions: Kirtland's Warbler Habitat Management as a Case Study', *Conservation Biology* 12, 5: 975–85.

May, R.M. 1977. 'Thresholds and Breakpoints in Ecosystems with a Multiplicity of Stable States', *Nature* 269: 471–8.

McCullough, D.R. 1996. 'Introduction', in McCullough, ed., *Metapopulations and Wildlife Conservation*. Washington: Island Press.

McLaren, B.E., and R.O. Peterson. 1994. 'Wolves, Moose, and Tree Rings on Isle Royale', *Science* 266, 2: 1555–8.

Meffe, G.K., and C.R. Carroll, eds. 1997a. *Principles of Conservation Biology*, 2nd edn. Sunderland, Mass.: Sinaur Associates.

————— and —————.1997b. 'What is Conservation Biology?', in Meffe and Carroll (1997a: 3–28).

Morin, P.J., and S.P. Lawler. 1995. 'Food Web Architecture and Population Dynamics: Theory and Empirical Evidence', *Annual Review of Ecology and Systematics* 26: 505–29.

Newmark, W.D. 1995. 'Extinction of Mammal Populations in Western North American National Parks', *Conservation Biology* 9: 512–26.

Noss, R.F. 1987. 'Corridors in Real Landscapes: A Reply to Simberloff and Cox', *Conservation Biology* 1: 159–64.

—————. 1996. 'Protected Areas: How Much is Enough?', in R.G. Wright, ed., *National Parks and Protected Areas: Their Role in Environmental Protection*. Cambridge, Mass.: Blackwell Science, 121–32.

————— and A.Y. Cooperrider. 1994. *Saving Nature's Legacy: Protecting and Restoring Biodiversity*. Washington: Island Press.

————— and B. Csuti. 1997. 'Habitat Fragmentation', in Meffe and Carroll (1997: 269–304).

—————, H.B. Quigley, M.G. Hornocker, T. Merrill, and P.C. Paquet. 1996. 'Conservation Biology and Carnivore Conservation in the Rocky Mountains', *Conservation Biology* 10, 4: 949–63.

—————, M.A. O'Connell, and D.D. Murphy. 1997. *The Science of Conservation Planning: Habitat Conservation Under the Endangered Species Act*. Washington: Island Press.

Odum, E.P. 1985. 'Trends Expected in Stressed Ecosystems', *Bioscience* 35: 419–22.

O'Neill, R.V., J.R. Krummel, R.H. Gardner, G. Sugihara, B. Jackson, D.L. DeAngelis, B.T. Milne, M.G. Turner, B. Zygmunt, S.W. Christensen, V.H. Dale, and R.L. Graham. 1988. 'Indices of Landscape Pattern', *Landscape Ecology* 1, 3: 153–62.

Parks Canada. 1998. *State of the Parks, 1997*. Report. Ottawa: Department of Canadian Heritage.

Parks Canada Agency. 2000. *Unimpaired for Future Generations? Protecting Ecological Integrity with Canada's National Parks, vol. 2: Setting a New Direction for Canada's National Parks*. Report of the Panel on the Ecological Integrity of Canada's National Parks. Ottawa.

Peterson, D.L., and V.T. Parker, eds. 1998. *Ecological Scale: Theory and Applications*. New York: Columbia University Press..

Petit, D.R. 1989. 'Weather-dependent Use of Habitat Patches by Wintering Woodland Birds', *Journal of Field Ornithology* 60: 241–7.

Pickett, S.T.A., and P.S. White. 1985. 'Patch Dynamics: A Synthesis', in S.T.A. Pickett and P.S. White, eds. *The Ecology of Natural Disturbance and Patch Dynamics*. San Diego: Academic Press, 371–84.

Power, M.E., D. Tilman, J.A. Estes, B.A. Menge, W.J. Bond, L.S. Mills, G. Daily, J.C. Castilla, J. Lubchenco, and R.T. Paine. 1996. 'Challenges in the Quest for Keystones', *Bioscience* 46, 8: 609–20.

Rapport, D.J., H.A. Reiger, and T.C. Hutchinson. 1985. 'Ecosystem Behavior Under Stress', *American Naturalist* 125: 617–40.

Riitters, K.H., R.V. O'Neill, and K.B. Jones. 1997. 'Assessing Habitat Suitability at Multiple Scales: A Landscape-Level Approach', *Biological Conservation* 81: 191–202.

Rodriguez, A., G. Crema, and M. Delibes. 1996. 'Use of Non-wildlife Passages across a High Speed Railway by Terrestrial Vertebrates', *Journal of Applied Ecology* 33:1527–40.

Senft, R.L., M.B. Coughenour, D.W. Bailey, L.R. Rittenhouse, O.E. Sala, and D.M. Swift. 1987. 'Large Herbivore Foraging and Ecological Hierarchies', *Bioscience* 37, 11: 789–99.

Shaw, J.H. 1985. *Introduction to Wildlife Management*. New York: McGraw-Hill.

Simberloff, D.S. 1974. 'Equilibrium Theory of Island Biogeography and Ecology', *Annual Review of Ecology and Systematics* (1974–5): 161–82.

———, J.A. Farr, J. Cox, and D.W. Mehlman. 1992. 'Movement Corridors: Conservation Bargains or Poor Investments?', *Conservation Biology* 6, 4: 493–504.

——— and J. Cox. 1987. 'Consequences and Costs of Conservation Corridors', *Conservation Biology* 1: 63–9.

Smith, P.G.R., J.G. Nelson, and J.B. Theberge. 1986. 'Environmentally Significant Areas, Conservation and Land Use Management in the Northwest Territories', Technical Paper Number 1, Heritage Resources Centre, University of Waterloo, Waterloo, Ont.

Soule, M.E. 1980. 'Thresholds for Survival: Maintaining Fitness and Evolutionary Potential', in Soule and Wilcox (1980: 151–69).

———. 1983. 'Application of Genetics and Population Biology: The What, Where and How of Nature Reserves', in *Conservation, Science and Society*. UNESCO-UNEP, 252–64.

———, ed. 1986a. *Conservation Biology: The Science of Scarcity and Diversity*. Sunderland, Mass.: Sinauer Associates.

———. 1986b. 'Conservation Biology and the Real World', in Soule (1986a: 1–12).

——— and B.A. Wilcox, eds. 1980. *Conservation Biology: An Evolutionary-Ecological Perspective*. Sunderland, Mass.: Sinauer Associates.Stanley, T.R., Jr. 1995. 'Ecosystem Management and the Arrogance of Humanism', Conservation Biology 9, 2: 255–62.

Terborgh, J. 1989. *Where Have All the Birds Gone?* Princeton, NJ: Princeton University Press.

Theberge, J.B. 1983. 'Consideration in Wolf Management Related to Genetic Variability and Adaptive Change', in L.N. Carbyn, ed., *Wolves in Canada and Alaska*. Canadian Wildlife Service Report Series, Number 45. Ottawa, 86–9.

———. 1989. 'Guidelines to Drawing Ecologically Sound Boundaries for National Parks and Nature Reserves', *Environmental Management* 13: 695–702.

———. 1995. 'Vertebrate Species Approach to Trans-Park Boundary Problems and Landscape Linkages', in T.B. Herman, S. Bondrup-Nielsen, J.H.M. Willison, and N.W.P. Munro, eds, *Ecosystem Monitoring and Protected Areas*. Proceedings of the Second International Conference on Science and Management of Protected Areas, 16–20 May 1994. Halifax, 526–36.

Tilson, R.L., and U.S. Seal, eds. 1987. *Tigers of the World: The Biology, Biopolitics Management, and Conservation of an Endangered Species*. Park Ridge, NJ: Noyes Publications.

Turner, M., and S.P. Bratton. 1987. 'Fire, Grazing, and the Landscape Heterogeneity of a Georgia Barrier Island', in M. Turner, ed., *Landscape Heterogeneity and Disturbance*. New York: Springer-Verlag, 85–101.

Turner, M.G., and R.H. Gardner, eds. 1991. *Quantitative Methods in Landscape Ecology*. New York: Springer-Verlag.

Vermeij, G.J. 1986. 'The Biology of Human-caused Extinction', in B.G. Norton, ed., *The Preservation of Species: The Value of Biological Diversity*. Princeton, NJ: Princeton University Press, 28–49.

Wilcove, D.S., C.H. McLellan, and A.P. Dobson. 1986. 'Habitat Fragmentation in the Temperate Zone', in Soule (1986a: 237–56).

Wilcox, B.A., and D.D. Murphy. 1985. 'Conservation Strategy: The Effects of Fragmentation on Extinction', *American Naturalist* 125: 879–87.

Wilson, P.J, S. Grewal, I.D. Lawford, J.N.M. Heal, A.G. Granacki, D. Pennock, J.B. Theberge, M.T. Theberge, D.R. Voigt, W. Waddell, R.E. Chambers, P.C. Paquet, G. Goulet, and B.N. White. 2000. 'DNA Profiles of the Eastern Canadian Wolf and the Red Wolf Provide Evidence for a Common Evolutionary History Independent of the Gray Wolf', *Canadian Journal of Zoology* 78, 12: 2156–66.

With, K.A. 1997. 'The Application of Neutral Landscape Models in Conservation Biology', *Conservation Biology* 11, 5: 1069–80.

With, K.A., and T.O. Crist. 1995. 'Critical Thresholds in Species' Responses to Landscape Structure', *Ecology* 76, 8: 2446–59.

Woodley, S., and J.B. Theberge. 1992. 'Monitoring for Ecosystem Integrity in Canadian National Parks', in J.H.M. Willison et al., eds, *Science and the Management of Protected Areas*. New York: Elsevier.

Woodwell, G.M. 1983. 'The Blue Planet: Of Wholes and Parts and Man', in H.A. Mooney and M. Gordon, eds, *Disturbance and Ecosystems*. Berlin: Springer-Verlag, 2–10.

Wootton, J.T. 1994. 'The Nature and Consequences of Indirect Effects in Ecological Communities', *Annual Review of Ecology and Systematics* 25: 443–66.

World Commission on Environment and Development. 1987. *Our Common Future*. Oxford: Oxford University Press.

World Conservation Strategy. 1980. Gland: ICUN-UNEP-WWWF.

Yahner R.H. 1988. 'Changes in Wildlife Communities Near Edges', *Conservation Biology* 2: 333–9.

KEY WORDS/CONCEPTS

ecology
ecological integrity
ecosystem
remote sensing
GIS
ecosystem management
anthropocentric
biocentric
grain
extent
landscape complementation
landscape supplementation
metapopulation concept
habitat fragmentation
habitat deterioration
overexploitation of species
isolated reserves
island biogeography
SLOSS
patch dynamics
corridors
matrix

heterogeneity
fragmentation
edge habitat
sedge
K-strategist
summit predator
montane
old-growth
tundra
prairie
cold desert
wetlands
minimum viable populations
1-per-cent rule
demography
stress ecology
uncertainty
catastrophe theory
adaptive management
stability
resilience

STUDY QUESTIONS

1. What is meant by the expression 'The ecological world is dynamic and nonequilibrial'?
2. What is meant by the expression 'Human presence must be included in conservation planning'?
3. What is meant by the expression 'Our understanding of biotic evolution has been too reductionist'?
4. What is the reasoning for using the term 'ecosystem management' as opposed to 'sustainable development'?
5. Why must any application of ecological thinking to parks necessitate 'thinking big'?
6. Discuss the influence of 'grain' and 'extent'on the analysis of ecological phenomena and park identification.
7. Discuss the factors putting metapopulations at risk.
8. What is meant by 'thinking connected'?
9. Discuss how island biogeography theory relates to arguments about the size and location of protected areas.

10. Comment on the role of corridors with respect to the viability of protected areas.
11. Describe the distinction between fragmentation and a natural matrix.
12. Why are roads of particular concern for conservation biologists?
13. List six key biological traits that make some species more vulnerable than others to human disturbances.
14. What habitat types are risk in Canada, and why?
15. Why does the 'species by species' approach have some limitations?
16. What types of 'fine filter species' deserve special attention?
17. Select a wildlife population found in a local park or protected area. Investigate the viability of this population, by identifying the level of protection within the park, and identifying possible risk factors.
18. Select a local park and discuss the size and configuration of the park through a consideration of island biogeography, SLOSS, patch dynamics, and corridors.

CHAPTER 5

Planning and Managing for Ecological Integrity in Canada's National Parks

Stephen Woodley

INTRODUCTION

National parks, viewed through the lens of the year 2000, might be described as a societal response to ecosystem decay. Throughout most of the history of national parks and equivalent protected areas, it was commonly thought that simply placing legal boundaries around areas was sufficient to protect them. The result would be healthy, self-regulating ecosystems unaffected by humanity's onslaught. This 'preservation' stage of park management was accompanied by the perception that national parks were 'natural' and or 'wilderness' and thus required no management. The revisions to the National Parks Act in 1988 introduced the term ecological integrity (Chapters 1, 2, and 9). This term provides a new model for managing protected areas. As a concept, 'ecological integrity' supersedes the notion of 'natural' as a management endpoint, which has several important ramifications. One of the key implications is that active management might be required in parks to maintain or restore ecological integrity.

During the early years of park establishment, Canadian National parks often were islands of civilization in a sea of wilderness. Park boundaries were only lines on a map and indistinguishable on the landscape. Today the impacts of forestry, agriculture, tourism, and urbanization have effectively isolated most parks as islands in a human-dominated landscape. Large-scale ecological insults, such as acidic precipitation and climate change, have no consideration for park boundaries. Ecosystem boundaries are difficult, if not impossible, to define. No matter where a park boundary is drawn, there will always be flows across the boundary. The flows may be water, nutrients, or animals. The essential fact is that parks are connected to a larger landscape and management must take that into account. Within parks, large-scale tourism facilities and road networks have been developed. It has become increasingly obvious that instead of being natural, self-regulating ecosystems, parks, and protected areas are remnant islands assaulted by a variety of human-caused stresses, originating both within and outside.

Historically, parks were considered to be 'natural' areas set aside for purposes of protecting and conserving representative, or unique, species and ecosystems. The stated goals of park management were simply to let nature take its course, with the implicit understanding that management would be minimal. However, there were

BOX 5.1 Ecological Integrity Statements

Ecological integrity has been a part of park policy since 1979. However, various definitions have emerged over the years. The Panel on the Ecological Integrity for Canada's National Parks (Parks Canada Agency, 2000: 1–15) suggests the following: 'An ecosystem has integrity when it is deemed characteristic for its natural region, including the composition and abundance of native species and biological communities, rates of change and supporting processes'.

For National parks, the Ecological Integrity Statement (EIS) plays a central role in setting out long-term management by identifying the basic and specific values of the ecosystem which the park is mandated to preserve in an ecological vision for the park. The statement also identifies issues relevant to achieving desired ecological conditions; setting and communicating ecological goals, indicators, objectives, and targets for acceptable conditions.

The quest for the protection or restoration of national parks' ecological integrity is an endless one. The EIS is the tool to be used to translate this immense task into more concrete, tangible goals and objectives. It provides a description of the key components of the ecosystems in a given park and their desired state in a 15-year time frame. The EIS is the means by which ecological integrity is defined for a particular park according to local conditions.

always many exceptions within the practice of minimal management. As late as the 1960's, predators, including bears, cougars, and eagles were shot in National parks. The stated goal of the day was to keep healthy populations of elk and mule deer, which were then considered threatened by the predators. Even today, wildfires continue to be suppressed in most protected areas in Canada.

Despite some past efforts that now seem misguided, simply letting nature take its course—'laissez faire' management—can be inconsistent with a goal of maintaining or enhancing ecological integrity. It is now well understood that many landscapes, in which parks are situated, especially in southern Canada, have been altered greatly from their historical condition. Active management may be needed to allow species or ecosystems to persist in parks where otherwise they might be lost. To the extent that a park may be the last stronghold for a particular species, if lost from the park that species may be lost from the larger region, too. Thus, if parks are to include species and ecosystems characteristic of the surrounding natural region, park landscapes and species populations may have to be actively managed for that species to persist.

In order to compensate for past or current actions, active management may be required in such areas as fire restoration, management of hyper-abundant native species, or elimination of non-native species. Active management should occur where there are reasonable grounds to believe that maintenance or restoration of ecological integrity will be compromised without it. Because of the difficulty in predicting ecosys-

BOX 5.2 Adaptive Management

Adaptive management is a formal process of 'learning by doing' for continually improving management policies and practices by learning from their outcomes. As stated by Walters (1997), 'It involves more than simply better ecological monitoring and response to unexpected management impacts.' In particular, it has been repeatedly argued (Holling, 1978, Walters, 1986) that adaptive management should begin with an effort to integrate existing interdisciplinary experience and scientific information into dynamic models that attempt to make predictions about the impacts of alternative policies. This modelling step is intended to serve three functions: (1) problem clarification and enhanced communication among scientists, managers, and other stakeholders; (2) policy screening to eliminate options that are most likely incapable of doing much good, because of inadequate scale or type of impact; and (3) identification of key knowledge gaps that make model predictions suspect'. For protected areas adaptive management offers a way to deal with the large amount of uncertainly surrounding ecosystem management. At its best, adaptive management integrates learning into its planning processes, to continually improve management for the protection of ecological integrity.

tem response, active management should be undertaken in national parks using adaptive management techniques. Public acceptability is also a key concern, and resources must be invested to raise public awareness of the issues before operations take place.

Ecological integrity as a goal in protected area management recognizes the need to manage parks for a particular ecosystem state. Ecological integrity as a management endpoint is a significant advance from the notion of 'natural'. It forces the use of ecosystem science in combination with societal wishes to define ecosystem goals. Moreover, ecological integrity recognizes ecosystems are self-organizing, dynamic entities. No one particular state or era in time is necessarily correct or ideally natural. Furthermore, protected areas management cannot attempt to recreate a particular era because most ecosystems are too dynamic and too complex. An era is distinguished by a range of conditions, such as disturbance history, levels of herbivores and predators, weather patterns etc. In some cases, it may be possible to maintain a similar ecosystem but it will never be exactly the same. For example, fire may be used in a landscape to maintain a successional stage, such as a grassland valley bottom. However, the serial stage is maintained for defined ecological objectives, such as providing winter forage, rather than simply to re-create a particular situation in time.

It has been a difficult transition for park managers to go from being protectors of nature—where nature always knew best—to actively managing ecosystems for a defined ecological goal. This chapter discusses the main types of active management used in Canadian national parks, with examples. Although the national parks' Guiding Principles (Parks Canada, 1994) are clear on the need for active management, it has been a difficult concept to put into operation across the national park system. Current policy on active management in national parks (ibid.: 34) has been defined thus:

> National park ecosystems will be managed with minimal interference to natural processes. However, active management may be allowed when the structure or function of an ecosystem has been seriously altered and manipulation is the only possible alternative available to restore ecological integrity.

ACTIVE MANAGEMENT

Active management in protected areas is complex. If the goal for a protected area is ecological integrity, a requirement will be populations of native species and the processes upon which they depend. Active management is aimed at maintaining or restoring a process, species, or community because (1) it is likely to disappear or has disappeared, or (2) it is not functioning within the expected range of variation for that ecosystem. Category 1 problems are easier to understand and include species reintroductions, such as peregrine falcon reintroductions to Fundy National Park and Pine Martin reintroductions to Riding Mountain National Park.

BOX 5.3 Reintroducing Peregrine Falcons to Fundy

During the 1980s, Fundy National Parks was a release site for a national recovery program for the Anatum subspecies of peregrine falcon. Eighty-four young birds were released from the park through a process called hacking. This was part of a national recovery plan for this species led by the Canadian Wildlife Service. The program was successful, with seven nesting pairs of breeding peregrines now re-established in the Bay of Fundy.

Other examples include community restorations, such as the restoration of prairie grasslands in Grasslands National Park. In some cases, park managers must mimic an entire ecological process. For example, to mimic the effects of predation on large mammals in Elk Island National Park where large carnivores are absent and cannot be reintroduced (it is too small) park managers regularly remove herbivores from the ecosystem. Category 2 problems are more complex and involve the enhancement of an existing species or ecological process to its former level. An example is the restoration of wildlife corridors in Banff's Bow Valley so that wolves and other predators have access to elk populations in and near the town of Banff (Kay et al., 1999).

Active management requires taking action in such potentially controversial areas as fire restoration or the control of hyper-abundant species. In complex ecological systems, there typically will be debate about why changes are occurring and whether or not such changes are detrimental to ecological integrity. Avoiding gridlock demands adaptive management. Under an adaptive management framework, actions can be taken simultaneously with testing for their alleged effects on ecological integrity. Through feedback loops, results of the actions can be used to adapt or change future actions for improved results. On-going parts of most park's management include: active adaptive management to restore fire, managing hyper-abundant native or non-native species, or upgrading infrastructure—where there are reasonable grounds to think that maintenance or restoration of ecological integrity will become compromised without active management.

Managing Hyper-abundant Species

Species can be defined as hyper-abundant when their numbers clearly exceed the upper range of variability that is characteristic of the ecosystem. Hyper-abundance or overabundance should be judged in context and can occur when a species caused ecosystem dysfunction or depressed or eliminated favoured species (McShea et al., 1997). This can happen when predators are removed from the ecosystem, or when there is a food subsidy, such as high raccoon populations caused by available garbage.

There has been considerable debate (McShea et al., 1997) about the management of hyper-abundant species, both inside and outside protected areas. The debate traces its historical roots to the early days of modern wildlife biology and the famous example of deer in the Arizona's Kiabob Plateau (Leopold, 1943). The determination of what constitutes a hyper-abundant species is difficult and an ongoing challenge to park managers. In several parks, Parks Canada is routinely managing hyper-abundant populations as discussed in the case studies below.

Some parks have lost key species that may have played a role in promoting the maintenance of others. One view holds that reduced abundance of large carnivores such as wolves from some parks has led to hyper-abundant populations of such prey species as elk and moose, and to significant changes in the abundance of other species (Kay et al., 1999). For example, Banff and Jasper have large problems with town-adapted elk and a dysfunctional predator-prey system—with resulting impacts on vegetation. Other species may be hyper-abundant because parks, as last enclaves, afford protection. Large populations are subsidized by extensive alternate food sources outside of the park. This is the case with deer in southern Ontario. Others, such as deer in Gwaii Haanas, were introduced to islands with both abundant food and few predators.

Case Study: Managing Ungulates in Elk Island National Park

The story of managing ungulate populations in Elk Island National Park begins with the construction of a 2.2-meter fence surrounding the park in 1905.

The original purpose of the fence was to keep animals, especially bison, in the park and prevent wild ungulates from feeding on neighbouring croplands. The park is a now rare mix of aspen parkland and prairie, supporting high densities of ungulates. Elks Island is only 194 km², too small to maintain a population of large carnivores such as wolves. An occasional wolf is seen in the park, but the surrounding agricultural landscape is inhospitable to wolves and grizzly bears. Thus, the park has a dilemma—how to manage this ecosystem in the absence of large carnivores. From the beginning, there was evidence that, in the absence of predators, ungulate population numbers would vary widely, with extremely high numbers causing soil erosion and eliminating some species of plants (Bork, 1993; Vujnovic, 1998).

The philosophy of managing ungulate populations has been changing since the park's inception. At the beginning, managers would allow numbers to increase to a point and then, based on the manager's field assessment, a surplus number was picked for slaughter. For example, historically there was a moose slaughter about every four years, now cancelled because of public concern. Also in the past, concern for diseases, such as brucellosis, resulted in large-scale test and slaughter operations. More recently the concept of ecological carrying capacity (allowing ungulates to self-regulate by minimizing annual removals of surplus) was explored to reduce management effort (Blyth and Hudson, 1987). The total ungulate population has gone from an estimated 1,982 in 1985 to 3,463 in 1999, an increase of 178 per cent (Cool, 1999). The current ungulate populations are some of the highest ungulate densities known to exist in North America, far exceeding free-ranging, year-round population densities for North American wildlife. This last 14 years is the longest period in the history of the park that ungulates were allowed to increase without a significant reduction in populations.

Several recent research studies have demonstrated the impacts of large numbers of ungulates on the park's ecosystem. Over-grazing was characterized by excessive and chronic trampling, causing topsoil removal and the exposing of mineral soil in grasslands, as compared to other rangeland sites outside of the park. These factors continue to contribute to the replacement of native plant species with non-native plants. The overall lack of mid-story and mature shrub species, such as beaked hazel chokecherry, saskatoon and dogwood, are indication of heavy use of woody material attributed to high stocking rates. Some age classes of certain species are also completely lacking such as Red Osier Dogwood. Some have been extirpated like rough fescue that once blanketed the area (Cool, 1999).

In 1997, the park hosted an Ecosystem Based Management Workshop, with a multi disciplinary team of experts and scientists from across North America. The key recommendation from the workshop was that the park should assume an adaptive landscape management approach, and allow landscape processes as a primary focus. Specifically, the reduction of ungulates would allow rangeland that appeared to be over utilized to recover; vegetation targets were also proposed to manage a gradient of vegetation across the park; and a science-based program involving peer review should proceed. Surplus populations of elk and bison are typically rounded up into holding facilities and released in non-park areas where wild populations are low, in co-operation with provincial wildlife managers. Surplus animals are also used in re-introductions (e.g., the Mackenzie bison sanctuary in the North West Territories). In recent years, there has been an increasing demand for elk and bison for private game ranching. Below are the targets for ungulates currently in use by Elk Island managers.

FIGURE 5.1 Capture can be a traumatic experience for wild animals.

FIGURE 5.2 Captured bison at Elk Island National Park await relocation.

TABLE 5.1 Projected Targets for Ungulates in Elk Island

Area of Park	Population Estimate of Animals	Change in Population
Elk main park	550–760	35% reduction of the 1998 population
Elk/wood bison area	130–202	
Plains bison	472–504	10–15 % reduction of fall population
Wood bison	241–272	50% reduction of the fall population
Moose main park	211–317	
Moose wood bison	96–200	
Deer main park	97–135	
Deer wood bison area	87–147	

SOURCE: Cool (1999).

The above numbers will be adjusted through an adaptive management process. Populations will be surveyed by air during the fall following a fixed protocol. The condition of vegetation, ungulate-caused erosion, and the incidence of disease will also be monitored. Three to five years will allow adequate time to monitor the response, and it will allow some flexibility to adjust targets correspondingly,

A range of complicating factors makes it difficult to manage ungulate populations within a relatively small area. High ungulate densities have a higher predisposition to the spread of both endemic and exotic diseases than do lower densities. Local cattle ranchers at Elk Island, for example, have requested that the park treat bison for Bovine Viral Diarrhea to mitigate the spread of the disease to their stock. There is also a concern for native diseases, specifically liver fluke and Avian tuberculosis. These diseases have the potential to cause rapid population declines. Also, they make the elk less desirable for transplanting to other wild areas.

There is a high level of public interest and concern around the management of ungulates. It is extremely difficult to round up and transport wild ungulates. With any handling of large wild ungulates, there is a high potential for injury both to animals and to park staff. Capture myopathy is an always-present side effect of handling wildlife. There is also public concern regarding an ungulate population crash due to diseases.

All the above factors illustrate the practical difficulties of actively managing large ungulates. However, in the absence of a protected area large enough to maintain viable predator populations, there is little other option than to manage populations. Elk Island's resource managers aim to maintain populations of ungulates within a range. Too high populations will have undesirable impacts in vegetation, cause erosion, and increase the incidence of disease transmission. If populations are too low there is a chance that they might disappear simply due to random stochastic processes. Small populations are also subject to undesirable genetic changes, such as inbreeding. So park managers of a relatively small park are forced into a juggling act to keep the ecosystem within a desired state of ecological integrity. Within this ecosystem there are no large carnivores or immigration. The park staff determine the process of emigration, which is, in fact, the key ecological variable being managed.

Case Study: White-tailed Deer Management in Point Pelee National Park

Point Pelee is a very small—only 15 km²—national park in southern Ontario,. Point Pelee is typical of many protected areas in southern Ontario and eastern North America in that there are problems caused by very abundant white-tailed deer. In the case of Point Pelee high densities of deer caused undesirable changes to the vegetation, including elimination of several species of rare Carolinian flora and the invasion of many exotic species of plants. Exotic species constitute 60 per cent of the entire park flora and dominate many disturbed sites. In 1992 Pelee National Park began reducing deer populations in the park, following a detailed assessment of the situation and considerable public consultation. The reduction is now an ongoing part of park management, with regular culling conducted by park staff. Overall, the park has been extremely successful at reducing locally abundant deer in the park with a series of culls over several years.

There are several reasons for the park's successful management of deer. First, there was a clearly articulated vision of ecological integrity in the park's management plan with a clear indication that high deer populations are inconsistent with protecting ecological integrity. The park is to be, so far as possible, representative of a functioning Carolinian ecosystem. As part of the vision, there were numerical targets for the post-cull population. The cull was conducted solely by staff and the park is closed during the cull to ensure public safety. This avoided the policy implications of allowing sport hunting in a national park. Park managers also invested in research into alternative methods of control, indicating clearly that they were aware of public sensitivities to shooting deer.

Conclusion: Managing Hyper-abundant Species

Clearly the management of so called 'hyper-abundant' species is fraught with many practical and policy pitfalls, as the case studies illustrate. Before any reduction is enacted, the reasons for the hyper-abundance must be thoroughly understood and clear objectives and numerical targets for the control program, as well as a reliable predictions of the impacts of the control measures, must be in place. There should be a monitoring system to examine the causes of hyper-abundance, the dynamics of the population being controlled, and the predicted impacts of the control measures. Finally, the management program should be conducted under an adaptive management framework where the original assumptions are regularly subject to review.

As long as the above conditions are met, it is reasonable to manage hyper-abundant species in protected areas. Of great significance are the consequences of not managing hyper-abundant species. Such species can cause erosion, alter plant communities, and even eliminate native species. Given that many protected areas worldwide are too small to maintain large predator populations or protect isolated populations, management of hyper-abundant species appears to be essential.

RESTORING FIRE AS AN ECOLOGICAL PROCESS

Excluding the arctic and the wet coastal parks, fire suppression has been identified as causing significant impact to ecological integrity in all other Canadian national parks. Fire is a pivotal ecological process in the boreal forest, grasslands, mountain Cordillera and even in the Carolinian and Acadian forests. Yet for most of the history of those parks, fire has been actively excluded and fought as a destroyer of ecosystems. Paradoxically, it is now abundantly clear that biodiversity exists because of fire, rather than in spite of, fire.

All protected area agencies have treated fire in the same way, active suppression. In National parks, the development of the Warden Service was largely to fight wildfires. However, the large size of the parks and slow transportation networks initially limited the amount of actual fire control. Beginning in the 1920's, new equipment was developed, hundreds of kilometers of fire roads were constructed, and networks of fire towers were erected. During this period it is likely that fire control began to alter the historical fire regime.

FIGURE 5.3 Fire crews have to be very vigilant when undertaking prescribed burns.

In the 1970's, the realization grew that parks were not always self-regulating, natural ecosystems. Instead of being considered 'natural', park ecosystems were increasingly seen as 'impaired' and active management was deemed necessary to correct the impaired condition. Attitudes towards fires began to change as fire was discovered to be an important dynamic element in the ecosystem. The Canadian Parks Service responded to the changing attitudes with a 1979 policy permitting active management or manipulation of the ecosystem, under certain well-defined conditions. With a new directive produced in 1986 and a comprehensive fire policy review called 'Keepers of the Flame', the Canadian Parks Service embarked on a new relationship with fire. For the first time, fire was officially restored to its 'natural role' by active management. Unregulated wildfire was considered impossible in most parks because of the values at risk, including public safety, protection of property (including neighboring lands with timber values) and rare species or habitat. Thus, the Canadian Parks Service began to use prescribed fire with an aim to restore the 'natural' fire regime. In most parks, unregulated natural wildfire continued to be eliminated.

While there are many examples of early use of prescribed fire in grasslands, the Canadian Parks Service began to formally use prescribed fire in the mid 1980's (White and Pengelly, 1992). Presently, prescribed burns have been conducted in 17 national parks in Canada. As a basis for the prescribed burn program, parks are required to prepare fire management plans and vegetation management plans. These plans are based on the historical role of fire in the park and a detailed set of vegetation management objectives.

BOX 5.4 Fire Management Plans

A fire management plan provides for the rational use and control of fire in a national park. It is based on an assessment of the fire history, fire risk to facilities and adjacent lands, and the role of fire in the ecosystem. In providing strategies for both use and control, the plan calls for the zoning of the park into units that typically are full — called suppression, containment, or observation, depending on the appropriate response to fire. These units are based on the fire risk, which is a function of fire behaviour in a particular fuel type and terrain, weather patterns, and sources of ignition, as well as the presence of people and facilities. A fire management plan also provides a monitoring strategy to assess the impacts of the fire regime, an environmental impact statement, and a public education and information strategy.

As the fire use program has developed in National parks, lessons have been learned, and many debates remain unresolved. One challenge relates to scale. First-generation fire management plans, fuel maps, and other planning aids all stopped at the park boundary, despite the obvious ecological and even operational irrelevance of the line. However, with the need to manage on a broader, more relevant scale, the question becomes 'how big?'. There is a dramatic change in the economic value of a tree, for example, when crossing a park boundary. On most lands surrounding national parks, fire is actively suppressed in favour of maintaining timber values. Under such conditions, the idea of ecosystem-based management (Chapter 12) becomes seriously challenged.

A central debate in the role of fires in parks revolves around the need to duplicate natural or historical fire regimes. The exact role of fire becomes mired in the question of the historical role of fire. There are some who argue that fire frequencies have not been altered by human fire suppression (see Johnson and Larsen, 1991). This line of argument assumes that fire is a process driven by climate and that present-day fire frequencies are unaltered, despite multi-million-dollar suppression efforts. The argument holds further that a few very large, intense fires make up the vast majority of acreage burned and that, therefore, prescribed burns are irrelevant and not in keeping with historical fire regimes. There are other researchers (Martel, 1994) who argue that human fire suppression and fire protection has definitely altered the fire regime and that prescribed fire is essential to recreate historical vegetation patterns. This dichotomy of viewpoints can paralyze an agency trying to develop a fire management program.

Increasingly it is recognized that there is no correct formula for fire management. It is not simply a matter of conducting a fire history study and then preparing a fire management plan to duplicate some historical fire frequency. Parks must seek individual solutions to fire management, depending on their own unique situations. In some cases it will be possible to keep entire parks, or large zones in parks, with fire frequencies unaltered by humans (discounting global warming). In these areas, lightning-caused fires can burn without any intervention. They will simply be monitored. This is the case in Nahanni National Park, situated in the northern boreal forest with little development on its boundaries. Some parks will have a mix of observation zones, full suppression zones, and evaluation zones. This complex scenario is being developed in Wood Buffalo National Park. Other parks, especially in the more developed regions of the country, will have to ensure fire is an ecosystem process by using only prescribed fire, as is the case in Elk Island National Park.

As an ecological process, wildfire is still below its historical range in most parks. In virtually all provincial and most national parks, full fire suppression remains the rule. Despite many successes, the combination of prescribed fire and wildfire stands at only 10 per cent of the historical long-term average. The internal goal in Parks Canada for fire restoration has been set at 50 per cent of the long-term historical average. Under an adaptive management framework, this appears to be a reasonable place to start. However, there will have to be huge changes in funding, staff, and public education in order to reach that target.

What is a reasonable solution to the question of managing wildfire? Individual parks must choose a combination of unregulated wildfire in observation zones; evaluation zones where response to fire is judged case by case, and prescribed fire. In all cases, fire management is a tool to manage vegetation. Canadian national parks' resource managers are wrestling with all these concepts as the role of fire in vegetation management unfolds and ecosystem-based management is developed further. Undoubtedly the road ahead will be difficult and we will have to experiment and adapt.

MANAGING ALIEN SPECIES

A working definition of an 'alien organism', developed by the Alien Species Focus Group, Environment Canada 1994 is: 'one that enters an ecosystem beyond its historic range, including any organisms transferred from one country or province to another' (Mosquin, 1997: 3). This definition, modified from the US National Park Service, implies no positive or negative impact by the alien organism. The definition includes organisms entering through natural range extension and dispersal, through deliberate or inadvertent introduction by humans, and as a result of habitat changes caused by human activity. Exotic species do not necessarily impair ecological integrity, so a further distinction is warranted, to the effect that 'alleged negative effects of invasive species are evaluated and demonstrated, in order to aid prioritization of exotic species designated for active management' (ibid.).

What constitutes an 'exotic' species, and when should an alien species be of concern? Most park managers have not developed a priority list of exotic species, nor have they established a list of appropriate control actions. Exotic species must be clearly categorized as to their history, potential for invasion into native ecosystems, and potential to effect negative change to ecological integrity. Many species, currently expanding their range as a result of human intervention, may have eventually reached national parks in the natural course of events. However, many other species that were purposely introduced are now at levels that make their eradication possible with current technology (e.g., the moose introduced to Newfoundland). If such an organism is shown to negatively affect ecological integrity, the 'exotic' designation should be retained in case an appropriate removal technology is developed in the future.

Determining the effect of exotic species on ecosystem structure and function is imperative. Many of these organisms may have neutral, negative, or positive ecosystem effects. It is well documented (Bight, 1998) that many exotic species, especially plants, are relatively benign—they do not invade and alter native ecosystems. From a management perspective it would be most efficient to be able to predict the probability that a newly detected exotic would invade and damage native ecosystems. Unfortunately there is currently no way of predicting how invasive an exotic species may be. Only early detection via monitoring, with an evaluation of ecosystem effects, can determine whether a species should be removed.

The majority of national parks in southern Canada report that 'exotic' organisms (invertebrates, fish, birds, mammals, and vegetation) cause major ecological effects (Parks Canada, 1997). Reported effects include elimination of species (e.g., native bull trout by exotic speckled trout in Rocky Mountain streams) and changes in the abundance of native species. In many national parks, exotic species make up 50 per cent of the total flora. And in the 1997 SOP report, 21 of 38 parks perceive that exotic vegetation represents a major stress, though it is not always clear whether these carry sound evidence of deleterious ecological effects or present merely aesthetic effects. Invasive species may be managed on either grounds, but Parks Canada does not presently have the scientific capacity to evaluate the nature of ecological effects and might waste precious resources managing non-problems.

Several parks have successfully removed invasive alien organisms threatening environmental integrity (EI) Gwaii Haanas NP successfully restored the native vegetation on off-shore islands by eliminating introduced mammals (black-tailed deer, raccoon, and Norway rat). Although there are currently many efforts underway to eliminate exotic species from national parks, most parks are unsure of what constitutes an exotic species or of when an alien species should be of concern to EI thereby initiating management actions. Most parks have not developed a priority list of exotic species, nor have they established a list of appropriate control actions.

Understanding the effect of exotic species on the ecological integrity of protected areas, especially under conditions of projected climate change, is of global importance. The spread of exotic or alien species is predicted to increase dramatically (Bight, 1998). The spread of exotic species likely will increase and present federal and provincial Acts and regulations do not address this proliferation. Some exotic organisms may affect biodiversity, a concern to all levels of government under the Biodiversity Convention signed by Canada.

Case Study: Eliminating Rats in Gwaii Hannas National Parks Canada

Norway Rats were unintentionally introduced onto 17 islands in the Haida Gwaii archipelago, which includes Gwaii Hannas National Park. As predators, rats devastated the breeding sea bird populations, eating eggs, young, and even adults of some species. Recently, three islands at the north end of the archipelago (Langara, Cox, and Lucy) were cleared of rats and Gwaii Haanas staff have conducted a similar eradication program on St James Island at the extreme south end of the islands. In the past it was considered impossible to eliminate rats from islands and this program is a breakthrough. The success of the program was a persistent program of trapping and using poison baits (Taylor et al., 2000). Monitoring for the return of rats at Cape St James is ongoing and there was no evidence of rats at baited traps or chew-sticks. No rat feces, tracks, or other sign of rats were found.

The aim of active removal of the Norway rat was to allow recovery of native seabird populations. The recovery of these populations will be monitored to evaluate the success of the program. However, there is no 'Defenders of the Exotic Rat' society. In other words, this is not a very controversial issue. The removal of other exotic species may involve considerably more public consultation. Fierce debates have been underway in the US, for example, regarding the removal of mountain goats from Olympic and Yellowstone National Parks. And what would be the response if efforts were made to keep the exotic moose out of national parks in Newfoundland?

MANAGEMENT OF HARVEST IN PROTECTED AREAS

Most Canadians assume national parks and protected areas are protected from harvest or resource extraction. In reality, most parks have some kind of active harvest or extraction. The most common type of harvest is that of sport fishing. However there are many other kinds of exceptions permitted in individual park establishment agreements (e.g., the harvesting of timber in Algonquin and the snaring of snowshoe hare and cutting of firewood in Gros Morne) or the recognized rights of First Nations. Below is a list of harvest in Canadian national parks.

TABLE 5.2 Harvesting Activities in National Parks

Type of Harvest or Extraction	Number of Parks Reporting Harvest
Aboriginal wildlife hunting/trapping	8
Non-Aboriginal wildlife harvest	6
Sport fishing	22
Commercial fishing	4
Problem or surplus wildlife	10
Domestic grazing	5
Domestic wood harvest	1

SOURCE: Parks Canada (1997).

Predicting the impacts of harvest of any population requires an ongoing assessment of the population levels, age, specific birth and death rates, an understanding of environmental variability, and a model projecting populations over time. This information is rarely, if ever, available for harvest or extraction projects in national parks. Even for sport fishing, there is rarely any comprehensive assessment of fishing pressure on fish populations.

BOX 5.5 Managing Sport Fishing in La Mauricie National Park

La Mauricie National Park is an excellent example of a well-managed sport fishery. Only 30 of 150 park lakes are open to fish for lake trout, bass, and pike. The remaining 120 are closed so there will be unexploited fish populations that can act as benchmarks. Because the demand for fishing is very high, fishing opportunities are allocated by a draw that takes place every morning during the May to Labour Day fishing season. In national parks, lead sinkers and jigs are strictly forbidden, as they can poison loons and waterfowl. Fishing limits are set according to age-specific assessments of fish populations as well as to assessments of the harvest.

CONCLUSION

In an ideal world, protected areas would be very large in size and managed with no human interference. They would be true benchmarks against which we could assess impacts on ecosystems outside protected areas. However, this is not the case. Most protected areas are too small to allow populations of large area-demanding species or area-demanding processes. Even the largest parks have trans-boundary issues. Apparently, the only solution to these problems is to use active management.

Active management is a major conceptual shift away from how protected areas historically have been managed and should not be taken lightly. There are many implications. Active management requires more precise definitions of management endpoints. Many protected area agencies now use ecological integrity as a management endpoint. Parks Canada requires the preparation of an ecological integrity statement for each national park, complete with detailed goals, objectives, and targets for management.

Active management is not a license to do anything in a protected area. It is an acceptance of the fact that key species and processes are missing in some protected areas and must be drawn into management. Active management will work best when there is clear prediction of cause and effect, a monitoring system, and an adaptive management framework that allows refinement and reconsideration. In an increasingly complex and human-dominated world, active management will be increasingly necessary as will programs to raise public awareness of the issues involved.

REFERENCES

Bight, C. 1998. *Life Out of Bounds: Bioinvasion in a Borderless World*. Worldwatch Institute. New York: Norton & Co.

Blyth, C.B., and R.J. Hudson. 1987. A Plan for the Management of Vegetation and Ungulates. Unpublished report. Parks Canada; Elk Island National Park, Fort Saskatchewan, Alta.

Bork, E.W. 1993. 'Interaction of Burning and Herbivory in Aspen Communities in Elk Island National Park', M.Sc. thesis, University of Alberta.

Cool, N. 1999. 'Elk Island National Park Ungulate Issue Analysis', Elk Island National Park internal document.

Holling, C.S., ed. 1978. *Adaptive Environmental Assessment and Management*. New York: John Wiley.

Johnson, E.A., and C.P.S. Larsen. 1991. 'Climatically Induced Change in Fire Frequency in the Southern Canadian Rockies', *Ecology* 71, 1: 194–201.

Kay, C.E., C.A. White, I.R. Pengelly, and B. Patton. 1999. *Long-Term Ecosystem States and Processes in Banff National Park and the Central Canadian Rockies*. Occasional Paper No. 9. Ottawa: Parks Canada.

Leopold, A. 1943. 'Deer irruptions', *Wisconsin Conservation Bulletin* 8: 3–11.

Martell, D.L. 1994. 'The Impact of Fire on Timber Supply in Ontario', *The Forestry Chronicle* 70, 2: 164–73.

McShea, W.J., H.B. Underwood, and J.H. Rappole. 1997. *The Science of Overabundance: Deer Ecology and Population Management*. Washington: Smithsonian Institution Press.

Mosquin, T. 1997. *Management Guidelines for Invasive Alien Species in Canada's National Parks.* Hull, Que.: Parks Canada Documentation Centre.

Parks Canada Agency. 2000. *Unimpaired for Future Generations? Protecting Ecological Integrity With Canada's National Parks: vol. 1, A Call to Action. vol. 2, Setting a New Direction for Canada's National Parks.* Report of the Panel on the Ecological Integrity of Canada's National Parks. Ottawa.

Parks Canada. 1994. *Guiding Principles and Operational Policies.* Ottawa: Minister of Supply and Services Canada. Cat. no. R62–275/1994E.

———. 1997. *State of Parks Report.* Hull, Que.: Parks Canada Agency Documentation Centre.

Taylor, R.H., G.W. Kaiser, and M.C. Drever. 2000. 'Eradication of Norway Rats for Recovery of Seabird Habitat on Langara Island, British Columbia', *Restoration Ecology* 8, 2: 151–60.

Vujnovic, K. 1998. 'Grasslands of the Aspen Parkland of Alberta', M.Sc. thesis, University of Alberta.

Walters, C.J. 1986. *Adaptive Management of Renewable Resources.* New York: Macmillan.

———. 1997. 'Challenges in adaptive management of riparian and coastal ecosystems', *Conservation Ecology* 1, 2: 1. Available at: <http://www.consecol.org/vol1/iss2/art1>.

White, C., and I.R. Pengelly. 1992. 'Fire as a natural process and a management tool: the Banff National Park Experience', in D. Dickinson et al., eds, *Proceedings of the Cypress Hills Forest Management Workshop.* Medicine Hat, Alberta, 3–4 Oct.

KEY WORDS/ CONCEPTS

ecological integrity
wilderness
minimum management
active management
laissez-faire management
adaptive management
alien organism
fire regime

STUDY QUESTIONS

1. Why do some people feel park management should be guided by the principle of 'let nature take its course'? List advantages and disadvantages of this approach.
2. List advantages and disadvantages of 'active' management.
3. Under what circumstances is active management appropriate?
4. Why is adaptive management a key principle in managing for ecological integrity?
5. How was adaptive management applied to the problems with elk, deer, and moose in Elk Island National Park?
6. Why is the culling of wildlife populations controversial?
7. Why was fire suppression used in past years? List advantages and disadvantages of this approach.

8. Why are prescribed burns controversial? List advantages and disadvantages of this approach.
9. Why do some people favour the approach of letting natural fires burn? List advantages and disadvantages of this approach.
10. What is a fire management plan?
11. Present arguments for and against hunting in national parks.
12. Present arguments for and against sport fishing in national parks.
13. Present arguments for and against hunting and trapping in national parks by First Nations peoples.

PART III

Social Science Theory and Application

I'd rather wake up in the middle of nowhere than in any city on earth.

Steve McQueen

Parks provide opportunities for people to experience the spiritual, aesthetic, and challenging attributes of a wild, natural setting. Paradoxically, the single greatest threat to ecological integrity is human use—or, more accurately, human misuse or overuse. Human settlements developed within parks, for example, the Banff and Jasper townsites, have profoundly altered the functioning of those parks' ecosystems. Not so obvious have been the environmental impacts of people hiking, skiing, canoeing, camping, or in other ways enjoying the backcountry areas of our parks. Loss of vegetation around campsites, deeply eroded trails, garbage, and the harassment of wildlife are some of the problems that occur in park backcountry areas. Some people have gone so far as to suggest that park environments should be strictly protected by forbidding any park visitation; on the other extreme are those who argue that humans have been a natural part of park ecosystems for thousands of years. However, the consensus of opinion is that some types of human visitation, at a low intensity and properly managed, are unlikely to harm park environments much. Further, it can be argued that park visitors become park advocates, the strongest supporters for the protection of parks—parks unused are parks unappreciated.

A second concern has to do with conflicts that sometimes occur between visitors. These may have to do with crowding. For example, the presence of too many other people in the same backcountry campground can take away from the opportunity of experiencing solitude or closeness to nature. Sometimes conflict is created by one type of activity interfering with another type of activity. This may happen when hikers find themselves dodging manure left by horses carrying people along the same trail.

A third concern related to visitor use of parks is the social impact of park visitors on communities located near parks. Often these impacts are positive in the sense that tourism generates revenues when people purchase food, gasoline, or other goods and services. However, sometimes these host communities resent the kinds of rowdy or other undesirable behaviours exhibited by some visitors. Park managers are now compelled to work more closely with surrounding communities to address these and other problems related to ecosystem management. Park managers have had to develop techniques for managing people in natural settings and techniques for interacting with nearby residents. Hence, this section of the book focuses on social science theory as it applies to the responsibilities of a park manager.

CHAPTER 6

Social Science, Conservation, and Protected Areas

Rick Rollins & Dave Robinson

INTRODUCTION

Over 80 per cent of Canadians participate in some form of nature-related activity such as camping and boating, and much of this activity takes place in national or provincial parks (Environment Canada, 1999). Further, nature-based tourism is a significant industry in Canada, employing many people and attracting considerable investments—in 1996 it accounted for American expenditures in Canada of $705.3 million, while 1996 Canadian expenditures in the US amounted to $236.1 million (Environment Canada, 1995). Although there is some debate about appropriate recreation and tourism use in parks and protected areas, there is a consensus that some forms of visitor use are acceptable or desirable. The major issue, then, is how to manage this use effectively in ways that protect park resources, provide for satisfactory visitor experiences, and create a constituency of supporters for park values.

Why do people seek out places like Gros Morne, Algonquin Park, the Nahanni River, Banff, or Pacific Rim? What kinds of activities do they pursue? What benefits flow from these experiences? What kinds of environmental impacts do park visitors create? In what ways do visitors contribute to or detract from the environmental sustainability of parks? What types of visitor services and facilities are desirable or appropriate? What types of experiences will or will not be provided in park settings? What conflicts occur between different user groups and why? To what extent are people willing to pay for parks through taxes or user fees? How much public support exists for protected landscapes compared to their use for other purposes like logging, ranching, or urban development? These types of questions have been explored by social scientists conducting research in Canada and elsewhere, so the intent of this chapter is to provide an overview of the contribution of social science to the management of protected areas. By social science we are referring to the theory and research that has been applied to park management from disciplines such as sociology, psychology, geography, economics, tourism, and leisure studies. This body of literature has contributed to the ongoing development of techniques for visitor management that are described in the next chapter and elsewhere in the book.

Many of our parks are besieged with requests to provide more and more visitor facilities, including trails, campgrounds, marinas, and downhill ski areas. There is also pressure placed on park managers to increase the level of overnight accommodation provided in parks, to include roofed structures, such as alpine huts, hostels, motels, hotels, and luxury resorts. Further, there is increasing demand to open parks to more visitors and different types of visitor activities. Proposed activities include camping, backpacking, rock-climbing, horseback-riding, hunting, fishing, all-terrain-vehicle use, canoeing, kayaking, sailing, waterskiing, scuba diving, downhill skiing, nordic skiing, and snowmobiling. In any given park some of these activities can be considered, but it is not possible to provide all types of visitor activities, services, and facilities—to do so would result in the loss of natural character and the conversion of parks to urban-looking landscapes. Park managers must decide which of these activities should be permitted, how much use should be allowed, where this use will be allowed, and how the use will be managed. In the face of an expanding set of visitor demands on parks, managers are challenged to articulate what purpose or role a park is to fulfill, and what balance between visitor use and resource protection is appropriate.

As well as environmental impacts created by visitors in parks, managers must deal with a variety of related issues including crowding, vandalism, and conflicts between user groups. These issues sometimes extend beyond park boundaries and impact upon adjacent land and nearby communities. Communities like Tofino near Pacific Rim National Park, and Canmore near Banff experience many tourism benefits due to their close proximity to popular national parks. However, these communities sometimes experience a number of visitor-related problems such as traffic jams and line-ups at grocery stores, gas stations, banks, and hospitals.

Hence, visitor management is a complex undertaking. In this book, the impacts of visitor use are examined within the topic of ecological integrity, where it is noted that most of the threats to ecological integrity stem from visitor activity within parks or human activity outside of parks impacting on park ecosystems. Therefore, it is apparent that the maintenance of ecological integrity requires an understanding of human behaviour as revealed in the social sciences. For example, when dealing with an issue such as the feeding of bears by park visitors, managers need an understanding of the social sciences in order to influence or regulate the behaviour of visitors, tourist operators and other groups and agencies who bring visitors to parks, host communities, other agencies, and within a park agency.

THE BEHAVIOURAL APPROACH

Social science research into visitor behaviour in parks and protected areas is described under a variety of headings, outdoor recreation, adventure tourism, adventure recreation, and ecotourism. What these terms have in common is the study of leisure behaviour: how people act and feel when not at work, when behaviour is freely chosen and intrinsically satisfying. Park agencies seek to provide satisfying leisure experiences that do not result in damage or lead to unacceptable change to the natural

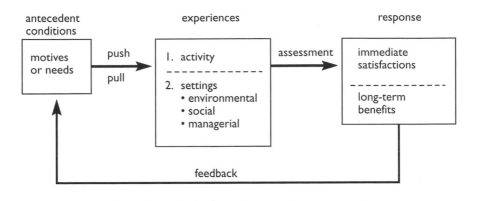

FIGURE 6.1 Behavioural model of outdoor recreation. After Mannell et al. (1999).

attributes of the area. Nevertheless, visitors sometimes describe their personal experiences as being unsatisfactory. This dissatisfaction can take several forms, including concerns about crowding, litter, and damage to park environments. Sometimes visitors express concerns about noisy or rowdy behaviour of other visitors, or conflict with other types of users (e.g., hikers with horseback riders, or skiers with snowmobilers). People also express concerns about facilities and services provided by park agencies, including complaints regarding the upkeep of campgrounds or trails, the quality of interpretive programs, or the availability of park wardens.

Social science researchers have examined these issues in order to understand outdoor recreation behaviour, and to assist park managers in their task of providing quality visitor experiences while protecting park environments. To summarize this research and show how it can be applied to park management issues, we begin with a description of the 'behavioural approach', illustrated in Figure 6.1. The behavioural approach proposes that people engage in specific activities in specific settings in order to realize a group of expected sociological benefits which are known, expected, and valued (Manning, 1999; Driver and Tocher, 1970). These benefits can be described as the various forces that push or pull people to seek out specific leisure activities and experiences. Researchers using motivational explanations are primarily concerned with what arouses or activates leisure behaviour, that is, with the forces in people that push them to engage in certain activities. Secondarily, researchers have examined characteristics of leisure activities and settings that pull people to select certain activities or settings over others (Mannell and Kleiber, 1997; Mannell, 1999). For example, some people may seek backpacking experiences in Jasper National Park because they are being pushed by motivational factors such as the 'need to escape urban life' and the 'need to be close to nature'. They may be pulled by the beliefs that the backcountry in Jasper is a natural setting devoid of urban characteristics and that relatively little crowding would be experienced. Hence, if these pushes and pulls were substantial, a person might select the behaviour of backpacking in Jasper. If the experience turned out as expected in terms of these push and pull motivations, the person would be satisfied with the experience and the feedback loop might result in the person seeking similar experiences at another time. If the experience turned out not as expected in terms of these anticipated motivating factors, the feedback loop would result in a lower probability that a similar experience would be selected in the future.

This model assumes that individuals usually have multiple motives for leisure experiences in general and for outdoor recreation in particular: to develop skills; to be close to nature, escaping daily routines, and so on. Motives are considered to activate behaviour in that a disequilibrium is created that generates a desire for something and an expectation that certain actions will reduce this disequilibrium. If the action or participation in a specific activity in a specific setting fulfills the need, then the experience of satisfaction provides positive feedback or satisfaction. A lack of satisfaction creates negative feedback that may lead to modification of behaviour or withdrawal from the activity. When a person's needs are active so that a person is energized to satisfy that need, they are called aroused motives (Mannell and Kleiber, 1997). Experiences in this model are defined as the interaction between an activity and a setting. People vary in their preference for type of activity. For example, some people may prefer backpacking rather than canoeing. People also vary in their preferences for different types of settings. Hence, the backpacking experience in Jasper National Park differs substantially from the backpacking experience provided on the West Coast Trail segment of Pacific Rim National Park. The canoeing experience in Algonquin Provincial Park differs from the canoeing experience in Whinisk Provincial Park. Recreational settings differ somewhat in appearance and character, and can be distinguished along three important parameters: (1) variability in environmental conditions (e.g., from modern to primitive conditions); (2) variability in social conditions (e.g., from isolation to crowded conditions); and, (3) variability in managerial conditions (e.g., from few regulations to many regulations).

The response component of the behavioural model is comprised of two types of benefits. The first type of benefit is the satisfaction of expected psychological motivations, such as developing skills, developing affiliations with others, escaping daily routine, adventure-seeking, and so on. The second type of benefit refers to ultimate or longer-term benefits—either personal or societal—which result from satisfying recreational experiences (e.g., enhanced self-esteem and self-identity, personal growth, family cohesion, and enhanced workplace efficacy). The behavioural model can be illustrated by contrasting the experience of wilderness hiking with the experience of family picnicking (Figure 6.2). Wilderness hiking may take place in a backcountry setting with few other people, no facilities, and few restrictions. On the other hand, a family picnic could take place in a frontcountry setting used by several other groups, and provided with many facilities and a number of rules and restrictions regarding behaviour and use of the area.

Level	Example 1	Example 2
1. Activity	wilderness hiking	family picnicking

2. Setting
  a. environmental setting
  b. social setting
  c. managerial setting
	• backcountry/wilderness
	• few people/groups
	• no restrictions
	• no facilities
		• frontcountry
		• many people/groups
		• some restrictions
		• many facilities

3. Motives	• risk-taking • challenge • physical exercise	• in-group affiliation • change of pace

3. Benefits
  a. personal
  b. societal
	• enhanced self-esteem
	• increased commitment
	  to conservation
		• family solidarity
		• increased work efficiency

FIGURE 6.2 Behavioural model illustrated with 'wilderness hiking' and 'family picnicking'. After Mannell et al. (1999).

Early outdoor recreation research in the 1960s focused on participation levels in various recreation activities, but more recent studies have explored other aspects of the behavioural model, notably the psychological benefits component (e.g., Driver and Brown, 1975; Manfredo, Driver, and Brown, 1983: Twynam and Robinson, 1997). Other researchers have begun to examine broader personal and societal outcomes. For examples of this work see the work by Haggard and Williams (1991) on leisure involvement and self identity; by Bruns (1998) regarding on-site and off-site benefits-based recreation/tourism management; by Ewert and Hollenhurst (1989) on adventure experience modeling; and, by Robinson (1992a) on the transfer of risk recreation benefits.

The behavioural approach has led to significant advances in the way visitor management is approached in many jurisdictions. For example, Clark and Stankey (1979) in their review of outdoor recreation research noted a consistent finding that people vary tremendously in attitudes and preferences for different types of outdoor recreation settings, presumably as a consequence of differing motivations or activity preferences. On the basis of these findings they concluded 'there was no such thing as the average camper' (Shafer, 1969) and reasoned that park agencies need to be providing different kinds of recreation opportunities, rather than uniform standardized settings. This led to the development of the Recreation Opportunity Spectrum (ROS), a system of zoning according to characteristics, such that outdoor recreation settings could be arrayed along a continuum from primitive to modern. In the ROS approach, different types of settings are created by varying the environmental, social, and managerial parameters of recreation settings. Details of this ROS approach are described in the next chapter.

FIGURE 6.3 Raeside's cartoon reveals differences in visitors' expectation and the values of park managers.

MOTIVATIONS FOR OUTDOOR RECREATION

The behavioural model is a useful outline of much of the kind of outdoor recreation theory and research that has assisted the human dimension of the management of parks and protected areas. However, motivational constructs are probably more complex than portrayed in Figure 6.3.

Leisure motives are identified by people when asked what needs they seek to satisfy through their leisure involvements. Researchers typically provide study participants with a list of reasons (or leisure motives) and ask them to rate the importance of each motive for their participation in various leisure activities. These reasons are generally referred to as expressed leisure motives (Mannell and Kleiber, 1997). Referring to Iso-Ahola's (1980) iceberg analogy (see Figure 6.4), Mannell and Kleiber illustrate how expressed leisure motives are often only part of a larger and more complex picture of what motivates people to engage in leisure activities. Many of the motives reported for leisure engagement are based on physiological, learned, and cognitive motives, and these in turn are influenced by the interaction of inherited char-

BOX 6.1 Measuring Visitor Satisfaction with 'Push' Factors

The measurement of visitor satisfaction in parks and protected areas has incorporated a number of methodologies reflecting the push and pull aspects of the behavioural approach. The figure below illustrates how satisfaction was assessed in Yoho National Park by using the 'push' element of motivation, the anticipated psychological benefits. Park visitors were asked to comment on 'how important' they felt about each motivational factor, and then 'how satisfied' they felt with each motivational factor (Rollins and Rouse, 1993). The resulting matrix allows managers to identify those important factors that are satisfied (success), those important factors that were not satisfied (need attention), and unimportant motivational factors (irrelevant from a visitor management perspective). For example, the motivation of seeking solitude was important to most visitors (81 per cent), but many visitors (36.1 per cent) did not feel this motivation had been achieved. The 'solitude' aspect of the Yoho experience is an area that is of concern and may require management attention. On the other hand, the motivation 'to be close to nature' was important to most visitors (92.5 per cent) and was achieved by most (79.5 per cent). Finally, the motive to 'meet new people' was viewed as not important by most visitors (83.6 per cent), and so can be viewed as irrelevant from a management perspective.

to be close to nature	
achieved	
1.4%	79.5%
not important	important
5.6%	13.0%
not achieved	

to meet new people	
achieved	
17.3%	10.7%
not important	important
66.7%	5.3%
not achieved	

solitude	
achieved	
4.1%	44.9%
not important	important
15.0%	36.1%
not achieved	

acteristics and socialization experiences. People are often unaware of these motives when reporting the reasons why they engage in specific activities; hence capturing these deeper motives presents a significant challenge to the researcher.

Despite the large number and types of motives that have been reported in the many studies of leisure behaviour, there is broad agreement that there are a relatively small number of basic types that operate (Graef et al., 1983; Fodness, 1994; Mannell

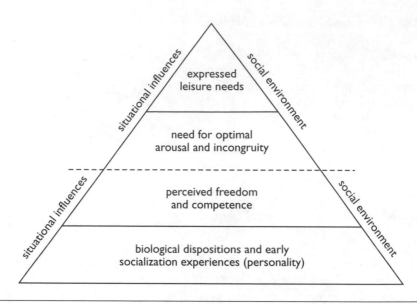

FIGURE 6.4 Iso-Ahola's levels of causality of leisure behaviour. After Mannell and Kleiber (1997).

and Kleiber, 1997). For example, Tinsley and Krass (1978) discovered that the 44 leisure needs they measured can be reduced to eight types:

self-expression	companionship
power	compensation
security	service
intellectual aestheticism	solitude

The multiple motives itemized in the widely used Recreation Experiences Preferences (REP) scales (see Driver, Tinsley, and Manfredo, 1991) have been reduced to 19 types, eight of which have been shown to be important to outdoor recreationists using parks and wilderness settings (Rosenthal, Waldman, and Driver, 1982):

exploration	escape role overload
general nature experience	introspection
exercise	being with similar people
seeking exhilaration	escaping physical stressors.

The work of Iso-Ahola (1982, 1989) has particular relevance to understanding outdoor recreational behaviours. Focusing on the social psychological aspects of personal and interpersonal rewards, Iso-Ahola (1982, 1989) has proposed that leisure participation is based on two motivational dimensions—seeking and escaping. These two motivational forces simultaneously influence people's leisure behaviour. Leisure activities may be engaged in because they provide opportunities for novelty or change from

BOX 6.2 Measuring Visitor Satisfaction with 'Pull' Factors

An alternate approach to the measurement of visitor satisfaction focuses more on the 'pull' aspect of motivation, as illustrated in the figure. Here visitors were asked to rate levels of satisfaction with the conditions experienced on the West Coast Trail region of Pacific Rim National Park (Rollins, 1998). Most visitors were satisfied with those aspects of the setting described at the top of the figure (information provided at the Pachena trailhead, information provided at the Renfrew trailhead, etc.) However, setting characteristics listed at the bottom of the figure were not as highly rated (frequency of staff patrols, garbage at campsites, condition of boardwalks, etc.).

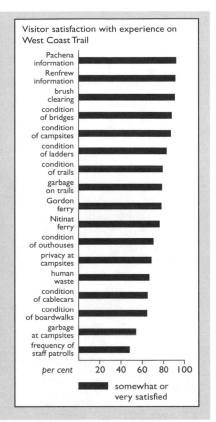

Visitor satisfaction with experience on West Coast Trail

daily routine and stress. The first dimension, escape, is seen as a powerful leisure motive due to the constraining nature of a person's life, particularly from his or her work. This aspect of motivation is based on the need for optimal arousal, in that individuals are considered to be constantly trying to escape from under-arousing and over-arousing. The second dimension, seeking, is the tendency to search out psychological satisfactions from participation in leisure activities. These satisfactions can be divided into personal (e.g., self-determination, sense of competence, challenge, learning, exploration, and relaxation) and interpersonal (e.g., social contact and connectedness) types. Iso-Ahola (1989) suggests that seeking and escaping motives both are forms of intrinsic motivation, undertaken without concern for some form of external reward.

Models of optimal experience—states of higher psychological involvement and absorption—have attracted substantial interest in the study of motives and experiences in outdoor recreation and leisure research (e.g., Tinsley and Tinsley, 1986; Robinson, 1992a, 1992b; Mannell et al., 1988, 1997). The most widely applied concept is Csikszentmihalyi's (1975, 1990) flow model. This model has a number of characteristics of conscious experience that define and operationalize optimal experience. The flow model was originally developed based on Csikszentmihalyi's (1975) work with people engaged in creative leisure activities (i.e., rock climbers, ballet dancers, chess players) and creative work activities (e.g., mathematicians, music composers, surgeons). The model describes the experiences gained when challenges equate well with a person's skill level. These optimal or flow experiences are invested with meaning and feelings of being powerfully in control, and are so intensely absorbing that self-consciousness is negated and the tracking of time is lost. Flow experiences may provide powerful opportunities for personal growth, and leisure settings are seen by many researchers as being particularly conducive to generating flow experiences (Csikszentmihalyi and Csikszentmihalyi, 1990). Csikszentmihalyi also contends that flow experiences in leisure settings can provide frames of reference for the transfer of benefits to other realms of life (social, work, family, and education). Robinson's (1992b) research with climbers illustrates this concept.

Csikszentmihalyi (1990) has represented his model in diagrammatic form (Figure 6.6) that illustrates the relationship between the key components of 'skills' and 'challenges', and how the interplay between these two components lead to the different experiences. Boredom (C2) occurs when skills are greater than challenges); anxiety (C4) occurs when skills are less than the challenges); and flow (C1) occurs when skills and

FIGURE 6.5 A raft gets swept onto a rock on the Firth River in Vuntut National Park reserve. Risk is an important element of wilderness recreation, and even the professionals can make mistakes. *Photo: P. Dearden.*

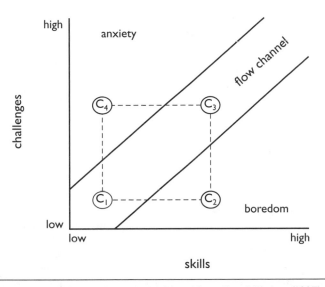

FIGURE 6.6 Czikszentmihaliyi's flow model. After Mannell and Kleiber (1997).

challenges are matched. C3 is a complex flow experience where skills and challenges are both operating at a higher level than in C1. The model gives emphasis to the dynamic nature and value of leisure experiences as vehicles for personal growth and discovery.

With the growing popularity and increasing number of participants in risk recreation in North America, a number of motivational models have recently been developed by leisure researchers to account for participation in this type of activity (Csikszentmihalyi, 1975: Ewert and Hollenhurst, 1989, Robinson, 1992a). These models suggest that though motivation is important, it is only part of the picture. For example, Robinson (1992a) has suggested a model of enduring risk recreation involvement. Important factors identified by the model include motives, personality difference, cognitive processes, and social influences—that is, both motivational and non-motivational conditions (Figure 6.7).

According to Robinson, two primary motivational dispositions are involved in determining if people are attracted to and stay involved in risk recreation activities. The first of these is the need for stimulation and the second is the need for autonomy (i.e., self-determination). However, the model also proposes that these motives 'serve only to provide a "potential" for risk recreation involvement' (Robinson, 1992a: 55). For example, other motives such as the need for 'affiliation' and 'need for recognition' contribute to the attractiveness of a risk recreation pursuit. In addition, conditions in people's social environment, such as the amount of certainty or predictability that exists in their daily life, may affect their willingness to engage in risk recreation. The more predictable and unchanging their everyday lives, the more likely they are to seek out the unpredictable in risk recreation.

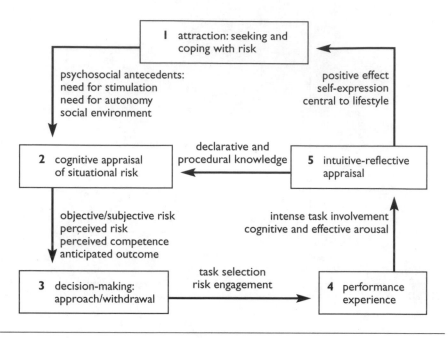

FIGURE 6.7 A risk recreation model. After Robinson (1992a).

Robinson's model also suggests that whether the arousal of the motives of sensation-seeking and autonomy lead a person to select risk recreation to satisfy these depends on several intervening cognitive processes—cognitive appraisal and decision-making. Essentially, these processes refer to how people come to judge the actual level of risk involved in participation relative to their perceived competencies (that is, knowledge and skills in the activity). This decision, furthermore is influenced by the level of risk that is acceptable to the person, which is, like a personality characteristic, a result of socialization experiences. If participation results in a successful flow-like experience, then the needs for stimulation and autonomy likely will be satisfied according to this model. However, continued or repeat participation is thought to depend on whether success in the activity reinforces aspects of self-identity or personality, such as 'I am adventurous' or 'I am self-sufficient'. At such a point, involvement may become 'serious leisure' occupying a place of centrality in the individual's life. In summary, this specific model demonstrates the importance of incorporating motivational explanations into a larger psychological framework if the complexity of leisure behaviour is to be understood. These models of visitor motivations demonstrate the approaches used by social scientists to understand why people select certain types of activities and types of park settings. Motivational approaches have contributed to the understanding of a number of visitor management issues, including crowding and conflict. These are discussed in the following section.

CROWDING IN OUTDOOR RECREATION

The increase in participation in outdoor recreation and nature-based tourism has resulted in crowding in many parks and protected areas in Canada. For example, visits to the West Coast Trail area of Pacific Rim National Park increased from a few hundred people in 1969 to about 8,000 people by 1984, by which time 34 per cent of visitors reported that they felt crowded (Rollins, 1998). The number of visitors floating the Colorado River through the Grande Canyon increased from 205 in 1960 to 22,000 in 1988 (Hendee et al., 1990). This growth in outdoor recreation throughout North America has led to concerns about crowding in natural settings. It was hoped that social science research would provide managers with scientific data from which it would be possible to reduce crowding problems, but the actual research into crowding has produced some surprising results.

Early conceptualizations of crowding postulated that visitor expressions of crowding in a natural setting would be directly proportional to the number of people in the setting at a given time. More people in a setting should create more reports of crowding; fewer people in a setting should result in less crowding. However, the research results in a number of studies showed very weak relationships between use levels and crowding. Researchers speculated that this unexpected result was due to faulty approaches in measurement—what should have been examined was contact levels

FIGURE 6.8 A commercial raft launch site just below Bow Falls on the Bow River and adjacent to the Banff Springs Hotel. Photo: Guy Swinnerton.

(the number of actual encounters) rather than visitor numbers or visitor densities (Shelby and Heberlein, 1986; Manning, 1999). It was reasoned that in the same park at the same time the numbers of encounters might vary from place to place with some people experiencing higher numbers of encounters than people in other parts of the same park. With this reasoning in place, the next generation of crowding research looked for relationships between crowding and the numbers of encounters people experienced. Surprisingly, these results did not turn out as expected either, with most studies reporting a very poor relationship between contact levels and crowding concerns. Manning (1999) provides a useful summary of over 30 crowding studies conducted between 1975 and 1997, all exhibiting this pattern of poor relationship between use levels, encounter levels, and crowding.

Reviews of these studies provided a number of possible explanations for such unexpected results (Heberlein, 1977; Jubenville, 1981; Stankey and McCool, 1984; Rollins, 1988; Manning, 1999). First, many of these crowding studies suffer from a type of sampling error referred to as displacement, whereby visitors who anticipate crowds decide to visit less crowded parks and are displaced by people who are more tolerant to higher contact levels (and less tolerant visitors are not included in the sample). Second, contacts more frequent than expected may lead to a change in the visitor's definition of the experience. For example, a 'wilderness area' may be re-evaluated as a 'semi-wilderness area' as a consequence of more contacts, and visitors may perceive a product shift and consequently may not feel crowded. Related to this product shift is a third concern sometimes described as the cognitive dissonance effect, which speculates that since recreation experiences are largely voluntary and self-selected, visitors will have invested time, money, and energy into their park experience. The last thing visitors will want to admit to themselves or to a researcher is that they felt crowded or unsatisfied with their experience. A fourth explanation is that use levels in some studies are not high enough to have a major impact on visitor experiences. Finally, it has been suggested that many visitors to natural settings are first-time visitors with no prior expectations or conceptual norms for appropriate use levels. For these people there is a tendency to view existing conditions as appropriate, regardless of the level of contacts experienced.

Some theorizing has used a social-psychological framework of social interference or behaviour constraint, which predicts that a situation will be evaluated as crowded when density or a related condition interferes with a setting (Schmidt and Keating, 1979; Gramann, 1982). The principle assumption of this model is that much of people's behaviour is motivated to achieve a variety of psychological states, as described in the previous section on motivation theories. Accordingly, perceptions of crowding may flow from blockage of some types of motivations, such as the desire for solitude, for stress release, or for social interaction within one's travel group. This theoretical position has led to the normative approach to crowding used in a number of more recent studies. The normative approach states that 'outdoor recreation visitors often have preferences, expectations, or other standards by which to judge a situation as crowded or not' (Manning, 1999: 122). A good example of this approach is illustrated

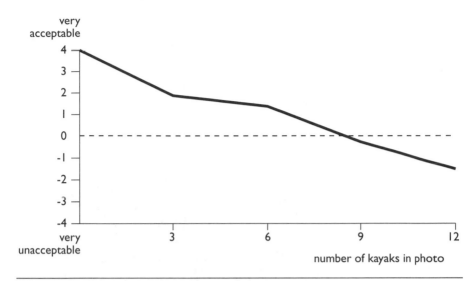

FIGURE 6.9 Kayaker norms for encountering kayaks in a wilderness setting in Gwaii Hanaas National Park Reserve. After Vaske et al. (1996).

in a study conducted in Gwaii Haanas National Park (Figure 6.9). In this study, kayakers in the park were interviewed and shown several photographs depicting the same marine setting, but the number of other kayaks was varied in each photograph (Vaske et al., 1996). After viewing each photograph, the respondents were asked to indicate whether they felt the number of kayaks in the setting was acceptable or unacceptable Using this method, an individual crowding norm was computed for each kayaker. These individual results were aggregated across the sample of kayakers to determine how much consensus or agreement exists between kayakers for different use levels. If a large degree of consensus exists, then it is possible to express this finding as a norm.

The curved line illustrated in Figure 6.9 is referred to as a 'norm curve' or 'contact preference curve'. The horizontal line in this figure represents the 'neutral position' or limit of toleration. Where the contact preference curve crosses the neutral position (when nine kayaks are encountered), the situation is only just tolerable. If the number of contacts exceeds this neutral position of about nine contacts, the experience would be viewed as unacceptable by most kayakers (assuming reasonable consensus in opinions). Fewer than nine contacts would be viewed as more acceptable. The most desirable situation depicted in these results occurs when the number of contacts with other kayakers is zero.

The validity of the normative approach depends on a number of factors. The first factor is the amount of consensus within the group. If a large amount of variability exists in tolerance for contacts with other kayakers, then it may be difficult to describe this curve as representing a norm. However, when consensus does not exist, it may

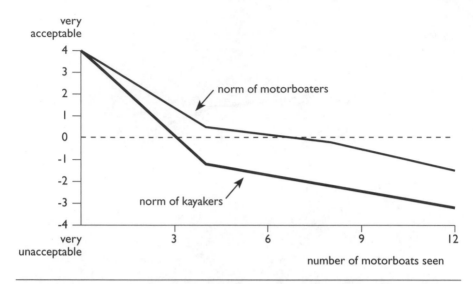

FIGURE 6.10 Kayaker norms versus motorboater norms for encountering motorboats in a wilderness setting setting in Gwaii Hanaas National Park Reserve. After Vaske et al. (1996).

be possible to identify subgroups that share within each subgroup a higher level of consensus than in the whole group. For example, the Gwaii Haanas data can be partitioned by examining responses of subgroups, such as motorboaters and kayakers (Figure 6.10). If motorboaters and kayakers had been lumped together as a single group, the results would have indicated little consensus regarding crowding norms.

The use of photographs to illustrate different encounter levels is a methodological improvement over earlier techniques, which asked respondents to indicate preferences for different encounter levels without a visual cue. However, a problem with the use of photographs is the ability of respondents to infer from a photograph what feelings they may actually experience when encountering different group sizes when traveling in their kayaks. Further, the number of times in a day one might encounter groups of this size before feeling crowded still remains to be determined.

A final concern with these approaches is the failure to come to terms with a deeper understanding of crowding as expressed in the behaviour constraint model: people may feel crowded when they encounter other people behaving in ways that interfere with their anticipated experience (Lee 1972; Schmidt and Keating ,1979; Gramann 1982). Encountering a large group of 10 backpackers at a campsite may be viewed as undesirable because of the anticipated noise level. However, it may not be the number of people per se that generates a crowding impact. If a group of ten backpackers were behaving very quietly, others may not feel crowded. This hypothesis remains largely untested, but it does suggest that part of the management of crowding might involve managing visitor behaviour in ways that reduce conflict with others.

In summary, the research into crowding suggests that level of interaction with other people during outdoor recreation experiences is an important component of satisfactory experiences. However, people vary somewhat in their preferences for different contact levels. This variability in contact preferences may be due to different motivations. Some people may be more highly motivated than others to 'get away from other people', as predicted by the behavioural model described earlier. Previous experience is another probable source of some variability in contact preferences, with more experienced visitors likely to be more sensitive to higher use levels. The size, behaviour, and 'alikeness' of other groups encountered are additional factors that may influence contact preferences and crowding (Manning, 1999).

Management responses to crowding vary. Quetico Provincial Park in northern Ontario is a large canoeing park characterized by a maze of lakes and rivers with endless possibilities for route choices. When crowding concerns emerged at Quetico, analysis of travel patterns revealed that crowding occurred in the more heavily used routes, related to higher visitor traffic through some access points into the park. Park managers used computer simulation models to predict likely contact levels that would result if some visitors were required to use other points of access into the park. After examining a series of these computer simulations, a quota system was established at each access point. If a canoeing party arrived at a certain access point to begin their trip and the daily quota was filled, the group was directed to another access point where the quota was not filled. Subsequent evaluation of this procedure demonstrated that reports of crowding diminished for Quetico while total use levels were actually increased through this more efficient spatial redistribution of visitors (Peterson, 1977; Peterson et al., 1977).

In the West Coast Trail region of Pacific Rim National Park, reports of crowding compelled park managers to develop a quota system as well (Rollins and Bradley, 1985). Unlike the Quetico example, the West Coast Trail is a single trail with very few route options, so a spatial redistribution strategy was not possible. Instead, what was developed for the West Coast Trail was a temporal redistribution system. This involved a daily quota of 52 people per day, split between the two ends of the trail so that 26 people per day per trail head were admitted into the park between 1 May and 30 September. This daily quota of 52 people per day was computed by redistributing the use from what had been a July-August concentration, to that of a May-September season. Previous use levels were estimated to be about 8000 people, so this total visitor level was divided by the total number of days between 1 May and 30 September, and the result was a daily quota of 52 people per day. Hence, annual use levels were kept constant, but daily use levels were greatly reduced in the peak season by shifting more visitors into the shoulder season. Subsequent evaluation of this quota system revealed high levels of satisfaction with the quota system and with encounter levels experienced while hiking, but some lingering concerns with encounter levels at campsites (Rollins, 1998).

Quotas established on the West Coast Trail and in Quetico are examples of management efforts to reduce crowding and sustain quality experiences, by applying crowding research into what is sometimes described as the 'carrying capacity model', discussed in the next chapter. Social carrying capacity is generally defined as the limit of use beyond which unacceptable impacts occur on the visitor experience—mainly crowding (Wagar, 1964; Shelby and Heberlein, 1986). A parallel strategy is the environmental carrying capacity model), aimed at determining the level of visitor use beyond which unacceptable impacts occur to park environments (water quality, loss of vegetation, compacted soils, disruption in wildlife, etc.). Park managers need to attend to both dimensions of visitor impacts, although this represents a challenging balancing act. To provide for total resource protection within the environmental carrying capacity model would result in no visitor activity whatsoever; to focus primarily on visitor needs and interests, including crowding, might result in unacceptable resource damage.

CONFLICT IN OUTDOOR RECRECREATION

Related to crowding are a number of other types of conflict that occur between people participating in different types or styles of outdoor recreation. One example of conflict in outdoor recreation was examined in a study of cross-country skiers and snowmobilers in Alberta (Jackson and Wong, 1982). It was apparent that the two groups were in conflict because the nature of each activity interfered with the other. Snowmobilers interfered with the sense of peace and quiet important to cross-country skiers, and cross-country skiers interfered with the sense of freedom and speed important to snowmobilers. Altogether, the two groups differed significantly in the importance attached to 11 of 18 motivations examined in the study. Many other types of conflict have been reported as follows: between canoeists and motorboaters; between hikers and motorcyclists, between hikers and horseback riders between hunters and fishers, between motorized rafters and oar-powered rafters; between fishers and water-skiers; between ORV users and non-users; between hikers and mountain bikers; between backcountry skiers and helicopter skiers; and between hunters and non-hunters (Manning, 1999).

Out of these studies has emerged a model of recreation conflict analogous to the social interference model suggested to explain crowding. Recreation conflict is generally viewed as stress created when recreation behaviour of one group of people interferes with another group in the achievement of recreation goals or motivations (Jacob and Schreyer, 1980; Gramann and Burdge, 1981; Ewert et al., 1999). Defined in this way, crowding can be seen as a special case of recreation conflict, and both can be understood within the general behavioural model described in Figure 6.1. When two groups of people decide to visit the same recreation setting to pursue different activities, the activities may interfere with each other because the two groups have different goals as determined by differing motivations. For example, a family may choose to go camping at a particular campground in order to achieve a close family experience. Another group consisting of young people may choose the same campground as a venue for letting off steam and having a late-night party in a setting where they anticipate being free of some of the restrictions they may find in a more urban venue. Obviously, the potential for conflict between these two groups would be very high. Sometimes the conflict is not equally perceived between groups. For the example above, the family camping group might be annoyed by the arrival of partying young people; whereas the teenagers may be unaffected by the presence of the family group and perhaps oblivious to the conflict created.

The general behavioural model provides a basic framework for explaining recreational conflict, but it is likely that more factors are involved, such as locus of control, goal specificity, goal importance, culture, individual schemata, and anticipated consequences (Ewert et al., 1999). Locus of control refers to the extent to which a person feels he/she has control over events. People with a high level of control are more likely to experience conflict as a precursor to taking actions to reduce conflict; while people with a lower locus of control may find other ways of coping with unexpected conditions in a recreation setting. Goal specificity can be quite general (to have a good time), or quite specific (to spend some quiet time with my family). People with higher goal specificity are predicted to have greater potential to experience conflict. Goal importance refers to the possibility that a person experiencing interference with a very important goal (e.g., to have quiet time with my family) might feel more conflict when encountering a noisy group than someone for whom this goal is not important. Culture refers to a learned system of beliefs, values, and feelings as expressed through shared norms. As illustrated in the normative approach to crowding, motorboaters in Gwaii Haanas form a sub-culture with a set of norms different from the kayaking sub-culture visiting the same area, resulting in a conflict situation for the kayakers (Figure 6.10). Individual schemata refer to the way people process information. For example, a backpacker may sometimes perceive incorrectly that heliskiers are rich and motivated to flaunt their affluence.

Anticipated consequences is another factor thought to influence conflict. In Neck Point Park, British Columbia, conflict arose between one group of park users (scuba divers, windsurfers, and others) demanding road access to the waterfront area of the park, and a second group (bird watchers, dog walkers, etc.), who wanted to keep the area roadless. Examination of perceived consequences of road access by the two groups revealed very different expected consequences (Rollins, Harding, and Mann, 2001). People supporting road access felt more people would enjoy the park, and scuba activity would be enhanced and safer. People opposed to road access felt a road would take away from the natural atmosphere, would make the park less safe for pedestrians, and lead to crowding and rowdy behaviour. Based on this understanding of visitor attitudes and perceptions, a satisfactory resolution was made possible by providing a road on the southern periphery of the park, minimizing the interaction of cars and pedestrians. Limited short-term parking was provided for just three vehicles in order to reduce concerns of crowding and rowdy behaviour. This example points to the need for managers to understand the basis of visitor concerns in order to develop strategies for managing visitor conflict.

VISITOR ATTITUDES, PERCEPTIONS, AND PREFERENCES

Sometimes 'attitude' is confused with 'satisfaction'. Leisure satisfaction refers to the 'after the fact assessment of an earlier [leisure] involvement or set of involvements' (Mannell, 1999: 238). Leisure attitude usually refers to positive or negative opinions people have regarding a leisure setting or activity. In the Neck Point example discussed above, attitudes were divided between people supporting road access into the park and people opposed to road access. Satisfaction, on the other hand, could be measured by examining actual experiences people describe after the road was put into Neck Point Park.

Attitudes can be defined as an enduring predisposition towards a particular aspect of one's environment, and is thought to consist of a cognitive component, an affective component, and a behavioural component (McDougall and Munro, 1994). This can be illustrated by considering attitudes towards a camping fee system proposed for Provincial Forest recreation sites in British Columbia (Rollins and Trotter, 2000). The affective component refers to feelings of like or dislike for a particular 'attitude object'. In this case, the attitude object is 'user fees in forest recreation sites'. Often the single item affective measure of like-dislike is used to measure attitude. However, more information about why people hold certain attitudes can be identified by including measures of the cognitive component, sometimes referred to as attitudinal beliefs or perceptions (Ajzen and Fishbein, 1980). Hence, the cognitive component of attitude in this example would consist of the relevant beliefs people hold about the consequences of establishing a user fee in forest service recreation sites. Positive attitudinal beliefs included 'would create more respect for sites', 'would lead to reduced vandalism', and 'would make people more willing to comply with rules and regulations'. Negative attitudinal beliefs included 'would lead to confrontations between visitors and fee collectors', 'would detract from freedom', and 'cost to collect fees would be too expensive'. An example of the behavioural component of attitude is 'I would camp less frequently if a user fee was introduced'. Attitudes towards user fees in Forest Service recreation sites were determined by measuring the extent to which people agreed or disagreed with each of these kinds of statements (Likert, 1970). Analysis of responses to these attitudinal questions indicated general support for a user fee although some people expressed concerns (agreed, but with negative attitudinal beliefs). These results made it possible for the BC Forest Service to develop an approach to user fees that addressed many of these concerns.

Another application of attitude theory is illustrated in a household survey conducted by BC Parks to determine attitudes towards setting aside more wilderness areas in British Columbia (BC Parks, 1994). Positive perceptions included protection of wildlife, preservation of biodiversity, places to conduct scientific studies, and stimulation of BC economy by tourists. Negative perceptions included possible loss of jobs, reduction in government revenues through fees and taxes from resource industries, and the restriction of some recreation activities since no roads would be allowed into these areas. The results of the study indicated that 61 per cent of respondents felt there was too little designated wilderness in BC, 3 per cent said there was too much wilderness, and 37 per cent said the amount of wilderness was about right. Repeated polling of this type provided convincing evidence of public support for creating more wilderness parks in BC, and contributed to government actions in the last decade to increase the amount of protected area from about 5 per cent to about 13 per cent of the provincial land-base.

Preference research has also provided useful information for park managers. For example, a study of public opinion regarding recreational uses in wilderness areas of BC (BC Parks, 1994) indicated high levels of support for canoeing, kayaking, backpacking, mountaineering and horseback riding. Low levels of support were found for ATVs, motorized boats, hunting, and snowmobiling.

Attitudinal research has been used to help develop procedures for managing wildlife and other resources in parks. For example, BC Parks developed a sport fishing policy in Bowron Lake Park based on a catch-and-release approach. This policy was made possible in part by the level of support determined from attitudinal studies with park visitors (BC Parks, 1995). Similarly, a bear management issue in Purcell Provincial Park was resolved by closing a backcountry campsite located too close to a calving area for black bears. This management action was facilitated by the strong support indicated from a survey of backcountry visitors to the park (BC Parks, 1997).

The use of surveys, public opinion polls, and the like can be very useful for documenting support or opposition for park management activities. This is particularly important in light of the observation that managers often hold different perceptions of park environments than do park visitors, and often managers are unaware that visitors have different opinions and perceptions (Clark et al., 1971; Hendee et al., 1990). Finally, it should be noted that opinions of park visitors or the general public may be based on misperceptions or misunderstandings, and this kind of finding can be identified in social science research.

VISITOR SEGMENTATION AND SPECIALIZATION

Many of the studies described in this chapter have illustrated a general finding that people vary tremendously in their motivations and goals, activities selected, and preferred setting attributes. This makes it difficult to plan for 'the average camper who doesn't exist', and has led to a number of studies aimed at better understanding the diversity evident in park visitors. The intent of this type of investigation is to determine if it is possible to identify subgroups or market segments of like-minded people within the more heterogeneous population of people who visit parks and protected areas. If this can be determined, then managers can better understand the needs and requirements of the different market segments. More park visitors may have satisfactory experiences, and fewer conflicts may occur.

One approach to segmentation is by visitor activity type. This activity approach is the basis of the 'Visitor Activity Management Process' (VAMP), developed by Parks Canada and described in the next chapter. Another approach is to segment people by setting preferences. This was the approach used in a study of backcountry visitors to

Yoho and Kootenay National Parks (Rollins and Rouse, 1993). In this study three distinct user groups were identified: a 'purist group' wanting no backcountry facilities, a 'semi-rustic group' expressing preferences for shelters, huts, firepits, and picnic tables; and a 'rustic' group who expressed more ambivalent preferences for camping facilities but were more supportive of horse facilities (corrals, grazing areas, etc). A similar approach was used in an examination of preferences for activities, settings, and psychological outcomes of visitors to forest areas in Northern Ontario. Several distinct market segments were revealed and labeled as enthusiasts, adventurers, naturalists, and escapists (Twynam and Robinson, 1997). Escapists, for example, indicated a higher preference for remoteness, unaltered nature, and a number of physically demanding and challenging activities such as climbing, canoeing, and kayaking. This group placed high importance on solitude, knowledge, and learning.

Another approach to segmentation has employed the approach of specialization. The concept of specialization speculates that some people will have more experience or attachment to an activity or setting than will other people, and this variability in specialization will influence issues such as perceived crowding, perceived environmental impacts, and other related attitudes and opinions. For example, an experienced canoeist who has paddled on several trips over a number of years in Algonquin Provincial Park is likely to be concerned if use levels should become much higher; whereas, a novice canoeist traveling through the same area at the same time may be less concerned. Recreation specialization has been defined as 'a continuum of behaviour from the general to the particular, reflected by equipment and skills used in the sport and activity setting preferences' (Bryan, 1977; Ewert, 1993). Several approaches have been used to measure specialization. One approach is to measure experience use history as determined through variables such as the number of times a canoeist has paddled in Algonquin Park; and the number of other canoeing trips taken (Schreyer et al., 1984). A second approach for measuring specialization focuses on psychological involvement with an activity (McIntrye, 1989; Dimanche et al., 1991), addressing factors such as interest, importance, pleasure value, and risk associated with an activity. A third approach is to measure specialization in terms of skill level (Donnelly et al., 1986; Ewert, 1994). Finally, specialization can also be measured as level of attachment to place (Williams et al., 1992). For example, in a study of wilderness use in the Clayoquot Sound area of British Columbia, concerns regarding visible logging increased as a function of attachment to place, with levels of concern varying from 52 per cent expressed from the low specialization group to 92 per cent for the high specialization group (Rollins and Connolly, 2001).

Presumably the specialization factor can be linked to the behavioural approach in the following way: people who are high specialists tend to have better developed motives and goals that are very important to them and not easily substituted, as compared to novices or people classified as low specialists. Further, high specialists will be more likely to develop a personal connection between anticipated goals and specific types of setting characteristics. For example, a high specialist might be disappointed to find an alpine hut in a favorite climbing area, and feel the preferred experience of self sufficiency has been diminished by this new facility. On the other hand, a novice climber who is just developing connections between personal motivations, climbing, and setting characteristics may not feel the same impact when encountering the same alpine hut.

As with other approaches to visitor segmentation, managers can apply the specialization principal to identify subgroups within a population of park visitors. Each sub-group identified through specialization approaches will be more similar in their views and expectations and may warrant a somewhat different management response. For example, ROS or LAC (described in the next chapter) might be employed such that different zones are created within a park to provide for a selection of more challenging canoe routes that will allow people of differing specialization levels to find a more appropriate route choice.

SOCIAL AND ECONOMIC IMPACTS OF PARKS AND PROTECTED AREAS

Most of the research on protected area management in Canada has been directed to issues related to ecological integrity or issues related to visitor management. Relatively little research attention has been given to the economic and social impacts of parks on nearby communities. Since parks tend to attract many visitors who are not residents of the area, these visitors (tourists) are likely to spend at least a little time in nearby host communities. Examples of host communities include Tofino, near Pacific Rim National Park, Marathon near Pukaskwa National Park, and the Innuit community of Pangnirtung near Auyittuq National Park in the Canadian Arctic.

While visiting these host communities, tourists may purchase goods and services, such as groceries, fuel, camping supplies, restaurant meals, or accommodation in a motel or hotel. Tourists may use other community services, such as banks, hospitals, and drug stores. Tourists may meet and interact with local residents in coffee shops, stores, and other local venues in ways that enrich the lives of local residents, who may welcome with interest the unique personalities and cultures afforded by encounters with visitors to their community as part of a park experience. These are all examples of positive interactions between park visitors and residents of host communities, interactions that could be characterized as providing economic benefits and social benefits to host communities. However, not all interactions are positive (Keough, 1989). Visitor numbers may stress local services not designed to handle the surge of summer visitors, creating parking problems and congestion in stores, banks, service stations, beaches, and other local attractions. Some tourists also feel less constrained while on holiday and are rude, condescending, rowdy, or obnoxious.

Sometimes visitors offend without meaning to offend, because they are unaware of local customs or sensitivities. For example, parks are often located in remote, rural communities, where lifestyles might not be as affluent as the lifestyles of visitors to host communities. This 'demonstration' effect may create stress within the host community when people aspire to a lifestyle difficult to obtain.

FIGURE 6.11 An aircraft equipped with tundra tires lands beside the Firth River in Vuntut National Park Reserve with a group of rafters. Aircraft accessibility is controversial in many parks. *Photo: P. Dearden.*

Finally, the presumed economic benefits are sometimes are not what has been anticipated. Perhaps tourism revenues only benefit some community residents, who are employed in services that tourists require; while other residents in the community may not receive such benefits and may in fact resent the benefits that other residents receive from tourism. Sometimes the jobs created by tourism go to non-residents, such as students, who are hired from urban areas to provide summer help for tourism operators. The tourism operators may not be local residents either, adding an additional drain of economic benefits away from host communities.

A general model of social impacts developed by Keough (1989) suggests that social impacts can be positive or negative, depending on (1) characteristics of visitors, and (2) characteristics of the host community. Visitor characteristics include numbers of visitors, length of stay, visitor attitudes, and visitor behaviours. Relevant characteristics of the host community include the type and extent of tourism infrastructure, community culture, values and norms, and the type of political organization (extent of local control over decision-making in the community).

Conflicts between park visitors and residents of host communities can be seen as a variation of the behavioural model (Figure 6.1), with the experience dimension (activities and settings) occurring within the host community rather than within the park. Presumably, conflict occurs when the behaviour of visitors blocks the goals and expectations that residents have developed regarding community values and ideals.

Social impacts of parks also involve economic factors. For example, a study of bird-watching in Point Pelee National Park revealed that most visitors were from the United States (48 per cent), who spent $3.2 million in the local area. These expenditures included the purchase of food, accommodations, and souvenirs. Local businesses reported hiring additional staff and extending hours of operation during the peak bird-watching season (Hvenegaard et al., 1989).

Another form of economic analysis of parks involves estimating the economic value of establishing new protected areas. The economic cost of creating new protected areas is usually computed from an analysis of lost revenues that might flow from other uses of the area, such as logging. Another form of economic analysis is a determination of public willingness to pay to purchase land for park use. A study conducted in British Columbia illustrates this approach (BC Parks, 1994). In a random household survey conducted by BC Parks in 1993, respondents were asked how much they would be willing to pay in increased household taxes and fees in order to double the amount of designated wilderness in the province from 5 per cent of the province to 10 per cent . The results of this study indicated that the mean willingness to pay increased taxes and fees for a doubling of wilderness was about $136 million. This amounts to a total of $174 million each year for park acquisition.

A third type of economic analysis involves an assessment of how much people are willing to pay to visit a protected area. In the early 1990s, fees were considered for the West Coast Trail in Pacific Rim National Park due to fiscal restraint practiced by the federal government and the high cost to maintain the trail. A visitor survey informed hikers that the cost to taxpayers to maintain the West Coast Trail was $65 per hiker, and asked respondents how much of this cost should be paid through a user fee (Rollins, 1998). Responses indicated that 85 per cent of the sample were willing to pay at least $25. As a result, a user fee system was established in the park.

'Willingness to pay' studies have been criticized on at least two levels: hypothetical bias, and strategic bias (Bishop and Heberlein, 1990; Johnson et al., 1990). Strategic bias refers to the tendency of respondents to deliberately provide a lower or higher willingness to pay response compared to their true feelings. Hypothetical bias refers to the difficulty many people have in assigning a monetary value to a commodity not normally sold or purchased in the market place. These criticisms seem particularly relevant to park issues. The West Coast Trail study attempted to mitigate hypothetical bias by providing hikers with the actual cost to manage the trail. Hikers could indicate what they felt was a reasonable user fee, given the information provided on the true cost of maintaining the trail. Strategic bias was addressed by providing a relatively low cost for the user fee. The maximum consequence of $65 compares favourably with other camping opportunities available in commercial campgrounds and provincial parks. Nevertheless, these and other criticisms of the validity of willingness to pay methodology suggest that such results should be treated with caution; perhaps only interpreting the results as an 'acceptance to pay' rather than a willingness to pay.

BOX 6.3. Perceived Community Impacts of Establishing a New Park in Cape Pele, New Brunswick

---

These issues were illustrated in a study of community perceptions of a proposed new park in Cape Pele, New Brunswick (Keough, 1990). Positive benefits as perceived by community residents included the creation of jobs, increased incomes, improved infrastructure (roads, parking), new or improved services, improved recreation facilities, increased opportunities for social encounters, and more attractive community. Perceived negative impacts included increased traffic, increase in local taxes, restriction of rights, increased noise, price inflation in stores, congestion of services and stores, congestion of beach facilities, change in character of village, inflation of land prices, and disputes over land acquisition.

CONCLUSIONS

We have presented some of the major areas of social science theory and research that address visitor management issues in parks and protected areas. The behavioural model (Figure 6.1) suggests that visitor behaviour can be understood in terms of visitor motivations, the psychological goals visitors develop as a consequence of those motivations, and how various activities and settings are perceived as facilitating the achievement of important goals. Visitor satisfaction is seen as the achievement of recreational goals, the degree of congruence between expectations and actual experiences. Issues such as crowding and conflict between groups can be explained in part through this model.

Social science research has demonstrated that people vary considerably in their motivations, and their preferences for different activities and settings. This finding suggests that quality of visitor experiences can be enhanced through zoning strategies aimed at better serving different market niches. These market niches can be refined and described through a variety of approaches to visitor segmentation, including the specialization approach. These insights have contributed to the development of a number of approaches to visitor management described in the next chapter: carrying capacity, Recreation Opportunity Spectrum (ROS), Limits of Acceptable Change (LAC), Visitor Impact Management (VIM), the Visitor Activity Management Process (VAMP), and the Visitor Experience and Resource Protection (VERP) framework. However, it is important to stress that park managers cannot act upon all visitor demands or preferences, no matter how well documented, if park resources are threatened by such actions.

Finally, it needs to be stressed that the protection of park ecosystems must take precedence over the provision of visitor experiences. However, the protection of park ecosystems requires the support and co-operation of park visitors, some of whom may be asked to do without certain facilities or services, or the opportunity to participate in certain types of activities in order to reduce environmental stresses. Protection of park environments also requires the support of local communities, located nearby or sometimes within parks. The involvement of visitors and the general public in the resolution of park issues can be facilitated by the selection of appropriate social science techniques, such as public meetings, expert panels, focus groups, surveys, and referendums. Increasingly, park managers are required to use these social science methods as part of the process of resolving park issues and gaining public support.

REFERENCES

Ajzen, I., and M. Fishbein. 1980. *Understanding Attitude and Predicting Social Behaviour*. Englewood Cliffs, NJ: Prentice-Hall.

BC Parks. 1994. *Wilderness Issues in British Columbia*. Victoria, BC: Ministry of Environment, Lands and Parks.

———. 1995. *Visitors Opinions About The Future Management of Bowron Lakes Canoe Circuit*. Victoria, BC: Ministry of Environment, Lands and Parks.

———. 1997. *Visitors Views About Management Issues in The Purcell Wilderness*. Victoria, BC: Ministry of Environment, Lands, and Parks.

Bishop, R.C., and T.A. Heberlein. 1990. 'The Contingent Evaluation Method', in R.L. Johnson and G.V. Johnson, eds, *Economic Valuation of Natural Resources*. Boulder, Colo.: Westview Press, 81–104.

Bruns, D. 1998. 'Benefits-Based Recreation-Tourism Paradigm Shifts', in M.E. Johnston, G.D. Twynam, and W. Haider, eds, *Shaping Tomorrow's North: The Role of Tourism and Recreation*. Thunder Bay, Ont.: Centre for Northern Studies, Lakehead University, 228–56.

Bryan, H. 1977. 'Leisure Value Systems and Recreation Specialization: The Case of Trout Fishermen', *Journal of Leisure Research* 9: 174–87.

Clark, R., J. Hendee, and F. Campbell. 1971. 'Values, Behaviour and Conflict in Modern Camping Culture', *Journal of Leisure Research* 3: 145–9.

——— and G. Stankey. 1979. 'The Recreation Opportunity Spectrum: A Framework For Planning, Management, and Research', USDA Forest Service Research Paper PNW-98.

Csikszentmihalyi, M. 1975. *Beyond Boredom and Anxiety: The Experience of Play in Work and Games*. San Francisco: Jossey-Bass.

———.1990. *Flow: The Psychology of Optimal Experience*. New York: Harper Perennial.

——— and L.S. Csikszentmihalyi. 1990. 'Adventure and the Flow Experience', N.J.C. Miles and S. Priest, eds, *Adventure Education*. State College, Penn.: Venture Publishing, 149–56.

Dimanche, F., M. Havitz, and D. Howard. 1991. 'Testing the Involvement Profile (IP) Scale in the Context of Selected Recreational and Touristic Activities', *Journal of Leisure Research* 23: 51–66.

Donnelly, M., J. Vaske, and A. Graefe. 1986. 'Degree and Range of Recreation Specialization: Toward a Typology of Boating Related Activities', *Journal of Leisure Research* 18: 81–95.

Driver, B.L., H.E. Tinsley, and M.J. Manfredo. 1991. 'The Paragraphs about Leisure and Recreation Experience Preference Scales: Results from Two Inventories Designed To Assess the Breadth of Perceived Psychological Benefits of Leisure', in Driver and G.L. Peterson, eds, *Benefits of Leisure*. State College, Penn.: Venture Publishing, 263–86.

——— and S.R. Tocher. 1970. 'Toward a Behavioral Interpretation of Recreational Engagements, With Implications for Planning', in B.L. Driver, ed., *Elements of Outdoor Recreation Planning*. Ann Arbor: University of Michigan Press, 9–31.

————— and P. J. Brown. 1975. 'A Socio-Psychological Definition of Recreation Demand, With Implications for Recreation Resource Planning', in *Assessing Demand For Outdoor Recreation*. Washington: National Academy of Sciences, 65–86.

Environment Canada. 1999. *The Importance of Nature to Canadians: Survey Highlights*. Ottawa: Minister of Public Works and Government Services Canada.

Ewert, A.W. 1993. 'Differences in the Level of Motive Importance Based on Trip Outcome, Experience Level and Group Type', *Journal of Leisure Research* 25: 335–49.

—————. 1994. 'Playing the Edge: Motivation and Risk-Taking in a High Altitude Wilderness-Like Environment', *Environment and Behavior* 26: 3–24.

————— and S. Hollenhorst. 1989. 'Testing the Adventure Model: Empirical Support for a Model of Risk Recreation Participation', *Journal of Leisure Research* 21: 124–39.

—————, R.B. Deiser, and A. Voight. 1999. 'Conflict and the Recreation Experience', in E.L. Jackson and T.L. Burton, eds, *Understanding Leisure and Recreation: Mapping the Past, Charting the Future*. State College, Penn.: Venture Publishing, 335–45.

Fodness, D. 1994. 'Measuring Tourist Motivation', Annals of Tourism Research 21: 555–81.

Graef, R., M. Csikszentmihalyi, and S.M. Gianino. 1983. 'Measuring Intrinsic Motivation in Everyday Life', *Leisure Studies* 2: 155–68.

Gramann, J. 1982. 'Toward a Behavioral Theory of Crowding in Outdoor Recreation: An Evaluation and Synthesis of Research', *Leisure Sciences* 5: 109–26.

————— and R. Burdge. 1981. 'The Effect of Recreation Goals on Conflict Perception: The Case of Waterskiers and Fishermen', *Journal of Leisure Research* 13: 15–27.

Haggard, L.M., and D.R. Williams. 1991. 'Self identity Benefits of Leisure Activities, in B.L. Driver and G.L. Peterson, eds, *Benefits of Leisure*. State College, Penn.: Venture Publishing, 103–20.

Heberlein, T.A. 1977. 'Density, Crowding, and Satisfaction: Sociological Studies for Determining Carrying Capacities', *Proceedings: River Recreation Management and Research Symposium*. USDA Forest Service General Technical Report NC-28, 67–76.

Hendee, J.C., G.H. Stankey, and R.C. Lucas. 1990. *Wilderness Management*. Golden, Colo.: North American Press.

Hvengaard, G.T., J.R. Butler, and D.G. Kristofak. 1989. 'Economic Values of Bird Watching at Point Pelee National Park, Canada', *Wildlife Society Bulletin* 17: 526–53.

Iso-Ahola, S.E. 1980. *The Social Psychology of Leisure and Recreation*. Dubuque, Iowa: W.C. Brown.

—————. 1982. 'Toward a Psychological Theory of Tourism Motivation: A Rejoinder', *Annals of Tourism Research* 12: 256–62.

—————. 1989. 'Motivation for Leisure', in E.L. Jackson and T.L. Burton, eds, *Understanding Leisure and Recreation: Mapping the Past, Charting the Future*. State College, Penn.: Venture Publishing, 247–79.

Jackson, E., and R. Wong. 1982. 'Perceived Conflict between Urban Cross-Country Skiers and Snowmobilers in Alberta', *Journal of Leisure Research* 14: 47–62.

Jacob, G.R., and R. Schreyer. 1980. 'Conflict in Outdoor Recreation: A Theoretical Perspective', *Journal of Leisure Research* 12: 368–80.

Johnson, R.L., N. Bregenzer, and B. Shelby. 1990. 'Contingent Valuation Question Formats: Dichotomous Choice Versus Open-Ended Responses', in R.L. Johnson, and G.V. Johnson, eds, *Economic Valuation of Natural Resources*. Boulder, Colo.: Westview Press, 193–204.

Jubenville, A. 1981. 'Role Segregation: A Conceptual Framework for Recreation Management Research', *Recreation Research Review* (Oct.): 7–15.

Keough, B. 1989. 'Social Impacts', in G. Wall, ed., *Outdoor Recreation in Canada*. Toronto: Wiley, 231–75.

———. 1990. 'Resident Recreationists Perceptions and Attitudes with Respect to Tourism Development', *Journal of Applied Recreation Research* 15, 2: 71–83.

Lee, R. 1972. 'The Social Definition of Outdoor Recreation Places', in *Social Behavior, Natural Resources, and the Environment*. New York: Harper & Row, 68–84.

Likert, R. 1970. 'A Technique for the Measurement of Attitudes', in G.F. Summers, ed., *Attitude Measurement*. Chicago: Rand McNally & Co., 149–56.

McDougall and N.W.P. Munro. 1994. 'Scaling and Attitude Measurement in Travel and Tourism Research', in J.R.B. Ritchie and C.R. Goeldner, eds, *Travel, Tourism, and Hospitality Research*, 2nd edn. Toronto: John Wiley.

McIntyre, N. 1989. 'The Personal Meaning of Participation: Enduring Involvement', *Journal of Leisure Research* 21: 167–79.

Manfredo, M.J., B.L. Driver, and P.J. Brown. 1983. 'A Test of Concepts Inherent in Experience-Based Setting Management for Outdoor Recreation Areas', *Journal of Leisure Research* 15: 263–83.

Mannell, R.C. 1999. 'Leisure Experience and Satisfaction', in E.L. Jackson and T.L. Burton, eds, *Understanding Leisure and Recreation: Mapping the Past, Charting the Future*. State College, Penn.: Venture Publishing, 235–52.

——— and D.A. Kleiber. 1997. *A Social Psychology of Leisure*. State College, Penn.: Venture Publishing.

———, J. Zuzanenk, and R.W. Larson. 1988. 'Leisure States and "Flow" Experiences: Testing Perceived Freedom and Intrinsic Motivation Hypotheses', *Journal of Leisure Research* 20: 289–304.

Manning, R.E. 1999. *Studies in Outdoor Recreation: Search and Research for Satisfaction*, 2nd edn. Corvallis: Oregon State University Press.

Peterson, G.L. 1977. 'Concepts and Methods for Designing Entry Station Quotas in the Quetico Visitor Distribution System', unpublished report. Toronto: Ontario Ministry of Natural Resources.

———, R.F. de Battencourt, and D.K. Wong. 1977. 'A Markov-Based Linear Programming Model of Travel in the Boundary Water Canoe Area', in *Proceedings: River Recreation Management and Research Symposium*. North Central Forest Experiment Station, St Paul, Minnesota, 342–56.

Robinson, D.W. 1992a. 'A Descriptive Model of Enduring Adventure Recreation Involvement', *Journal of Leisure Research* 24: 52–63.

———. 1992b. 'The Adventure Recreation Experience: Subjective State Dimensions and the Transfer of Benefits', *Journal of Applied Recreation Research* 17: 12–36.

Rollins, R. 1998. 'Managing for Wilderness Conditions on the West Coast Trail Area of Pacific Rim National Park', in N.W.P. Munro and J.H.M. Willison, eds, *Linking Protected Areas with Working Landscapes*. Proceedings of the Third International Conference on Science and Management of Protected Areas, Wolfville, NS, 643–51.

——— and G. Bradley. 1986. 'Measuring Recreation Satisfaction with Leisure Settings', *Recreation Research Review* 13, 1: 22–7.

————, R. Harding, and M. Mann. 2001. 'Resolving Conflict in an Urban Park Setting: An Application of Attitude Theory', *Leisure*.

———— and J. Rouse. 1993. 'Segmenting Backcountry Visitors by Setting Preferences', in J.H.M. Willison, S. Bondrup-Nielsen, H.T.B. Drysdale, and N.W.P. Munro. *Science and the Management of Protected Areas*. Wolfville, NS: SAMPA, 485–98.

———— and S. Connolly. 2001. 'Visitor Perceptions of Clayoquot Sound: Implications from a Recreation Specialization Model', *Science and the Management of Protected Areas*.

———— and W. Trotter. 2000. 'Public Attitudes Toward User Fees in Provincial Forest Lands', *Leisure* 24: 139–59.

Rosenthal, D.H., D.A. Waldman, and B.L. Driver. 1982. 'Construct Validity of Instruments Measuring Recreationists' Preferences', *Leisure Studies* 5: 89–108.

Schmidt, D.E., and J.P. Keating. 1979. 'Human Crowding and Personal Control: An Interpretation of Research', *Psychological Bulletin* 86: 680–700.

Schreyer, R., D. Lime, and D. Williams. 1984. 'Characterizing the Influence of Past Experience on Recreation Behavior', *Journal of Leisure Research* 16: 34–50.

Shafer, E., Jr. 1969. 'The Average Camper Who Doesn't Exist', USDA Forest Service Research Paper NE-142.

Shelby, B., and T.A. Heberlein. 1986. *Carrying Capacity in Recreation Settings*. Corvallis: Oregon State University Press.

Stankey, G.H., and S.F. McCool 1984. 'Carrying Capacity in Recreation Settings: Evolution, Appraisal, and Application', *Leisure Sciences* 6, 4: 453–73.

Tinsley, H.E.A., and R.A. Kass. 1978. 'Leisure Activities and Need Satisfaction: A Replication and Extension', *Journal of Leisure Research* 10: 191–202.

———— and D.J. Tinsley. 1986. 'A Theory of Attributes, Benefits, and Causes of Leisure Experiences', *Leisure Sciences* 8: 1–45.

Twynam, G.D., and D.W. Robinson. 1997. 'A Market Segmentation Analysis of Desired Ecotourism Opportunities', Natural Resources Canada, Canadian Forest Service, Great Lakes Forestry Centre, Sault St Marie, Ont.. NODA/NFP Technical Report TR-34.

Williams, D., D. Patterson, J. Roggenbuck, and A. Watson. 1992. 'Beyond the Commodity Metaphor: Examining Emotional and Symbolic Attachment to Place', *Leisure Sciences* 14: 29–46.

Vaske, J.J., M.P. Donnelly, W.A. Freimund, and T. Miller. 1996. 'The 1995 Gwaii Haanas Visitor Survey', HDNRU Report No. 26, School of Forestry, University of Montana.

Wagar, J.A. 1964. 'The Carrying Capacity of Wildlands for Recreation', *Forest Science Monograph* 7, 1: 1–24.

KEY WORDS/CONCEPTS

nature-based tourism
social science
leisure behaviour
environmental impacts
behavioural approach
motives
intrinsic motivation
benefits
environmental conditions
social conditions
managerial conditions
Recreation Opportunity Spectrum (ROS)
zoning
Iceberg Theory
Flow Theory
crowding
normative approach
displacement

product shift
cognitive dissonance
social interference
behaviour constraint
spatial redistribution
temporal redistribution
locus of control
goal specificity
goal importance
environmental impacts
social impacts
community impacts
demonstration effect
leisure satisfaction
leisure attitudes
segmentation
specialization

STUDY QUESTIONS

1. Describe the behavioural approach, using an activity familiar to you (e.g., skiing, mountain-biking, scuba diving, fishing).
2. Discuss how the 'behavioural approach' provides the conceptual underpinning of ROS.
3. Discuss why an understanding of visitor motivations is important for a park manager.
4. Crowding is a frequently reported concern, yet it is difficult to determine how to manage to reduce crowding in parks. Discuss.
5. Critique the normative approach to the measurement of crowding.
6. Discuss how conflict can be understood in terms of the behavioural model.
7. Using an outdoor activity familiar to you, describe how 'specialization' could be involved within this activity. How might this specialization influence the selection of preferred setting characteristics.
8. Select a park familiar to you and then identify a community nearby where visitors to this park might stop. Discuss ways this community might benefit/suffer from these park visitors.

CHAPTER 7

Visitor Planning and Management

R.J. Payne & Per W. Nilsen

INTRODUCTION

The relationship among carrying capacity, visitor management, and ecosystem management in the context of Canadian national parks and protected areas is the subject
of this chapter. Parks, as well as other protected areas, are distinctive in that while
they are established to protect representative and significant natural areas of importance, they also are expected to offer visitors opportunities to understand, appreciate,
and enjoy a natural and cultural heritage. Managing this contradiction between protection and use is the chief enterprise of protected area managers. It is in this context
that visitor management is significant.

'Carrying capacity'—the notion that there is a limit to the number of visitors that
can use park areas—is an attractive idea. It possesses an intuitive appeal that has led
many people to place it at the very centre of theories and prescriptions that focus on
the human use of natural environments. For environmental managers especially, it
promises scientific justification for difficult decisions that inevitably involve competing human interests as well as incomplete knowledge of the natural environment. US
researchers polled National Park Service managers who were responsible for backcountry management in national parks (Manning et al., 1996a). Among the problems managers reported was the deterioration of campsites and trails. The researchers
(Manning et al., 1996b: 144-5). went on to identify three trends:
• backcountry impacts were primarily related to recreational use; negative visitor
  experiences and crowding were becoming issues; and,
• carrying capacity was '. . . a pervasive but unresolved issue'.

The following approaches to visitor management are discussed in this chapter:
Recreation Opportunity Spectrum (ROS), Limits of Acceptable Change (LAC), Visitor
Impact Mangement (VIM), Visitor Activity Management Process (VAMP), and Visitor
Experience and Resource Protection (VERP). The approach used is to compare each of
these management frameworks to the traditional carrying capacity model, and then to
describe the relationship between visitor management and ecosystem management.

CARRYING CAPACITY

Carrying capacity is a venerable idea. Modern definitions reflect the most important dimensions of the concept: An environment's carrying capacity is its maximum persistently supportable load (Catton, 1986 cited in Rees, 1998); and, '... carrying capacity ... assumes that there are a finite number of people who can be supported without degrading the natural environment and social, economic, and cultural systems and, as such, is an indirect measure of the maximum level of stress that an ecosystem can maintain' (Barbier, Burgess, and Folke, 1994 cited in International Institute for Sustainable Development, 1995).

Daniel Botkin (1990: 20), however, points out that in 1849 a Belgian scientist, Pierre-François Verhulst, first discussed the S-shaped logistic growth curve that describes how a population grows to its limits. All other things being equal, those limits set the carrying capacity for that population in that environment. The definitions cited above contain the essential kernels of Verhulst's S-curve. Each also offers other elements that have come to be accepted as part of the meaning of carrying capacity. 'Load' might be numbers of people, as in the second definition, but it might also be cattle, voles, or sewage effluent. Going beyond an environment's carrying capacity produces a response: in the second definition, the response is the degradation of that environment. The second definition also mentions 'stress' and, in doing so, introduces the causal relationship of 'stress-response', a direct and traceable cause-and-effect link, which forms a main theme in ecological science. Lastly, the second definition provides the significant observation that natural and social systems are interrelated: overshooting carrying capacity causes a response in the ecosystem that in turn affects elements of the social system.

Another important aspect of carrying capacity is that it must be tied to some purpose or goal and capacities may differ depending on these goals. In other words, there may be many different versions of carrying capacity. At the very least, it is reasonable to say that a particular expression of carrying capacity must be firmly associated with a specific purpose. To discuss carrying capacity without discussing its purpose, then, would be misleading and inappropriate. In summary, the following may be said of carrying capacity:
- it can be defined as 'an environment's maximum persistently supportable load';
- it may be employed at a variety of scales; and,
- it is always associated with a purpose or goal.

CARRYING CAPACITY AND PROTECTED AREAS

Carrying capacity was introduced into the parks, recreation, and tourism literature by Wagar (1964). Three variations of carrying capacity might be applied in national park settings. One, *design (or physical) carrying capacity*, is an architectural/engineering adaptation that specifies particular levels of use in or for facilities. In national park settings, it might be utilized to manage roads in frontcountry areas. For example, if roads were designed for light automobile traffic but were being used by many more cars than expected or by many large recreational vehicles, it would be reasonable to say that the carrying capacity of those roads had been exceeded, causing consequent problems of maintenance and public safety. In the example of a visitor centre, the numbers of visitors at one time may be such that fire safety becomes an issue because the building was not designed with the number of exits necessary for the number of visitors using the facility at the same time.

In 'mid-country' or even backcountry areas, design carrying capacity may assist managers in meeting ecological integrity goals and satisfying visitor expectations. In Point Pelee National Park, for instance, a boardwalk gives many visitors access to areas of the marsh they would otherwise not see and does so in a manner that minimizes their effects upon marsh ecology. In Pacific Rim National Park, boardwalks and ladders help visitors to experience the backcountry qualities of the West Coast Trail while serving to minimize the environmental impacts of their visits. Especially in frontcountry settings, design carrying capacity offers managers of parks and protected areas alternatives to actions that limit human use. Design carrying capacity also illustrates clearly the importance of the purpose of an area in determining a threshold beyond which degradation occurs or problems arise. Although design carrying capacity offers useful solutions, it also might pre-dispose managers towards modifying the natural environment in favour of human use, regardless of the objectives declared for the setting. When design carrying capacity solutions are implemented in wilderness settings, they can themselves facilitate the decline of the very values they were implemented to protect—wilderness values.

A second variant, *ecological carrying capacity*, is more familiar. In national parks, ecological carrying capacity refers to the capability of the natural environment to withstand human use. Ecological carrying capacity, therefore, represents an early form of environmental impact assessment. When proposing to develop a visitor opportunity in a national park, Parks Canada is required to investigate whether the development will have environmental effects and, if so, take steps to mitigate them. While environmental impact assessment may appear straightforward, there are thorny scientific and management issues that require attention.

A third form, *social carrying capacity*, has received a good deal of attention in the parks' literature and in management practice. Social carrying capacity acknowledges that visitors respond to the social, as well as to the natural environment in parks, as discussed in Chapter 6 (the 'behavioural model'). Social carrying capacity focuses on the experiences visitors have in the park. For some visitors, too many other people, people who are different in their interests, or people who are too different in their behaviours constitute negative influences. Such negative influences disturb their own enjoyment. Managing social carrying capacity requires that managers not only appreciate the interactions of visitors in national parks but, also, that they have ideas about what those interactions should be.

Ecological Carrying Capacity

Although ecological carrying capacity is the variant that most obviously applies in park settings, it has been employed much less than its cousin: social carrying capacity. To appreciate why this is the case, one must understand that determining ecolog-

ical carrying capacity involves finding answers to not one but three questions. Answers are needed to the following:
- What is the ecological impact of human use in a particular ecosystem?
- Does the impact change the character of the ecosystem?
- Is the change, if any, an acceptable change?

The first of these questions may be answered by scientific research, assuming that it is possible to develop a causal relationship between human use and ecological impact.

The second question, however, requires different sorts of data and information. What was the condition of the ecosystem before it was disturbed by human use? Was that previous condition a 'natural' state or was it also caused by some human interference? Is the cause of the disturbance something that national park managers may influence through their actions? Nelson (1968) raised several of these questions in relation to Banff National Park three decades ago. The recent Banff-Bow Valley Study (Page et al., 1996) has served only to sharpen them.

The third question requires something completely different if it is to be answered. It is not a scientific question; rather it is a 'values' question (Becker et al., 1984). An 'acceptable change' implies that national park managers have established a range of desired conditions and can then judge the change, determining if it is 'good' or 'bad'. While Parks Canada has produced management plans for national parks for a number of years, it is evident from the Banff-Bow Valley experience that Parks Canada has not been prepared until recently to judge whether the changes to park ecosystems have been desirable or undesirable.

The trails in the Lake O'Hara area in Yoho National Park have been the focus of monitoring efforts since 1983 (Yoho National Park, 1997). The area is a popular one with backcountry travellers. Managers hoped to be able to utilize baseline data in order to direct maintenance and rehabilitation efforts on the trails. It is recognized that human use is responsible for trail degradation. Human use data or information is currently collected through the backcountry permitting system. However, no analysis has been conducted that might pinpoint the threshold at which human use begins to produce negative environmental effects. Moreover, no levels of acceptable impacts have been specified by managers, although it is evident that deteriorating trail conditions moved them to act. Are the deteriorating trail conditions visually unpleasant or are they also indicative of deteriorating ecological integrity? The assumption is that visual impact means ecological impact and that ecological impact constitutes a decline in ecological integrity. Thus, all three of the ecological carrying capacity questions in the Lake O'Hara area are not being answered by the monitoring program.

Kachi and Walker (1999) have surveyed work being conducted in Canadian national parks on human use management. Their results indicate that a focus on ecological carrying capacity is common. For example, in Gwaii Haanas National Park (1999), staff examined visitor impacts on backcountry campsites in a subjective manner, determining that 52 of 75 sites required management intervention. A part of that intervention includes setting standards, which, when exceeded, demand remedial actions by managers. It is questionable, however, whether monitoring by itself will point to the causes of degradation. Without those causes, it is difficult for managers to determine what actions to take in response.

Drysdale (1995) outlines the data management and monitoring work underway for some time in Kejimkujik National Park. While this initiative is not focused directly on ecological carrying capacity, the resulting databases provide the park's management team with opportunities to undertake analyses to provide answers to specific questions.

Parks Canada and many other parks agencies generally have been unable to answer questions two and three. Ecological carrying capacity therefore has not been seriously applied in parks and protected areas. There are signs, however, (e.g., the Kejimkujik data management initiative; the Lake O'Hara Trail Monitoring Program) that Parks Canada is prepared to identify acceptable levels of ecological integrity (through ecological integrity statements, see Chapter 5) and to manage national parks in ways to maintain or to attain those levels over the long term.

Social Carrying Capacity

Social carrying capacity has received the majority of attention by researchers and like the ecological variant, concerns itself with three questions:

- what is the social impact of human uses of a particular ecosystem?
- does that impact change the nature of recreation experiences available in that ecosystem?
- is the change, if any, an acceptable one?

Social carrying capacity focuses on the relationships among users of a park or protected area. That these users may be having an ecological impact is not an issue for social carrying capacity. The possibility, however, that the numbers or the behaviours of some visitors may affect the recreational experience of other visitors is at the heart of social carrying capacity.

The literature on social carrying capacity is characterized by a concern with wilderness and backcountry recreation situations, a fact that reflects the management responsibilities of American protected areas agencies, especially the US Forest Service (Hendee et al., 1990). The changes in thinking about social carrying capacity in wilderness areas mirror changes in thinking about wilderness itself. With the passage of the Wilderness Act in 1964, managers were required to define wilderness in meaningful terms for management. Social scientists pointed out that people's perceptions and understandings of wilderness differed and that defining wilderness ought to take such differences into account (Stankey, 1973). A good deal of research was conducted into crowding (e.g., Lime et al., 1995) and conflict (e.g., Schreyer 1990), revealing that a number of demographic, social, and economic variables influenced whether people felt crowded or in conflict with other users in recreational settings. It became clear that it was ineffective to base management actions on definitions that were so changeable. Something more firmly based in science was required. The following definition appears in the Wilderness Act:

A wilderness, in contrast with those areas where man and his own works dominate the landscape, is hereby recognized as an area where the earth and its community of life are untrammeled by man, where man himself is a visitor who does not remain. An area of wilderness is further defined to mean in this Act an area of undeveloped Federal land retaining its primeval character and influence, without permanent improvements or human habitation, which is protected and managed so as to preserve its natural conditions and which (1) generally appears to have been affected primarily by the forces of nature, with the imprint of man's work substantially unnoticeable; (2) has outstanding opportunities for solitude or a primitive and unconfined type of recreation; (3) has at least five thousand acres of land or is of sufficient size as to make practicable its preservation and use in an unimpaired condition; and (4) may also contain ecological, geological, or other features of scientific, educational, scenic, or historical value (Sec. 2c).

Note that the addition of the size criterion gives an operational dimension to the definition that allows measurement and determination of what does not constitute wilderness as well as what might. The particular contribution of social carrying capacity lies in defining 'encounter norms' (Vaske et al., 1986), standards by which managers might evaluate crowding in backcountry or wilderness settings.

FIGURE 7.1 Management should try to accommodate different types of recreation and recreationists in national parks, but are there limits? The Columbia Icefields, Jasper National Park. *Photo: P. Dearden.*

More recently, managers have recognized that there is a need to address social carrying capacity in frontcountry settings, especially in those occupied by day users. Some such studies (e.g., Heberlein and Alfano, 1986) have encountered a significant barrier, namely the considerable diversity in motivations, expectations, and knowledge among people in frontcountry settings. Attempting to set standards for conditions of visitor experience has been daunting.

Social carrying capacity has been widely connected to recreational conflict—that is, two groups of recreationists so different in themselves, in their activities, and/or in their attachments to the natural environment that one of them becomes dissatisfied or even displaced. Duffus and Dearden (1990, 1993), for example, suggest that as visitor numbers grow for whale-watching activities at Robson Bight Ecological reserve on Vancouver Island that the nature of the visitors changes as a result of social carrying capacities. Initially, when visitor numbers are low there is a high proportion of specialized whale-watchers. As numbers increase, the proportion of generalists also increases, changing the nature of the experience; and the more demanding visitors are displaced as their social carrying capacity is reached. This analysis should be distinguished from that of social carrying capacity related to the interaction between visitors and residents (see, for example, Canestrelli and Costa, 1991).

Carrying capacity is not only a venerable idea; it is also a popular one, with the public and protected area managers alike. Now that it has been examined, the question remains: Does carrying capacity have a role in national park management?

Some writers, including Wagar himself (1974), have suggested that perhaps the focus should be on conditions in the environment (i.e., a qualitative approach) rather than on the level of stress (i.e., a quantitative approach) being applied to the environment (Washburne, 1982; Vaske, 1994; Rees, 1997). Such a shift of focus would change carrying capacity, but might also render it more useful to park managers. Others are not in agreement, continuing to advocate a 'traditional' carrying capacity approach to managing human use of natural environments for recreation and tourism (e.g., Butler et al., 1993; Williams and Gill, 1991; Heberlein et al., 1986).

Shelby and Heberlein (1984: 434, 441) suggested an approach to carrying capacity that still is worthy of attention. They defined carrying capacity as: 'the level of use beyond which impacts exceed acceptable levels specified by evaluative standards'. Their approach required managers to take three actions:
- specify management parameters (i.e., something that managers could manipulate) for an area;
- specify impact parameters relevant to an area; and
- collect data at regular intervals to describe the existing situation.

Shelby and Heberlein maintained that only within this context is it reasonable to employ the idea of carrying capacity. Note that they did not differentiate between ecological and social carrying capacity. Rather, they felt the approach was as useful for one as the other. More than that, they offered two other realizations: that carrying capacity is tied to particular sites or landscapes and that social and ecological expressions of carrying capacity may be closely related.

Elsewhere, the recognition of the multi-purpose nature of park management has led the US National Park Service (1997a: 30) to define carrying capacity in the following manner: ' . . . carrying capacity is the type and level of visitor use that can be accommodated while sustaining the desired resource and social conditions that complement the purpose of a park unit and its management objectives'.

The link between carrying capacity and management purpose has seldom been more overtly stated. Such a definition still contains the kernels of carrying capacity identified earlier. It also pays attention to management purposes, facilitating results-based management and accountability. Moreover, the definition hints at responses to carrying capacity issues as being more than limiting human use (Cole et al., 1987). Management responses may be 'direct' or 'indirect' (Hendee et al., 1990), where direct responses refer to techniques aimed at regulating behaviour, and indirect responses refer to techniques aimed at influencing behaviour (Table 7.1). Direct approaches include zoning of incompatible uses, providing increased enforcement of regulations, limiting use levels, and restricting certain types of activities. Indirect approaches include 'hardening' (i.e., applying gravel for levelling the ground and eliminating surface water) campsites, providing visitor information (i.e., educating visitors about appropriate behaviour), and charging fees.

TABLE 7.1 Examples of Indirect and Direct Management Strategies

INDIRECT MANAGEMENT TECHNIQUES

Physical Alterations

1. Improve or neglect access.	At Point Pelee National Park, a 1.25-km stretch of East Road was removed so that it can revert back to a natural state, resulting in an increase in natural habitats, reconnection of habitats, and a decrease in road kills. Elsewhere in the park, the East Road was improved by widening and resurfacing, in order to accommodate two-way traffic.
2. Improve or neglect campsites.	At Kejimkujik National Park each of the backcountry campsites is equipped with a fireplace, picnic table, outhouse toilet, and gravel tent pad. Camping is only permitted at these designated campsites.

Information Dispersal

1. Advertise recreation opportunities in nearby areas.	At La Maurice National Park, visitors are encouraged to visit Les Forges du Saint Maurice National Historic Site. At Point Pelee National Park, visitors are informed of other birding opportunities, available at sites such as Hillman Marsh Conservation Area, Wheatley Provincial Park, and Kopegaron Woods Conservation Area.

INDIRECT MANAGEMENT TECHNIQUES   continued

2. Provide minimal impact education.	Mingan Archipelago National Park Reserve has initiated an awareness program on the impact of interfering with seabirds, and navigation ethics in the Mingan Archipelago.

Eligibility Requirements

1. Charge constant entrance fees.	Mount Revelstoke National Park charges a $4.00 entry fee. Pacific Rim National Park Reserve charges a fee of $70 for hiking the West Coast Trail, and an additional $25 for ferry services across two rivers.
2. Charge differential fees.	Kouchibouguac National Park charges $13 for unserviced sites from 16 May to 27 June and from 2 September to 13 October. The fee at these same sites from 28 June to 1 September is $16.25.

DIRECT MANAGEMENT TECHNIQUES

Increased Enforcement

1. Impose fines.	In any national park, a visitor who is convicted of hunting is subject to fines of up to $150,000.00 or to six months imprisonment, or both.
2. Increase surveillance.	The Gwaii Haanas Watchman program was developed out of concerns for protecting old Haida village sites from vandalism and other damage. Watchmen are posted at several sites to make visitors aware of the significance of the sites and how to visit the sites without leaving a trace.

Zoning

1. Separate incompatible uses.	In Jasper National Park, horseback riders are not permitted at picnic sites, campgrounds, or car-accessible campgrounds.
2. Temporal zoning.	At Bruce Peninsula National Park, motorboats are prohibited on Cyprus Lake from 15 June–15 September, but canoes and sailboards may be used anytime.

Rationing Use Intensity

1. Rotate use.	Quetico Provincial Park varies the number of back-country permits provided at each access point.
2. Require reservations.	Of the 50 backcountry permits issued daily for the Chilkoot Trail, 42 can only be obtained with a reservation. Similarly, the West Coast Trail has a daily quota of 52 backcountry permits, of which 40 are available by reservation.
3. Assign campsites.	In Jasper National Park, backcountry camping is allowed only in designated campsites. The same approach is used in Kejimkujik National Park.

DIRECT MANAGEMENT TECHNIQUES   continued

4. Limit size of groups.	At Pacific Rim National Park Reserve, no more than 52 people per day are allowed to enter the West Coast Trail, and no single group can have more than 9 members.
5. Limit length of stay.	Bruce Peninsula National Park has imposed a maximum length of stay of 14 days at campgrounds.
Restrictions on Activities	
1. Restrict type of use.	A fishing ban is in effect for all streams and rivers in Glacier National Park.
2. Restrict camping practices.	On the Chilkoot Trail, visitors must pack out everything they pack in, make use of the grey water pits that are provided, and use camping stoves rather than campfires.
3. Restrict collecting.	In the Broken Groups Islands unit of Pacific Rim National Park, visitors are not allowed to collect shells from the beaches.

SOURCE: Adapted from N. Kachi and K. Walker (1999).

CARRYING CAPACITY AND VISITOR MANAGEMENT FRAMEWORKS

Carrying capacity is clearly a well-established term in the field of recreation, parks, and tourism management. Documented difficulties in its implementation, however, have led researchers and managers to look beyond carrying capacity (Stankey and McCool, 1989) in search of appropriate management methodologies. That Giongo et al. (1993) could conclude that visitor management is a poorly developed art in the world's parks and protected areas indicates that there is still much work to be done in shaping carrying capacity into an effective tool for managers. However, several visitor management frameworks have been used in North American park systems.

Table 7.2 outlines the connections between the five visitor management frameworks (VMFs) and carrying capacity. Drawing upon the published work of Payne and Graham (1993) and Nilsen and Tayler (1998), the intentions in this section are:
- to outline five common visitor management frameworks;
- to sketch their connections with carrying capacity; and,
- to consider their utility in park and protected area management.

The Recreation Opportunity Spectrum Framework

The Recreation Opportunity Spectrum (ROS) (Clark and Stankey, 1979, 1990) is a direct descendent of social carrying capacity (Driver et al., 1987; Driver, 1990). It does not, however, address ecological carrying capacity. Using standards that describe recreation 'settings' or areas, the ROS framework systematically divides up a landscape to produce

TABLE 7.2 A Comparison of Visitor Management Frameworks (VMFs)

VMFs	Related to Carrying Capacity?	Scope	Scale	Applications
ROS	Yes; social carrying capacity	Social	Landscape	Four Mountain Parks, Yoho National Park, Pukaskwa National Park
VAMP	No	Design and Social	Landscape and Site	Various National Parks, Heritage Canals, Visitor Risk Management, Appropriate Activity Assessment
VIM	Yes	Social and Ecological	Landscape and Site	Columbia Icefields, Jasper National Park
LAC	Yes; through its connection to ROS	Social and Ecological	Landscape	Yoho National Park, Chilcoot Trail National Historic Park
VERP	Yes	Social and Site	Landscape Ecological	None

SOURCE: After Payne and Graham (1993); Nilsen and Tayler (1998).

a continuum or spectrum of recreation opportunities ranging from primitive (wilderness) through urban (developed). The supply of opportunities identified in this way is compared with visitors' demands for opportunities, with managers having the opportunity to match supply and demand where possible and permissible under legislation and policy. Often, however, ROS is only employed to describe the supply of opportunities and to help set associated management objectives.

ROS is based on the idea that people participate in recreational activities in specific settings to achieve desired experiences and benefits (see the discussion of the 'behavioural model' in Chapter 6). People vary in the their preferences for setting characteristics, so the emphasis in ROS is to provide for a variety of setting types, as defined by the types of factors listed in Figure 7.2. Hence, human modification, access, user interaction, and management regime lie at the heart of ROS. Variation among these factors determines the nature of the setting in which the activities occur. By manipulating these factors—for example, by providing trail access to an area previously without a trail—settings can be managed to produce the desired results.

The ROS is a unique framework. It can best be appreciated at a landscape (rather than site) level, where its technique of applying social carrying capacity is especially effective in wilderness and backcountry environments. The ROS is also a systematic land-planning and management framework, requiring that planners and managers who use it accept its underlying, powerful rationale. This management-planning orientation is in direct contrast to the more problem-oriented approach adopted by the other frameworks reviewed here.

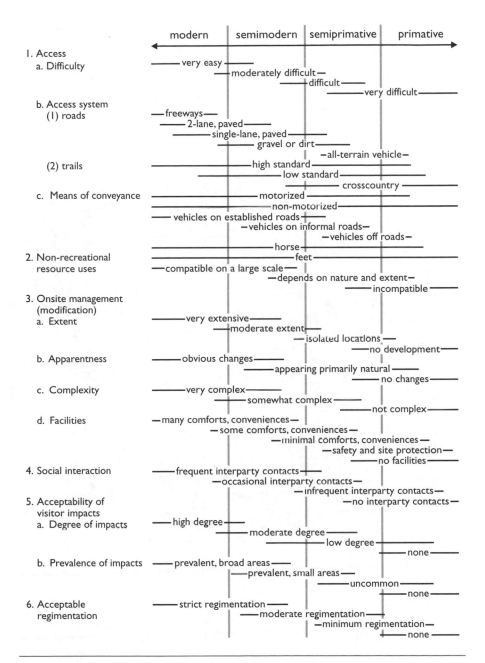

FIGURE 7.2 The Recreational Opportunity Spectrum (ROS) showing the relationship between the range of opportunity setting classes and management factors. Source: Clark and Stankey (1979).

BOX 7.1 Applying the ROS for Visitor Opportunity Assessment in Canadian National Parks

---

The ROS is an excellent tool for estimating the supply of visitor opportunities that may be available in a park or protected area.

In their application of the ROS for this purpose in Yoho and Pukaskwa National Parks, Payne et al. (1997) emphasized the importance of existing modifications to the natural environment in determining the supply of visitor opportunities.

In Yoho National Park, the Trans-Canada Highway and the transcontinental railway line in the Kicking Horse Valley so modify the natural environment in physical and social terms that visitor opportunities are largely those of the front-country variety. The influence of these human modifications extends well away from the valley floor where they are located, due to the steep sides of the Kicking Horse Valley itself. The sights and sounds of cars, buses, trucks, and trains are obvious and remain so some distance up the valley sides.

Human influences also intrude from outside Yoho's boundaries, especially in the north-west and the west, where the park abuts Crown land used during the winter by snowmobilers.

Wilderness opportunities are restricted to the higher elevations and to those parts of the park in the north-east and the east where the presence of Banff National Park provides protection for backcountry opportunities.

This analysis has implications for Yoho's attempts to designate wilderness areas under the new National Parks Act.

There are few explicit applications of the ROS in Canadian national parks. There is evidence of its use in backcountry areas of the four mountain parks (Canadian Parks Service, 1986); it was also employed more recently in assessing visitor opportunities in Yoho and Pukaskwa National Parks (Payne et al., 1997).

It could be argued however, that the zoning system developed for national parks resembles ROS (Chapter 9), in that five types of zones are included: Zone 1 (Special Protection); Zone 2 (Wilderness); Zone 3 (Natural Environment); Zone 4 (Outdoor Recreation); and, Zone 5 (Park Services). These zones are intended to provide a range of visitor opportunities, although the greatest emphasis is placed on Zone 1 and Zone 2 (Parks Canada, 1994b).

The Visitor Activity Management Process

The Visitor Activity Management Process (VAMP) was developed by Parks Canada in the late 1980s to complement its existing Natural Resource Management Process. While VAMP has no obvious roots in carrying capacity, several aspects help to provide this framework with exceptional capability. Furthermore, this capability affords a basis upon which discussion of both ecological and social carrying capacity issues and possible solutions may begin.

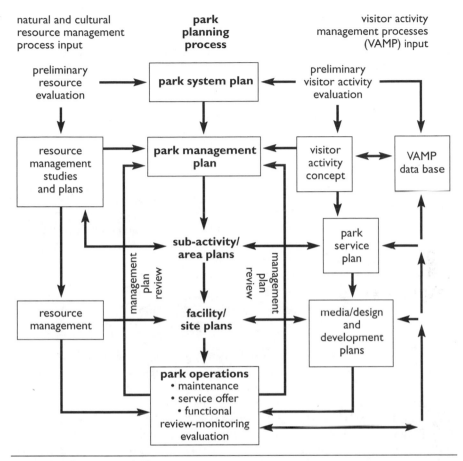

FIGURE 7.3 The national park planning process, showing the role of the Visitor Activity Management Process (VAMP). SOURCE: Parks Canada (1986).

The VAMP framework revolves around visitor activity profiles. A visitor activity profile connects a particular activity (for example, cross-country skiing) with the social and demographic characteristics of participants, with the activities' setting requirements, and with trends affecting the activity. For cross-country skiing, the visitor activity profile used by Parks Canada is composed of four subactivities: recreation/day-use skiing, fitness skiing, competitive skiing, and backcountry skiing. Differences among participants' socio-demographic characteristics, equipment, and motivations, as well as their setting needs, make each of these sub-activities—all involving cross-country skiing—quite unique. More importantly for planning and management, these distinct variations require differing levels of service and have differing environmental effects. Competitive skiing, for instance, requires creating courses that meet standards set by cross-country skiing associations. On the other hand, backcountry skiing requires no changes to the landscape, since the natural setting is such a large part of what these skiers want.

VAMP's power is seen first in its focus on visitor activities as a means of understanding and managing human use of parks and protected areas. Activities such as camping are well understood by participants and managers alike. Moreover, such activities contain more specialized components; camping, for example, may be sub-

---

BOX 7.2 Using VAMP in Appropriate Activity Assessment

The principle that not all types of activities are appropriate in parks and protected areas is well established for Canada's national parks.

Appropriate activity assessment goes back to the early 1980s when both VAMP and an approach to appropriate activity assessment were under development (Nilsen, 1994). A process to assess an activity's appropriateness was developed and tested using activities such as hang gliding, dog sledding, and trail bicycling. VAMP had a significant influence on the criteria selected for appropriate activity assessment at the national level.

The approach strove to be comprehensive and interactive, using a workshop approach involving Parks Canada staff and stakeholders to develop a national position regarding an activity. Applying the approach highlighted several issues. These included an underestimation of the complexity of the task, a lack of supporting social science data, and intensive political lobbying.

The public consultations of the early 1990s leading to the current *Parks Canada Guiding Principles and Operating Policies* focused considerable attention on the issue of appropriate activities. Using the lessons learned from the initial foray into appropriate activities assessment and the experience of implementing VAMP at both the management planning and operational (service) planning level a *Proposed Framework for Assessing the Appropriateness of Recreation Activities in Protected Heritage Areas* (Parks Canada, 1994) was developed. It focuses on assessment at the park/site level and has been used extensively in park management planning and in activity-specific situations.

Considerable experience has been gained in appropriate activities assessment within Parks Canada. More work is required as demonstrated by the Banff-Bow Valley Study and, more recently, by the Panel on Ecological Integrity of Canada's National Parks (Parks Canada, 2000). Parks Canada is committed to review the appropriateness of visitor activities during the management planning process with public consultation. In addition there is a commitment to update and finalize the 1994 proposed framework in response to the Panel's recommendations.

divided into frontcountry and backcountry variants, based on the associated settings and services. Not surprisingly, campers themselves differ in their motivations for participating in these forms of camping. The detailed understanding of a visitor activity provided by VAMP also enables Parks Canada to decide whether the activity is an appropriate one for a national park. Using the VAMP framework, Parks Canada is able to tailor opportunities, programs, services and facilities to specific visitor activity groups and, in turn, to specific areas (e.g., Pukaskwa National Park Management Plan; Rideau Canal Service Plan). Parks Canada has utilized the VAMP framework in two other important initiatives, one focusing on risk management (Parks Canada, 1998b) and the other on appropriate activity assessment (Parks Canada, 1994c).

While not always explicitly spatial in orientation, VAMP does provide an opportunity to define service objectives and levels of service (standards) to address social carrying capacity. It relies on the Natural Resource Management Process and the Environmental Impact Assessment Process to address elements more related to ecological carrying capacity. Like other VMFs, the ongoing challenge is to ensure integration of functional processes for overall park management goals and objectives.

The Visitor Impact Management Framework

The Visitor Impact Management (VIM) framework was developed by researchers in concert with the National Parks and Conservation Association, an American non-government organization specializing in park issues (Graefe, 1990, Graefe et al., 1990a, Graefe et al., 1990b).

As its name suggests, VIM exemplifies a concern for managing visitor impacts on the natural environment in parks. Consequently, the VIM framework displays a strong connection to carrying capacity and, especially, to ecological carrying capacity. However, VIM also attempts to deal with social carrying capacity (e.g., Vaske, 1994), a feature that re-enforces the tentative links between social and ecological carrying capacities. The revision of carrying capacity presented by Shelby and Heberlein (1984) also is prominent. VIM features requirements for managers to specify ecological standards for park areas, to determine effective ways to monitor conditions in those areas, to identify problems when standards are not achieved, and to act to restore or maintain desired conditions. In this, VIM echoes features of LAC and anticipates those of the Visitor Experience and Resource Protection (VERP) framework.

Eight steps comprise the Visitor Impact Management (VIM) Framework (Figure 7.4):

Step 1. Review existing databases.
Step 2. Review management objectives.
Step 3. Select key impact indicators.
Step 4. Select standards for key impact indicators.
Step 5. Compare standards and existing conditions.
Step 6. Identify probable causes of impacts.
Step 7. Identify appropriate management strategies.
Step 8. Implement the best strategy.

basic approach: systematic process for identification of impact problems, their causes, and effective management strategies for reduction of visitor impacts

conditions for use: integrated with other planning frameworks or as management tool for localized impact problems

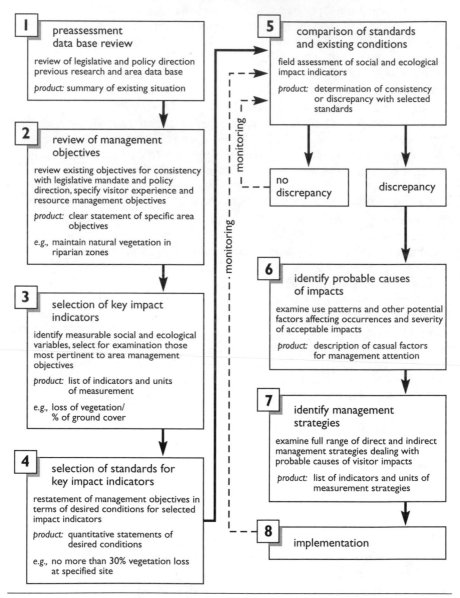

1 preassessment data base review

review of legislative and policy direction previous research and area data base

product: summary of existing situation

2 review of management objectives

review existing objectives for consistency with legislative mandate and policy direction, specify visitor experience and resource management objectives

product: clear statement of specific area objectives

e.g., maintain natural vegetation in riparian zones

3 selection of key impact indicators

identify measurable social and ecological variables, select for examination those most pertinent to area management objectives

product: list of indicators and units of measurement

e.g., loss of vegetation/ % of ground cover

4 selection of standards for key impact indicators

restatement of management objectives in terms of desired conditions for selected impact indicators

product: quantitative statements of desired conditions

e.g., no more than 30% vegetation loss at specified site

5 comparison of standards and existing conditions

field assessment of social and ecological impact indicators

product: determination of consistency or discrepancy with selected standards

monitoring

no discrepancy

discrepancy

6 identify probable causes of impacts

examine use patterns and other potential factors affecting occurrences and severity of acceptable impacts

product: description of casual factors for management attention

7 identify management strategies

examine full range of direct and indirect management strategies dealing with probable causes of visitor impacts

product: list of indicators and units of measurement strategies

8 implementation

FIGURE 7.4 The Visitor Impact Management (VIM) process. SOURCE: Graefe (1990).

BOX 7.3 Applying VIM in the Columbia Icefields

The application of VIM to the Columbia Icefields (Vaske, 1994) was intended to assist in the development of area plans for the Columbia Icefields, the most heavily visited day use in Jasper National Park. The Icefields are located adjacent to the heavily travelled Icefields Parkway, which provides access between Banff and Jasper. At the time of the study there was a Parks Canada information centre and commercial snowcoach tour operation to the Athabasca Glacier operated by the Brewster Corporation. The study provided input to a major redevelopment of the area including the construction of a new Icefields Centre, which contains snowcoach staging facilities and a Parks Canada visitor centre.

All seven steps of the VIM framework were applied. Ecological and facility impacts were not the limiting capacity indicators, especially in light of the new facility. Of greater concern was the social carrying capacity, particularly of snowcoach users. Specific management objectives concerning the number of snowcoach users and their learning experiences were identified. Measurable indicators for management objectives, with a key indicator being perceived crowding, were specified. Standards for the crowding indicator were set. Comparing existing conditions to the crowding standard using survey data revealed that crowding was not a problem for the intensively managed glacier experience. However, crowding was a concern in the visitor facilities. Probable causes of the problem situation such as prior experience, visitor expectations, norms, and cultural differences were examined.

The application of the VIM framework at the Icefields demonstrated that, while the level of crowding on the glacier had not exceeded the determined management standard, crowding at the visitor facilities was a problem. This situation has since been addressed through the new facility development.

Shelby, Vaske, and Donnelly (1996) undertook further data collection and analysis in 1996 in consideration of more recent carrying capacity research. They suggested that changes in the crowding standard be considered given its stronger basis in theory and empirical data.

VIM is definitely a spatial framework and works best in site-specific situations rather than in landscapes, although it can be utilized with ROS or LAC at the landscape level.

Applications in Canadian national parks are limited to Vaske's (1994) use of VIM at the Columbia Icefields in Jasper National Park (Box 7.3).

The Limits of Acceptable Change Framework

The Limits of Acceptable Change (LAC) framework was developed by the US Forest Service to complement the ROS (Stankey et al., 1985; Knopf, 1990; McCool, 1990a; McCool, 1990b). Essential steps in the LAC process (Figure 7.5) are listed below:

Step 1. Identify area concerns and issues.
Step 2. Define and describe management objectives.
Step 3. Select indicators of resource and social conditions.
Step 4. Inventory resource and social conditions.
Step 5. Specify standards for resources and social conditions.
Step 6. Identify alternatives.
Step 7. Identify management actions for each alternative.
Step 8. Evaluate and select an alternative.
Step 9. Implement actions and monitor conditions.

The LAC can be considered an extension and elaboration of ROS. Like ROS, it is concerned with identifying opportunities for a variety of recreation experiences, through the provision of a variety of settings. LAC goes beyond ROS by specifying indicators and standards for both resource conditions and social conditions for each type of setting or zone. The requirement for monitoring commits the managing agency to specify a management response when monitoring suggests an 'unacceptable change'. Significant in the LAC process is the inclusion of 'stakeholders'—those individuals and organizations with an interest in the management of the area. These stakeholders work with the management team to determine the range of settings, indicators, standards, and management responses.

The LAC framework includes several features it shares with other VMFs:
• a problem orientation;
• an inventory of existing conditions;
• a determination of standards; and
• monitoring to see that standards are met.

Like the ROS, LAC is most appropriately used at the landscape scale. LAC, however, differs from ROS in that it is problem-oriented. This orientation is well illustrated by a LAC application in Yoho National Park (see also Elliot, 1994).

BOX 7.4 Using LAC in the Yoho Valley, Yoho National Park

When managers in Yoho National Park put controls on road access into Lake O'Hara, the result was increased traffic and use of the nearby Yoho Valley area.

The Yoho Valley offers two sorts of opportunities for heritage experiences to visitors. On the one hand, it is a frontcountry area for campers and day-visitors. On the other, it provided direct access into the backcountry of the upper Yoho River and the higher elevations beyond. More visitors congested the frontcountry area; more visitors also found their ways onto the trails leading into the backcountry, effectively producing a mixture of true backcountry users and frontcountry visitors.

Although the LAC application in Yoho was not completed, it did serve to focus managers' thinking on the ecology of the area, on the sorts of opportunities for experiences they wished for visitors there and on ways to monitor whether such experiences were being provided. Moreover, the LAC application also showed managers that social and ecological issues were linked in the Yoho Valley, allowing them to focus not only on the social but also the ecological conditions there.

Completing the LAC application in the Yoho Valley and identifying solutions to the problems occurring there would require that park managers confer with frontcountry and backcountry users to develop mutually acceptable indicators and monitoring mechanisms. This co-operative, consensual dimension of LAC marks it as radically different from ROS, and, indeed, from the other VMFs.

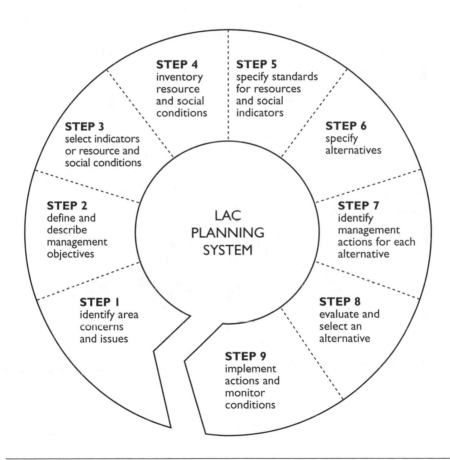

FIGURE 7.5 The Limits of Acceptable Change (LAC) planning system. SOURCE: Hendee et al. (1990).

The Visitor Experience and Resource Protection Framework

A newcomer to the VMF ranks, the Visitor Experience and Resource Protection (VERP) framework answers a need within the US National Park Service for an integrative management process (Manning, 2001; United States National Park Service, 1997a; 1997b; Manning et al., 1996a; Manning et al., 1995a; Manning et al., 1995b). The VERP framework builds on and combines several aspects of other VMFs in attempting to integrate social and ecological carrying capacity issues with appropriate indicators and standards of quality. VERP contains nine components (Manning, 2001):

BOX 7.5 Implementing VERP in Acadia National Park

Jacobi and Manning (1999) applied the Visitor Experience Resource Protection (VERP) framework in Acadia National Park where roads originally established for horse and carriage had become the focus for a variety of visitor activities. The advent of the mountain bike exacerbated an already crowded situation and threatened to create recreational conflict. Complaints to park managers cited the crowding on the carriage roads and specified behaviours (e.g., high speed by mountain bikers when among walkers) that were rude and perhaps dangerous. The persistence of the complaints and the lack of action by park managers threatened to lower the quality of the recreational experience for many visitors.

Using the VERP framework, Jacobi and Manning confirmed that the problem was one of social rather than ecological carrying capacity. The solution that VERP helped to create centred on two questions: what level of visitor experience should the park seek to attain; and, what percentage of visitors should have that level of experience. Providing a solution required that visitor experience be measured, a social science question, and that a management question, an appropriate target level for visitor experience, be determined.

The solution established a limit of 3000 users per day on the carriage road system, implying higher likelihoods of encounters at nodes and lower likelihoods along sections of the network. In addition to answering the question of crowding, this limit would reduce the probability of conflict. However, additional indicators were designed for anti-social behaviours, affording another means to evaluate the success of the solution. Monitoring, the authors emphasize, is a critical activity to ensure the quality of the visitor experience.

Step 1. Assemble a project team, consisting of planners, managers, and researchers.

Step 2. Develop a public involvement strategy.

Step 3. Develop clear statements of park purposes, significance, and primary interpretive themes. This step sets the stage for the rest of the process.

Step 4. Map and analyze the park's important resources and potential visitor experiences.

Step 5. Identify potential management zones that cover the range of desired resource and social conditions consistent with the park's purpose.

Step 6. Apply the potential management zones on the ground to identify a proposed plan and alternatives. The park's purpose, significant resources, and existing infrastructure are included at this stage of analysis.

Step 7. Select indicators of quality and associated standards for each zone. A monitoring plan is developed at this stage.

Step 8. Park staff compares desired conditions with existing conditions to address discrepancies.

Step 9. Identify management strategies to address discrepancies (see Table 7.1).

Strategies should favour indirect techniques where possible. Monitoring of conditions is ongoing.

The relationship between VERP and carrying capacity is unequivocal: 'According to current NPS [National Park Service] guidance, general management plan will qualitatively address carrying capacity by describing visitor experiences and resource conditions by zone' (United States National Park Service, 1997a: 5).

VERP shares with LAC and VIM the requirement for park managers to specify social and ecological standards, to monitor conditions, to identify problems, and to find remedial solutions.

VERP is an integrative tool and clearly applicable at both landscape and site levels, features that make it an attractive instrument for park managers. Applying VERP, however, has proven to be difficult, primarily because managers find it taxing to identify both social and ecological conditions in park zones.

While VERP has been used by park managers at Isle Royale, Acadia, and Arches National Parks in the US, it has not yet been applied in Canadian national parks.

Summary of Visitor Management Frameworks

There are several points concerning the visitor management frameworks that bear emphasizing:

- carrying capacity is at the root of all VMFs;
- LAC, VIM, and VERP incorporate the revised version of carrying capacity;
- recent VMFs incorporate social and/or ecological standards;
- recent VMFs require monitoring to track the achievement of standards;
- recent VMFs function at both the landscape and site scales; and,
- depending on the management situation, VMFs may be combined to produce a more powerful tool.

CARRYING CAPACITY AND ECOSYSTEM MANAGEMENT

The initiative to manage ecosystems in parks and protected areas can be traced to Agee and Johnson (1988) who introduced the term 'ecosystem management' and suggested what might be involved in implementing such a management philosophy (see Chapter 12). Ecosystem management raises a problem that many parks and protected area agencies have only begun to deal with: visitors. While managing visitors has certainly been a growing concern, it is clear from the frameworks discussed earlier that agencies are still searching for a method that is simple but effective. Nepstad and Nilsen (1993) make the point that any serious consideration of ecosystem management in parks and protected areas must include an understanding of human use patterns in the past and in the present. Others, such as Freemuth (1996), suggest that for ecosystem management to be effective, it will be necessary for it to reflect social values.

In Parks Canada, there is a growing realization that ecological problems in national parks are related to human uses and to facilities that support those uses both inside and outside park boundaries (Parks Canada, 1995; Page et al., 1996). Parks Canada (1999) defines ecosystem management as:

> Ecosystem management provides a conceptual and strategic basis for the protection of park ecosystems. It involves taking a more holistic view of the natural environment and ensuring that land use decisions take into consideration the complex interactions and dynamic nature of park ecosystems and their finite capacity to withstand and recover from stress induced by human activities. The shared nature of ecosystems also implies that park management will have effects on surrounding lands and their management.

Links with Ecological Carrying Capacity

Earlier, we referred to carrying capacity as defined by Shelby and Heberlein (1984: 441) as 'the level of use beyond which impacts exceed acceptable levels (our emphasis) specified by evaluative standards'. But, we may ask, Impacts upon what? Evaluative standards about what? Parks Canada has answered these questions by referring to the National Parks Act and National Parks Policy (Department of Canadian Heritage, 1994), which direct the agency to place ecological integrity at the top of a list of several goals. Parks Canada has made progress not only in defining ecological integrity but also in recognizing that the ecological integrity of national parks will be affected by circumstances specific to each park. Assessing ecological integrity in a national park entails examining three broad indicators: biodiversity, ecosystem functions, and stressors (Parks Canada, 1998c: 24). Using these indicators, the most recent State of the Parks Report available assigns an overall ecological integrity rating to national parks: Vuntut National Park has a ranking of 1, indicating a high level of integrity; Gros Morne National Park, at 3, receives a moderate ranking; Point Pelee National Park, at 5, shows the effects of its small size and its location in a highly developed agricultural region.

Links with Social Carrying Capacity

National parks are about more than ecological integrity. People look to national parks for recreation opportunities and national park managers attempt not only to accommodate visitors but also to attract them. The same questions about impacts and evaluative standards may be asked here with respect to social carrying capacity. The answers to these questions, however, are not nearly as forthcoming as they are in reference to ecological carrying capacity.

By categorizing 'human land-use patterns', including 'land use maps, roads, densities, [and] population densities' as stressors (Parks Canada, 1998c: 24), two things are apparent. In the first place, Parks Canada does not have a precise understanding of human use. Such factors certainly are part of human use, but so too are numbers of visitors, their activities (and especially the technologies associated with them), and the areas where visitor activities occur. In the second place, the formulation may suit ecological carrying capacity to a degree, but it not does not address social carrying capacity at all.

The Shelby/Heberlein suggestions for carrying capacity include both ecological and social variations. Under social carrying capacity, impacts could be impacts of one group of visitors on another group; evaluative standards could be those that direct managers towards providing certain experiences in opportunities, facilities, programs, and services. Earlier, a review of visitor management frameworks indicated how well ingrained the Shelby/Heberlein suggestions were in several frameworks. Neither the frameworks nor the Shelby/Heberlein suggestions seem to fit particularly well into Parks Canada's version of ecosystem management. Data and information on human use is not available or not used to set social standards; and, no evaluations are carried out to determine whether those standards are met. Parks Canada's use of visitor management frameworks has not progressed to this level.

Moreover, while the nature of ecological data and information needed to support ecosystem management is clear, the same is not true of human use data. The issue of human use data has received some attention in Canada and internationally (Machlis, 1995; Hornback et al., 1997; Payne, 1997), but those discussions seem not to be reflected well in the current Parks Canada efforts.

In short, there is nothing in the Shelby/Heberlein formulation that discriminates against social carrying capacity or in favour of ecological carrying capacity. The approach, inherent in several of the visitor management frameworks, is not applied in its entirety in the Parks Canada formulation of ecosystem management.

Integrating Social and Ecological Dimensions

Merely stating that ' . . . people are part of ecosystems and [that] human conditions are shaped by, and in turn, shape ecosystems' (Driver et al., 1995) is not enough if that truth is not reflected in management frameworks and practices. Concern about the lack of integration of the social and ecological dimensions of managing parks and protected areas is hardly a recent dilemma. In their paper, Driver and his associates propose a framework that bears a strong resemblance to the Shelby/Heberlein carrying capacity formulation. The key, in their view, is maintaining a focus upon a particular area—perhaps a greater park ecosystem (e.g., Central Rockies Ecosystem; Greater Yellowstone Ecosystem). Such a (large-scale) spatial focus forces managers to consider ecological and social facts together.

Several examples of human use of particular spatial units are readily available. In Banff National Park, area planning utilizes grizzly bear habitat areas as critical spatial units. In Yoho National Park, grizzly bear-human contacts in the Lake O'Hara area forced Parks Canada to go beyond monitoring to examine the social and ecological dimensions of this problem and to suggest solutions (Petersen, 1998). Wright and Clarkson (1995) discuss a study of recreation use on major rivers in Jasper National Park designed to determine ecological impacts of human use and to discover the extent to which such riverine activities contribute to visitors' understanding, appreciation, and enjoyment of their national park visits. Both studies address the reality facing park managers: understanding ecological impacts is not sufficient; human use must be understood as well before managers respond. In developing responses, managers also need to consider an array of direct and indirect strategies with carrying capacity being only one part of a solution

These examples represent particular problems in two national parks. To suggest that they might guide management actions in other national parks might be placing too

FIGURE 7.6 Recreational conflicts occur when different activities, such as fly fishing and kayaking, come into contact. *Photo: Jim Butler.*

much weight on the specifics of the situations. However, it is important to point out that the spatial focus in each case forced ecological and social factors to be considered together rather than separately. Managers might make use of similar spatial contexts in integrating these two dimensions. The zones in park management plans come to mind as appropriate spatial units upon which such integration might be focused.

CONCLUSION

This chapter began as an attempt to come to terms with carrying capacity, a very attractive idea in the parks and protected areas field. Carrying capacity was shown to be complex, including variations such as ecological, social, and design carrying capacity. These most popular variations address different but related aspects of the human use of parks and protected areas. In the academic literature, social carrying capacity has received the largest share of study. Ecological carrying capacity in contrast has become a form of environmental impact assessment. More than 30 years of academic and practical work has determined that if carrying capacity is to be a useful tool in a park manager's arsenal, it is necessary to recognize that it has both a scientific and a value basis. It is the latter of these that has frightened managers away. In its modern form, carrying capacity may offer an opportunity to confront the protection-use dilemma that is at the heart of managing parks and protected areas.

An investigation into the relationship between carrying capacity and visitor management frameworks (VMFs) revealed that several of the VMFs cover both ecological and social carrying capacity. Moreover, these frameworks operate from the same bases as the modern version of carrying capacity. The relationships between carrying capacity and the various visitor management frameworks discussed was demonstrated to be close.

Finally, carrying capacity was considered in relation to ecosystem management, a new paradigm in the management of parks and protected areas. Ecological carrying capacity fits very well into current ecosystem management formulations. Social carrying capacity, on the other hand, fits poorly, not because of any inherent difficulties in the modern carrying capacity model, but rather because the formulation of ecosystem management treats human use as a stressor and as nothing more.

REFERENCES

Agee, J.K., and D.R. Johnson. 1988. *Ecosystem Management for Parks and Wilderness*. Seattle: University of Washington Press.

Becker, R., A. Jubenville, G.W. Burnett, and A.R. Graef. 1984. 'Fact and judgement in the search for a social carrying capacity', *Leisure Sciences* 6, 4: 475–86.

Botkin, D.B. 1990. *Discordant Harmonies: A New Ecology for the Twenty-first Century*. New York: Oxford University Press.

Butler, R., D.A. Fennell, and S.W. Boyd. 1993. *Canadian Heritage Rivers System Recreational Carrying Capacity Study*. Ottawa: Canadian Parks Service.

Canadian Parks Service. 1986. *In Trust for Tomorrow: A Management Framework for Four Mountain Parks*. Ottawa: Supply and Services Canada.

Canestrelli, E., and P. Costa. 1991. 'Tourist Carrying Capacity: A Fuzzy Approach', *Annals of Tourism Research* 18, 2: 295–311.

Clark, R.N., and G.H. Stankey. 1979. *The Recreation Opportunity Spectrum: A Framework for Planning, Management and Research*. Seattle: Pacific Northwest Research Station, USDA Forest Service, General Technical Report PNW-98.

——— and ———. 1990. 'The Recreation Opportunity Spectrum: A Framework for Planning, Management and Research', in Graham and Lawrence (1990: 127–58).

Cole, D.N., M.E. Petersen, and R.C. Lucas. 1987 *Managing Wilderness Recreation Use: Common Problems and Potential Solutions*. Ogden, Utah: Intermountain Research Station, USDA Forest Service, General Technical Report INT-230.

Department of Canadian Heritage. 1994. *Parks Canada: Guiding Principles and Operational Policies*. Ottawa: Supply and Services Canada.

Driver, B.L. 1990. 'Recreation Opportunity Spectrum: Basic Concepts and Use in Land Management Planning', in Graham and Lawrence (1990: 159–83).

———, P.J. Brown, G.H. Stankey, and T.G. Gregoire. 1987. 'The ROS Planning System: Evolution, Basic Concepts and Research Needs', *Leisure Sciences* 9: 201–12.

———, C.H. Manning, and G.R. Super. 1995. 'Integrating the Social and Biophysical Components of Sustainable Ecosystems Management', in J.E. Thompson, ed., *Analysis in Support of Ecosystem Management*. Ecosystem Management Analysis Center, USDA Forest Service, Washington, DC.

Drysdale, C. 1995. 'Coordinated Ecological Research and Monitoring Systems: The Kejimkujik Model', in Herman, Bondrup-Nielsen, Willison, and Munro (1995: 180–7).

Duffus, D.A., and P. Dearden. 1990. 'Non-consumptive Wildlife Oriented Recreation: A Conceptual Framework', *Biological Conservation* 53: 213–31.

——— and ———. 1993. 'Killer Whales, Science and Protected Area Management in British Columbia', *The George Wright Forum* 9: 79–87.

Elliot, T.E. 1994. 'Attitudes toward Limiting Overnight Use of the Chilkoot Trail National Historic Site', MSc. thesis, University of Montana.

Freemuth, J. 1996. 'The Emergence of Ecosystem Management: Reinterpreting the Gospel?', *Society and Natural Resources* 9, 4: 411–17.

Giongo, F., J. Bosco-Nizeye, and G.N. Wallace. 1993. *A Study of Visitor Management in the World's National Parks and Protected Areas*. Fort Collins: Colorado State University.

Graefe, A.R. 1990. 'Visitor Impact Management', in Graham and Lawrence (1990: 213–34).

———, F.R. Kuss, and J.J Vaske. 1990a. *Visitor Impact Management: A Review of Research*. National Parks and Conservation Association, vol.1, Washington, DC.

———, ———, and ———. 1990b. *Visitor Impact Management: The Planning Framework*. National Parks and Conservation Association,vol. 2, Washington, DC.

Graham, R., and R. Lawrence, eds. 1990. *Towards Serving Visitors and Managing Our Resources*. Waterloo, Ont.: Tourism Research and Education Centre, University of Waterloo and Canadian Parks Service, Environment Canada.

Heberlein, T.A., G.E. Alfano, and J.J. Vaske. 1986. 'Using a Social Carrying Capacity Model to Estimate the Effects of Marina Development at the Apostle Islands National Lakeshore', *Leisure Sciences* 8, 3: 257–74.

Hendee, J.C., G.H. Stankey, and R.C. Lucas. 1990. *Wilderness Management*, 2nd edn. Golden, Colo.: Fulcrum Publishing.

Herman, T., S. Bondrup-Neilsen, J.H.M. Willison, and N.W.P Munro, eds. 1995. *Ecosystem Monitoring and Protected Areas: Proceedings of the Second International Conference on Science and the Management of Protected Areas*. Wolfville, NS: Science and the Management of Protected Areas Association and the Centre for Wildlife and Conservation Biology, Acadia University.

Hornback, K., N. McIntyre, and P.F.J. Eagles. 1997. *Best Practice Guidelines for Public Use Measurement and Reporting at Parks and Protected Areas*. Gland: World Commission on Protected Areas, IUCN.

International Institute for Sustainable Development. 1995. Carrying Capacity. <http//:www.iisd.org/ic/info/ss9506.htm>

Jacobi, C., and R. Manning. 1999. 'Crowding and Conflict on the Carriage Roads of Acadia National Park: An application of the Visitor Experience and Resource Protection Framework', *Park Science* 19, 2: 22–6.

Kacki, N., and K. Walker. 1999. *Status of Human Use Management Initiatives in Parks Canada*. Ecosystem Management Branch, Hull, Que.: Parks Canada.

Knopf, Richard C. 1990. 'The Limits of Acceptable Change (LAC) Planning Process: Potentials and Limitations', in Graham and Lawrence (1990: 201–11).

Lime, D.W., S.F. McCool, and D.P. Galvin. 1995. 'Trends in Congestion and Crowding at Recreation Sites', in J. Thompson, D.W. Lime, B. Gartner, and W.M. Sames, comps, *Proceedings of the Fourth International Outdoor Recreation and Tourism Trends Symposium and the 1995 National Recreation Resources Planning Conference*. St Paul: University of Minnesota Press, 87–96.

Machlis, G.E. 1995. *Usable Knowledge: A Plan for Social Science and the National Parks*. Washington: US National Park Service.

Manning, R.E., 2001. 'Visitor Experience and Resource Protection: A Framework for Managing the Carrying Capacity for National Parks', *Journal of Park and Recreation Administration* 19, 1: 93–108.

———, N.L. Ballinger, J. Marion, and J. Roggenbuck. 1996a. 'Recreation Management in Natural Areas: Problems and Practices;, *Natural Areas Journal* 16, 2: 142–6.

Manning, R.E., D.W. Lime, M. Hof, and W. Freimund. 1995a. 'The Visitor Experience and Resource Protection (VERP) Process: The Application of Carrying Capacity to Arches National Park', *The George Wright Forum* 12, 3: 41–5.

———, ———, ———, and ———. 1995b. 'The Carrying Capacity of National Parks: Theory and Application', in J. Thompson, D.W. Lime, B. Gartner, and W.M. Sames, eds, *Innovations and Challenges in the Management of Visitor Opportunities in Parks and Protected Areas*. Waterloo, Ont.: Heritage Resources Centre, University of Waterloo, Occasional Paper #26, 9–21.

McCool, S.F. 1990a. 'Limits of Acceptable Change: Evolution and Future', in Graham and Lawrence (1990: 185–93).

———.1990b. 'Limits of Acceptable Change: Some Principles', in Graham and Lawrence (1990: 195–200).

Munro, N.W.P, and J.H.M. Willison, eds. 1998. *Linking Protected Areas with Working Landscapes Conserving Biodiversity*. Wolfville, NS: Science and the Management of Protected Areas Association.

Nelson, J.G. 1968. 'Man and Landscape Change in Banff National Park: A National Park Problem in Perspective', in Nelson, ed., *Canadian Parks in Perspective*. Montreal: Harvest House, 63–96.

Nepstad, E., and P. Nilsen. 1993. 'Towards a Better Understanding of Human/Environment Relationships in Canadian National Parks', Ottawa: Supply and Services Canada, National Parks Occasional Paper No. 5.

Nilsen, P., and G. Tayler. 1998. 'A Comparative Analysis of Human Use Planning and Management Frameworks', in Munro and Willison (1998: 861–74).

Page, R.S., Bayley, D. Cook, J. Green, and B. Ritchie. 1996. *Banff-Bow Valley: At the Crossroads*. Hull, Que.: Supply and Services Canada.

Parks Canada. 1994a. *Park Management Guidelines: Pacific Rim National Park Reserve*.

———. 1994b. *Guiding Principles and Operational Policies*. Ottawa: Minister of Supply and Services Canada.

———. 1994c. *A Proposed Framework for Assessing the Appropriateness of Recreation Activities in Protected Heritage Areas*. Ottawa: Department of Canadian Heritage.

———. 1995. *State of the Parks: 1994 Report*. Ottawa: Department of Canadian Heritage.

———. 1998b. *Parks Canada Visitor Risk Management Handbook*. Available at: <http://parkscanada.pch.gc.ca/library/risk/english/tdmvrme.html>.

———. 1998c. *State of the Parks: 1997 Report*. Ottawa: Department of Canadian Heritage.

———. 1999. Ecosystem Management. Available at: <http://parkscanada.pch.gc.ca/natress/ENV_CON/ECO_MAN/ECO_MANE.HTM>.

Payne, R.J. 1997. *Visitor Information Management in Canada's National Parks*. Ottawa: Natural Resources Branch, Parks Canada.

———, A.P. Carr, and E. Cline. 1997. 'Applying the Recreation Opportunity Spectrum (ROS) for Visitor Opportunity Assessment in Two National Parks: A Demonstration Project', Natural Resources Branch, Parks Canada, Occasional Paper No. 8.

——— and R. Graham. 1993. 'Visitor Planning and Management in Parks and Protected Areas', in P. Dearden and R. Rollins, eds, *Parks and Protected Areas in Canada: Planning and Management*. Toronto: University of Toronto Press, 185–210.

Petersen, D. 1998. 'Allocation of Land Resources between Competing Species—Humans and Grizzly Bears in the Lake O'Hara Area of Yoho National Park, in Munro, Willison, and. Martin (1998: 478–91).

Rees, W.E. 1997. *Revisiting Carrying Capacity: Area-Based Indicators of Sustainability*. Available at: <http://dieoff.org/page110.htm>.

Schreyer, R. 1990. 'Conflict in Outdoor Recreation: The Scope of the Challenge to Resource Planning and Management', in J. Vining, ed., *Social Science and Natural Resource Recreation Management*. Boulder, Colo.: Westview Press, 13–31.

Shelby, B., and T.A. Heberlein. 1984. 'A Conceptual Framework for Carrying Capacity Determination', *Leisure Sciences* 6, 4: 433–51.

——— and ———.1986. *Carrying Capacity in Recreational Settings*. Corvallis: Oregon State University Press.

———, J.J. Vaske, and M.P. Donelly. 1996. 'Norms, standards, and natural resouces', *Leisure Sciences* 18, 2: 103–23.

Stankey, G.H. 1973.'Visitor perception of wilderness recreation carrying capacity', research paper INT-142. Ogden, Utah: USDA Forest Service, Intermountain Forest and Range Experimental Station.

————, D.N. Cole, R.C. Lucas, G.L. Peterson, and S. Frissel. 1985. *The Limits of Acceptable Change System for Wilderness Planning*. Ogden, Utah: USDA Forest Service, Intermountain Research Station, General Technical Report INT-176.

————and S.F. McCool. 1989. 'Beyond Social Carrying Capacity', in E.L. Jackson and T.L Burton, eds, *Understanding Leisure and Recreation: Mapping the Past, Charting the Future*. State College, Penn.: Venture Publishing.

United States National Park Service. 1997a. *VERP: A Summary of the Visitor Experience and Resource Protection (VERP) Framework*. Denver: Denver Service Center, US Department of the Interior.

————. 1997b. *The Visitor Experience and Resource Protection (VERP) Framework: A Handbook for Planners and Managers*. Denver: Denver Service Center, US Department of the Interior.

Vaske, J.J. 1994. *Social Carrying Capacity at the Columbia Icefield: Applying the Visitor Impact Management Framework*. Ottawa: Parks Canada, Department of Canadian Heritage.

————, B. Shelby, A.R. Graefe, and T.A. Heberlein. 1986. 'Backcountry Encounter Norms: Theory, Method and Empirical Evidence', *Journal of Leisure Research* 18, 3: 137–53.

Wagar, J.S. 1964. *The Carrying Capacity of Wild Lands for Recreation*. Washington: Society of America Foresters, Forest Science Monograph 7.

————. 1974. 'Recreational Carrying Capacity Reconsidered', Journal of Forestry 72: 274–8.

Washburne, R.F. 1982. 'Wilderness Recreational Carrying Capacity: Are Numbers Necessary?', *Journal of Forestry* 80, 11: 726–8.

Williams, P.W., and A. Gill. 1991. *Carrying Capacity Management in Tourism Settings: A Tourism Growth Management Process*. Tourism Development Agency, Alberta Economic Development, Edmonton. Available at: <http://www.gov.ab.ca/edt/tda/capmgment.htm>.

Wright, P.A., and P. Clarkson. 1995. 'Recreation Impacts on River Ecosystems: Assessing the Impacts of River Use on the Biophysical and Social Environment', in Herman, Bondrup-Neilsen, Willison, and Munro (1995: 299–303).

Yoho National Park. 1997. *Lake O'Hara Trail Monitoring Program*. Available at: <http://www.worldweb.com/ParksCanada-Yoho/TrailMonitor/English/index.htm>.

KEY WORDS/CONCEPTS

tragedy of the commons
limits to growth
carrying capacity
physical carrying capacity
ecological carrying capacity
social carrying capacity
acceptable change
visual impact
wilderness
encounter norms
recreation conflict

Recreation Opportunity Spectrum (ROS)
Visitor Activity Management Process
  (VAMP)
Visitor Impact Management (VIM)
Limits of Acceptable Change (LAC)
Visitor Experience and Resource
Protection Framework (VERP)
direct management strategies
indirect management strategies
ecological integrity
ecosystem management

STUDY QUESTIONS

1. Discuss the confusion that sometimes occurs between visual impacts and ecological impacts (ecological integrity).
2. Compare 'design carrying capacity', 'ecological carrying capacity', and 'social carrying capacity'.
3. 'Ecological carrying capacity has not been seriously applied in parks and protected areas'. Discuss.
4. Compare 'indirect management actions' with 'direct management actions'. Which approaches do you think would work best in a national park, and why?
5. Compare ROS and carrying capacity.
6. Compare VAMP and carrying capacity.
7. Compare LAC and carrying capacity.
8. Compare VIM and carrying capacity.
9. Compare VERP and carrying capacity.
10. Compare VAMP and ROS.
11. Examine the National Park Zoning system, and compare this with the approach to zoning developed within ROS.
12. A significant component of LAC is the inclusion of 'stakeholders' as part of the planning process. Discuss strengths and weaknesses of this approach. What other forms of public participation are possible? Discuss strengths and weaknesses of each.
13. Examine a park management plan of your choice, and outline the extent to which the plan uses visitor management concepts described in this chapter. Critique the visitor management strategies described in the plan.

CHAPTER 8

Interpretation and Environmental Education

James R. Butler & Glen T. Hvenegaard

Get as near the heart of the world as I can.
—John Muir, 1871

INTRODUCTION

Interpretation and environmental education have been fundamental to the original concept of national parks and wilderness protection. At first, energetic volunteers led nature walks and gave interpretive talks. Later, forward-thinking administrators facilitated the hiring of interpreters in parks and laid the organizational foundation for interpretation throughout the park system. Today, interpretation, in its many forms, is employed in almost all protected areas, providing important benefits to visitors, the natural environment, and the park agency. This chapter traces the history of interpretation in North America, highlighting important trends, definitions, and principles, and examines, with Canadian and international examples, how interpretation improves environmental protection and visitor experiences.

ORIGINS

The first appeal for a 'Nation's Park' in 1833 by American artist George Catlin, who called for an area 'preserved for its freshness of nature's beauty', included the assumption that the area would have to be understood to be appreciated. This implication was reaffirmed by Nathaniel P. Langford, co-leader of the Yellowstone expedition, which in 1870 led to the establishment of Yellowstone National Park. As Langford wrote, 'while you see and wonder, you seem to need an additional sense, fully to comprehend and believe'.

During this same period, a then little-known sawmill operator in the Yosemite Valley by the name of John Muir was diversifying his income by leading early park tourists on nature hikes. One of his followers wrote, 'Never was there a naturalist who could hold his hearers so well, and none had so much to tell.' Influenced by the wilderness of Yosemite, Muir would find his niche as an influential spokesman for wilder-

FIGURE 8.1 Visitor scanning for wildlife, Firth River, Vuntut National Park. 'Interpretation should fill visitors with a greater sense of wonder and curiosity.' *Photo: P. Dearden.*

ness preservation. While working in the Yosemite Valley, Muir would hone his interpretive skills and his understanding of the ecology and dynamics of wildland ecosystems. He wrote during this time, 'I'll interpret the rocks, learn the language of flood, storm and avalanche. I'll acquaint myself with the glaciers and wild gardens, and get as near the heart of the world as I can.' As far as we know this was the first use of the word interpret in a park context.

James Harkin, the first Director of Canada's Dominion Parks Branch (Chapter 2), was an admirer of Muir and used his words in Canada's first national parks policy documents and annual reports, to clarify the value of wilderness and the philosophy and purpose of national parks (Hendersen, 1994). Harkin considered national parks to be 'outdoor museums', suggesting their important interpretive value (Taylor, 1997).

The fundamental role for interpretation in national parks was reaffirmed when the US National Parks Service was established as a distinct bureau, five years after the Dominion Parks Branch in Canada, to supervise and formalize policies for America's first national parks. The report on the establishment of this agency and its first uniform policies in 1916 (written by R.B. Marshall) stated that national parks were not designed solely for the purpose of recreation; they also possess an educational value that cannot be estimated. In his initial annual report, the US Park Service's new director, Stephen T. Mather, further emphasized this final point: 'One of the chief functions of the national parks and monuments is to serve educational purposes.'

FIGURE 8.2 An interpreter interacts with his audience on Bonaventure Island, Quebec. *Photo: G. Hvenegaard.*

Returning east by railroad in 1919, Mather made a special trip from Yosemite to stop at Lake Tahoe to investigate some interpretive programs in progress at the Fallen Leaf Lodge (Weaver, 1982). Filled with the frustrations of managing the challenges and threats to the fragile Yosemite environment, his attention was drawn to the popularity of interpretive presentations at the lodge by Professors Harold C. Bryant and Loye H. Miller from the University of California. They were part of a fresh initiative only a few weeks old, being conducted in co-operation with the California Nature Study League and the State Fish and Game Commission. They were assisted in this program by a Sacramento patron, Mr C.M. Goethe, who had been impressed by the interpretative guides he had met on vacation in Europe. Mather, upon observing the success of this program, responded with such enthusiasm that he wanted to move the entire show immediately to Yosemite. He was told that none of this could happen until the next summer. All parties agreed and the following summer, Miller and colleague, Harold Bryant, became the first park naturalists employed by a government agency, working in Yosemite. Private interpretive programs had already begun within the national parks in a more informal manner, and Mather in his 1919 annual report specifically mentioned eight instances of campfire education already underway that summer (Shankland, 1970). Thus began a tradition that would, in spite of wavering commitments and administrative cutbacks, continue within American and Canadian national parks to the present time.

SHIFTS IN EMPHASIS

Since the 1920s, interpretation in parks has become considerably more sophisticated in planning and technological applications, and eventually in systems planning and interagency co-operation and co-ordination (Box 8.1). Important shifts in interpretive focus over this period may be divided into three phases. In phase one (beginning with the earliest interpretive programs), park interpretation was concerned with acquainting visitors with the natural features in the park, often the most dramatic, majestic, and exceptional. The emphasis was in providing explanations for these phenomenon, often as examples of the wonders of God's creation.

BOX 8.1 History of Park Interpretation in North America

1784   First natural history museum to utilize interpretive techniques opens in Philadelphia, with Charles Wilson Peale exhibiting wildlife collections from the American west.

1869   First park interpretive book, The Yosemite Guidebook, is published by California State Geologist, J.D. Whitney.

1870s   John Muir leads groups on interpretive hikes into Yosemite backcountry.

1887   Scottish caretaker and guide, David Galletly, conducts visitors through the lower Hot Spring cave, Banff. These are the first formal interpretive walks conducted by an interpreter in a Canadian national park.

1889   Enos Mills, the father of nature guiding, formalizes and teaches principles of nature guiding in Rocky Mountain National Park, Colorado. He later wrote *Adventures of a Nature Guide and Essays in Interpretation*.

1895   First park interpretive museum, and first museum in any national park, is established at Banff.

1904   First park interpretive trail is established at Yosemite; Lt. Pipes of the Army Medical Corps establishes a trail with labelled trees and other plants.

1905   C.H. Deutschman, who discovered Nakimu Caves in Glacier National Park, British Columbia, begins to conduct visitors through the cave system.

1911   Evening campfire programs and tours of park features are well established in several Canadian and US national parks, but all are conducted by concessions.

1914   First Canadian National Park interpretive publications appear in Banff.

1915   Esther Burnell Estes becomes first licensed woman interpreter in the US.

1918   US establishes its first park museum in Mesa Verde, Colorado, with exhibits and lectures given; the next museum opens in 1921, in Yosemite.

1919   Nature guiding becomes popular in Rocky Mountain resorts in US. Steven Mather, Director of US Parks Service, institutionalizes interpretation in the US national parks system.

1920	First US Park Service interpretive programs begin with government-employed interpreters in Yosemite and Yellowstone.
1929	First seasonal interpretive programs begin in the Rocky Mountain National Parks of Canada, with the appointment of J. Hamilton Laing.
1931	Grey Owl employed as interpreter by Parks Canada at Riding Mountain, Manitoba; later transferred to Prince Albert, Saskatchewan.
1944	Early interpretive events conducted in Banff; wildlife warden, Hubert Green, feeds aspen cuttings to beavers of Vermilion Lakes before 25–30 tourists nightly while discussing beaver life history.
1954	Interpretive programs begin in provincial parks of Ontario.
1958	First co-ordinated interpretive service established in Ottawa for Canada's national park system.
1964	First permanent naturalists located in Canadian Rocky Mountain national parks.
1969	First Canadian wildlife interpretation centre opens at Wye Marsh, near Midland, Ontario.
1983	Hector Ceballos-Lescuráin, a naturalist tour operator in Mexico, coins 'ecotourism' (ecology-based tourism promoting positive environmental ethics). This preferred form of tourism for parks and nature reserves will soon grow to be the fastest-rising sector of the tourism industry. There will soon be more employment opportunities for interpreters in the private sector of the tourism industry than in the public sector of parks, forests, and urban nature centres (the former principal employment source).
1985	A national Canadian assembly on national parks and protected areas, formed to mark the Centennial of Canada's national parks, encourages the development of more interpretive programs.
1988–1994	Governmental downsizing efforts result in drastic budget cuts for interpretive staff and services in Canada's national parks.
1990s	Scattered attempts to 'privatize' interpretive services, particularly in provincial parks. Quality of services and professionalism decline. Important 'windows of opportunity' are lost or diminished to reach thousands of visitors whosupport protected area initiatives.
1991	The Canadian Environmental Advisory Council (1991) advises Parks Canada to dedicate more resources to support interpretation and education programs that increase public awareness of the intrinsic values of protected areas.
2000	Panel on the Ecological Integrity of Canada's National Parks recommends that interpretation have ecological integrity as its core purpose and that interpretive funding in national parks be doubled.

In phase two (during an era of higher ecological awareness, beginning in the late 1950s and early 1960s), interpretation expanded to stress interrelationships, ecology, and the landscape in general, even when these were less dramatic than high-profile features like hot springs or waterfalls. Management issues also received greater attention. Communication was focused, however, only on what existed within the park boundary.

Phase three was defined by an expansion of park interpretation to foster a broader environmental consciousness among park visitors and the public at large. This involved a shift from an internal, within-the-frame viewpoint to a greater external awareness of the ecosystems surrounding the park. This phase was influenced greatly by the photograph of earth from outer space in 1969, the emergence of the green peace movement, and by heightened interest in ecology and ecosystems in general. This was also a period when environmental education emerged as an important and critical interdisciplinary subject taught in school systems throughout North America.

This new 'ecological mission' of park interpretation, with its shift of emphasis from the park in isolation to ecological perspectives beyond the limits of the park boundary, paralleled the development of several new policy and management perspectives that were occurring in national parks as part of a redefinition of their role in society as critical and important ecological landscapes. The 'new' ecological interpretation affirmed the perspective that national parks, which had come to be revered as benchmarks of the natural environment (to be compared and contrasted to landscapes where renewable resource activities such as logging are undertaken), cannot survive independent of the surrounding landscapes. A federal vehicle was needed to reach the public in a campaign to support a national environmental strategy, and national park visitors were recognized as a more highly educated segment of the population, with greater receptivity to environmental education and a disproportionately higher influence on decision-making. Untouched national park environments were recognized as one possible basis for building a new philosophy and ethical system with park interpretation as the key communication tool. Such a reorientation, although a long-term goal, was recognized by many as critical to the protection of the ecological integrity of national parks and, by association, of the larger environment.

This federal responsibility was well expressed by Parks Canada (1997: 1): 'In a world of rapid change, our parks, historic sites, and marine conservation areas are seen as models of environmental stewardship and as an important legacy to be preserved for future generations. They represent one of the most positive, tangible and enduring demonstrations of the federal government's commitment to the environment'.

DEFINITION AND PURPOSE OF PARK INTERPRETATION

In addition to its historical roots, the role of park interpretation is shaped by legal and policy documents as well as visitors' needs and interests. In legislation, national parks are for the 'benefit, education and enjoyment' of the people of Canada (Government of Canada, 1990). The National Parks Policy further outlines the goals, methods, content, and target audiences of interpretation (Parks Canada, 1994: 37). Specifically, the national parks are to provide programs to encourage and assist Canadians in 'understanding, appreciating, enjoying and protecting their national parks'.

Interpretation should provide essential facts about the area, its program, and its facilities, and to help the visitor understand, appreciate, and enjoy not only nature but the area as a whole. By doing so, interpretation helps to minimize uncertainty and to maximize opportunity for visitors. A well-rounded interpretation program serves to awaken public awareness of park purposes and policies and strives to develop not only a concern for preservation but a different approach to life.

The general model of the interpretation-protection interface begins with awareness and progresses from insight to knowledge, understanding, appreciation, respect, love, and, finally, to preservation (Canadian Environmental Advisory Council, 1991; Parks Canada, 1998a). Thus, interpretation is not the mere transfer of information to others, nor is it only a catalogue of things to see and do. Interpretation should fill visitors with a greater sense of wonder and curiosity. It should leave the visitor both better informed and with a desire to know more. Finally, interpretation should provide challenges or opportunities to act upon this new-found sense of respect, so that the ecological integrity of national parks and the surrounding environments will benefit.

The degree to which a visitor enjoys and values his or her experience in a park depends largely upon the individual's perception of that area's environment. For this reason, interpretive approaches should be designed to enhance the visitor's perception of these landscapes and ultimately to be a positive influence on the interactions between visitor and the ecosystem.

Tilden (1977: 8) first defined interpretation as 'an educational activity which aims to reveal meanings and relationships through the use of original objects, by firsthand experience, and by illustrative media, rather than simply to communicate factual information'. Interpretation in parks differs from information in that it deals with meanings and relationships as well as with hard facts, although informational publications and signs are, of course, important components of park interpretation. A number of similar definitions exist (see Sharpe, 1982), but typically embrace the following attributes generally found within all interpretive services:

1. It is on-site, emphasizing first-hand experiences with the natural environment (e.g., a park interpretive centre will introduce, clarify, and direct the visitor to the outdoors for direct interactions between visitors and the park environment, unlike a museum in the city, which functions as the destination).
2. It is an informal form of education (i.e., interpretation does not employ a rigid, classroom-style approach).
3. It deals with a voluntary, non-captive audience (i.e., visitors participate by choice during their leisure time).
4. Visitors normally have an expectation of gratification (i.e., they want to be rewarded or to have a need or want satisfied).

5. It is inspirational and motivational in nature (i.e., interpretation does not present just factual information).
6. Its goals are expansion of knowledge, shifts in attitude, and alterations in behaviour of visitors (i.e., visitors should increase their understanding of and their appreciation and respect for the park environment).
7. It is an extrinsic activity (e.g., an interpretive sign or exhibit along the trail side, which are not natural or innate to the setting), based on the intrinsic values of the landscape (e.g., a waterfall, a calypso orchid, or the song of a red-eyed vireo). Interpretation facilitates understanding, appreciation, and protection of the park's intrinsic landscape values.

COMMUNICATION AND LEARNING PRINCIPLES

Interpretation is simply one specific expression of a much broader realm of communications critical to the management and planning of all parks and protected areas. Other important realms of communication involve internal communications with agency staff, emergency information procedures, and other forms directed to the external public through planned publicity, advertising, research, working through the print and electronic media, public participation processes, and dealing with the ominous presence of what has come to be termed biopolitics. Communication has been described as 'the successful transmission of thoughts or ideas, without significant distortion, so that understanding is achieved' (Fazio and Gilbert, 1981: 77).

Interpretation in protected areas is both a science and an art. As a science, it relies on proven learning principles and current understanding in psychology, sociology, communications, and education; it requires familiarity with the area's people and with the motivations of visitors. In addition, it must communicate to the public about such areas as geology, palaeontology, anthropology, geography, zoology, and botany. This combination of natural and social sciences is applied in a park setting.

Art enters the picture during the stage of interacting with the audience. The process, procedures, and rationale for selecting a given concept may be based in the sciences, but the effective communication and presentation of that concept requires art. Elements such as drama, visual design, and music improve visual and verbal communications. Sometimes complex relationships can be introduced in an entertaining fashion in order to arouse the visitor's interest; more refined treatments of specific concepts may then follow. Because interpretation involves meanings and relationships, it strives for a holistic approach rather than merely presenting isolated facts.

Since audiences are seldom homogeneous, interpretation must appeal to visitors of all ages and backgrounds, experiences, and personalities. For example, Stewart et al. (1998) suggest at least a four-part typology of potential users of interpretive sources: (1) seekers, who actively search for interpretation sources; (2) stumblers, who come across interpretation sources by accident; (3) shadowers, who are chaperoned by other people through interpretation sources; and (4) shunners, who either avoid or are uninterested in interpretation. Each type of interpretive user poses unique

FIGURE 8.3 Living interpretation at one of Canada's most famous sites, the fortress of Louisbourg, Nova Scotia. *Photo: G. Hvenegaard.*

challenges and opportunities to interpretive planners and staff. This may require a variety of interpretive programming strategies to reach a variety of audiences on a variety of levels. Knowing the characteristics of park visitors requires well-planned and executed research.

Important communication principles have been summarized by Dick et al. (1974), Sharpe (1982), and Beck and Cable (1998). Communication, and the tendency to change opinion, will be improved by understanding and integrating three components of the interpretive experience: the communicator, the message, and the receiver. First, communication is improved if the communicator is well-informed, intelligent, and trust-worthy; is well-liked; states an opinion in agreement with the receiver; gets and holds the attention of the receiver; and uses credible sources. As one example, Manfredo and Bright (1991) found that users of the Boundary Waters Canoe Area Wilderness were more persuaded by information packets if they were perceived to be credible.

Second, messages are more effective if they are well spoken; or aptly phrased; gain the attention of the receiver; are understandable; relate to the interests of the receiver; present a moderate, versus substantial, difference in opinion; cater to diverse interests; recommend an appropriate course of action for the receiver; and, for complicated messages, state conclusions clearly. Overall, the experience should be rewarding and fun for the receiver. To provide one example, Morgan and Gramann (1989) found that the

FIGURE 8.4 Self-guiding trail booklets are one way to inform a large number of visitors about a park. *Photo: G. Hvenegaard.*

effectiveness of interpretive programs (in this case reflecting improved attitudes towards snakes) was not related to the amount of information. The level of involvement, especially a combination of exposure, modelling, and direct contact, was much more important in improving attitudes towards snakes (see also Guy et al., 1990). Similarly, for interpretive exhibits, Bitgood and Patterson (1993) found that, to increase reading time, labels should minimize the number of words used, enlarge letter size, avoid distractions, and be relevant to and placed near the objects being discussed.

Third, acceptance of the interpretive message is more likely if the receiver exposes him/herself to communications of interest; is made to feel at ease; is motivated by group membership; and continues discussion on the issue with like-minded people. For example, Manfredo and Bright (1991) also found that less experienced wilderness canoeists (i.e., with less confidence about the area or with canoeing in general) were more persuaded by information than more experienced canoeists.

Orams (1996) outlines a model for interpretation programs that emphasizes the affective (i.e., attitudes, feelings, emotions, and value systems) and cognitive (i.e., knowledge and perception) domains. Including the affective domain in a program recognizes that knowledge alone does not change attitudes and values; they need to be addressed directly. Using the cognitive domain, an interpretive program can develop cognitive dissonance or a dynamic disequilibrium by 'throwing people off balance', thus creating a 'teachable moment' (Forestell, 1991) and causing people to ask 'how, why, and when' questions. Interpretive programs should then provide a motivation to act and an opportunity to act. The success of this process is measured through evaluation and feedback.

INTERPRETATION AS A MANAGEMENT TOOL

Park interpretation programs generally make some reference to the role of interpretation in environmental protection. One of the main benefits of interpretation is to preserve 'a significant historic site or natural area by arousing citizen concern. Interpretation may motivate the public to take action to protect their environment in a sensible and logical way' (Sharpe, 1982: 9).

Managers may use interpretation to minimize negative impacts on the natural environment. For example, interpretation can emphasize that rare species have been severely impacted by off-trail use; however, managers should be aware that this can result both in increased understanding of the issues and in increased searching, and subsequent off-trail use, for those same rare species (Cialdini, 1996). Interpretation can also assist park management by developing programs and facilities that will aid in minimizing destructive behaviour and enforcement problems, while guiding visitors towards designated and selected locations. Interpretation can minimize accidents by emphasizing common public safety concerns in the park. As Boxes 8.2, 8.3, and 8.4 suggest, park agencies should view interpretation as one of several approaches needed to ensure the preservation of the park environment, including protective facility design, proper legal designation, and a real commitment to enforcement.

Interpretation can promote public understanding of an agency's goals and objectives. Interpretation can demonstrate, by example, the agency's and nation's philosophies and beliefs about conservation, wildlife protection, environmental preservation, and the innate value of its natural and cultural heritage. This will hopefully improve public image and solidify public support for the agency's goals. The park agency may also choose to highlight, through interpretation, the values and issues of concern to the parent government department.

BOX 8.2 Benefits of Interpretation

In Kananaskis Country, Alberta, one year after starting an innovative poster campaign illustrating commonly-picked flowers (e.g., 'Wanted ALIVE not dead'), the number of visitors reprimanded by park staff for picking flowers decreased by 50 per cent (Wolfe, 1997).

After noting an increase in bears frequenting campsites, staff at Peter Lougheed Provincial Park, Alberta initiated a 'Bear Paw Program'. They placed bear paw-shaped cards (with information from the bear's perspective) on the tables of campers who left their campsites in an unsuitable manner. Within one year, the number of problem campsites had decreased significantly (Wolfe, 1997).

In the 1970s, Staff at Dinosaur Provincial Park, Alberta, noted low visitor compliance to restricted area signs. Within days after organizing interpretive hikes into interesting areas outside of the restricted area, the number of visitors observed within the restricted areas decreased nearly 90 per cent (Wolfe, 1997).

In 1979, rangers in the Elbow district of Kananaskis Country were concerned about a random camping area known as Paddy's Flats. It had gained a reputation as a 'party area', with campers giving little regard to regulations. The situation reached a climax one weekend in June when the only management the rangers and RCMP could provide was to stop all new campers from going into the area and to stop all campers from coming out. Very soon after, the campground was closed, and converted to a designated campsite with self-registration. The next spring, an interpretive program began with Saturday night amphitheatre programs and Sunday morning walks, emphasizing entertainment and creating a family atmosphere. Management messages about bears, campsites, dogs, and respecting neighbours were discretely slipped into these programs. By the end of the summer, the interpretive programs combined with the campsite formalization had achieved its goal; the campsite was declared a 'family campground' (Gamble, 2000).

Near the Bonneville Lock and Dam, along the Columbia River, at least one person had drowned for five years in a row. The drownings resulted from improper anchoring. Sturgeon anglers were using anchor ropes that were too short in the deep, fast-moving water; the bows of the boats were simply pulled under the water. In response, interpreters developed new 'safe anchoring' posters and passed them out to anglers. In addition, interpreters placed large signs at boat ramps, developed an interactive video, and made contacts with supply stores. Five years after the 'Safe Anchoring in Current' initiative, nobody has drowned (Barry, 1993).

Interpretation can change visitor attitudes towards a resource management agency. In 1982 and 1983, visitors to the Petawawa National Forestry Institute's Visitor Centre were asked about their attitudes towards activities of the Canadian Forestry Service (e.g., management, prescribed burning, harvest rates, and timber focus). After visiting the centre, the attitudes about most of the agency's activities changed, by at least a small amount, in the desired direction (Cable et al., 1987).

BOX 8.3 Interpretation to Manage Dolphin-Watching in Australia

Researchers in Australia conducted an innovative study to measure a number of impacts of interpretive programs. At a resort in Tangalooma, Australia, about 40 km east of Brisbane, growing numbers of tourists arrive to hand-feed wild bottlenose dolphins. Resort staff, who run the dolphin feeding program, developed a management strategy to minimize the associated risks and to control interactions between dolphins and tourists. This strategy was developed in 1992 and operated in 1993. Some of the related rules include: only supervised entry allowed into the feeding area, limited amount of fish fed to dolphins, no touching or swimming with dolphins, contact time minimized, people with colds or flu not allowed to feed dolphins, and no photography in or near the water. One staff member made sure that tourists wanting to feed dolphins disinfected their hands before touching the fish, and another staff member helped people feed the dolphins. Only informal instructions were provided.

In 1994, a structured interpretive program was implemented with three main features. First, a Dolphin Education Centre provided a variety of information and served as the location where tourists could collect a limited number of free tokens, which allowed visitors to feed dolphins later that night. Second, people with tokens were given an educational briefing about the dolphins and the rules regarding feeding. Third, a public address system allowed staff to talk to feeders and observers during the feeding sessions (focusing on the behaviour and ecology of dolphins, and related environmental responsibilities of visitors).

Researchers observed and videotaped feeding sessions before and after the new interpretive program. Researchers recorded inappropriate behaviour and cautions throughout the sessions (Orams and Hill, 1998). For this study, the 1993 visitors were the control group and the 1994 visitors were the experimental group. Standardized to 100 feed events, the number of touches in the control group, 6.7, dropped to 1.2 in the experimental group. As well, the number of staff cautions dropped from 2.6 to 1.2, and the number of other inappropriate behaviours dropped from 3.2 to 1.1.

At the same time, researchers measured the impact on the tourists themselves (Orams, 1997). Tourists were questioned both during their experience and 2-3 months after. Although high levels of enjoyment exist for both groups, the interpretive program increased the level of enjoyment for the experimental group, especially their desire for more information. Based on a test, the knowledge level of the experimental group (which was exposed to the interpretive program) was significantly higher than the control group. Environmentally-conscious attitudes also increased among visitors. The control and experimental groups did not significantly differ in their intentions to participate in environmentally friendly behaviour. However, the experimental group increased their actual environmentally friendly behaviour by removing beach litter, making donations, and becoming involved in environmental issues.

BOX 8.4 Interpretation to Manage Vandalism at Writing-On-Stone Provincial Park, Alberta

Recognized as a significant international cultural resource, Writing-On-Stone Provincial Park, Alberta, contains several hundred petroglyphs (rock carvings) and numerous pictographs (rock paintings) created by First Nations people at least 300 years ago. Many carvings have been vandalized by the public, arousing the concern of park managers, among others. Interpretation subsequently received increased attention in the park and the interpretive program put more emphasis on environmental protection, with a follow-up study to determine if interpretive programming helped motivate people to protect such fragile features.

Groups of park visitors saw an interpretive program, which emphasized the significance of the native petroglyphs and the consequences of vandalism. The next day at the rock art site, a researcher posed as a vandal pretending to carve his initials on the petroglyph wall and recorded the level of reaction by the visitors. Another researcher interviewed the same visitors shortly afterwards to obtain their reactions. The interviewer gave the visitors an opportunity to report the act of vandalism, without prompting them to do so. The reactions of those who had been exposed to the interpretive program were compared to the reactions of those who had not (Butler, 1980). Those who attended the program demonstrated significantly stronger reactions against the vandal than those who had not attended. They accounted for 73 per cent of the high-level reactions, those that called for confronting the vandal. Of those in the control group who also exhibited a strong reaction against vandalism, a majority also had attended interpretive programs in the park before the experiment. If we count this group with the experimental group, together they accounted for 82 per cent of the strongest levels of reaction against the vandal.

INTERPRETATION AND ECOTOURISM

There is an obvious potential link between interpretation and ecotourism, a newly-labelled form of park use. The Ecotourism Society (1991: 1) defines ecotourism as:

> purposeful travel to natural areas, to understand the culture and natural history of the environment, taking care not to alter the integrity of the ecosystem, while producing economic opportunities that make the conservation of natural resources beneficial to local people.

Ecotourism usually refers to non-consumptive activities, such as birding, whale-watching, nature photography, and botanical study. As such, ecotourism is reliant on natural features in relatively undisturbed sites, such as parks and protected areas (Hvenegaard, 1994).

The broader goals of ecotourism are to conserve the environment and improve the welfare of local people (Hvenegaard and Dearden, 1998a). Accomplishing these goals is complicated by many social, economic, environmental, and educational issues, involving a network of protected areas, natural attractions, ecotourists, ecotourism infrastructure, and local people (see Hvenegaard and Dearden, 1998b). Of importance here, however, in terms of reaching these goals, is the role of interpretation in maximizing the positive impacts and minimizing the negative impacts of ecotourism (see Bramwell and Lane, 1993).

A few examples can illustrate this role. First, interpretation can help to reduce environmental impacts by highlighting appropriate activities and sensitive areas. Interpreters often describe various species and habitats that are of concern, due to disturbance or overuse. Second, interpretation can be used to alleviate social impacts by involving local communities and re-directing traffic. For example, in response to high use levels at Point Pelee National Park, 'Operation Spreadout' seeks to inform visitors of other nearby attractions. Third, by providing additional opportunities for visitors, interpretation can improve local economic impacts by increasing the number of days that visitors stay in an area. As well, interpretation can emphasize opportunities to contribute to conservation. Ecotourists tend to donate more money to conservation than other tourists, but they need additional interpretation to encourage them to do so (Hvenegaard and Dearden, 1998a). Finally, interpretation responds to the ecotourists' need for awareness and understanding of a park's natural features. Visitors to Grassland National Park, for example, are primarily motivated to learn more about the environment (Saleh and Karwacki, 1996).

INTERPRETIVE PLANNING

Without planning, interpretive programs can become ineffective or redundant. Several planning models are available for interpretation. The model by Sharpe et al. (1994) involves seven logical steps. The interpretive planner should work with other

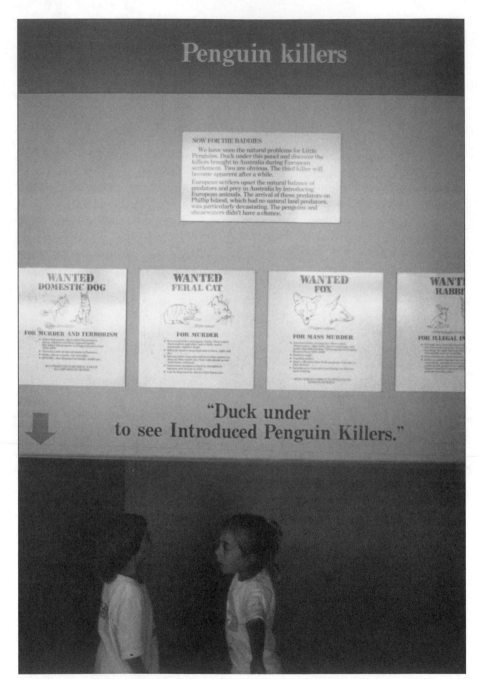

FIGURE 8.5 A critical aspect of interpretation is to orient the message and delivery to the audience. Here we see signs designed to appeal to a younger audience. *Photo: G. Hvenegaard.*

management specialists to determine objectives, take inventory, analyze data, synthe-size alternatives, develop the plan, implement the plan, and evaluate and revise the plan. Throughout the planning process, planners should consider each objective of interpretation and make appropriate connections among them.

Another interpretation planning model by McArthur (1998) requires three key stages for successful interpretation. The first stage is to define a target audience, gain-ing an understanding of group makeup, demographics, motivations, expectations, and satisfactions. The second stage is to determine the content and structure of the interpretive message. This is considered within the hierarchy of interpretive themes, concepts, and messages. The third step is to select a technique; a later section describes the many possibilities along with their advantages and disadvantages.

The latter model is applicable to interpretive efforts in Canada's national parks. First, visitors can be grouped according to park usage, trip behaviour, and attitudes towards park management, or demographics. Visitor types are best analyzed at the park level, and planners often use techniques from the Visitor Activity Management Process (Chapter 7). Knowing the demographic and attitudinal characteristics of each group assists interpreters in planning, marketing, and evaluating interpretive activities.

Second, the content of interpretive messages is guided by national policy and adapted to individual parks. At the national level (Parks Canada, 1998b), the purpose of interpretation is to encourage visitors to appreciate, understand, and support:

- Canada's system of nationally significant heritage places;
- the essence of each heritage place and how it is significant to the country and rel-evant to individuals; and
- the need to protect heritage resources. Although not precisely stated in that docu-ment, the protection of ecological integrity should be the primary purpose for interpretation (Parks Canada Agency, 2000).

Thus, across the system, interpretation focuses on messages about the national park system, about ensuring ecological integrity, and about issues of national signif-icance. Individual parks then highlight national and park-specific issues as they relate to these messages. For example, each park could interpret the status of completing the national parks system, how the park is representative of its natural region, and why the park is of national significance. Similarly, each park could interpret species that are endangered at the national level and that are found in the park. Messages should com-plement current site-level management practices to promote ecological integrity. Interpretive messages should also be placed in a regional or national context, and relate to broader environmental issues (Parks Canada, 1994), such as global warming, acid rain, recycling, and water quality.

Finally, each park chooses the mode of delivering each interpretive message. In times of cutbacks, choosing an interpretive technique is heavily influenced by fund-ing and staffing. However, subject to these constraints, an interpretive technique should be chosen for its ability to reach the target audience, effectively interpret the target message, and fulfil the broader goals of interpretation.

FORMS OF INTERPRETATION

In selecting a form of interpretation, interpreters should have a deep understanding of the needs of the visitor, of the natural environment, and of the agency (Sharpe et al., 1994). Interpreters should consider the visitors' need for orientation, use of other facilities, group size, potential impact, need for warning about dangers, varying lengths of stay, language barriers, and varying backgrounds. As well, related to the park environment, interpreters should consider the relevant interpretive theme, appropriate timing of events, vulnerability of park features, and impacts of permanent versus temporary developments. Finally, interpreters should consider how the interpretive effort furthers the park agency's goals, and the agency's investment, maintenance, and replacement costs. Box 8.5 provides a list of organizations and publications that examine many of these issues.

BOX 8.5 Interpretation Organizations and Publications

Organization	Publication	Web site
Interpretation Canada	*Interpscan*	www.interpcan.ca/
National Association for Interpretation	*Journal of Interpretation*	www.interpnet.org/
Association for Heritage Interpretation	*Interpretation*	www.heritageinterpretation
Association for Experiential Education	*Journal of Experiential Education*	www.aee.org.uk/ index.htm
n/a	*Canadian Journal of Environmental Education*	ayamdigut.yukoncollege.yk .ca/programs/cjee.htm
North American Association for Environmental Education	*Environmental Communicator*	naaee.org/index.php

Personal Services

Interpretation services may be both personal and non-personal in nature. Non-personal services include displays, exhibits, signs, trails, and publications. Personal services involve direct contact between the interpreter and the public. These activities fall into two categories; informational duty and presentation duty.

Informational duties include services that tell the visitor where specific facilities and opportunities are located and how to make use of them. Information services staff are not interpreters (although interpreters often perform information service duties), in that they do not present programs, conduct walks, or otherwise interpret the natural and cultural environment. They are, however, front-line representatives of the park and the agency.

Presentation duties entail scheduled services that are provided by specifically trained people. In this era of hi-tech gadgetry, human interpreters remain one of the most popular and effective forms of interpretive communication. Scheduled events might include guided tours, slide shows, prop talks, evening campfire programs, and many other activities planned to take place at a predetermined time and advertised accordingly.

Guided tours are extremely useful to encourage interactions between visitors and the natural environment. Slide shows, videos, and other audiovisual aids used by staff are effective ways to convey abstract messages through 'substitute experiences'. They can also be used to set moods and demonstrate perspective. Prop talks, using objects or artifacts as focal points of a talk, can also provide valuable first-hand involvement. Dramatic presentations generally require more elaborate production, but can prove highly effective and entertaining. They are popular for historical topics, and they can create high interest and accommodate large audiences.

Point duty involves stationing an interpreter at a prominent feature or gathering place (i.e., a waterfall attraction, or a concentration of wildlife) during periods of high visitation. Travelling point duty or roving duty is similar, except that travelling point duty implies interpreting along the way. The interpreter walks through an area, informally interpreting sites through casual conversation at points where people naturally choose to pause.

Impromptu events are not formally scheduled but they are planned; which is to say they are impromptu only from the standpoint of the spectator. They are far more formalized and better rehearsed than roving duties. The sudden arrival of an interpreter on a beach with table, aquarium, net, bioscope, and sample jars will draw a crowd as the interpreter invites visitors to look close up at sand particles and aquatic invertebrates.

Living interpretation entails the demonstrating of a historical lifestyle or a contemporary culture that is different from that of the visitors'. Living interpreters in period costumes and authentic, reconstructed settings carry out day-to-day activities, showing visitors how people actually lived (or still live, in other cultures) and demonstrating crafts or skills, often with technical information or authentic products as an additional feature.

Extension programs are presentations of natural and cultural interest, taken into communities or schools or communicated through media such as newspapers, radio, or television, with the intention of expanding the audience for an interpretive message.

Non-personal Services

The presentation of a natural area's features and story also relies on inanimate interpretative aids such as park facilities and publications.

Visitor Centres

The visitor centre is essentially a communication facility. Through a variety of personal and technical media visitors are briefed about the area, its regulations, its values, opportunities for the visitor, special features, the area's role in the overall park system, and how visitors can best enjoy and understand the dynamics of the immediate environment. It also serves as a repository for park information for both visitors and staff.

Exhibits

Exhibits used in parks may include dioramas, artifacts, reconstructions, and models. Exhibits in visitor centres must be versatile so they can be changed frequently over the years and with the season. Panels with dry-mounted photographs, rear-lighted transparencies, and backlit, self-activated projector exhibits are all highly suitable, since they are readily adapted for changing themes.

Most formal exhibits would be located in the visitor centre; but kiosks (an outdoor consolidation of several exhibit panels, usually under a roof) are often set at appropriate locations along trails or near features whose explanation is too complex for a normal sign.

Signs

The use of signs is the most basic form of interpretive service. Interpretive signs are self-pacing; that is, readers can browse at their own speed and read only what they are interested in. A number of considerations govern what to say in the sign and why a sign should be there in the first place. Is the message significant and worth telling? Is the message simple and easy to understand? Is the message accurate and brief? Is the style of writing appropriate for the occasion? Does the message evoke a response in the visitor?

Interpretive Trails

Interpretive trails are self-guided, generally using signs or leaflets for information. 'The self-guided trail, in natural and human history interpretation, is a device that places visitors, usually in family-sized groups, in direct contact with the park or forest resources. A self-guided trail, in contrast to a conducted tour, means that the visitors are on their own; there is no one to guide them through the trail experience. The self-guided trail is a meandering footpath along which the visitor's attention is drawn to interesting or unusual features, which might otherwise be overlooked or not fully appreciated' (Sharpe, 1982: 299).

Publications and Web Sites

Publications and web sites can present a topic in greater depth than other methods. Publications can be taken home as souvenirs and referred to many times. Web sites can be referenced at home or in recreational vehicles, allowing the visitors to become better informed about unique park features, opportunities, and services prior to their visit. Today, time is one of the greatest limitations faced by the park visitor. The greater the extent of interpretive information that can be accessed online (including advertisements of forthcoming interpretive programs), the more impressive and meaningful will be the park experience. Few parks currently utilize this technology in an effective outreach manner, although some have developed extremely effective interactive programs accessible in the visitor centre itself.

Environmental Education

Environmental education should be an essential component of the overall interpretive effort. Such programs are developed principally for schools. Personal services include teacher training and conducted events led by volunteers and park staff. Non-personal services include pre- and post-trip resource kits, brochures on self-guided field studies, exhibits developed specifically for children, and CD programs and videos to be used in the classroom before the field trip.

In its broadest perspective, environmental education attempts to convey knowledge about the whole environment and its associated problems, suggestions as to how to help solve these problems, skills that can be transferred to others, and motivation to work towards solutions. The environmental education component of a park cannot by itself do all this. It should concentrate on providing an awareness, appreciation, and understanding of the immediate environment by permitting first-hand observation and personal involvement with the park.

School Field Trips to the Park

One of the primary benefits of a field trip is to enhance classroom activities and broaden students' perspectives. It is, therefore, important to develop park experiences as an extension of the classroom program. Field trip planning guides should be developed and distributed to potential visiting groups to help them plan their trip and ensure a successful experience.

CONCLUSION

Interpretation in North America has an amazing history of inspirational, dedicated, and professional staff. Moreover, interpretation fulfils several important goals, which are guided by legislation, policy, and visitor interests and needs. Significant and tangible benefits result from park interpretive efforts; these accrue to the visitor, park environment, park agency, and ecosystem beyond the park boundary.

Unfortunately, the full importance of interpretation is not often reflected in a park's staffing and budgetary priorities. Evidence for this comes in many forms. For example, as budgets rise or fall, interpreters are often the last to be hired, and the first to be fired. Many full-time interpreters have been replaced by seasonal employees (Parks Canada Agency, 2000). Budgets have been severely cut, forcing staff to rely on the least costly, and in many cases, least-effective, interpretive methods, when such programs survive at all. In recent years attempts have been made by several provincial governments to privatize programs in a regretable political trend to convert park operations from public domain to profit-motivated privatization.

In many parks, interpretation is under-utilized as a park management service. Reasons for this are many. First, few managers, the principle budget officers, actually possess a background in interpretation, public education, or communications, leading to a poor understanding of interpretation's potential and role in the ecological and visitor management mandates of parks. Second, interpretation is generally poorly integrated into the park planning and management efforts, resulting in, for example, interpretive staff located in buildings that offer little interaction with other park operational staff. Third, managers are rarely familiar with the published research documenting the benefits of interpretation. Without knowledge of the evidence of the positive impacts of interpretive services upon park operations, visitor satisfactions, and ecological management, such managers rarely consider these services as an important management tool, nor do they actively promote and advance these services in setting or arguing for budgetary priorities. Programs are also poorly supported because of a lack of useful information on park user demographics and preferences; interpretive content is often narrowly or inappropriately focussed; unimaginative communication techniques are often used; and evaluation is generally lacking (Sharpe, 1982; Nyberg, 1984; Wolfe, 1997; McArthur, 1998).

As a further constraint on the expanse and support of interpretive programs, the unique and intrinsic features of individual parks are poorly celebrated from a systems perspective or poorly aligned to the seasonal specialties of the calendar year; environmental education opportunities with local schools seem more reluctantly accommodated than encouraged and facilitated; almost no parks adopt an 'ecological-model-for-society' approach, and training opportunities are limited and rarely encouraged.

To deal with these constraints, several improvements are needed. The importance of interpretation needs to be elevated by increasing organizational links, increasing funding, developing professional full-time staff, reaching a wide range of people, using appropriate and innovative communication methods, and clearly defining key messages (Canadian Environmental Advisory Council, 1991; Parks Canada Agency, 2000).

Effective interpretation is essential to the successful management and operation of a park or protected area. Natural areas cannot survive as islands. Their survival is closely tied to people's attitudes, beliefs, and way of life. Public support, at both the political and community level, is necessary to help an area succeed in meeting its conservation and preservation goals.

An important goal of any protected area is to give local residents and visitors information to increase their awareness and understanding of the area's natural values and to relate these experiences to modern life. Achieving this goal will result in informed people who have a deeper appreciation for their area's natural and cultural heritage, and who transfer these values and experience into their daily lives. Attitudes towards the environment are learned, not inborn.

Protecting parks and wilderness areas is, in many ways, comparable to a library acquiring important works to ensure the availability of the literature of the past and present. Acquisition and protection are indeed important, but the books have to be read and understood for their true worth to be realized. While the librarian (or manager) may conserve the volumes, the visitor must also be shown how to read them. Most visitors to parks and wilderness settings today lack the experience to 'read' such places adequately. Their visits are comparable to passing through a corridor of valuable books, nine-tenths of which are unreadable. Interpretation resolves this dilemma. It guides the visitor to discover the wonders contained within these volumes, to 'experience this sense of wonder' as Rachel Carson described it, to be moved emotionally and mindfully along the path of discovery, to be motivated to want and to understand more, and to experience in the volumes of nature's wealth and complexity an upwelling of pride in our heritage and an inner sense of belonging and richness in our personal lives.

REFERENCES

Barry, J.P. 1993. 'Anchoring Safely in Current: An Example of Using Interpretation to Solve a Management Problem', *Legacy* 4, 4: 22.

Beck, L., and T.T. Cable. 1998. *Interpretation for the 21st Century: Fifteen Guiding Principles for Interpreting Nature and Culture.* Champaign, Ill.: Sagamore Publishing.

Bitgood, S.C., and D.D. Patterson. 1993. 'The Effects of Gallery Changes on Visitor Reading and Object Viewing Time', *Environment and Behaviour* 25, 6: 761–81.

Bramwell, B., and B. Lane. 1993. 'Interpretation and Sustainable Tourism: The Potential and the Pitfalls', *Journal of Sustainable Tourism* 1, 2: 71–80.

Butler, J.R. 1980. 'The Role of Interpretation as a Motivating Agent Toward Park Resource Protection', Ph.D. dissertation, University of Washington.

Cable, T.T., D.M. Knudson, E. Udd, and D.J. Stewart. 1987. 'Attitude Changes as a Result of Exposure to Interpretive Messages', *Journal of Park and Recreation Administration* 5, 1: 47–60.

Canadian Environmental Advisory Council. 1991. *A Protected Areas Vision for Canada.* Ottawa: Minister of Supply and Services Canada. Cat. no. EN 92-14/1991E.

Cialdini, R.B. 1996. 'Activating and Aligning Two Kinds of Norms in Persuasive Communications', *Journal of Interpretation Research* 1, 1: 3–10.

Dick, R.E., D.T. McKee, and J.A. Wagar. 1974. 'A Summary and Annotated Bibliography of Communication Principles', *Journal of Environmental Education* 5, 4: 1–13.

The Ecotourism Society. 1991. 'The Ecotourism Society's Definition', *The Ecotourism Society Newsletter* 1, 1: 1.

Fazio, J.R., and D.L. Gilbert. 1981. *Public Relations and Communications for Natural Resource Managers.* Toronto: Kendall/Hunt Publishing.

Forestell, P.H. 1991. 'Marine Education and Ocean Tourism: Replacing Parasitism with Symbiosis', in M.L. Miller, and J. Auyong, eds, *Proceedings* of the 1990 Congress on Coastal and Marine Tourism. Newport, Oreg.: National Coastal Resources Research & Development Institute, 35–9.

Gamble, D. 2000. Personal Communication. Natural Resource Conservation Officer, Alberta Environmental Protection, Camrose, Alta, Aug.

Government of Canada. 1990. National Parks Act. Ottawa: Minister of Supply and Services Canada. Cat. no. YX76-N14/1989.

Guy, B.S., W.W. Curtis, and J.C. Crotts. 1990. 'Environmental Learning of First-Time Travellers', *Annals of Tourism Research* 17: 419–31.

Henderson, G. 1994. 'James Bernard Harkin: The Father of Canadian National Parks', *Borealis* 5, 2: 28–33.

Hvenegaard, G.T. 1994. 'Ecotourism: A Status Report and Conceptual Framework', *Journal of Tourism Studies* 5, 2: 24–35.

———— and P. Dearden. 1998a.'Ecotourism Versus Tourism in a Thai National Park', *Annals of Tourism Research* 25, 3: 700–20.

———— and ————. 1998b. 'Linking Ecotourism and Biodiversity Conservation: A Case Study of Doi Inthanon National Park, Thailand', *Singapore Journal of Tropical Geography* 19, 2: 193–211.

McArthur, S. 1998. 'Introducing the Undercapitalized World of Interpretation', in K. Lindberg, M.E. Wood, and D. Engeldrum, eds, *Ecotourism: A Guide for Planners and Managers*, vol. 2. North Bennington, Vt: The Ecotourism Society, 63–85.

Manfredo, M.J., and A.D. Bright. 1991. 'A Model for Assessing the Effects of Communication on Recreationists', *Journal of Leisure Research* 23, 1: 1–20.

Morgan, J.M., and J.H. Gramann. 1989. 'Predicting Effectiveness of Wildlife Education Programs: A Study of Students' Attitudes and Knowledge toward Snakes', *Wildlife Society Bulletin* 17: 501–9.

Nyberg, K.L. 1984.'Some Radical Comments on Interpretation: A Little Heresy Is Good for the Soul', in G.E. Machlis and D.R. Field, eds, *On Interpretation: Sociology for Interpreters of Natural and Cultural History*. Corvallis: Oregon State University Press, 151–6.

Orams, M.B. 1996. 'Using Interpretation to Manage Nature-Based Tourism', *Journal of Sustainable Tourism* 4, 2: 81–94.

————. 1997. 'The Effectiveness of Environmental Education: Can We Turn Tourists into "Greenies"?', *Progress in Tourism and Hospitality Research* 3: 295–306.

————and G.J.E. Hill. 1998 'Controlling the Ecotourist in a Wild Dolphin Feeding Program: Is Education the Answer?', *Journal of Environmental Education* 29, 3: 33–8.

Parks Canada. 1994. *Parks Canada Guiding Principles and Operational Policies*. Ottawa: Minister of Supply and Services Canada.

————. 1997. *National Parks System Plan*, 3rd edn. Ottawa: Minister of Supply and Services Canada. Cat. no. R64-197/1-1997E.

————. 1998a. *State of the Parks, 1997 Report*. Ottawa: Minister of Supply and Services Canada. Cat. no. R64-184/1997E.

————. 1998b *The Role of Heritage Presentation in Achieving Ecological Integrity*. Ottawa: Minister of Supply and Services Canada.

Parks Canada Agency. 2000. *Unimpaired for Future Generations? Protecting Ecological Integrity with Canada's National Parks*, vol. 2: *Setting a New Direction for Canada's National Parks*. Report of the Panel on the Ecological Integrity of Canada's National Parks, Ottawa. Cat. no. R62-323/2000-2E.

Saleh, F., and J. Karwacki. 1996. 'Revisiting the Ecotourist: The Case of Grasslands National Park', *Journal of Sustainable Tourism* 4, 2: 61–80.

Shankland, R. 1970. *Steve Mather of the National Parks*. New York: Alfred A. Knopf.

Sharpe, G.W. 1982. 'An Overview of Interpretation', in Sharpe, ed., *Interpreting the Environment*, 2nd edn. New York: John Wiley & Sons, 3–26.

————, C.H. Odegaard, and W.F. Sharpe. 1994. *A Comprehensive Introduction to Park Management*, 2nd edn. Champaign, Ill.: Sagamore Publishing.

Stewart, E.J., B.M. Hayward, and P.J. Devlin. 1998. 'The "Place" of Interpretation: A New Approach to the Evaluation of Interpretation', *Tourism Management* 19, 3: 257–66.

Taylor, C.J. 1997. 'Defining National Parks: J.B. Harkin and the National Parks Branch', *Research Links* 5, 1: 5.

Tilden, F. 1977. *Interpreting Our Heritage*. Chapel Hill: University of North Carolina Press.

Weaver, H.E. 1982. 'Origins of Interpretation', in G.W. Sharpe, ed., *Interpreting the Environment*, 2nd edn. New York: John Wiley & Sons, 28–51.

Wolfe, R. 1997. 'Interpretive Education: An Under-Rated Element of Park Management?', *Research Links* 5, 3: 11–12.

KEY WORDS/CONCEPTS

interpretation

first-hand experience

informal education

extrinsic activity

intrinsic value

communication

visitor motivation

ecotourism

interpretive planning

personal interpretive services

impersonal interpretive services

guided talks

prop talks

dramatic presentations

point duty

impromptu events

extension programs

visitor services

exhibits

interpretive signs

interpretive trails

interpretive publications

environmental education

STUDY QUESTIONS

1. Compare the three phases of historical development of park interpretation in Canada and the US.
2. List the major attributes of interpretation.
3. List the major benefits of interpretation.
4. Discuss why interpretation is both a science and an art.
5. Describe four types of potential users of interpretive services.
6. Describe how each of the following can make interpretation more effective: the communicator; the message; and the receiver.
7. Discuss the impact of interpretation on the experience of dolphin-watching in Australia.
8. Discuss the impact of interpretation on the behaviour of visitors to Writing-on-Stone Provincial Park.
9. Discuss the role of interpretation in achieving the objectives of ecotourism.
10. 'In many parks, interpretation is under-utilized'. Discuss.
11. Select a park in your area. Review and critique the range of interpretive services provided.
12. Join a guided walk provided by interpreters in a park setting. Discuss the techniques used by the interpreter. Comment on what worked/ did not work.

PART IV

Putting it Together

Enter Glacier National Park and you enter the homeland of the grizzly bear. We are uninvited guests here, intruders, the bear our reluctant host. If he chooses, now and then, to chase somebody up a tree, or all the way to hospital, that is the bear's prerogative. Those who prefer, quite reasonably, not to take such chances, should stick to Disneyland in all its many forms and guises.

Edward Abbey, The Journey Home

This section applies the conservation theory and social science theory developed in the previous section to the management of parks and protected areas. Part of this analysis is an explication of values, and woven into it is a consideration of the changing historical perspectives on parks and protected areas.

The section begins with a description of how national parks are managed in Canada, reviewing the legislation, policies, and procedures developed by Parks Canada. Of particular interest here is the approach to systems planning, ecological integrity, and visitor management. This overview is followed by a chapter that looks in more depth at Canada's most famous park and its environs, Banff. Although beset by most of the problems that face the national park system, Banff is also showing leadership in surmounting these challenges and offers valuable lessons to other parks in the system.

Chapter 11, Site Management, deals with the connection between values and the type of management responses that might be made to significant issues regarding Canadian parks. Bridging several different issues through the use of case studies, it illustrates how both ecological and social science information are required to address many park management problems.

The section concludes with a discussion of ecosystem-based planning as the overarching framework within which integrated park management can be achieved.

Ecosystem planning views the management of parks from the perspective of the larger ecosystem or landscape in which parks are found. Parks are not large enough to protect all species and natural processes. Even the very large parks are impacted by external forces, such as acid rain and global warming. Furthermore, many species travel across park boundaries and are affected by conditions found outside of parks. The ecosystem approach recognizes that humans at some level of activity are a natural component of most ecosystems and cannot be ignored in the pursuit of ecological integrity. This includes the interaction of park visitors with park environments, as well as the interaction of parks with adjacent human communities.

CHAPTER 9

Managing the National Parks

Pamela Wright & Rick Rollins

INTRODUCTION

Millions of people explore the national parks of Canada each year. They clamber to lookouts, gaze from belvederes, and rest at scenic pull-offs that highlight special features. Other visitors probe deeper within national parks, perhaps travelling for days by canoe, horseback, or on foot with a backpack. Visitors may encounter park staff, providing information and interpretation to visitors, or enforcing park regulations. Sometimes, commercial guides or outfitters lead groups into national parks providing their clients with a unique experience that an experienced guide can bring.

Some people are concerned about the amount of recreation and tourism that occurs in national parks. They are concerned that the numbers of park visitors, their behaviour, and the services and facilities visitors require or demand will erode the very qualities of a natural setting the park is intended to protect. For example, the behaviour of bears, elk, and other wildlife may change in response to campers leaving garbage, taking photos, or establishing trails and campsites in places that interfere with wildlife feeding or other range requirements. In some parks, townsites have developed over the years to support a booming nature-based tourism industry, but the negative impact these developments have on park ecosystems is now becoming better understood. These concerns are exacerbated by the growing realization that parks are threatened by human activity in adjacent lands: hunting, farming, ranching, logging, petroleum extraction, and urban development. Parks are now viewed as part of larger ecosystems in which wildlife cross back and forth across park boundaries.

Hence, the job of managing the national parks has become a complex undertaking. The issues can be reduced to the following kinds of considerations.
- What is the purpose of national parks? What values are guiding park management decisions? (Chapters 1 and 11)
- Where should national parks be located, and how many are needed? How large must they be, and how are boundaries to be resolved? (Chapters 3, 4, and 14)
- How are natural resources in parks to be managed? (Chapters 5, 10, 11, and 12)
- How is visitor use of parks to be managed? (Chapters 6, 7, and 8)
- How are decisions made about management issues? (Chapters 1, 2, 11, and 15)

FIGURE 9.1 Horse-drawn carriages stand ready to whisk visitors from the Banff railway station to hotels such as the Banff Springs (1913). Because it owned both the hotel and the railway station, the Canadian Pacific Railway held considerable influence over park visitors. Other hotels expressed resentment over the CPR's influence during this period, particularly when they learned the CPR was advising tourists that the Banff Springs was the only hotel in town. *Photo: Canadian Parks Service.*

- How will park managers resolve conflicts with adjacent communities and land-owners? What relationships will be established with Aboriginal communities? (Chapters 13 and 12)

Chapter 8 provides an overview of the direction created by legislation and by policy and then considers some of the primary management concerns described above.

LEGISLATIVE DIRECTION

Legislation and policy form two of the primary tools that guide management. Legislation is in the form of acts or laws and is approved by legislature and must be followed by the government, by its citizens, and is enforced by the court system. Legislation is generally broad in scope and vague in details. It has often been described as the tool that enables policies and practices and that gives guidance on what can be done, but not usually the details on how it is to be done.

National Parks Act

Several key pieces of legislation guide the management of national parks but at their core is the National Parks Act. Prior to 1930, each national park was established by an individual Act and management was subject to whatever stipulations were contained

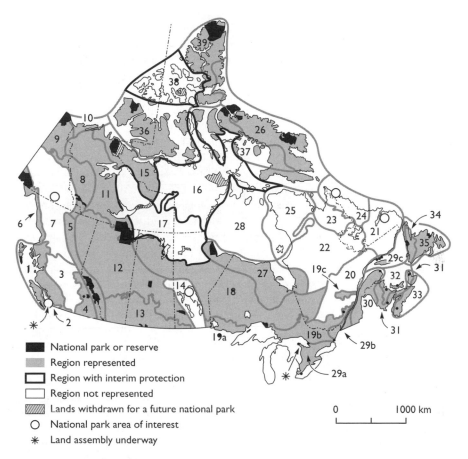

National park or reserve

Region represented

Region with interim protection

Region not represented

Lands withdrawn for a future national park

National park area of interest

Land assembly underway

0   1000 km

1 Pacific Coast Mountains
2 Strait of Georgia Lowlands
3 Interior Dry Plateau
4 Columbia Mountains
5 Rocky Mountains
6 Northern Coast Mountains
7 Northern Interior Plateaux
  and Mountains
8 Mackenzie Mountains
9 Northern Yukon
10 Mackenzie Delta
11 Northern Boreal Plains
12 Southern Boreal Plains
   and Plateaux
13 Prairie Grasslands
14 Manitoba Lowlands
15 Tundra Hills

16 Central Tundra
17 Northwestern Boreal Uplands
18 Central Boreal Uplands
19a West Great Lakes–St Lawrence
   Precambrian Region
19b Central Great Lakes–St Lawrence
   Precambrian Region
19c East Great Lakes–St Lawrence
   Precambrian Region
20 Laurentian Boreal Highlands
21 East Coast Boreal Region
22 Boreal Lake Plateau
23 Whale River
24 Northern Labrador Mountains
25 Ungava Tundra Plateau
26 Northern Davis Region
27 Hudson–James Lowlands

28 Southampton Plain
29a West St Lawrence Lowland
29b Central St Lawrence Lowland
29c East St Lawrence Lowland
30 Notre Dame–Megantic
   Mountains
31 Maritime Acadian Highlands
32 Maritime Plain
33 Atlantic Coast Uplands
34 Western Newfoundland
   Highlands
35 Eastern Newfoundland
   Atlantic Region
36 Western Arctic Lowlands
37 Eastern Arctic Lowlands
38 Western High Arctic
39 Eastern High Arctic

FIGURE 9.2 Terrestrial system plan for Parks Canada, showing degree of representation.

within that legislation. The National Parks Act was first established in 1930 with a major set of amendments made in 1988. With the passing of the 1930's Act, comprehensive rules for the management of every national park were set. In October of 2000, the Canada National Parks Bill (Bill C-27) was approved in Parliament. In this chapter, references are to the consolidated act of 1988 unless otherwise noted.

Purpose of Parks

The National Parks Act states that 'Parks are hereby dedicated to the people of Canada for their benefit, education, and enjoyment, subject to the provisions of this Act and Regulations, and such Parks shall be maintained and made use of so as to leave them unimpaired for the enjoyment of future generations.' This purpose statement contains several noteworthy points. That Parks are dedicated to the public good is clear, but what is also clear is the intent to maintain the ecological values of these areas. The use of the dedication 'for future generations' and of the desired status 'unimpaired' provided the initial impetus for management and protection of the ecological values within national parks. Early conceptualizations of appropriate use and enjoyment and what would impair national parks was not based on the current numbers of people that visit parks, the competing demands for use of the parks, the increasing stresses and pressures placed on parks from the outside nor on our understanding of the complex ecological systems that support and are supported by parks. As a result, there has been much debate and difficulty aimed at reconciling human use within national parks. Subsequent changes in policy and legislation have sought to contemporize our understandings of these situations and to further clarify the purpose.

Publication of the 1979 policy statement for the agency, the National Park Act Amendments of 1988, the subsequent revised Guiding Principles and Operational Policies of 1994 and the Parks Canada Agency Act (1998) have successively indicated that ecological integrity (and historical or commemorative integrity for historic sites) should be Parks Canada's first consideration and are to be regarded as 'prerequisites against use' (Parks Canada Policy, 1979: 12). Further clarification of the purpose of parks and consolidation of ideas from the Guiding Principles and Operational Policies and the Parks Canada Agency Act (discussed in more detail in other sections of this chapter) is made in the 2000 Canada National Parks Bill. Section 8 (2) in this bill states that 'maintenance or restoration of ecological integrity, through the protection of natural resources and natural processes, shall be the first priority of the Minister when considering all aspects of the management of parks.' This wording is intended to be broader still than that included in the 1988 amendments, where it could be questioned that the imperatives of ecological integrity be applied only to park zoning and visitor use in a management plan. To resolve confusion regarding terms and to resolve debates concerning the actual definition of ecological integrity, the bill defines ecological integrity as follows: 'ecological integrity means, with respect to a park, a condition that is determined to be characteristic of its natural region and likely to persist, including abiotic components and the composition and abundance of native species and biological communities, rates of change and supporting processes.'

The result of these evolving purpose statements is an agency mandate that is clear about intent and priority within its mandate. Correspondingly, the definitions of what activities and pursuits constituted 'benefit, education and enjoyment' have evolved from a very broad definition that included a wide variety of activities including extractive activities. As attitudes changed, the range of activities started to be limited to outdoor recreation activities and extractive uses were largely omitted. Later still, only those outdoor activities with a minimum or non-consumptive impact on the environment were allowed. Today, one of the continuing and primary challenges of park managers is determining where, what type, and how much use should be allowed in order to provide for 'use without abuse' of the national parks.

Comprehensive Policies

Strategic direction for parks has come at the national level through the creation of a systems plan for the completion of the national park system, a comprehensive policy document, and more recently a national reporting system. The first two elements—the systems plan and the policy documents—are discussed in separate sections later in this chapter. Both are broadly enabled through legislation but detail on requirements for either has not been provided in the Act. The requirement for a national monitoring report card for National parks is a result of the 1988 amendments to the Act. The Act calls for a report to Parliament 'on the state of the parks and progress towards establishing new parks' (section 5.1.5) every two years. These State of Parks reports released to date in 1990, 1994, 1997, and 2000 provide an overview of the status towards completion of the national park system and the ecological integrity of national parks and commemorative integrity of national historic sites and monuments.

Park Management

At the individual park level, the Park Management Plan is the primary tool for directing management. Management plans are required by law and must be tabled in the House of Commons within five years of park establishment. The revised Act further clarifies the requirements stating that:

> 11(1) The Minister shall, within five years after a park is established, prepare a management plan for the park containing a long-term ecological vision for the park, a set of ecological integrity objectives and indicators and provisions for resource protection and restoration, zoning, visitor use, public awareness and performance evaluation, which shall be tabled in each House of Parliament.

More recently, the preparation of business plans at the corporate (entire Agency) and individual park levels has been added to the required direction for management (Parks Canada Agency Act, 1998). These business plans set out the financial accountabilities and short-term actions of the Agency providing a potential tracking mechanism for monitoring.

Two new clauses in the Canada National Parks Bill will provide further legislative direction for park management. The first clause calls for legislative protection for wilderness areas within parks providing a higher level of security and protection of ecological values in the majority of each park. Although the intent of this clause was included in the 1988 amendments, no wilderness areas had been legislated through 1999. The revised Act is intended to make the mechanism easier and to require the legislation of these areas.

> Where a management plan that exists at the time this Act comes into force sets out an area of a park as a wilderness area, the Minister shall recommend to the Governor in Council that the area be declared a wilderness area within two years of the coming into force of this Act.

The second clause represents a much more fundamental shift in the intent of park management and calls for the Agency to recognize that to achieve its purpose it must work proactively and co-operatively with landowners, communities, and resource managers outside of parks. The legislative recognition that parks can no longer be managed as islands will, if effective, enable a fundamental change in the ways in which park values must be protected.

> For the purposes of maintaining or restoring ecological integrity, the Minister shall, where applicable, (1) work co-operatively with federal and provincial ministers and agencies, local and Aboriginal governments and organizations, bodies established under land claims agreements, representatives of park communities, private organizations, individuals and landowners in or adjacent to a park; and (2) participate in the development and implementation of processes and programs that may reasonably be expected to affect ecological integrity, including research, education, land use planning, and environmental assessments.

Park Regulations

Regulations for national parks are made by Cabinet and include such regulatory powers as: the powers to make detailed rules governing the protection of flora and wild animals; public safety; management of fishing; public works; traffic; domestic animals; control of fires; firearm discharge, and licensing. While these regulations are applied through planning and management activities, Section 2 of the National Park Act states that a park warden is an 'officer appointed under the Public Service Employment Act whose duties include the enforcement of this Act'. Among their other duties, wardens have the powers of peace officers in regards to violations of park regulations by residents or visitors. Park wardens also have the authority to enforce a number of other regulations from other statutes. Penalties and fines associated with violations have been increasing over time as deterrents or punishments of infractions.

DIRECTION PROVIDED BY POLICY

Policies are statements of intent for management and are usually much more detailed and explicit than legislation. Although policy direction should be followed by the bureaucracy, it is not directly enforceable in the courts. Any guideline expressed in the National Parks Act can be enforced in the courts, whereas policy cannot. Policy guidelines provide extremely important direction for the day-to-day planning and management of national parks. The national park policy (Canadian Heritage, 1994) describes the rationale for national parks and the philosophy for managing them. The first comprehensive policy document was passed in 1964 with the latest most comprehensive revisions published in 1994. The purpose of national parks contained in the legislation is further elaborated in these policy documents. The policies state that:

> Protecting ecological integrity and ensuring commemorative integrity take precedence in acquiring, managing, and administering heritage places and programs. In every application of policy, this guiding principle is paramount. The integrity of natural and cultural heritage is maintained by striving to ensure that management decisions affecting these special places are made on the grounds of sound cultural resource management and ecosystem-management practices.

The guiding principles and detailed activities policies contained within the policy document provide guidance with respect to the following essential considerations: the national park system and establishment of national parks; management planning; ecosystem-based management; public understanding, appreciation, and enjoyment of national parks; historical activities; infrastructure; and land tenure and residency. Details of the pertinent policies with respect to implementation and challenges are discussed in other chapters. The statement of guiding principles contained within this document provides an overview of the direction for management activities. Important concepts discussed in these guiding principles include:

- the paramountcy of protecting ecological integrity and commemorative integrity;
- managing on an ecosystem-basis and managing parks as part of larger ecosystems and not as islands;
- providing leadership and demonstrating through example environmental and heritage ethics and practices;
- protecting new parks and historic sites based on a systems approach, informed by science and on a co-operative basis;
- recognizing that education through a variety of approaches is the key to longer-term success of the protection of park values;
- basing management decisions on the best-available knowledge;
- providing appropriate, basic, and essential services for park visitors within the objectives of maintaining ecological integrity;
- providing opportunities to build public understanding and make sound decisions through public involvement, co-operation, and collaboration with a full range of levels of government and interest groups;

- ensuring the accountability of Parks Canada for adherence to these principles through State of the Parks reporting.

Although Parks Canada published its comprehensive policies in the 1994 document, new policy direction, largely in the form of ministerial statements, has since been forthcoming that is of primary importance. These policy directions often come in the form of individual issues and are harder to track. Some of the most recent and prominent policy decisions include: the revenue policy (Parks Canada, 1998a); a principle of 'no net environmental impact' for park communities within national parks along with other policies designed to regulate use and development (Canadian Heritage, 1998); a policy statement preventing the expansion of ski areas within national parks, policies to restrict existing ski area capacity to within current Long Range Plans and to review those capacity figures, and a restriction on the development of any new ski areas within national parks; and an announcement on a moratorium on commercial development outside of park communities within National parks (Canadian Heritage, 1998). Forthcoming policy statements are expected on policy direction for existing outlying commercial accommodations for the Mountain Parks.

WHERE TO LOCATE NATIONAL PARKS AND HOW MANY ARE NEEDED?

One of the most controversial aspects of national parks is their location and number. The fierce debate over the establishment of a Gwaii Haanas National Park and Haida Heritage Site on South Moresby Island, BC, illustrates this point. The involvement of several levels of government and stakeholder groups (Dearden, 1987) played a part in the final decisions about the park. Conservation groups recognized the ecological significance of the area and wanted to see a large national park established to provide maximum protection to it. The tourist industry argued that the creation of a national park would serve as a focus for tourism. Opposed to this notion was the forest industry, which wanted to harvest the valuable old-growth temperate rainforest within the area. The Haida Nation, whose traditional territory the area is within, wanted the area protected, but their concerns did not exactly mirror those of the tourism industry or the conservation community; they value the area for its spiritual significance to their culture. The provincial government was reluctant to give up any territory to the federal government as a national park and would have preferred some other solution. The debate over Gwaii Haanas was fiercely fought and drawn-out with interests polarized, protests staged over harvest activities, and arrests made.

The issue was resolved with the signing of a memorandum of understanding in 1987 between the federal government and the government of British Columbia. This was followed by the Canada-British Columbia South Moresby Agreement, signed in 1988, which provided compensation to the forest industry and other industries as well as funds for a regional economic initiative, based on tourism and small business development in the Queen Charlotte Islands (Environment Canada, 1991). Perhaps the most significant aspect of the agreement was the signing of an agreement between Canada and the Haida Nation in which the Haida Nation and the Government of Canada agree to manage the area as a national park while continuing to disagree over ultimate ownership of the land.

The solution will endure as one of the most unique in national park creation worldwide and a turning point in the process of establishing new national parks. Gwaii Haanas signalled the increasing role and importance that First Nations now have in park creation and the need for the development of a common vision and agreement from all parties on the protection of ecological integrity. Every potential national park is established in the context of complexity of ownership and jurisdiction, existing land use, and competing values and visions for the land. As a result, it has become imperative to define some sort of process and rationale for establishing new national parks.

Systems Planning

Canada's early national and provincial parks were set aside as opportunities arose. These lands were preserved for their scenic beauty, revenue potential from tourism, wildlife, or other wonders of nature. Growth in the number of parks for the first half of the century was not part of a system plan and certainly not explicitly linked to protecting biodiversity. The initial ideas of systems planning suggested that each province or regional area should have a protected area. Gradually more ecological rationale has crept in. The creation of a systems planning framework was an effort to develop a rational basis for establishing national parks. In 1971, a national parks systems plan was approved as a basis for deciding where national parks were needed (National and Historic Parks Branch, 1971; Environment Canada, 1990). These natural regions were based generally on broad physiographic characteristics and defined as: 'natural landscapes and/or environments of Canada which may be separated from other such landscapes and environments by surface features which are readily observable, discernible, and understandable by the layman as well as by scientists and others more familiar with the natural features of Canada' (National and Historic Sites Branch, 1971: 3).

In the 1980's, this natural region approach was updated to give it a broader ecological foundation that focused on the idea of using ecoregions with the notion that establishing a representative protected area within each would capture the typical range of variability of landforms, vegetation, and wildlife and therefore help conserve the native biodiversity of the region. The plan classified the land mass of Canada into 39 natural regions each with its own characteristic vegetation patterns, landforms, climate, and wildlife. Parks Canada's progress towards its commitments to represent these natural regions have been significant with the creation of a number of new national parks, particularly in the Canadian Arctic and as a result of land claim settlements. However, many natural regions still are not represented. (Figure 9.1). A parallel systems plan for National Marine Conservation Areas was released in 1996 although little progress has been made towards representation (Chapter 14).

Endangered Spaces

In 1989, the World Wildlife Fund and the Canadian Parks and Wilderness Society launched a campaign to rally public support and public policy towards representing each of the country's 486 ecoregions (a much finer scale classification system than the Parks Canada system of 39 regions) with a protected area (Hummel, 1989). In 1992, the Endangered Spaces goal became public policy with the signature by the Tri-Council of Environment, Parks, and Wildlife Ministers (federal, provincial, and territorial ministers) to the 'Statement of Commitment to Complete Canada's Network of Protected Areas'. This statement committed the governments to completing the terrestrial protected areas network by 2000. Despite a doubling in the amount of protected land in Canada in the last decade—a significant achievement—the target has not been met and Canada ranks 36th in terms of total area legally protected from industrial development. Many of the methods used to identify representative areas pre-dated many of our modern principles of conservation biology. Common criticisms are that the Parks Canada approach based on 39 natural regions defines regions that are generally far too large and diverse for a single national park to adequately represent, consequently, most ecoregions still need more adequate representation. In reality, the adequacy of representation of the protected areas systems depends on the scale of analysis, the strength of the candidates, the degree to which candidate areas are unimpaired, the willingness of the levels of government to protect the area, and the legislative and management tools used to protect the areas.

Establishing a New Park

Identifying, selecting, and establishing new national parks has proven to be a complex exercise, although the normal sequence of events can be summarized in five steps:

1. Identify representative natural areas within the natural regions;
2. Select potential park areas, known as "Natural Areas of Canadian Significance;"
3. Assess park feasibility;
4. Negotiate a new park agreement;
5. Establish a new national park in legislation.

In the past, establishing a new national park in legislation, thus allowing the full authority of Parks Canada to manage the park, has been a difficult process taking upwards of 20 years. The Canada National Parks Bill (Bill C-27) contains a revised park establishment process that allows a new national park to be added very quickly to the legislation within months rather than years.

New national parks must be established with the co-operation of the provinces and territories that must, under current legislation, make formal transfer of the land to federal jurisdiction. Provincial governments have been reluctant to surrender lands to the federal government, thereby slowing the process of creating new national parks. First Nations governments also have a key role to play in negotiating new parks within traditional territories and the recent establishment of parks such as Aulavik, Sirmilik, and Tuktut Nogait in the North are testimony to not only the increasingly important role of First Nations but also the new and creative ways that must be sought for park establishment. National parks established through land claims agreements, while perhaps increasing the overall management complexity, may indeed be examples of park creation that allows for parks to be managed in a way that takes into account the greater park ecosystem. For example, in Ivvavik National Park in Yukon established through the Inuvialuit Final Agreement, the local hunter and trapper committees, the north-slope Wildlife Management Advisory Committee, and other mandated boards and councils all play a role in regional integration of the park.

Foregoing Options

Competing resource values such as forestry and mining on provincial Crown land and urbanization on private land mean that options for new park creation are being foreclosed. The ultimate location, size, shape and condition of the new parks have a significant effect on the ability of a park to maintain ecological integrity, consequently the negotiation for new parks is exceptionally important. The Mealy Mountain area of Labrador has been proposed since the 1970s as a candidate national park, representing the East Coast Boreal Region. The area is part of an Innu land claim and the Innu Nation supports the establishment of this park. As of yet, however, the provincial government, while pledging in 1992 to help establish the park, has yet to launch the feasibility study. Meanwhile, Phase III of the Trans-Labrador highway is slated to traverse the proposed national park. If the road is built through the proposed area prior to the completion of the feasibility study, resource users will gain access and legal rights to the land, thereby compromising the park values as well (potentially) as the land claim negotiations with the Innu Nation (Parks Canada Agency, 2000a). The Canadian Environmental Advisory Council (1991) characterized the problem as: 'Establishing protected areas in isolation from regional planning and decision-making processes is not an effective way to ensure the maintenance of their long-term ecological integrity. Past experience has shown that surrounding communities, landowners, and commercial developers systematically encircle and encroach on protected areas. The result is often the loss of protected areas values and demands for inappropriate uses of these resources.' Clearly, to achieve the protected areas goals a more co-operative and inclusive approach by Parks Canada is required. The Auditor General of Canada's report on national parks (1996: 13–19) noted, however, that: 'By simply waiting for other governments and local communities to adopt favourable positions, Parks Canada is reducing the likelihood of achieving representation in several natural regions and maintaining ecological integrity'. Both the Auditor General's report and the Ecological Integrity Panel report noted that by the nature of the process they use, Parks Canada may be encouraging other jurisdictions to adopt a defensive position at the outset. The challenge is to facilitate the development of a common vision with the relevant governments or communities within which a new national park could be created before the identification of a candidate area. Based on this common vision, stronger interim protection measures negotiations (such as withdrawal from mining claims), meant to ensure park conservation values, are not lost during the slow process of negotiations.

TOWARDS A NATIONAL PROTECTED AREAS STRATEGY

National and provincial parks, wildlife management areas, heritage rivers, conservation easements, wilderness areas, marine conservation areas, special management areas established under First Nation's land claims, along with a host of other conservation tools make up some of the components of a system of protected areas. But is it really a 'system'? Is the designation and management of these areas co-ordinated to ensure that collectively they meet the nation's needs and its international obligations for the conservation of biodiversity, wilderness, ecological integrity, sacred lands and waters, and for recreation? To achieve the national conservation objectives, Canada needs a comprehensive national protected areas systems plan that folds in the myriad layers of conservation goals within a co-operative implementation plan. A true protected areas systems approach includes:

- Representative core areas in each eco-region, designed to play a key role in maintaining ecological integrity;
- Protection of special natural and cultural features and landscapes;
- Protection of wildlife habitat and species populations throughout the country;
- Protection of rare and endangered species throughout their ranges;
- Maintenance of ecological connectivity between protected areas;
- Management of human use outside of protected areas in ways that help conserve biodiversity as well as ecosystem functions (Parks Canada Agency, 2000a).

BOX 9.1 Other Legislation and Constitutional Guidance

The National Parks Act and associated Agency Act are not the only legislated guidance for the management of national parks. Several other important pieces of legislation have direct implications for specific management actions such as those associated with the enforcement of rules and regulations referred to in the section on park regulations.

Canadian Environmental Assessment Act (CEAA)

CEAA is federal legislation that requires environmental screening, assessment, and review of projects involving federal land or federal dollars. The environmental assessment process is a key mechanism for examining use and development decisions within national parks and Parks Canada has associated directives guiding the procedures used for environmental assessments. Although a strong tool, in practice the environmental assessment of a project is de facto a final review resulting only in recommendations on ways to mitigate the effects of proposed projects. In a review from 1998 to 1999, only 6 of 962 Parks Canada projects registered with CEAA were rejected through the environmental assessment process. The new (Parks Canada, 1998a) Management Directive 2.4.2 Impact Assessment requires that projects not undergo environmental assessment until the project is proven to be in compliance with Parks Canada legislation, policies, and directives. This directive, if fully implemented, may go a long way towards strengthening the utility of the CEAA tool for park management.

Marine Legislation

While Canada's system of terrestrial national parks is one of the oldest and best established in the world, progress towards establishment of a Marine Protected Areas system has lagged substantially behind. In the past decade some progress has been made towards the establishment of legislative guidance for Marine Protected Areas including the Canada Oceans Act passed in 1996. Critical to full implementation of a Marine Protected Areas strategy will be passage of a national marine conservation area act that was unsuccessfully put forward in 1999.

Species at Risk

Unlike many other counterparts including the United States, Canada lacks a major legislative tool, an endangered species act, to protect biodiversity. In 2000 federal legislation for the protection of threatened and endangered species, the Species at Risk Act, or SARA (Bill C-33) was proposed but was not passed prior to the dissolution of the Parliament for the 2000 federal election. Conservation groups however criticized the proposed act as it currently stands for inadequately addressing the needs of threatened and endangered species for issues from 'What species matter?' to 'Should the law apply across all jurisdictions and ownerships?' If comprehensive legislation protecting species at risk were passed, it would provide an important tool, now lacking, for the protection of threatened and endangered species both within and outside of national parks. Such legislation would also obligate Parks Canada to a series of actions to protect species.

Constitutional Guidance

Aboriginal rights, land claims, and treaties that are enabled under the constitution provide guidance, with authority that overarches legislation and policy, regarding the establishment and management of national parks with respect to Aboriginal Peoples. As Aboriginal rights are clarified and land claims and treaties signed or modernized, there arise new challenges and new opportunities for approaches to national park management. These issues, discussed in more detail in Chapter 12, affect where and how national parks are established and how they are managed.

How Parks Are Managed

Legislation and policy form the foundation for management in the national parks with that foundation translated into park-specific direction through the development of plans. Parks Canada currently divides planning activities into three tiers: strategic, implementation, and work planning. While there are many types of plans in each tier, the key focus here will be on: the Park Management Plan at the strategic tier; the Business Plan at the implementation tier level; and specific work plans at the third tier.

Park Management Plans

Park management plans provide the essential direction for park managers. The legislation section of this text outlines that management plans are required to be prepared within five years of park establishment and tabled in the House of Commons. Detailed management planning guidelines have been prepared by the Agency (Parks Canada Agency, 2000b) to ensure consistency and standardization in plan preparation from everything from required elements to be contained within the plans to guidance

---

BOX 9.2 Contents of a National Park Management Plan

1. Forward
2. Recommendation Statement
3. Executive Summary
4. Table of Contents
5. Introduction
6. Role of National Park in the National Park System
7. Planning Context
8. Vision and Strategic Goals
9. Managing for Ecological Integrity
10. Protection of Cultural Resources
11. Heritage Presentation
12. Visitor Use and Services
13. Park Communities
14. Transportation and Utilities
15. Administration and Operations
16. Partnerships and Public Involvement
17. Park Zoning and Wilderness Area Declaration
18. Summary of Environmental Assessment
19. List of Contributors
20. References

on the level and types of appropriate public participation that should be undertaken to develop the plans (see Box 9.2). Both the policy statements and the 1988 Act amendments state that maintenance of ecological integrity must be the first consideration in management planning. This increased focus on ecosystem-based management for ecological integrity will result in a fundamental shift in park management planning. To date, most plans can best be described as human use and development plans with the relationship of visitor opportunities and allowable developments and activities tied only loosely to the underlying ecological resource. Newer plans and associated guidelines are calling for a much more explicit focus and priority on ecological integrity and within that foundation a vision and objectives for human use. The revised National Park Act calls for a requirement that Park Management Plans contain a 'long-term ecological vision for the park, a set of ecological integrity objectives and indicators and provisions for resource protection and restoration, zoning, visitor use, public awareness and performance evaluation'.

Two areas in management planning that will become the focus of future work are: (1) the streamlining of planning processes to meet the primary mandate, and (2) more effective and appropriate forms of public consultation and involvement.

Parks Canada currently engages in the development of so many different types of plans and strategies that making a logical linkage between plans is exceptionally difficult (Charron, 1999). Not only does this overwhelming number of plans result in continuous planning and a lack of action but it can overwhelm and confuse the public. Additionally, accountability for the purpose of parks is very difficult to track. This wealth of plans has emerged based often on good rationale. Since the early 1980s with an increased emphasis on ecosystem-based management and ecological integrity, a series of plans or strategic documents including ecosystem conservation plans, ecological integrity statements, and vegetation and aquatic management plans have arrived on the scene. Similarly, at various times there has been an increased focus on human use—from marketing, to communications, to community outreach, to visitor activities management. Often the response has been that each component has been afforded separate plans. Parks Canada is now tasked with the challenge of consolidating planning to ensure that ecological and commemorative integrity are the core of all planning and decision-making and can be tracked throughout all activities. Revised management planning guidelines are beginning to make that translation, but work remains if the next generation of park management plans is to reflect this change.

Public involvement and participation in park management planning has been required for many years, but the nature of that involvement and the forums for participation have greatly evolved. Management for the national parks is entering a new era of more inclusive forms of decision-making, not mere consultation. This evolution away from traditional consultation processes (such as written submissions and public hearings) to more co-operative or consensus processes (such as round tables or other multi-stakeholder processes) is both opportune and problematic. Clearly a more participatory democracy in which citizens are more invested in the management

FIGURE 9.3 In front of the Wikkaninish interpretation centre in Pacific Rim National Park Reserve a full-scale wedding is taking place. Is this an appropriate activity to be encouraging in national parks? *Photo: P. Dearden.*

of national parks and in which managers are more responsive to the knowledge and concerns of the citizenry sounds ideal. These civics-based approaches acknowledge the range of values and interests held by different parties that will be necessary to manage parks not as islands but as core protected areas connected to working landscapes. However, some of the early attempts by Parks Canada to engage in these more participatory processes were naïve entries where the impacts—in terms of the ability of the agency to uphold legislation and policy and to form lasting relationships— were unclear. Parks Canada needs to be skilled and understanding of the advantages and disadvantages of various processes so that the mandate of parks is upheld and participants come together to share common values and alternative strategies and interests in how to meet this mandate (Chapters 6 and 7).

Park Zoning

One of the principle techniques developed for managing national parks is the park zoning system (Box 9.3). Park zoning reflects different intensities of visitor use, although in all places ecological integrity is to be the main priority. It is clear that Zones I (Special Preservation) and Zone II (Wilderness) are intended to provide the highest level of protection, although the only specific guideline is that motorized access will not be

BOX 9.3 Zoning System for National Parks

Zone I. Special Preservation

- Contain or support unique, threatened , or endangered natural or cultural features, or among the best examples of features that represent a natural region
- Motorized access and circulation will not be permitted

Zone II. Wilderness

- Extensive areas that are good representations of a natural region
- Perpetuation of ecosystems with minimal interference is key
- Require few if any rudimentary services and facilities
- Visitors will experience remoteness and solitude
- Visitor activities will not conflict with maintaining the wilderness
- Motorized access and circulation will not be permitted
- A variety of direct and indirect management strategies will be used to manage visitors

Zone III. Natural Environment

- Provide outdoor recreation opportunities requiring minimal services and facilities of a rustic nature
- Motorized access may be allowed, but will be controlled
- Public transit will be preferred

Zone IV. Outdoor Recreation

- Limited areas that are capable of accomplishing a broad range of opportunities
- Activities, services, and facilities will impact ecological integrity to the smallest extent possible
- Defining feature is direct access by motorized vehicle

Zone V. Park Services

- Communities in existing national parks that contain a concentration of visitor services and support facilities
- Major park operation and administration functions may also be found

Adapted from Parks Canada (1994b). Guiding Principles and Operational Policies.

BOX 9.4 Selected Resource Management Policies

- Ecosystem management provides the conceptual and strategic basis for the protection of park ecosystems.
- Decision-making associated with the protection of park ecosystems will be scientifically based on internationally accepted principles and concepts of conservation biology.
- An integrated database will be developed for each national park, along with research and environmental monitoring. Data requirements will regularly extend beyond park boundaries.
- Human activities within a national park that threaten ecological integrity will not be permitted.
- Sport hunting will not be permitted.
- Sport fishing may be permitted.
- Fish stocking will be discontinued.
- National parks will make efforts to prevent the introduction of exotic plants and animals.
- National park ecosystems will be managed with minimal interference in natural processes.
- Manipulation of naturally occurring processes such as fire, insects, and disease may take place if no alternative exists;
  — if there will be serious adverse effects on neighbouring lands;
  — if major park facilities, public health, or safety will be threatened; or
  — if management of certain natural features or cultural resources otherwise cannot be achieved.
- Integrated management agreements will be made with adjacent landowners and land management agencies.

Adapted from Parks Canada (1994b). Guiding Principles and Operational Policies.

allowed in these two zones. Zone III through to Zone V allow for more facilities and services, presumably to deal with higher numbers of visitors. The intent of the zoning system is to emphasize Zones I and II, such that each national park consists mainly of these two zones. In addition, the 1988 amendment to the National Parks Act specified that Zone II wilderness boundaries would be protected under legislation, whereas the designation of other zones is subject to national park policy.

Management of Natural Resources

While one of the major vehicles for protecting park resources is the zoning system, a number of policies guide planning and management. Managing for ecological integrity within a framework of ecosystem management requires a number of specific management guidelines, as indicated in the listing of relevant policies in Box 9.4.

FIGURE 9.4 The Icefields Centre in Jasper National Park. The Centre is a public-private partnership between Parks Canada and Brewster Tours. See Edward Abbey's *Desert Solitaire* (1968: ch. 5) for some comments on Coke machines in parks! *Photo: P. Dearden.*

Visitor Management in National Parks

The greatest negative impact on ecological integrity in national parks is thought to be visitors, and the facilities built in some parks to support their recreation and tourism. Yet, the provision of appropriate visitor activities is an important function of national parks. Box 9.5 lists a number of policies developed to guide visitor management in national parks.

Business Plans

The main planning tool at the implementation level is the business plan. The Business Plan is a three-year plan written at the Field Unit level combining planning for national parks and national historic sites. The Plan is the key accountability mechanism between the Field Unit Superintendent and the Chief Executive Officer of Parks Canada and it spells out both the specific actions that Parks will take to implement the park management plan during that time period as well as the financial requirements, including revenues, to implement that plan. Current critiques of business plans are that these plans do not currently translate well into implementation plans for the maintenance and restoration of ecological integrity, because targets and performance indicators for ecological integrity are often expressed in broad terms only, if at all. Secondarily, existing budget divisions (service lines) do not currently parallel those used in describing ecosystem-based management activities. Further detail on business plans is discussed in later sections in this chapter dealing with finance and accountability.

Work Plans

Work plans represent the detailed set of tasks and actions that are prescribed for a particular functional area within a park, such as an urban outreach plan or a fire management plan. These plans typically contain detailed actions over a fairly short horizon (1–3 years). The work planning function is an important part of daily operations and is the final stage where direction from legislation and policy through systems and management planning is translated into action. Although these plans typically are not prescribed or required, guidance for them can be found in policy and guidelines. Important aspects often addressed through specific work plans, such as fire management and restoration plans and visitor use management, are discussed in detail in other chapters.

Evaluation and Reporting—The Missing Tier

In the current management planning structure for Parks Canada at the individual park, or field unit level, the feedback loops of evaluation and reporting are largely missing from the structure. Current legislation calls for management plans to be reviewed every five years, however the nature or scope of that review is not stated. Often that review is less of an evaluation or reporting and mostly a redraft of the plan if significant changes are required. The biannual State of the Parks Report, written at the national level, provides the only mechanism to evaluate or report on park-specific actions. The general move towards a process of adaptive management, or formalized learning and evalua-

BOX 9.5 Selected Visitor Management Policies

- The Visitor Activity Management Process (VAMP) (Chapter 7) will be used to determine appropriate visitor activities, facilities, and services in national parks.
- VAMP will be predicated on social science information, and will be integrated with natural and cultural information.
- Not every kind of use requested by the public will be provided.
- Provincial, territorial, municipal, and private agencies will be encouraged to provide complimentary opportunities that respect shared ecosystems.
- The practice of ecotourism will constitute an important mutual linkage with other land management agencies and private interests.
- Each park may develop a variety of outdoor recreation opportunities, but these must conform to the park zoning plan.
- A minimum of built facilities will be permitted.
- An integrated visitor activities data base will be developed and kept up to date for each national park.
- Risk control measures will consider the experience needs of the visitor and promote visitor self-reliance accordingly.
- Parks Canada will use a variety of 'direct' and 'indirect' management strategies for managing public use. Direct strategies include rationing use, restricting activities, and law enforcement. Indirect activities include facility design, information dispersal, and cost-recovery mechanisms. (See Chapter 7.)
- Any built facilities in a national parks will be designed such that the scale, site, accessibility, and function are in harmony with the setting.
- Non-motorized means of transportation will be favoured.
- Aircraft will not be allowed in national parks unless reasonable travel alternatives are not available.
- Trails and roads may be constructed if their primary function is to serve park purposes.
- New commercial skiing areas will not be permitted in national parks.
- Through interpretation and public education, both within and outside national parks, Parks Canada will provide the public with interesting and enjoyable opportunities to observe and discover each parks natural, cultural, and historical features (Chapter 8).
- Interpretation and education will be used to inform visitors of park management issues and practices.
- Interpretation and education will be used to relate park themes to broader environmental issues, to provide the public with knowledge and skills to make environmentally responsible decisions.

Adapted from Parks Canada (1994b). Guiding Principles and Operational Policies.

tion from management action, is becoming a common discussion point within agencies adopting an ecosystem-based management approach. Translating these discussions into evaluation and reporting mechanisms is the next step. The institution of a formalized park-based evaluation and reporting mechanism, an individual state-of-the-park report that would be conducted at least prior to management plan review has been recommended as a mechanism to improve this shortfall (Parks Canada Agency, 2000a). One park, Banff, has taken a leadership role in providing an annual reporting in a public forum of its actions and progress towards achieving its objectives and this example coupled with a park-based evaluation report could serve as models for improving the evaluation and reporting level from other parks.

ADMINISTRATION: HOW MANAGEMENT IS STRUCTURED

The purpose of this chapter has been to examine national park legislation, policy, systems plans, and management direction for parks. Legislation and policy provide direction for Parks Canada in managing the national parks and provide for the Canadian public a framework for debating the purpose and rationale for various management actions. To fully understand how national parks are managed, we must, however, also understand the management culture: the bureaucracy of the Parks Canada Agency. Recent reviews and critiques of Parks Canada have indicated that the organizational culture of the Agency is the single biggest factor and barrier in affecting management (Parks Canada Agency, 2000a; Searle, 2000).

Creation of a New Agency

Since the 1980s, Parks Canada has undergone a series of rapid reorganizations, moves, re-naming and downsizing that have left their mark on the organization. In 1993, Parks was shifted from its older home in the Department of the Environment to reside in the Department of Canadian Heritage. In the spring of 1999, Parks Canada became a separate operating agency—a unique structure within the government. While the Parks Canada Agency still reports to the Minister of Canadian Heritage, it has greater autonomy particularly with respect to fiscal management and revenue generation. In the midst of these switches, the familiar icon named 'Parks Canada' made a short-lived but ineffective shift to the 'Canadian Parks Service'. The creation of the Agency status provides an opportunity to attempt new creative management structures as well as a chance to renew the organization. However, setting a new direction may be challenging for an organization with decreasing resources and an established management cadre. The new Agency status could provide opportunities to pursue creative fiscal practices, but it may lead to an increased reliance on cost-recovery and revenue generation at the expense of the core of the mandate.

Jurisdiction

With national parks, authority for park management emanates from the National Parks Act. This Act gives clear authority to the Minister of Canadian Heritage through to the Agency through the Parks Canada Agency Act. The Chief Operating Officer (CEO) of the Agency, the executive board, field unit and park superintendents and park wardens are cited in either the National Parks Act or the Parks Canada Agency Act as being involved in some way with the routine responsibilities of managing each park, regulating activities, leases, licenses, camping permits, and so on. Although a separate operating agency, the CEO still reports directly to the Minister and cabinet and the Minister's office and assistant deputy minister (ADM) have considerable authority and responsibility with respect to policy and legislation. The National Parks Act and policy provide general direction and authority, however, most of the day-to-day management decisions in the park are guided by directives and regulations passed pursuant to the Act. Within the Agency, the Field Unit Superintendents are directly accountable to the executive and CEO for decisions and actions at the park level.

Although Parks Canada has sole jurisdiction over national parks, park managers are by no means completely autonomous. Parks Canada must also take direction from central agencies, including the Treasury Board, on such areas as program expenditures, personnel policies, and the management of real estate. In addition to direction from these central agencies, an increasing number of parks have been created through formal co-operative management agreements (e.g., Gwaaii Haanas National Park and Haida Heritage Site) with First Nations and as a result park managers may share responsibility for some or all parts of park management activities with duly appointed representatives or councils. For example wildlife management activities within many of the newer northern national parks have mandated involvement in management from local or regional wildlife councils. Similar arrangements exist for a host of resource issues in an increasing number of parks.

The Organizational Structure

The Parks Canada Agency has responsibility for National Parks, National Historic Sites, and a range of other designations including, among others, Historic Canals and Canadian Heritage Rivers. The area of the Parks Canada Agency with jurisdiction over National Parks is currently made up of an Executive Board, Service Centres, and Field Units (Figure 9.5). The Executive Board is headed by the CEO along with a number of executive positions including the Directors General (East and West), the National Office Program Directors General, the Executive Directors of Quebec and the Mountain Parks, as well as Directors of Human Resources and of Communications. One significant change to this structure was amended in 2000—the addition of a new position of Director General for Ecological Integrity, who will serve as the point person for ensuring the first priority is placed on restoration and maintenance of ecological integrity. Setting policy and direction that reflects the mandate of national parks is responsive to field staff concerns and meets the needs of politicians.

In the past, regional offices were spread across the country to provide technical and professional support on a range of issues from planning, to data management to environmental assessment assistance. In the mid 1990s the organizational structure of the Agency was flattened with one principle effect being the removal of the regional offices. In their place there are service centres that have substantially reduced numbers of professional and technical staff.

The core of the Agency operations occurs at the Field Unit level managed by a Field Unit Superintendent. These Field Units are of varying size and spatial area and are made up of a combination of National Park(s), National Historic Site(s), and National Historic Canal(s). Depending on the size and location, some parks also have a Park Superintendent with specific focus on the National Park. This new Agency

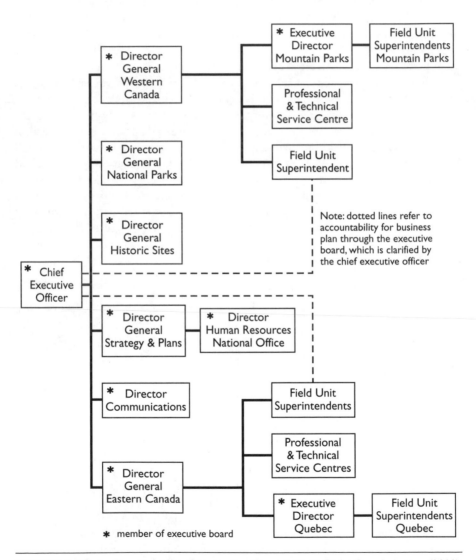

FIGURE 9.5 Parks Canada Agency, Organization Chart. SOURCE: Parks Canada Agency (2000).

with a more flattened organizational structure has been critiqued as resulting in highly politically responsive but balkanized units with a focus so broad from historic sites to monuments to parks that no one purpose is well served.

The structure of management at the National parks level is less standard and varies to some degree from park to park and from region to region. Job positions or functions common to most units include:

- Park Superintendent
- Chief Park Warden and warden staff
- Park Ecologist(s) or Ecosystem Secretariat
- Heritage Interpretation/Communication specialists and staff
- Business Management staff including operations, maintenance, personnel, finance
- Park Planner (often a shared position within a field unit or service center)

At the park level, the job requirements are many and varied and the staffing levels low. Increasingly, park staff are being called upon to work outside of park boundaries and to develop new relationships placing even more demands on staff time.

A Daily Profile

One of the emerging management challenges within National parks is that for each staff category or position, protecting ecological integrity should be 'job one'. For example, the park wardens and ecologists or Ecosystem Secretariat provide expertise and guidance in ecological issues and management. Resource conservation staff and wardens are instrumental in ensuring that park visitors comply with the requirements and laws that protect ecological integrity—from conducting environmental assessments to apprehending poachers. Interpretation and outreach staff should raise awareness and knowledge about the role of the park within the greater ecosystem, and encourage appropriate action by park visitors and partners. Maintenance and cleaning staff affect management directly through their choice and use of environmentally safe cleaning products and indirectly by demonstrating to the public the relationship between environmental awareness and individual actions. Affecting the cultural shift within the organization to enable the focus on the core of the mandate is the primary challenge for the Agency within the next few years. Box 9.6 outlines the major types of positions found in national parks, and the responsibilities associated with each position.

Financial Management

Traditionally, Parks Canada, like other government departments, was given an annual allocation from treasury on the discretion of Parliament. These allocations are based on work plans and multi-year operational plans prepared within parks and across regions. Budget plans are generally divided into operating plans, the ongoing costs associated with operating the park, such as salaries and standardized expenses, and capital projects such as the construction or refurbishment of visitor centres and new trails. The passage of a Parks Canada Revenue Policy and the creation of the Parks Canada Agency launched the organization into a new era of financial management.

BOX 9.6 A Day-to-Day Profile

Park Superintendent

Park Superintendents spend much of their time out of the Park at meetings and in consultations with various community groups, industry associations, and various levels of government.

- Annual budgeting plan.
- Review seasonal personnel requests for Warden Service.
- Attend negotiation meeting with Park Aboriginal Liaison Officer and local First Nation about traditional use and co-operative management of shellfish resources.
- Respond to phone inquiry from headquarters regarding monthly revenue targets from park fees.
- Meet with Chief Park Warden and operations staff regarding increase in public safety issues and vandalism in Birch Campground.
- Schedule a meeting with Provincial and Industry representatives to discuss the proposed forest management plan.
- Attend an evening meeting in the adjacent town regarding community concerns over community access and boat use in the Sound.

Park Warden

Depending on their skills and the needs of the park, wardens have a variety of responsibilities and skills including public safety, operations, communicating with the public, resource management activities, and conducting environmental assessments.

- Patrol shift in front-country including checking self-pay fee station in campground.
- Respond to emergency call regarding aggressive elk in campground—involved arranging transport for injured person and incident report assessment.
- Follow-up in the campground talking to visitors about appropriate human use during calving season.
- Planning for next day's vegetation inventory field work in Burnt Mountain.

Heritage Interpreter

Heritage interpreter, park naturalist, and outreach co-ordinator are among the names for park staff whose first responsibility is communication with the public. Historically interpreters have been involved primarily with traditional park interpretive programs, however, today they are communicating ecological messages to a range of audiences both inside and outside the park.

- Make presentation to regional Real Estate Board members on corridors for wildlife, greenspace, and property values.
- Work with team members and school teachers to develop outreach materials for the urban school Park Edu-kit.
- Meet with wardens to revise ecological and public safety messages for boating in the park.
- Prepare a public service announcement on safety during elk calving season for the local radio station.
- Talk to university graduate student regarding threatened and endangered species in the park.

Park Ecologist

Park ecologists, or in some locations the ecosystem secretariats, are often the primary co-ordinators of research, monitoring, and restoration efforts conducted by everyone from wardens to volunteer groups to heritage interpreters.

- Review methods and write contract for university study of impacts of recreation on grizzly bears.
- Provide technical advice on environmental assessment being prepared by wardens on the proposed filming of a TV commercial in the park.
- Negotiate with transport companies for compensation from the aquatic impacts of an oil spill on the highway bisecting the park.
- Catch Superintendent and Chief Park Warden in the hall to schedule a meeting to discuss the ecological impacts of park staff use of ATVs for trail maintenance.
- Chair an evening meeting of the Model Forest Association to discuss co-operative woodlot management and biodiversity issues.

The Parks Canada revenue policy introduced in the mid-1990s means that most National parks are involved in revenue generation with respect to charging fees for various products and services of both commercial and personal benefit. The foci of the revenue policy are several, although the general intent appears to be to provide funding, through traditional governmental appropriations, for the core mandate of the Agency, and to ensure that public goods are paid for from the public purse. Guiding principles within the revenue policy state that revenue initiatives will ensure long-term sustainability of ecological integrity and commemorative integrity; be consistent with market demand for services; and deliver services in a cost-efficient manner. Services operated or provided to benefit only select individuals who choose to consume or use those services (private goods) will have fees charged for them.

The fundamental principle guiding Parks Canada's revenue policy is that tax dollars pay for the cost of establishing and protecting national parks and national historic

sites; those who use them, will pay for the additional personal or commercial benefits they receive. Services providing both a public good and a personal benefit, such
as heritage presentation programs in parks and sites, will be financed through a combination of tax-based appropriations and fees (Parks Canada Revenue Policy, 1996).

Revenue generation targets and plans are developed on an annual basis for each
Field Unit and approved by the Agency executive as part of annual Business Planning
approvals. The portion of individual park budget's that these targets represents varies
considerably from year to year and from park to park. Some parks with high visitation (e.g., Jasper and Banff) generate an amount in revenue sometimes equal to the
parks' operating budgets. In contrast, Gwaii Haanas, a park with significantly lower
levels of visitation generates only about 2 per cent of its total budget. Revenue targets
are not meant to directly offset expenditures within parks with an intent to make
parks self sufficient, as this would violate the intent of government to provide through
traditional appropriations funding for the core mandate of parks. Instead revenue
resources are distributed by complicated funding schemes to help fund new park
acquisitions and to subsidize parks with lower visitation levels. If targets are exceeded,
the excess amount is re-allocated by the Executive Board. If a revenue target is not met,
the Field Unit must reduce expenditures by an equivalent amount.

From its inception the revenue policy of Parks Canada has been controversial both
inside and outside of the agency. Critiques from the public and opposition politicians cite concerns that fees will be accessible only to the élite in Canadian society and
not to the disadvantaged. Other critiques state that charging entrance or public goods
fees in parks amounts (considering the general appropriations that come from the
public's income tax) to double taxation. Within the Agency, employees have cited
concerns that revenue generation activities in some parks are driving activities or levels of activities that are in conflict with the maintenance of ecological integrity. An
example is the renewal of the lease on a golf course despite evidence in the *State of the
Parks 1997 Report* (Parks Canada, 1998b) that golf courses can have negative ecological impacts. Parks management are challenged to determine mechanisms that ensure
revenue targets are appropriately set and that these revenue targets neither prevent
people from visiting parks nor generate a motivation-and-reward system for managing in contravention to the primary purpose of National parks.

Decline in Funding

The funding scenario for the organization has also dramatically changed in the last
decade. In the early 1990s a unique five-year funding program (ending in 1996–7),
the Green Plan, provided an envelope of money that supported the creation of new
parks and sites as well as many ecological initiatives related to inventory, monitoring,
research, and education. Despite this funding boost, by 1998–9, Parks Canada saw an
annual amount of $104 million or 25 per cent reduction from 1994–5. This funding
decline was further exacerbated by the fact that a number of new parks or park reserves,
new National Marine Parks, and new park study areas were created over the same time
period. The result of this funding decrease was a major reorganization—with associ-

ated staffing declines, an increased focus on cost-recovery policy, and reduced subsidies to users who receive specific services. Entrance fees to parks were increased and new fees introduced. Today funding for Parks Canada for all operations hovers around $350 million of core funding and approximately $75 million in revenue. A recent study by the World Conservation Monitoring Centre of global protected areas budgets and staffing (James, 1999) show that while Canada is one of the world leaders in the amount of land in protected area status it has significantly less staff (13 staff/1000 km^2 in Canada compared to an average of 27 staff/1000 km^2 in developed countries) and budgets ($1,017/km^2 in Canada compared to an average of $2,058/km^2 in developed countries) than many other developed and some developing nations. With the creation of many new parks still on the agenda and an increasingly complex management job, staffing and budgetary requirements must be made adequate to do the job. The Ecological Integrity Panel noted that just to address the recommendations within their present capabilities would require an additional $330 million over five years.

Towards Greater Accountability

Clear legislation and policy are not sufficient without strong accountability mechanisms. Accountability mechanisms from the parliamentary level to the personnel level provide the means of ensuring that laws, policies, and plans are being followed and are effective. In reality, the purpose and utility of accountability measures varies based on the mechanism and on whom the accountability measure holds accountable and at what level. Accountability mechanisms within Parks Canada may ensure its staff's compliance with laws, policies, and plans or, accountability mechanisms could be designed to measure the effectiveness of the laws, policies, and plans themselves, which is a measure of the legislators and policy-makers. Some accountability mechanisms serve both purposes.

At the parliamentary level, accountability mechanisms have traditionally consisted of those associated with budgetary processes and the tabling of park management plans. To date, the latter has been generally more a formality than a useful means of accountability. Perhaps one of the most significant elements of the 1988 amendments to the Parks Act was the introduction of a new, system-wide accountability mechanism: the amendment stated that the minister was required to report to Parliament every two years on the state of the parks. The State of the Parks (SOP) reports are designed to report on progress towards completion of the systems plan, the state of the protection of park resources both ecological and commemorative, and the state of service to the public. State of the Parks reports have been improving in quality over the years with a better information base gradually being built to inform them. Their purpose can be both the extent to which Parks Canada complies with its laws, policies, and plans (such as reporting progress towards the completion of the systems plan), but also on the effectiveness of the actions Parks Canada has taken. This effectiveness or feedback monitoring component, currently expressed in the SOP reports as the status of ecological integrity within the parks and the stresses facing the parks, is a crucial part of holding Parliament and the Agency accountable for making progress towards maintaining or restoring ecological (and for historic sites, commemorative) integrity. Strengthening the science and knowledge base that informs the SOP reports is a need recognized both inside and outside of the Agency. Developing means and mechanisms to ensure that the SOP is duly considered by Parliament, perhaps by the Standing Committee on Heritage, and that Parliament and the Agency are held responsible for the results of the report is an area that needs continued work.

Within the Agency, the major accountability mechanisms in addition to the SOP report are the systems plan and corporate plan, at the level of the entire Agency, and the Park Management Plan and business plan, at the field unit level. Although all of these mechanisms can be used to hold managers and the executive accountable for actions, both the Auditor General's reviews of the Agency and the Ecological Integrity Panel's reviews suggest that substantial improvements are needed to ensure, first, consistency between plans and strategies and, secondarily, translation of these into effective accountability mechanisms.

The issue of fiscal accountability throughout the Agency is a priority. The move from one department to another, the creation of the Agency status, the restructuring and flattening of the organization, the change in government accounting systems, the introduction of the revenue policy, and a myriad of other events have resulted in a confusing fiscal accounting situation. Both the Auditor General and the Ecological Integrity Panel noted exceptional difficulty in obtaining rigorous, comparable, or reliably formatted data on financial systems. The Panel was unable to tell, for example, the amount of money spent on the core of the mandate, which is the maintenance and restoration of ecological integrity. A new system to track expenditures with better sub-categories that enable better identification of expenditures specifically related to ecological integrity activities implemented by Parks Canada in 1998–9 fiscal year and with upcoming reviews by the Auditor General may result in significant progress on financial accountability mechanisms.

In respect to personnel, performance reviews provide the major tool for accountability. While the scale of this accountability mechanism is the smallest, it is perhaps one of the most important and often neglected. Common critiques of the Agency are that job descriptions, requirements, and associated performance reviews throughout the Agency in all positions and categories should reflect the purpose of National parks. Each individual, from janitorial services to the CEO, needs to be held accountable for the ways in which his or her job contributes to the achievement of the purpose of National parks. Strong accountability mechanisms, including performance reviews, punishments, rewards, and awards will cascade up the chain into strong accountability mechanisms for the Agency as a whole.

Not to be neglected in a discussion of accountability mechanisms is the increasingly important role that the public are having in affecting Parks Canada. These accountability mechanisms are not formalized, but through public participation, litigation, lobbying, and campaigning citizens are holding the government, the minister and the Agency accountable for its actions. In a much broader context, public responsibility and personal accountability for actions that are in keeping with the purpose of National parks are the cornerstone to protecting park values.

CONCLUSION

That Canadians support the concept of National parks and of protecting wilderness and natural settings there is little doubt. Consistently, national polls and media coverage affirm the public's intense regard for parks and opposition to threats against parks. Confusion still remains, within the Parks Canada Agency and within the public at large, concerning how best to manage these areas. Part of this confusion can be attributed to the persistence of historical practices or to the needs for such facilities as town-sites, golf courses, or ski areas that are inconsistent with protecting national parks. Another source of confusion is the disjoint between legislation and practice. In the midst of the Ecological Integrity Panel's deliberations and hearings a winter road through the centre of Wood Buffalo was advocated by policy-makers. Furthermore, relatively small management actions inconsistent with the values and practices parks are trying to maintain can have a large negative influence on the public image of the Parks. The presence of mowed grass and non-Native, somewhat urban, landscaping at the entrance to Fundy National Park among others and the widespread lack of sustainable or green technologies or facilities (such as composting toilets, recycling bins, and alternative energy sources) contradict the intent of legislation and policy. From legislative and policy direction to individual maintenance activities park management is a challenging responsibility.

Fundamental to the management of the national parks system is the process of determining where new parks should be located and how many are needed. With the recognition of growing stresses on parks from within and from land management outside of parks, the notion that parks once established will self-manage has been dispelled. The human footprint is everywhere from the clogging of the Bow Valley wildlife corridor with highways, towns, and developments to the generation of airborne pollutants in cities that are deposited thousands of miles a way in the pristine high alpine lakes of national parks or in the fatty tissue of a marine mammal within Saguenay Fiord National Marine Conservation Area. In Canada today we face the reality that protecting the right areas will not by itself allow 'nature to heal itself'. The stresses placed on parks are too many and too great for us to be sure that their integrity will persist without active management.

The administrative, decision-making, and accountability structures within Parks Canada have been the source of many past problems. Decision-making must deal with the realities of the legislation and policies that govern management and with the conservation science that should inform decision-making and with the interests and wishes of the public and politicians. Reconciling these competing interests within the legislative and policy structures is a continuing challenge. Looking forward, each national park plan should be scrutinized for optimal achievement of the intent of the legislation and policies. Taking such a leap forward will require revolutionary changes in areas such as: human use management; the role of science in decision-making; and the need to protect ecological values both within and outside of national parks. Corresponding changes in Agency structure, decision-making processes, and accountability mechanisms will be required.

ACKNOWLEDGEMENTS

This chapter is based on work by Paul Eagles and by Rick Rollins in an early edition of this book (Chapters 4 and 5) and on the collective writings of the Ecological Integrity Panel.

REFERENCES

Auditor General of Canada. 1996. Chapter 31: *Canadian Heritage-Parks Canada: Preserving Canada's National Heritage*. Ottawa: Report of the Auditor General of Canada to the House of Commons.

Canadian Environmental Advisory Council. 1991. *A Protected Areas Vision for Canada*. Ottawa: Minister of Supply and Services.

Canadian Heritage. 1994. *Parks Canada: Guiding Principles and Operational Policies*. Ottawa: Minister of Supply and Services.

Canadian Heritage. 1998. *State of the Parks, 1997*. Ottawa: Minister of Public Works and Government Services Canada.

Charron, L. 1999. *An Analysis of Planning Processes of Parks Canada*. Prepared for the Panel on the Ecological Integrity of Canada's National Parks.

Dearden, P. 1987. 'Mobilizing Public Support for Environment: The Case of South Moresby Island, British Columbia', in *Need-to-Know: Effective Communication for Environmental Groups*. Proceedings of the 1987 Annual Joint Meeting of the Public Advisory Committees to the Environmental Council of Alberta. Environment Council of Alberta, 62-75.

Environment Canada. 1990. *National Parks Systems Plan*. Ottawa: Supply and Services Canada.

———. 1991. *State of the Parks: 1990 Report*. Ottawa: Supply and Services Canada.

Hummell, M. 1989. *Endangered Spaces*. Toronto: Key Porter Books.

James, A. 1999. 'Institutional Constraints to Protected Area Funding', *Parks* 9, 2: 15-26.

National and Historic Sites Branch. 1971. *National Parks Systems Planning Manual*. Ottawa: Information Canada.

Parks Canada. 1994a. *Parks Canada Guide to Management Planning*. Internal Document. Ottawa.

———. 1994b. *Guiding Principles and Operational Policies*. Ottawa: Parks Canada.

———. 1996. *Revenue Policy*. Internal Document.

———. 1998a. *Management Directive 2.4.2, Impact Assessment*. Internal Document.

———. 1998b. *State of the Parks, 1997*. Ottawa: Minister of Public Works and Government Services.

Parks Canada Agency. 2000a. *Unimpaired for Future Generations? Protecting Ecological Integrity with Canada's National Parks,* vol. 2: *Setting a New Direction for Canada's National Parks*. Report of the Panel on the Ecological Integrity of Canada's National Parks, Ottawa.

———. 2000b. *Parks Canada Guide to Management Planning*. Ottawa: Minister of Public Works and Government Services Canada.

Searle, R. 2000. *Phantom Parks*. Toronto: Key Porter Books.

KEY WORDS/CONCEPTS

Bill C-27
legislation
policy
regulations
systems plan
Endangered Spaces Campaign
park management plan
zoning system
business plan

work plan
park superintendent
park warden
heritage interpreter
park ecologist
financial management
revenue policy
State of the Parks Report

STUDY QUESTIONS

1. Describe the evolution of 'appropriate activities' in national parks.
2. Distinguish between 'legislation', 'policy', and 'regulations'.
3. During the winter of 2001, a debate surfaced regarding the carrying of firearms for law-enforcement purposes by national park wardens. Some people in the Agency supported this idea, but others were opposed. Develop a position on this issue by examining relevant sections of national park legislation, policies, and regulations together with any media accounts of the debate.
4. What is the significance of 'species at risk' legislation for Parks Canada?
5. Discuss the significance of the 'Endangered Spaces Campaign'.
6. Critique the systems planning approach used by Parks Canada listing both positive and negative features.
7. Examine a recent national park management plan for evidence of 'ecological integrity', 'ecosystem management', and 'appropriate activities'.
8. Comment on the changes to Parks Canada as a result of the new 'agency structure'.
9. Outline the funding crisis facing national parks.
10. What is romantic or naïve about the expression that 'if we protect the right areas, nature will take care of the rest'?
11. What is the purpose of the zoning system developed by Parks Canada? Compare this with the type of zoning described in ROS (Chapter 7).
12. What circumstances described in National Park policy allow for the manipulation of naturally occurring processes? Discuss viewpoints both supporting and opposing this policy.
13. Discuss advantages and disadvantages of the policies for allowing motor vehicle access into national parks.
14. Contrast the development and approval process for 'business plans' with 'work plans'.
15. Compare the roles of park warden, heritage interpreter, and park ecologist.

CHAPTER 10

Case Study: Banff and the Bow Valley

Guy S. Swinnerton

INTRODUCTION

The Banff-Bow Valley is situated within Banff National Park, which has been described as 'one of the world's most significant protected areas' (Banff-Bow Valley Study, 1996b: 1; Figure 10.3). However, at the time of its establishment in 1885, Banff National Park was primarily perceived as having the potential to become an important tourism destination (see Bella, 1987; Lothian, 1987; Lowry, 1994). As a result of development over the past century, today's visitors to Banff National Park frequently look upon the area primarily as an international tourism 'icon' (see Banff-Lake Louise Tourism Bureau, 2000; Ritchie, 1998, 1999c) rather than recognizing its ecological significance (Canadian Parks Service, 1991b) within the Canadian Rocky Mountain Parks World Heritage Site.

Many national parks and protected areas within Canada, as well as globally, have become important destinations for tourism and the settings for a variety of nature-based recreation activities (see Swinnerton, 1999). However, the conflict between protection and human use, and the tendency to treat parks as commodities, is being more widely recognized and addressed as an increasing variety of activities and associated development place additional pressures on park environments (Lowry, 1994, Parks Canada Agency, 2000a; 2000b).

In Canada, increasing concern has been expressed about the growing threat to the ecological integrity of most of the national parks within the system (see Canadian Parks Service, 1991a, 1991b; Parks Canada, 1998a; Parks Canada Agency, 2000a, 2000b). For example, the first *State of the Parks Report* (Canadian Parks Service, 1991b: 28) referred to the problem in the following manner:

> A balance between visitor service facility development and the protection of land resources is essential. The prime example of where this balance is threatened is in the montane environment. The loss of the montane, or valley bottom environment in the Banff, Jasper, Yoho, Kootenay complex has been well documented and remains a problem with no ready solution.

Nevertheless, nearly a decade later, considerable controversy persists over the gravity of the threats to the ecological integrity of Canada's first National park and whether or not a crisis really exists. On the one hand, environmentalists and scientists are

FIGURE 10.1 View from Sulphur Mountain showing the Town of Banff and illustrating its critical position within the montane zone, and the constricted nature of wildlife corridors. *Photo: Guy Swinnerton.*

adamant that the ecological health of Banff National Park (see Banff-Bow Valley Study, 1995d; Green, 1996b) and many of the other national parks is already seriously compromised (Parks Canada Agency, 2000a; 2000b). At the same time, advocates for public enjoyment and tourism within the national parks, such as the Association for Mountain Parks Protection and Enjoyment (AMPPE), are skeptical about the magnitude of the problem and feel that many of the restrictions on development and human use are unnecessary and unwarranted (see AMPPE, 1999; Corbett, 1998; Sillars, 1996; Urquhart, 1998a). Following a fact-finding visit to Banff National Park in October, 1994, the Senate of Canada's Standing Committee on Energy, the Environment and Natural Resources commented that it had, '. . . heard first hand how the desires of local businesses and conservation interests are on a collision course. Each has a very different view of the role of a national park' (Senate of Canada, 1996: 39).

Acknowledgment that the ecological integrity of the Bow Valley could be permanently impaired on account of the continued increase in visitation and infrastructure development, resulted in the then Minister of Canadian Heritage, Michel Dupuy, announcing the Banff-Bow Valley Study in March 1994. Its mandate was to 'assess the cumulative environmental effects of development and use in the entire Bow River watershed inside the Park' (Banff-Bow Valley Study, 1996b: 1). The final technical report, *Banff-Bow Valley: At the Crossroads*, was released by the Minister of Canadian Heritage, Sheila Copps on 7 October 1996.

The Banff-Bow Valley Study is recognized as one of the most important events in the evolving history of Banff National Park. Sheila Copps, in the Minister's Message contained in the new Banff National Park: Management Plan (Canadian Heritage, Parks Canada, 1997), noted that not only were many of the recommendations of the Banff-Bow Valley Study incorporated in the new management plan, but that the Study made a unique contribution to both understanding the role of science in decision-making and the importance of effective public involvement. Moreover, by observing that the management plan could be a model for all the national parks in Canada for generations to come, she expressed tacit acknowledgment of the relevance of the Banff-Bow Valley Study beyond the confines of Banff National Park.

A number of existing studies have already examined or commented on the Banff-Bow Valley Study from a variety of perspectives, including both the decision-making process that was adopted and the substance of the Study (see Hodgins and Cook, 1999; Page, 1997; Ritchie, 1998, 1999a, 1999b; Urquhart, 1998a). The purpose of this chapter is to outline the circumstances that led to the Banff-Bow Valley Study, to examine the Study itself and to provide an overview of the recommendations that were contained in the Final Report. Reference is also made to the new management plan that was subsequently prepared for Banff National Park and that provided the government's formal response to the Final Report of the Banff-Bow Valley Study. Finally, some of the implications and ensuing developments that have evolved from, or were influenced by the Banff-Bow Valley Study and the new park management plan are noted in Box 10.3. Amongst these are the 'capping' of commercial growth within the Town of Banff, the more open and transparent process adopted for decision-making, including the development review process being followed in the Four Mountain Parks, the adoption of a Heritage Tourism Strategy, the development of guidelines for ski areas and outlying commercial accommodations and hostels, and the increased priority being given to protecting ecological integrity.

HISTORICAL BACKGROUND AND CONTEXT

A detailed review of this historical background is beyond the scope of this chapter, and readers are instead directed to the more detailed analysis afforded by studies such as those of Bella (1987), Banff-Bow Valley Study (1996b), Belland and Zinkan (1998), Dearden and Berg (1993), Hart (1999), Hildebrandt (Banff-Bow Valley Study, 1995c), Lothian (1987), and Chapter 2 in this book. Nevertheless, the significance of the Banff-Bow Valley Study would be largely lost without some appreciation of this historical background and context.

Belland and Zinkan (1998) in their examination of the evolution of heritage tourism and Canada's Rocky Mountain Parks divide the time since 1885 into four periods: 1885–1950s, 1960–70s, 1980–90, and the 1990s. Their time frame has been adopted for this overview. Integrated into this time frame are the seven major themes or events identified by Hildebrandt (Banff-Bow Valley Study, 1995c) as being significant to the more recent history of the Banff-Bow Valley. They are: (1) auto-tourism and the opening of the Trans-Canada Highway in the early 1960s; (2) winterizing the Banff Springs Hotel in the late 1960s; (3) Banff National Park and the Olympics in the 1960s; (4) public participation and the 1979 Parks Canada Policy Document; (5) Parks Canada's move from the Department of Indian Affairs and Northern Development to the Department of the Environment in 1979 and its subsequent move to the Department of Canadian Heritage in 1994; (6) Parks Canada and business development in the 1980s; and (7) incorporation of the town of Banff in 1990. However, in order to provide a continuous temporal picture, Box 10.1 is provided.

BOX 10.1. Historical Outline of Significant Events Influencing the Banff-Bow Valley Area

---

1885: November 28th: Order in Council establishing a 26-sq.-km reservation around the Banff hot springs
1887: Rocky Mountain Parks Act to establish the boundaries for a more extensive 672-sq.-km park
1981: Four Mountain Parks planning program initiated
1984: Canadian Rocky Mountain Parks World Heritage Site designated
1986: In trust for tomorrow: A management framework for Four Mountain Parks
1988: Banff National Park Management Plan approved
1988: National Parks Act Amendments
1990: Incorporation of the Town of Banff
1994: Parks Canada: Guiding Principles and Operational Policies
1994: Banff-Bow Valley Study announced

Belland and Zinkan (1998) note with reference to the first period that they identify (1885–1950s), that from the outset, and extending up to the middle of the twentieth century, Canada's Rocky Mountain National Parks, and specifically Banff, were promoted for public enjoyment and the economic return that could be derived from the promotion of tourism. Even though the National Parks Act of 1930 officially confirmed the dual mandate of protection and public enjoyment, the latter continued to take priority.

The second period, the 1960s and 1970s, was also characterized by the growth of mass tourism and the continuing development of the necessary infrastructure and facility-based attractions for the growing numbers of visitors to Banff and the other Mountain Parks. Active involvement by the National Parks Service in supporting this growth continued, particularly during the 1960s (Banff-Bow Valley Study, 1995c). However, it was during this period that people began to question the appropriateness of many of the developments taking place and the ensuing loss of the 'natural values' of the mountain parks. Reflecting these concerns, were 1964 and 1979 National Park

Policy documents that signified acknowledgement of the special qualities of the parks and need for their protection (see Banff-Bow Valley Study, 1995c; Belland and Zinkan, 1998). The 1979 policy document included the statement: 'Ecological and historical integrity are Parks Canada's first considerations and must be regarded as prerequisites to use' (Parks Canada, 1979: 12).

Nevertheless, during the 1980s Banff National Park, and specifically the town of Banff, experienced further development pressures and business activity. According to the 1981 census, Banff had a population of 4,627 permanent residents (Parks Canada, 1986) and the visitation level to the Park in the early 1980s fluctuated in excess of 3.5 million (Banff-Bow Valley Study, 1996b).

In 1981 the Four Mountain Parks Planning Program was initiated with the intent of providing a long-range management framework for Banff, Jasper, Yoho, and Kootenay National Parks (Parks Canada, 1986). The framework received approval in 1986 and provided the direction and context within which individual management plans were subsequently prepared for each of the four individual Mountain Parks. The management plan for Banff National Park was approved in 1988 (Canadian Parks Service, 1988). In recognition of the global significance of the Four Mountain Parks and selected adjacent provincial parks, the area was designated the Canadian Rocky Mountain Parks World Heritage Site in 1984.

Of more immediate significance to the on-going management of Banff National Park were the amendments to the National Parks Act (1988) that incorporated into legislation the growing concerns for ecosystem protection and wildlife management and that priority must be given to protection in reconciling the dual mandate of protection and use. Particularly relevant to the Banff situation was the inclusion in the Amendments of guidelines for the incorporation for the townsites of Banff and Jasper and the prevention of any new ski areas within national parks.

During the first half of the 1990s a number of important planning and policy changes were to take place prior to the initiation of the Banff-Bow Valley Study itself. One of these was the incorporation of the town of Banff in 1990. The Town of Banff Incorporation Agreement that was signed by the Government of Canada and the Province of Alberta and took effect in January 1990 transferred most municipal government powers, including planning functions, from the Federal Government to an elected Banff Town Council. Although the Town of Banff became a municipality of the Province of Alberta, the Federal Government through the Minister of Canadian Heritage and Parks Canada retained authority over most environmental matters. Moreover, the Town was not permitted to extend the current boundary, and the Minister of Canadian Heritage was to be the final approval authority for the General Municipal Plan (see Banff-Bow Valley Study, 1995a, 1995c, 1996a; Town of Banff, 1998).

A General Municipal Plan (GMP) was adopted at the time of the incorporation agreement. The primary focus of the GMP was to provide a planning framework for addressing local community services, together with residential, commercial, and infrastructure requirements within the boundaries of the Town (see Banff-Bow Valley Study, 1995b, 1995d; Government of Canada and the Government of Alberta, 1989).

FIGURE 10.2. Park visitors and a street scene in Banff. *Photo: Guy Swinnerton.*

In 1994 the Minister of Canadian Heritage, Michel Dupuy, signed a new policy statement entitled Parks Canada: Guiding principles and operational policies (*Canadian Heritage*, 1994). Of particular relevance to the Banff-Bow Valley were policy directives on ecological and commemorative integrity, the management of visitor activities, tourism, and the type and scale of development acceptable within national parks (Banff-Bow Valley Study, 1995c, 1996b; Canadian Heritage, 1994). With reference to ecological and commemorative integrity the policy document includes the following statement: 'Protecting ecological integrity and ensuring commemorative integrity takes precedence in acquiring, managing, and administering heritage places and programs' (Canadian Heritage, 1994: 16). Ecological integrity is defined as, 'a condition where the structure and function of an ecosystem are unimpaired by stresses induced by human activity and are likely to persist' (Canadian Heritage. 1994: 119).

Although the policy provides for continued public understanding, appreciation, and enjoyment of the national parks, it also clarifies the types of visitor activities that are appropriate within such areas. Specifically, permissible activities are those that promote an appreciation of the park's purpose, respect the integrity of the ecosystem, and require a minimum of built facilities (Canadian Heritage, 1994). Hildebrandt (Banff-Bow Valley Study, 1995c), Belland and Zinkan (1998), and the Banff-Bow

Valley Task Force (Banff-Bow Valley Study, 1996b) have commented on the empathetic treatment that tourism received in the policy. The importance of tourism in contributing to the national economy and local communities is recognized. While acknowledging this importance, Parks Canada's role is seen as co-operating with the tourism sector to promote a sustainable tourism industry that respects and fosters the primary purpose of national parks with regard to maintaining and enhancing ecological and commemorative integrity.

THE BANFF-BOW VALLEY STUDY

In 1993 Parks Canada commenced an internal review of the management plans for the four Mountain Parks of Banff, Jasper, Kootenay, and Yoho (Parks Canada, 1994). This undertaking was the initial stage of the required process to review the national park management plans on a quinquennial basis. The five-year update was seen as providing an opportunity to measure the progress of implementing the 1988 plans, to consider the implications of changing environmental, social, and fiscal conditions, and to initiate an ecosystem-based management approach (Parks Canada, 1994).

In 1991 the Town of Banff had an estimated total population of 7,615 of which 5,688 were permanent (Banff-Bow Valley Study, 1996b). According to Parks Canada figures, the number of person visits to the Park between April 1993 and March 1994 was 4.2 million, and of this number 3.4 million visited the Town of Banff (Pacas, 1996). At the same time, commercial space within the Town of Banff had shown persistent growth. As observed by the Task Force, one of the consequences of these visitor numbers and the growth in the commercial sector is that 'Banff National Park and the Town of Banff generate significant benefits to Alberta and Canada through the economic activity they generate in the region' (Banff-Bow Valley Study, 1996b: 57). At the beginning of the 1990s direct visitor expenditures was in excess of $505 million per annum, and over three-quarters of this amount was generated by expenditures within the Town of Banff itself. Of particular concern to those people primarily interested in protecting the ecological integrity of Banff National Park was the future outlook for the Park if these patterns of growth and their cumulative effects were to continue. Subsequent visitation projections undertaken in conjunction with the Banff-Bow Valley Study suggested that if the annual growth rate experienced since 1950 were to continue, visitor numbers would reach 10.3 million in 2020 and 21.6 million by 2045 (Banff-Bow Valley Study, 1996b).

To environmental scientists as well as NGOs representing conservation interests, the requirements set out in the amendments to the National Parks Act, 1988 and the directions included in the 1994 National Parks Policy giving precedence to the protection of ecological integrity, provided more than adequate direction and powers to Parks Canada regarding the position it should be taking to the increasing pressures on the park environment. At the same time, commercial and tourism interests, including the three ski resorts within the Banff National Park, were arguing that they had to expand their operations to achieve economies of scale and to stay competitive in both

FIGURE 10.3 Banff and the Bow Valley.

the North American and global market (Corbett, 1998). Whereas some people were of the opinion that Parks Canada's apparent inability to deal with the management issues facing Banff National Park was largely a reflection of lack of resources resulting from continuing budget cuts (see Borbey, 1997; Parks Canada Agency, 2000b), 'to the NGOs, it appeared the government was impotent when it came to enforcing its own policies' (Banff-Bow Valley Task Force, 1996b: 8).

The circumstances directly responsible for the initiation of the Banff-Bow Valley Study are cogently summarized in the technical report of the Banff-Bow Valley Task Force (ibid., 15–16).

Management and governance are at the centre of the current issue in dispute. Park managers, caught in a difficult political position between the aspirations of environmental groups and of the business community, allowed both to proceed with their plans and expectations. Parks Canada backed away from addressing the contradictions between the two positions and let each feud with the other in public.

The two positions became increasingly polarized and it became evident that Parks Canada was in no position to reconcile the acrimony and underlying issues through the conventional park management planning process. As a result, the Minister of Canadian Heritage, Michel Dupuy, announced the Banff Bow Valley Study in March 1994. The initial intention was that the Study would be completed by June 1996.

THE BANFF-BOW VALLEY STUDY: OBJECTIVES AND PROCESS

The specific terms of reference for the Banff-Bow Valley Study was as follows:

> The Bow Valley Study will be a comprehensive analysis of the state of the Bow Valley watershed in Banff National Park. The study will provide a baseline for understanding the implications of existing and future development and human use, and the impact of such on the heritage resources. The study will integrate environmental, social and economic considerations in order to develop management and land use strategies that are sustainable and meet the objectives of the National Parks Act. (Ibid.: 2)

Three major objectives were identified:
- to develop a vision and goals for the Banff Bow-Valley that will integrate ecological, social, and economic values;
- to complete a comprehensive analysis of existing information, and to provide direction for future collection and analysis of data to achieve ongoing goals; and
- to provide direction on the management of human use and development in a manner that will maintain ecological values and provide sustainable tourism.

In addition to the three major objectives, the Study was requested to recommend strategies to the Minister that:
- recognize areas where existing land use activities are appropriate, areas where development and use have exceeded the ecological or social capacity of the area, and areas where additional activities are possible;
- maintain or enhance the area's tourism potential consistent with the Park's ecological integrity objectives;
- fill critical information gaps and support sustainable management and use practices in the future;

- provide a set of key indicators useful for assessing changes in the integrity of the Banff-Bow Valley and possible thresholds beyond which ecological integrity cannot be maintained;
- reduce existing detrimental environmental effects and prevent/reduce adverse effects of future development, park operations, and other land use activities (ibid.).

One of the most distinctive ways in which the Banff-Bow Valley Study differed from the approach to the preparation of conventional park management plans was that the Minister assigned the responsibility of directing the Study to a Task Force, the membership of which was independent of government. Another characteristic of the approach to be used in the Study—that was unprecedented in the history of Canada's National parks—was the level of provision for public participation. The minister had stressed the importance of consulting the Canadian public both as an integral part of the overall process and also in the formulation of the final recommendations (Ritchie, 1999a, 1999b, 1999c).

The Task Force identified six major tasks that needed to be undertaken in order to address the Study's objectives. These were:

- develop a program to involve the public
- collect and assess existing information about the Banff-Bow Valley
- draft a Vision, Principles, and Values for the Valley
- identify and assess key issues
- draft specific objectives and actions
- prepare recommendations for the Minister of Canadian Heritage

PUBLIC PARTICIPATION AND THE ROUND TABLE

Shared decision-making including consensus-building, as demonstrated through a 'round table' approach, has become widespread as a means to effective conflict and dispute resolution in issues involving natural resource planning and the allocation of public lands (see Dodds and Fenton, 1999). A critical dimension of this approach includes the transition from simply consulting the public to ensuring that they are actively involved in making decisions. Equally important is for all participants to adopt an 'interests' perspective rather than the more traditional 'positions' approach to addressing issues (see Fisher and Ury, 1991).

Hodgins and Cook (1999) in their review of the public participation process associated with the Banff-Bow Valley Study identify three main elements, information-sharing, consultation, and public interest negotiation. Whereas Parks Canada had traditionally used the first two elements in the preparation of park management plans, the inclusion of public interest negotiation was a new departure. In Hodgins and Cook's estimation, 'the public involvement program ... was perhaps the greatest success-with potentially the most lasting legacy-of the task force's work' (Hodgins and Cook, 1999: 53).

The procedures and processes for public interest negotiation process, by means of the round table approach, evolved during the fall of 1994. The Banff-Bow Valley

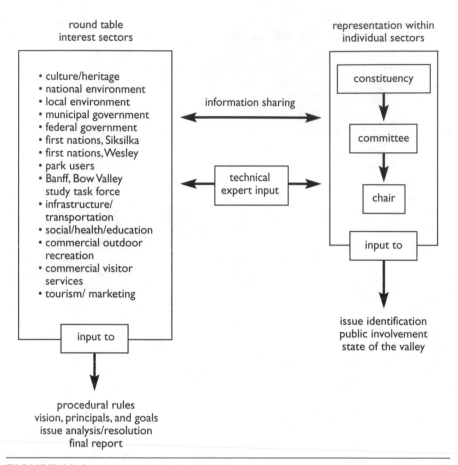

FIGURE 10.4 Banff-Bow Valley Round Table.

Round Table was intended to be the primary mechanism for identifying, analyzing, and resolving the issues encountered in the Banff-Bow Valley. In February 1995, The Minister of Canadian Heritage opened the first meeting of the Round Table (see Figure 10.4). Although the two First Nations representatives attended the initial meetings of the round table, they subsequently withdrew from the process. The Round Table met formally for two or more days each month between February 1995 and March 1996.

An initial objective of the Banff-Bow Valley Task Force was to develop goals and a vision for the Bow Valley in Banff National Park that would bring together ecological, social, and economic values. In December 1995, the Round Table unanimously agreed to submit its vision to the Task Force. The core vision was as follows:

The Bow valley in Banff National Park reveals the majesty and wildness of the Rocky Mountains. It is a symbol of Canada, a place of great beauty, where nature is able to flourish and evolve. People from around the world participate in the life of the valley, finding inspiration, enjoyment, livelihoods, and understanding. Through their wisdom and foresight in protecting this small part of the planet, Canadians demonstrate leadership in forging healthy relationships between people and nature. The Banff-Bow Valley is, above all else, a place of wonder, where the richness of life is respected and celebrated. (Banff-Bow Valley Study, 1996b: 21)

The core vision was expanded through a series of statements relating to central themes, values, and principles. This vision was used by the Task Force in conjunction with the other information sources it had available to draft the final report with recommendations that was eventually submitted to the minister.

RESEARCH AND ANALYSIS

To complement and provide in-put into the work of the Round Table, the Task Force commissioned the following studies for the *State of the Banff-Bow Valley: A Compendium of Information*:

- Historical analysis
- Governance model review
- Development decisions in the Banff National Park
- Review of the research management framework
- Discussion paper on governance and land management
- Visitor behaviour research
- Tourism outlook project
- Ecological outlook project
- Cumulative effects assessment
- Futures outlook project
- Identifying appropriate activities for Banff National Park

Ritchie (1998, 1999a, 1999b, 1999c) has examined the tourism and human use dimensions of the Banff-Bow Valley Study in considerable detail and Pacas et al. (1996) provide a detailed description of the issues relating to ecological projects and the working relationships between the Round Table, the Task Force, Technical Working Groups, and a Scientific Review Committee.

Even though the time-lines for the overall study were stringent and had implications for the workings of the Round Table and the scientific research and analysis that could be undertaken, the Banff-Bow Valley Study incorporated an overall process, research methodologies, and knowledge that were innovative and ground-breaking both in the ecological area and, to a more limited extent, in the field of human dimensions research in parks and protected area management.

BOX 10.2. Key Conclusions of the Banff-Bow Valley Task Force

1. While Parks Canada has clear and comprehensive legislation and policies, Banff National Park suffers from inconsistent application of the National Parks Act and Parks Canada's Policy.

2. Despite the fact that ecological integrity is the primary focus of the National Parks Act and Parks Canada's Policy, we found that ecological integrity has been, and continues to be, increasingly compromised.

3. While scientific evidence supports conclusion #2 above, a significant percentage of the population find it difficult, based on what they see around them, to understand the ecological impacts that have occurred.

4. The current rates of growth in visitor numbers and development, if allowed to continue, will cause serious, and irreversible, harm to Banff National Park's ecological integrity. Stricter limits to growth than those already in place must be imposed if Banff is to continue as a national park.

5. More effective methods of managing and limiting human use in Banff National Park are required.

6. To maintain natural landscapes and processes, disturbances such as fire and flooding must be restored to appropriate levels in Banff National Park.

7. There are existing anomalies in the Park, such as the Trans-Canada Highway, the Canadian Pacific Railway, and the Minnewanka dam.

8. We are proposing the refocusing and upgrading of the role of tourism. Tourism in Banff National Park will, to a greater extent, reflect the values of the Park, and contribute to the achievement of ecological integrity and the quality of the visitor experience.

9. We acknowledge that mountain tourism in Alberta will continue to expand. Any new, related facilities will have to be located outside national park boundaries.

10. Current growth in the number of residents, and in the infrastructure they require, is inconsistent with the principles of the national park. Revisions to the General Municipal Plan for the Town of Banff must address these inconsistencies and the needs for limits to growth.

11. Public scepticism and lack of trust in the decision-making process has led to the polarization of opinion. There must be an overhaul of the development review process.

12. Visitors must be better informed about the importance of the Park's natural and cultural heritage, the role of protected areas and the challenges that the Park will face in the third millennium.

13. Improvements in Parks Canada's management is central to the successful future of Banff National Park. This should begin with a comprehensive revision to the Banff National Park Management Plan that will reflect the recommendations of this report.

14. We believe that current funding will be inadequate to implement the recommendations of the Task Force and maintain normal operations in Banff National Park.

TASK FORCE CONCLUSIONS AND RECOMMENDATIONS

The Task Force completed its work in just over two years, and the final report, *Banff-Bow Valley: At the Crossroads*, was released in October 1996. Over 400 pages in length, it includes a discussion on the process, an examination of the research and documentation on which the final report was based, and most importantly the 500 recommendations that the Task Force made to the minister. Box 10.2 provides an abbreviated version of each of the 14 key conclusions using the exact words of the Task Force (see Banff-Bow Valley Study, 1996b: 11–12).

OFFICIAL RESPONSE AND STAKEHOLDER REACTIONS TO THE BANFF-BOW VALLEY REPORT

The response of the Minister of Canadian Heritage, Sheila Copps, to the Banff-Bow Valley Study reflected an internal assessment of the recommendations in terms of those that could be acted upon and those that were considered as being rather more 'extreme' and that were unacceptable to Parks Canada for economic and other reasons (see Searle, 2000; Urquhart, 1998b). Accompanying the news release that announced the completion of the Banff-Bow Valley report was a document: *Highlights of Minister's Direction for the Banff Bow Valley and Response to the Bow Valley Study Report* (Canadian Heritage, 1996). The minister endorsed the overall intent and direction of the Final Report: This position was outlined through six themes: (1) a place for nature; (2) a place for visitors; (3) a place for community; (4) a place for heritage tourism; (5) a place for open management; and (6) a place for environmental stewardship. Selected components of these six themes will be briefly noted.

Under 'a place for nature' it was acknowledged that the ecological integrity of the Banff Bow Valley was paramount to all decisions involving the National Park. Reflecting this priority, the minister announced that no new lands would be released for commercial development and that priority would be given to wildlife corridors. To this end the airstrip, bison paddock, and the cadet camp were to be closed. In addition, ski-run development would be in accordance with approved long-range plans.

The theme 'a place for community' acknowledged the close historical relationship between the Park and the communities of Banff and Lake Louise. However, the minister indicated that in the case of the Town of Banff, a community plan should be prepared by 31 March 1997 that would cap the Town's population at 10,000. The role of Banff National Park in providing opportunities for education and enjoyment was addressed under the theme of 'a place for visitors'. This theme acknowledged that, although ecological integrity would remain 'the foundation of all national parks' (Canadian Heritage, 1996: 4), provision for, and enhancement of the visitor experience, including opportunities to learn about the Park, must be accommodated.

Central to the 'place for heritage tourism' theme was the minister's observation that all visitors to the Park should be made aware of its being a special place, and that a heritage tourism strategy should be developed to facilitate this objective. The importance of tourism in contributing to the economy and as an employment generator was also acknowledged. One of the major concerns associated with the Town and Banff and the

Park was the decision-making process and environment within which it took place. The minister addressed these concerns under the theme 'a place for open management' and called for clear and open decision-making including a transparent development and review process. She responded to some of the more contentious recommendations contained in the Final Report, as far as the commercial and business community were concerned, by stating that Parks Canada did not foresee the need to expropriate properties or to relocate commercial accommodation within the boundaries of the Town of Banff. Finally, under this theme she directed that 'a revised comprehensive park management plan, providing clear direction for the future of Banff National Park, will be tabled in Parliament in 1997' (Canadian Heritage, 1996: 5).

The sixth theme, 'a place for environmental stewardship', confirmed that because of the Bow Valley's location within a World Heritage Site it had to exemplify leadership in environmentally friendly practices. Specific reference was made to the fact that Parks Canada would lead by example in this undertaking.

Stakeholder reactions to the Final Report of the Banff-Bow Valley Study Task Force and the minister's response extended across the complete spectrum from strong support to concern that the underlying intent of the recommendations was to suppress commercial interests and to make the Park less accessible to visitors. 'The environmental community was, for the most part pleased' (Searle, 2000: 57). However, some environmentalists felt that the Task Force did not go far enough in its recommendations to provide direction for how to manage human use in a finite landscape.

While many of the business leaders were on side regarding the general tone of the Final Report, specific recommendations that addressed actions to re-establish the ecological integrity of the Park, and which the minister supported, such as the closure of the airstrip, led to subsequent on-going litigation. Sillars (1996) refers to the opinions expressed by Brad Pierce, President of the Association for Mountain Parks, Protection and Enjoyment (AMPEE), 'I think that what they've done is created a doomsday scenario to advance what would be otherwise politically unacceptable solutions, without exploring other options' (Sillars, 1996: 17).

One of the recommended actions put forward by the Banff-Bow Valley Task Force was that Banff National Park Management Plan should be revised to include the recommendations of the Task Force (Banff-Bow Valley Study, 1996b). However, the Minister of Canadian Heritage announced that although some of the recommendations would be implemented immediately, others would require further deliberation. The minister established an advisory committee to assist Parks Canada in developing implementation strategies and specifically the incorporation of the recommendations into a revised management plan.

Findings of the implementation advisory committee were presented at public information sessions in January 1997. The end product of this process was the document, Parks Canada's Response to the Bow Valley Study (Parks Canada, 1997). The response was organized in terms of the six major themes used by the minister and provided clarification on the proposed key actions. One addition, however, was the inclusion of a new section that addressed the theme of 'a place of cultural significance'. This growing recognition of the importance of cultural resources within Banff National Park was subsequently demonstrated through the approval of a Cultural Resource Management Plan for the park (Parks Canada, 1998b).

In the meantime, the concerns expressed by the Task Force over the state of Banff National Park were further vindicated by the Auditor General of Canada, whose report to the House of Commons pointed to similar problems regarding the lack of protection of ecological integrity throughout the National Park system (Auditor General of Canada, 1996). At the end of January, the Standing Committee on Energy, the Environment and Natural Resources (Senate of Canada, 1997) returned to Banff as a follow-up to an earlier visit that had taken place in 1994. In its report, the Committee commented on the increase in mutual respect and level of consensus that had been achieved as part of the Banff Bow-Valley study process.

BANFF NATIONAL PARK MANAGEMENT PLAN

Sheila Copps tabled the new management plan for Banff in the House of Commons on 17 April 1997. The Banff National Park management plan (Canadian Heritage, Parks Canada, 1997) was the culmination of a process, the outcome of which was largely determined by the recommendations of the Banff-Bow Valley Task Force and confirmed by the unequivocal stance of the minister at the time of its release. In broad terms, continuity of direction and purpose was evident. However, for some people, the management plan reflected Parks Canada's continued reluctance to confront in a resolute and comprehensive way the fundamental issue of increasing visitor numbers to the National Park (Searle, 2000).

There is a strong temptation to trace the continuity between the recommendations made by the Banff-Bow Valley Task Force and the key actions stipulated in the management plan and to provide some numerical assessment of the level of accord. The figure of over 70 per cent has been referred to in this regard. Such an assessment, however, undermines the importance of recognizing the interrelatedness of so many of the recommendations. The minister's message that prefaces the Banff National Park Management Plan recognizes that although Banff National Park is, 'first and foremost, a place for nature', it is also a place for people, a place for heritage tourism, a place for community and a place for environmental stewardship. However, the priority that must be given to protecting the ecological integrity of the park is clearly confirmed.

The structure and format of the management plan follows very closely the six themes referred to by the minister in 1996 and subsequently followed by Parks Canada in its response to the Banff-Bow Valley study. In keeping with the intended purpose of all National park management plans, the plan provides guidance and overall direction 'for the next 10 to 15 years and will serve as a framework for all planning within the park' (Canadian Heritage, Parks Canada, 1997: 5). The role of the plan in establishing key directions that should be followed in the preparation of management plans for the other parks that make up the Rocky Mountains World Heritage Site is also recognized.

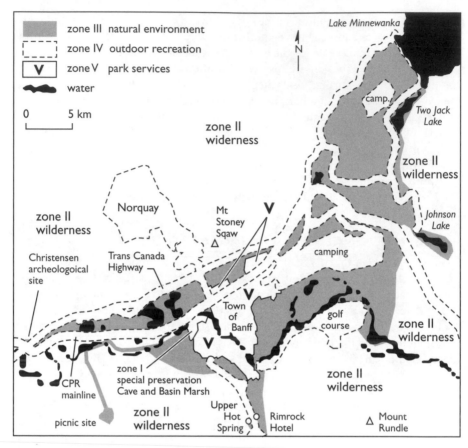

FIGURE 10.5 Zoning map of Banff town site.

Each of the theme areas within the plan is addressed through an overview statement, the development of a series of strategic goals, and their elaboration in terms of objectives and key actions. The spatial context for these intended actions is the park zoning system that the management plan notes remains similar to that contained in the earlier 1988 management plan.

Reference is made to the significance and vulnerability of the montane ecoregion within Banff National Park. The management plan re-emphasizes the importance of the montane ecoregion to wildlife and specifically in terms of wildlife corridors. Fundamental to this cause for concern is the fact that less than 4 per cent of the park area is within this zone and much of it is already highly impacted and fragmented because of human use and development associated with the Town of Banff, the Trans-Canada Highway, and the CP Railway (Canadian Heritage, Parks Canada, 1997; Nelson, 1994; Pacas, 1996). A clear indication of this problem is evident from one of the zoning maps accompanying the management plan and which refers to the area surrounding the Town of Banff (Figure 10.5).

In many ways the new Banff National Park Management Plan may be considered one of the most important watersheds in the planning and management of the Park. The Plan represents the culmination and official embodiment of many of the recommendations contained in the Final Report of Banff-Bow Valley Task Force. At the same time, it provides the guidelines and modus operandi for Banff National Park into the future. Box 10.3 indicates some of the implications and outcomes that have become evident in the time that has elapsed since the Plan was approved.

BOX 10.3. Selected Implications and Outcomes of the Banff Park Management Plan

- The Town of Banff Community Plan
- Draft Guidelines for the Development and Operation of Ski Areas in Banff and Jasper National Parks
- The Development Review Process and Open Management
- Banff-Bow Valley Heritage Tourism Strategy
- Redevelopment Guidelines For Outlying Commercial Accommodations and Hostels in the Rocky Mountain national parks
- Report of the Panel on the Ecological Integrity of Canada's National Parks

---

CONCLUSION

This chapter has traced the factors that led to the establishment of the Banff-Bow Valley Study, the process that was followed in undertaking the Study, and the recommendations that eventually were made. The chronological review also examined the ensuing management plan for Banff National Park and noted the subsequent events that followed its implementation. It has been a complicated and convoluted process, yet the intensity of the debate and the strength of conviction of the various interest groups involved are evident. Clearly demonstrable is the important impact that the Banff-Bow Valley Study had on succeeding actions both in terms of process and in matters of substance not only for Banff National Park but also for National parks in Canada generally.

Despite the ability of the Round Table to agree upon a core vision for the Bow Valley in Banff National Park, subsequent events have shown that disparate views and opinions exist when the intent of the vision is applied in the context of real and tangible issues. For example, although AMPPE contends that it supports the conservation mandate of Canada's mountain parks, its perspective towards human use management and controlling development is very different to that being advocated by environmentalists, natural scientists, and the recommendations contained in the Report of the Panel on Ecological Integrity, and even some of the proposals contained in Bill

FIGURE 10.6 Wildlife overpass. *Photo: Guy Swinnerton.*

C-27. Moreover, the inclusion in the Panel's Report of the comment that there is no dual mandate with regards to national parks but one single mandate to protect ecological integrity (Parks Canada Agency, 2000b) is clearly contrary to AMPPE's view of the role of National parks. Likewise, a letter to the editor of *Communiqué*, Canada's Tourism Monthly, by Greg McKnight, Executive Director, Banff-Lake Louise Tourism Bureau, provides further evidence of the conflict that continues to exist. According to McKnight (2000: 2), Canada's National parks are under serious threat from, ' well-funded professional extremists dedicated to restricting visitors to places like Banff and Jasper National Parks.' Unfortunately, because of the inability of Parks Canada to undertake its own research or fund independent research (see Parks Canada Agency, 2000b), the research that is being undertaken by consultants and university scientists is invariably criticized for being biased and representative of such extremist positions.

Parks Canada has not gone unscathed in the on-going debate concerning its real commitment to protecting the ecological integrity of Banff National Park. The apparent paradox between park policy and legislation and actions on the ground is not new. This incongruity is attributed in part to the trend towards privatization and a business plan approach that focuses on greater financial self reliance at the individual park level (McNamee, 1997; Parks Canada Agency, 2000b; Swinnerton, 1999). In the case of Banff National Park, environmental groups point to inconsistency and lack of action in implementing policy and statements of intent (Searle, 2000). The approved expansion of Chateau Lake Louise is one outstanding example that environmental groups make frequent reference to. In addition, scientists who had previously been involved in the

Banff-Bow Valley Study have continued to chastise park managers for neglecting their responsibilities to protect the ecological integrity of the parks (Struzik, 2000). On the other hand, interests that favour more active involvement in promoting and marketing public enjoyment and human use within the park criticize Parks Canada for being unduly influenced by so-called environmental extremists. Consequently, it appears that the benefits of the dialogue and mutual respect that were generated as part of the Round Table process during the Banff-Bow Valley Study have been significantly eroded. These relationships have been replaced by a considerable amount of skepticism and mistrust, if not hostility, among the various stakeholders. Other problems relate to the process and nature of decision-making. While there have been improvements, mistrust continues to be associated with the degree of openness in decision-making and with the sharing of information in a timely manner.

Another fundamental issue is the number of visitors to Banff National Park and particularly the numbers that are concentrated in the Banff-Bow Valley. Although a variety of approaches and techniques have been used with success to manage human use within protected areas (Chapters 6 and 7), they do not have unlimited capacity to deal with constantly increasing numbers of visitors, irrespective of the types of activities and experiences being sought. Groff (1996) has discussed the role of demarketing in reducing the demand and, therefore problems, of crowding and overuse in national and state parks in the United States. The Panel on the Ecological Integrity of Canada's National Parks (Parks Canada Agency, 2000b) in its discussion of use and enjoyment of the National parks recommended that Parks Canada cease the product marketing of these protected areas. In contrast, although the Banff/Lake Lake Louise Tourism Bureau is one of the lead participants implementing the Heritage Tourism Strategy and its 2000 Business Plan (Banff/Lake Louise Tourism Bureau, 2000) refers to the initiatives it has taken to make visitors aware of Banff National Park being a special place, its strategies are predominantly focused on aggressively attracting increasing numbers of visitors to the park.

Unfortunately, there appears to be a disinclination to accept the fundamental fact that visitors ultimately impact the environment and 'consume places' (see Urry, 1995). Compounding this problem is that, even though the Banff-Bow Valley Study raised people's consciousness of the problems of the Bow Valley, there remains a reluctance to accept the reality that aesthetics or general appearance of a landscape is a very limited indicator of its biological health and ecological integrity (see Banff-Bow Valley Study, 1996b; Parks Canada Agency, 2000a, 2000b; Sellars, 1997). The 'tourists gaze' (see Urry, 1995), particularly in the context of mass tourism, has little inclination or incentive to go beyond this relatively superficial assessment of the state of the environment within which tourism occurs.

One of the criticisms that has been raised by commercial recreation and tourism interests is that many of the decisions being made by Parks Canada are based on inadequate information especially in relation to the economic and human dimensions of the problems being faced within the Banff-Bow Valley (see AMPPE, 1999, 2000). This criticism has been raised in relation to many of the recommendations made by the

Banff-Bow Valley Task Force and subsequent actions taken by Parks Canada. The need for more research on ecological integrity and especially the human dimensions of National park management is undeniable (see Parks Canada Agency, 2000b; Praxis Inc., 1998). However, such shortcomings should not be used as an excuse for taking no action to protect park ecosystems or for the adoption of a more permissive attitude towards development (Lemons, 1995; Nilsson and Grelsson, 1995). The importance of pursuing a precautionary approach was one of the recommendations to come out of the Banff-Bow Valley Study.

The Panel on Ecological Integrity (Parks Canada Agency, 2000b: 1–8) in its vision for Canada's National parks aspires to a situation where 'Canadians and guests from around the world embrace the notion of use without abuse' within this country's National parks. While the Banff-Bow Valley Study made significant progress towards finding an acceptable balance between human use and ecological integrity, the attainment of a really workable consensus continues to remain elusive.

ACKNOWLEDGEMENTS

The author acknowledges the opportunity afforded to him to participate in the Banff-Bow Valley Study as a member of the Scientific Review Committee. In addition to informal discussions with numerous people involved with the Banff-Bow Valley over the years, particular appreciation is extended to the people who consented to be interviewed and who provided invaluable insight and information that specifically facilitated the writing of this chapter. They are: Dave Dalman, Manager, Ecosystem Secretariat, Parks Canada, Banff National Park; David Day, Partner and Senior Consultant, IRIS Environmental Systems, former Superintendent of Banff National Park; Eva Katic, Senior Development Officer, Parks Canada, Banff National Park; Neil MacDonald, Community Advisor/Planner, Western Canada Service Centre, Parks Canada; Mike McIvor, President, Bow Valley Naturalists; Brad Pierce, President, Association for Mountain Parks Protection and Enjoyment (AMPPE); Dave Poulton, Conservation Director, Canadian Parks and Wilderness Society, Calgary/Banff Chapter; Jillian Roulet, Park Planner, Parks Canada, Banff National Park; Cameron Spence, Senior Manager Marketing/Communications, Banff/Lake Louise Tourism Bureau; and Pamela Veinotte, Manager, Heritage Tourism Mountain Parks, Parks Canada. Unless specified otherwise, the opinions and views expressed in the chapter are those of the author.

REFERENCES

Association for Mountain Parks Protection and Enjoyment (AMPPE). 1999. Presentation to the Roundtable Forum on the Banff National Park Management Plan, 15–16 Oct., Banff, Alberta. Available at: <http://www.amppe.org/amppe/rndtable0210.htm>. Accessed 24 Mar. 2000.

———. 2000. Submission to the House of Commons Standing Committee on Canadian Heritage regarding Bill C-27: An Act respecting the National Parks of Canada. Ottawa, 18 May. Available at: <http://www.amppe.org/amppe/commons0518.htm>. Accessed 16 Aug. 2000.

Auditor General of Canada. 1996. *Canadian Heritage: Parks Canada: Preserving Canada's Natural Heritage. 1996 Report of the Auditor General of Canada.* Nov., Chapter 31. Available at: <http://www.oag-bvg.gc.ca/domino/reports.nsf/html/9631ce.html>. Accessed 6 July 2000.

Banff-Bow Valley Study. 1995a. *A Review of the Governance Model of the Banff-Bow Valley.* Prepared by Coopers & Lybrand Consulting, Calgary, for the Banff-Bow Valley Task Force. Banff, Alta.

———.1995b. *Tourism Outlook Project.* Prepared by Coopers & Lybrand Consulting, Calgary, for the Banff-Bow Valley Task Force. Banff, Alta.

———. 1995c. *An Historical Analysis of Parks Canada and Banff National Park, 1968–1995.* Prepared by W. Hildebrandt for the Banff-Bow Valley Study Task Force. Banff, Alta.

———.1995d. *State of the Banff-Bow Valley.* Compiled by D. Bernard, C. Pacas, and N. Marshall for the Banff-Bow Valley Task Force. Banff, Alta.

———. 1996a. *Development Decisions in Banff National Park: How Are They Made, and How Could They Be Improved?* Prepared by L. A. Taylor for the Banff-Bow Valley Task Force. Banff, Alta.

———. 1996b. *Banff-Bow Valley: At the Crossroads.* Technical Report of the Banff-Bow Valley Task Force. Edited by R. Page, S. Bayley, J.D. Cook, J.E. Green, and J.R.B. Ritchie. Prepared for the Honourable Sheila Copps, Minister of Canadian Heritage. Ottawa: Minister of Supply and Services Canada.

Banff-Lake Louise Tourism Bureau. 2000. *2000 Business Plan.* Banff, Alta: Banff-Lake Louise Tourism Bureau.

Bella, L. 1987. *Parks for Profit.* Montreal: Harvest House.

Belland, G., and C. Zinkan. 1998. 'Heritage Tourism in Canada's Rocky Mountain Parks: A Case in Education and Partnership', in N.W.P. Munro and J.H.M. Willison, eds, *Linking Protected Areas with Working Landscapes Conserving Biodiversity.* Proceedings of the Third International Conference on Science and Management of Protected Areas. Wolfville, NS: Science and Management of Protected Areas Association, 616–25.

Borbey, P. 1997. 'The Parks Canada Business Plan', in Munro (1997: 47–53).

Canadian Heritage. 1994. *Parks Canada: Guiding Principles and Operational Policies.* Ottawa: Minister of Supply and Services Canada.

———. 1996. *Highlights of Minister's Directions for the Banff-Bow Valley and Response to the Bow Valley Study Report.* Ottawa: Canadian Heritage.

Canadian Heritage, Parks Canada. 1997. *Banff National Park: Management Plan.* Ottawa: Minister of Public Works and Government Services Canada.

Canadian Parks Service. 1988. *Banff National Park: Management Plan.* Calgary: Environment Canada, Canadian Parks Service.

————. 1991a. *State of the Parks: 1990 Profiles*. Ottawa: Minister of Supply and Services Canada.

————.1991b. *State of the Parks: 1990 Report*. Ottawa: Ministry of Supply and Services Canada.

Corbett, B. 1998. 'The Battle for Banff: Environmentalists Take Off the Gloves', in I. Urquhart, ed., *Assault on the Rockies: Environmental Controversies in Alberta*. Edmonton: Rowan Books, 129–36.

Dearden, P., and L.D. Berg. 1993. 'Canada's National Parks: A Model of Administrative Penetration', *Canadian Geographer* 37, 3: 194–211.

Dodds, G., and G. Fenton. 1999. 'A Consensus Approach to Management Planning: An Evaluation of the Effectiveness for Riding Mountain National Park, Manitoba, Canada', in Harmon (1999: 41–7).

Fisher, R., and W. Ury. 1991. *Getting to Yes: Negotiating Agreement without Giving In*, 2nd edn. New York: Penguin Books.

Government of Canada and the Government of Alberta. 1989. Town of Banff Incorporation Agreement.

Green, J., C. Pacas, L. Cornwell, and S. Bayley, eds. 1996a. *Ecological Outlooks Project. A Cumulative Effects Assessment and Futures Outlook of the Banff Bow Valley: Final Report.* Prepared for the Banff-Bow Valley Study. Ottawa: Department of Canadian Heritage.

————, ————, ————, and ————. 1996b. 'Restoring Ecological Integrity in the Banff Bow Valley Region', in Green et al. (1996a: 11–i–11–74).

Groff, C. 1996. 'Demarketing in Park and Recreation Management',. in W.F. Kuentzel, ed., *Proceedings of the 1996 Northeastern Recreation Research Symposium*. Radnor, Penn.: USDA, Forest Service, General Technical Report-NE–232, 173–7.

Harmon, D., ed. 1999. *On the Frontiers of Conservation*. Proceedings of the 10th conference on research and resource management in parks and on public lands. Hancock, Mich.: George Wright Society.

Hart, E.J. 1999. *The Place of Bows: Exploring the Heritage of the Banff-Bow Valley, Part I to 1930*. Banff, Alta: EJH Literary Enterprises.

Hodgins, D.W., and J.D. Cook. 1999. 'The Banff-Bow Valley Study: Breaking the Public Policy Grid Lock', in Harmon (1999: 52–7).

Lemons, J. 1995. 'Ecological Integrity and National Parks', in L. Westra and Lemons, eds, *Perspectives on Ecological Integrity*. Boston: Kluwer Academic Publishers, 177–201.

Lothian, W.F. 1987. *A Brief History of Canada's National Parks*. Ottawa: Minister of Supply and Services Canada.

Lowry, W.R. 1994. *The Capacity for Wonder: Preserving National Parks*. Washington: Brookings Institution.

McKnight, G. 2000. Letter to the editor. *Communiqué* 4, 6: 2.

McNamee, K. 1997. 'Who Will Be Left Standing: The Beggars or the Bears?', in Munro (1997: 86–8).

Munro, N., ed. 1997. *Protecting Areas in Our Modern World*. Proceedings of a workshop held as part of the IUCN World Conservation Congress, Montreal, Oct. 1996. Halifax, NS: Parks Canada.

Nelson, J.G. 1994. 'The Spread of Ecotourism: Some Planning Implications', *Environmental Conservation* 21, 3: 248–55.

Nilsson, C., and G. Grelsson. 1995. 'The Fragility of Ecosystems: A Review', *Journal of Applied Ecology* 32, 4: 677–92.

Pacas, C. 1996. 'Human Use of the Banff Bow Valley: Past, Present and Future', in Green et al. (1996a: 3–i–2.F–1).

———, L. Cornwell, and J. Green. 1996. 'Process and Strategic Direction—Measuring Ecological Integrity', in Green et al. (1996a: 2–i–2.D–3).

Page, R. 1997. 'The Process of the Banff Bow Valley Study: Managing Controversy', in Munro (1997: 119–24).

Parks Canada. 1979. *Parks Canada Policy*. Ottawa: Minister of the Environment.

———.1986. *In Trust for Tomorrow: A Management Framework for Four Mountain Parks*. Ottawa: Minister of Supply and Services Canada.

Parks Canada. 1994. *Four Mountain Parks: Five Year Plan Updating: Spring 1994*. Ottawa: Canadian Heritage, Parks Canada.

———.1997. *Parks Canada's Response to the Bow Valley Study*. Department of Canadian Heritage.

———.1998a. *State of the Parks: 1997 Report*. Ottawa: Minister of Public Works and Government Services Canada.

———.1998b. *Banff National Park: Cultural Resource Management Plan*. Banff, Alta: Parks Canada.

Parks Canada Agency. 2000a. *Unimpaired for Future Generations? Protecting Ecological Integrity with Canada's National Parks*, vol. 1, *A Call to Action*. Report of the Panel on the Ecological Integrity of Canada's National Parks. Ottawa.

———. 2000b. *Unimpaired for Future Generations? Protecting Ecological Integrity with Canada's National Parks*, vol. 2, *Setting a New Direction for Canada's National Parks*. Report of the Panel on the Ecological Integrity of Canada's National Parks. Ottawa.

Praxis, Inc. 1998. *Summary of the Kootenay and Yoho National Parks Science Workshop, October 1998*. Prepared for Parks Canada, Kootenay and Yoho National Parks. Radium, BC.

Ritchie, B.J.R. 1998. 'Managing the Human Presence in Ecologically Sensitive Tourism Destinations: Insights from the Banff-Bow Valley Study', *Journal of Sustainable Tourism* 6, 4: 293–313.

———. 1999a. 'Crafting a Value-Driven Vision for a National Tourism Treasure', *Tourism Management* 20: 273–82.

———.1999b. 'Interest Based Formulation of Tourism Policy for Environmentally Sensitive Destinations', *Journal of Sustainable Tourism* 7, 3, 4: 206–39.

———.1999c. 'Policy Formulation at the Tourism/Environment Interface: Insights and Recommendations from the Banff-Bow Valley Study', *Journal of Travel Research* 38: 100–10.

Searle, R. 2000. *Phantom Parks: The Struggle to Save Canada's National Parks*. Toronto: Key Porter Books.

Sellars, R.W. 1997. *Preserving Nature in the National Parks: A History*. New Haven: Yale University Press.

Senate of Canada. 1996. *Protecting Places and People: Conserving Canada's Natural Heritage*. Standing Senate Committee on Energy, the Environment and Natural Resources. Ottawa.

———. 1997. *Report of the Committee's Fact-Finding Visit to Banff*. Standing Committee on Energy, the Environment and Natural Resources. Ottawa.

Sillars, L. 1996. 'Are Parks Preserved for—or from—Ordinary Mortals?', *Alberta Report* 28, 46: 16–18.

Struzik, E. 2000. 'Fire Mountain Parks Bosses, Scientists Advise Minister: Animals Being Killed by Cars and Trains', *Edmonton Journal*, 15 Mar., A10.

Swinnerton, G.S. 1999. 'Recreation and Conservation: Issues and Prospects', in E.L. Jackson and T.L. Burton, eds, *Leisure Studies: Prospects for the Twenty-first Century*. State College, Penn.: Venture Publishing, 199–231.

Town of Banff. 1998. *Banff Community Plan: Our Town Our Future*. Banff, Alta: Town of Banff.

Urquhart, I., ed. 1998a. *Assault on the Rockies: Environmental Controversies in Alberta*. Edmonton: Rowan Books.

———.1998b. 'Doing Solomon's Job: The Banff Bow-Valley Task Force', in Urquhart (1998a: 137–8).

Urry, J. 1995. *Consuming Places*. London: Routledge.

KEY WORDS/CONCEPTS

State of the Parks Report
Association For Mountain Parks Protection and Enjoyment (AMPPE)
Banff-Bow Valley Study
ecological integrity
sustainable tourism
Auditor General's Report (1996)
Banff Park Management Plan

STUDY QUESTIONS

1. Discuss the significance of the location of Banff townsite.
2. Discuss the significance of the 'incorporation' of Banff townsite.
3. Outline the impact of the early history of Banff on the recent problems in the park.
4. Discuss the significance of the ski industry to Banff.
5. Discuss the significance of townsite expansion on ecological integrity.
6. Comment on the impact on Banff of the Trans-Canada Highway.
7. What is unique about the Banff-Bow Valley Study, compared to other park management processes?
8. Comment on the type of public involvement used in the Banff-Bow Valley Study.
9. Outline the main conclusions of the Banff-Bow Valley Study. Comment on each.
10. Summarize the response of the Heritage Minister to the Banff-Bow Valley Study.
11. Summarize the stakeholder's reaction to the Heritage Minister.
12. What concerns remain concerning the 1997 Banff Management Plan?
13. Comment on the statement 'there remains a reluctance to accept the reality that aesthetics or general appearance of a landscape is a very limited indicator of its biological health and ecological integrity.' Why is this perspective particularly relevant in Banff?
14. Comment on the more recent history, beginning in 2001, of park management activities in Banff. To what extent are these activities consistent with the recommendations of the Banff-Bow Valley Study?

CHAPTER 11

Environmental Management

Paul F. J. Eagles

INTRODUCTION

The management of the natural environment of a park is an essential aspect of park administration. National and provincial parks were often, but not always, established because of a natural resource that attracted attention. For example, the creation of a new provincial park in 1970 in Ontario's Hudson Bay Lowlands was for the protection of significant, low-Arctic tundra ecosystems. The presence of an impressive population of polar bears gave the park its name—Polar Bear Provincial Park.

The management of people is also an essential aspect of park administration. Parks are always established by government with the support of some aspect of society. The support may be for direct use purposes, such as recreation, or indirect use purposes, such as environmental protection. The support may be for cultural purposes, such as in the creation of a National Historic Park. The human management aspect may involve a wide array of groups, such as: park visitors, local residents, Aboriginal groups, tourism businesses, local governments, and park employees.

The significance assigned to a natural environment and to a cultural environment during the park's start-up phase guides management policies for many years. After park establishment the value of the resources is often increased by a heightened level of knowledge followed by appreciation. Sometimes values emerge and are developed long after park establishment. Hence, all parks are cultural phenomena. They are ideas in the form of landscapes. They are attitudes or values represented by laws, policies, and plans. This chapter describes a selection of management actions at the site level, actions reflecting these values, laws, policies, and plans. The discussion here is an extension of the previous sections of the book dealing with conservation theory and social science theory as applied to parks.

HOW PARK VALUES SHAPE THE APPROACH TO SITE MANAGEMENT

It is important to recognize that the phrase 'natural resource management' is value-laden. A resource is something that is seen to be of value to people. Following that concept, a natural resource is a part of nature that is seen to be of value. For example, trees are usually considered to be a natural resource because of the valuable substances that they contain, such as wood and fibre.

However, parts of nature that people do not see as of immediate use are not considered to be natural resources. Is the squirrel that lives in the tree called a natural resource? Not usually, unless someone wants to hunt it, to eat it, or to view it. The concept of a natural resource is inherently anthropocentric—human-centred. Something achieves this status when people decide that it is of use and therefore is of value.

In recent decades, the term natural resource management has broadened as a changing philosophy of nature starts to include more concern for the processes and for all elements of the environment, whether on not they are of immediate use to humans. Within most parks all living and non-living features are given value. This value is ascribed because all elements of nature are seen as being part of the biosphere and therefore part of functioning ecosystems. And since all people depend upon the biosphere for survival, all parts of the biosphere may be vital to that survival. The phrase 'environmental management' is now being used to indicate a broader emphasis on all aspects of the environment, not just those already perceived as natural resources.

Dorney (1989) points out that this change in emphasis is a change from a marketing point of view, preoccupied with 'growth' and 'progress', to an ecological point of view, based on the maintenance of equilibrium between man and nature. This latter view is merging with the concept that all of nature is of value because it exists. It does not have to be of known use to human kind, or even to be known. Its value inheres in its existence.

The concept of management is also value-laden. To manage is to guide or to control. Typically, it involves the setting of goals, the marshalling of resources, and the taking of actions to fulfil those goals. It is inherently manipulative. An essential component of park management is the process used to outline goals. All subsequent management actions flow from those goals. This chapter outlines both the processes to outline goals and specific management issues that confront park managers at the national, provincial, regional, and municipal levels.

Parks represent many cultural, social, and environmental values. Some people like to believe that it is possible to make decisions in a value-free way. They often state this philosophy within the context of 'using a 'scientific' approach. However, all decisions require the setting of priorities, and all priorities are based on some set of values. The defining of values in reference to the known environmental resources in a park is achieved through a variety of measures. Ecological function is considered and role in the ecosystem is assessed. Scarcity of the resource is significant. The aesthetic qualities of a feature often are relevant. For example, the public may in general find the the Grizzly Bear more aesthetically pleasing and may therefore value it more highy than the Black Widow Spider.

Commercial value is not a first priority, but impinges importantly in parks. However, the market for parks has some different characteristics from that used in general resource exploitation. Within parks, the natural environment does not have to be removed from its surroundings and modified to become marketable. There is a market for observing nature in situ. Some people do wish to see big trees, alive and growing in the forest. Some wish to view the Spotted Owls and other creatures that live among the big trees. These folks are willing to travel to the park to see nature. Others will pay for books with stories and pictures of the trees and owls. Others will purchase videos and watch television shows on these subjects. Some just wish to know that the trees and the owls exist, even if they never have the opportunity of seeing them. Some will join groups that study trees and owls. Others will join groups that take political action lobbying for tree and owl preservation. All of these desires create a market for the products that a park has to offer—observation, learning, reflection, and conservation action.

Determining the value of an element of the cultural or the natural environment in a park is important, but difficult. A discussion of some of the factors used in arriving at such a definition may help to reveal some of the nuances in this debate.

One school of thought considers all aspects of a park of value, simply because they exist. All species, all landscapes, and all ecological processes are held to have inherent value. This concept has often been referred to as part of the environmental management activities in Canadian national parks.

This concept, as part of the underlying philosophy of national parks management, is taken a step further in the application of 'process management'. The ecological processes that flow naturally through an ecosystem are taken to be the determinants of value. The concept recognizes how little we know really of how ecosystems function. In the light of that awareness, surely the most prudent course of action is to study and follow the ebb and flow of nature as it exists. Practically, this belief leads to a policy of non-interference in the affairs of nature. Management assumes a position of 'hands-off' nature as much as possible. Therefore, environmental management, in this context, implies the study of nature and the management of the park visitor as the first priorities. Study—to better understand the processes. Visitors—directed so they do not interfere with the natural processes.

Another school of thought considers that all aspects of a park are of value, but not of equal value. An endangered species is accorded higher value than a common species. A species at the edge of its range is of higher value than a species in the centre of its range. A species, landscape, or natural phenomenon that is attractive to the visitors is given precedence. An unusual scene is considered more beautiful than a plain scene. Many such assessments of value contribute to the design of park facilities.

The determination of such values is demonstrated when a visitor facility or program is conceived. The building of a road to a point of interest in a park is a typical action. The assignment of significance to an area of a park so that it becomes a point of interest is a determination of value. One place in nature is assigned more value than some other place. Therefore, other points are deemed less valuable. The road is destructive to some feature of the park. The road will be located on areas that are determined to be of less value.

A romantic idea persists that parks are isolated islands in a sea of tranquillity, but a more accurate view is that parks are but one component of the world's biosphere.

This biosphere is under assault by human society and its activities. Therefore, it is not possible to leave nature to its own purposes in a park because the influences coming from outside the park are too big and too important to be ignored.

WHO DETERMINES VALUE

The determination of value is a major part of natural resource management in parks. Critically important is the method used to assess this value. Who assigns value and how the value is assigned are central issues.

A typical approach is to let the park staff assign value. Most park agencies have highly trained staff who have spent years in the study of natural resources. They often know a lot about the environment and about human culture. They are familiar with the existing agency policies. They typically have specialized and highly technical knowledge. They are emotionally involved with the park. They often feel very strongly about the significance of various park resources. Shouldn't they be given the job?

Or, possibly, independent experts should assign value. Canadian society is blessed with a high degree of expertise in many fields. All aspects of natural and cultural resource issues are known to highly trained people in universities, in schools, in government, and in industry. These people have valuable information and insight that can be brought to bear on a natural resource issue. Maybe they should be given this job because of the strong technical component.

Another approach is to let the politicians assign value. In Canada's democratic system of government all park managers have a political master. These people were elected to represent a group of people in a ward or a riding. The government then appointed them to a position of power over the parks. It is extremely rare in Canada for any person to be elected directly to a board or commission that governs parks. Such positions are almost always through indirect election or appointment. These politicians are popular in their community. They were elected to carry out certain policies and are quite familiar with the views of their constituents. Perhaps they are in the best position to do the job.

Maybe it would be best to let the local community assign value. The people immediately around the park are directly affected by whatever uses or policies are put into place. Often other resource uses, such as those that are extractive, are forgone with the establishment of the park. The park affects the local economy. The park visitors travel through, visit, and impact on the local community. The local people may know the park area well. They have probably lived there for a long time and have seen nature in its many seasons. They are probably already demanding a say in any resource policy. Maybe they should assign the value to the resources.

Or, maybe it is best to let the park visitors assign value. The visitors are keenly interested in the park. They have taken their valuable leisure time to come to see the park. They pay for the privilege of visiting. In older parks they may have been visiting the parks over very long periods and have developed unique perspectives. A visitor is often very appreciative of the park and its unique features. Visitors are very willing to give their opinions and often demand to be heard. Some might argue that the park has been established for the use of the visitors. They have a unique position from which to determine resource value.

The potential park visitors form an important group. There are many people inclined to visit who have not yet been able to visit the park. It is distinctly possible that the park policies are creating an impediment to their visit. Maybe the fees are too high. Maybe the activities that they most desire are not allowed. Maybe they are physically challenged and need special facilities. Maybe they want a more relaxed atmosphere and fewer crowds. They might want to encourage certain species of wildlife. Such people are often interested in providing their ideas on how the natural resources should be valued and managed. The potential park visitors might wish to assign value.

Parks are, in fact, run by large governments, such as the provincial and federal governments. These parks cater to a wide geographical area. The argument can be made that provincial park policies should reflect the view of the people across the entire province. Correspondingly, national park policies should reflect policies of the entire country. Many parks have resources of world-wide significance and are in essence important to all people. Therefore, possibly all people should have a say in the assignment of value to park resources.

In practice, parks management is influenced to some extent by each of the above constituencies. Natural and cultural resource decision-making must be considered within such a context. A decision-making system must be developed that realistically and effectively provides an opportunity for all people in all constituencies to participate. No one group should dominate. It is worth mentioning that the soundness of the decisions will be determined by the validity of the values and the extent of the knowledge of the involved public. It is therefore critically important that the ecological and cultural roles of parks be effectively communicated to the public. In actual fact, every major decision in parks' environmental and cultural management is ultimately subject to determination by formal political process. How many people support a particular decision is the telling point for democratic governments. All fledgling park managers must be aware of this fact. The public could be made more aware of this fact.

There is not yet an adequate procedure for the participation of all peoples in the determination of resource value. It is an accident of past politics that a certain ecosystem is found in a particular country. The survival of the world's genetic diversity is important to all people. Why should not Canadians be involved in the management of parks elsewhere in the world? Why should not people elsewhere have a say in the management of Canadian parks? Practically speaking, it will be some time until the ecological recognition of parks as part of the world's biosphere affects the functioning of political systems. For the foreseeable future most of the environmental management decisions will be made within the context of the country or the state. Maybe at some time in the future the context will be broadened to include a broader, world-wide constituency.

Values and the determination of values influence how parks are managed. This influence is described in the following section in three dimensions: environmental management; cultural and historic management; and, recreation and tourism management.

ENVIRONMENTAL MANAGEMENT

Typical forest management on Crown land outside parks may involve a forester, who sees the trees as the primary focus of attention. Those trees that produce the most valuable commodity for the market are given the highest importance. The goal of management is to produce as many of those trees in as short a time as possible. The entire ecosystem is manipulated towards that goal. Species that interfere with the resource tree are persecuted. For example, tree herbivores are killed. Competing plants are called weeds and are removed if possible. Abiotic elements of the environment are manipulated to produce maximum growth. For example, fertilizers and water may be added. Imperfect individuals of the important species are culled. This type of management regime is inherently simple. The goals are clear and unambiguous—to produce quickly a lot of a particular species. This is a typical approach to resource management.

What are the implications of such an approach? The most important implication is that the values of the parts of the ecosystem are determined by the marketplace. Those parts with the highest monetary value are given an elevated stature within the management regime. This concept is ecologically illiterate if applied to all landscapes. The values of all parts of the ecosystem are not taken into account in the assessment of importance.

The Spotted Owl controversy is an example of the implications of the typical resource management approach. The rain forests of western North America extend from northern California along the coast through Oregon, Washington, British Columbia, and Alaska. This area of rich soils, abundant moisture, and temperate climate encourage the growth of magnificent forests of very old, very large trees. Douglas Fir, Giant Sequoia, and Western Red Cedar trees attain a majesty of size and form. The trunks of these trees may produce valuable wood products. Therefore, the trees are a much sought after natural resource. The trees have been cut since the last century at a prodigious rate and the amount of old-growth forest remaining is shrinking rapidly.

The Spotted Owl lives in these forests, as far north as southwestern British Columbia (Godfrey, 1986). The Spotted Owl has a large territory of several hundred hectares and is dependent upon the old growth trees. The bird has no commercial value. It is not made into any household product and is presumably not very good to eat. Therefore, the commodity marketplace sees it as an externality, an irrelevance. The Spotted Owl does not live in the cut-over forest, only in the old growth forest.

The question now asked in the United States and Canada is: 'How many Spotted Owls should be allowed to live in the world?' Every Spotted Owl pair that survives takes valuable timber production out of the natural resource economy. The timber industry views the idea of preserving millions of dollars worth of trees for a few owls as, at the very least, silly, and more emphatically, as capitalistic heresy.

However, the ecology point-of-view sees that the owl has a role to play in the ecosystem and it thus achieves value. The owl exists and therefore is of value. It achieves its right to exist by being. Humans have no right to destroy this species. Another line of ecological argument is that the owl is an indicator of a mature ecosystem that should be preserved because of the enormous value inherent in the age and stability of that system.

The debate reached the highest level of officialdom in the United States and Canada in the early 1990's. Discussions in the US involved the listing of the bird as an endangered species under national endangered species legislation. No such debate occurred in Canada, because Canada does not have national endangered species legislation. A hard-fought debate between short-term economics and long-term species preservation occurred. The outcome by 2000 was a virtual cessation of logging on public lands in the northwestern states of the USA. This meant that no old-growth logging occurs in all classes of public land, including national parks, and national forests. However, a compromise was arrived at, with logging continuing on private land.

Throughout the world debates similar to that over the Spotted Owl are raging around the management of the few remaining natural areas. The protection of some of these areas as parks is one of the options, along with agriculture, forestry, and urbanization as other options. The understanding of the ecosystem and the values placed on this knowledge are inherent parts of management. The values being placed on the ecosystem and its parts are the conceptual underpinning for all the resource-allocation decisions.

CULTURAL AND HISTORICAL MANAGEMENT

All parks are cultural phenomena. There is one special set of parks that has clearly identified cultural values, those of cultural and historic conservation: historic parks. The earliest Canadian National Historic Parks and sites emphasized significant political events and personalities. Sites that represented significant military events were heavily represented, such as those representing the early French-English wars, and the British-American wars. Sites representing important political figures, such as Prime Ministers, were popular.

Later the idea of representation was expanded to include a much broader sector of society. Therefore, sites representing influential immigrant groups, important industries, and vibrant local cultures were developed. Canada's program of historical commemoration now recognizes nationally significant places, persons, and events. Historic sites give Canadians a sense of the development of Canada as a nation. Locally, they also are important cultural icons and provide important regional economic development.

All national parks in Canada have a cultural and historic component, in addition to their environmental values. These parks often contain artifacts of millennia of human occupation and activity. Their cultural values to Canadians represent a melding of both the natural environment and human experience on these landscapes. Park management in the historic sites must be cognisant of the environmental values of the sites. Similarly, managers in national parks must understand the historic and cultural values of the natural environments.

Over thousands of years people have lived on and interacted with the Canadian environment. Canada's national historic site system represents a huge range of time periods, events, and ideas. L'Anse aux Meadows National Historic Site in Newfoundland contains the only authenticated Viking settlement in North America. It dates from approximately 1000 AD. Port-Royal National Historic Site in Nova Scotia

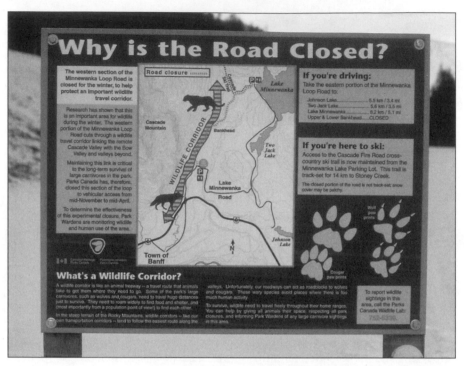

FIGURE 11.1 Often compromises have to be made in terms of recreation access in order to maintain ecological integrity, as shown here in Banff National Park.

contains the restored early French habitation from 1605. The Cave and Basin National Historic Site in Banff National Park contains warm thermal springs, and is the birthplace of the National parks system in Canada in 1885. The Bar-U Ranch National Historic Site is a historic ranch in the Alberta foothills. The ranch operated from 1882 to 1950. These four examples include Scandinavian and French immigration to Canada, the birth of the national park system and a regionally important lifestyle and economic activity.

RECREATION AND TOURISM MANAGEMENT

As discussed in Chapters 6, 7, and 8, most parks have a role in producing products that are desired by people. These products can be used consumptively, such a duck hunted in a wildlife preserve, or used appreciatively, such as a duck viewed in a provincial park.

One of the most abundant use of products is through recreation and tourism. Virtually all parks have some form of recreational use. This varies from low-density hiking and canoeing in wilderness parks, to high-density beach and other facility use in recreation parks. Eagles et al. (2000) found 115,323,513 visitor days of recreation spent in 1996 in the national parks, national wildlife areas, and the provincial parks of Canada. This works out to 3.9 days of park visitation per person in Canada, a very impressive figure. This study further calculated an economic impact of between $120.47 to $187.69 (Canadian funds) per day, of park use per person per day of activity. Therefore, the overall economic impact was between $13.9 and $21.6 billion in that year in Canada. This makes the production of recreation by the parks of Canada one of Canada's largest economic activities.

The way parks are managed will have a profound effect on the quality of visitor experiences. Rules, regulations, facilities, and type of supervision shape the type of visitor attracted to a park, the types of activities possible or allowed, visitor density, visitor impacts on park resources, and visitor satisfaction. Further, the values expressed by visitors have an impact on the way parks are managed, as will the values of other 'stakeholders', as described earlier. Within this context of values-driven management, we have examined three aspects of park management: environmental, historical-cultural, and recreation-tourism. Now we can use this context to review a number of selected case studies to illustrate these concepts.

BEACH EROSION: THE POINT PELEE CASE STUDY

Beach management in Point Pelee National Park provides an example of an active management issue. This park is a long, funnel-shaped sand spit projecting south into Lake Erie. The entire length of the peninsula is outlined by sandy beaches. The northern edge of the park abuts farm fields that were once extensive marshes, but were drained for the special vegetable products that they could produce.

In recent decades the lake level has fluctuated widely. In the late 1980s and again in the late 1990s it reached record high levels. During storms, the wave damage was extensive as the waters swept into the dryland forests at the tip and eroded areas of marshlands that previously had been protected behind barrier beaches.

Some people said that the water level changes were a phenomenon of nature and that remedial engineering action was inappropriate. Other people pointed out that Point Pelee was made entirely of sand that has been deposited by the lake currents. The source of this sand was eroded cliffs elsewhere along the shore. In recent decades this sand source was altered as engineering works were erected to stop this erosion, thereby depriving the park of its continuous source of sand. Therefore, part of the beach erosion in the park was the result of human interference in a natural system outside the park. Therefore, remedial action was an alternative as the changes were not entirely natural. A third line of argument stated that no matter what the reasons for the changes were, the entire system was too poorly known for accurate predications to be made. And the engineering works would probably not work at any rate, and might have serious, unanticipated impacts.

So here we have a classic example of the types of questions that must be faced. What is causing the change? Is the change the result of forces of nature or of human intervention? If intervention is anticipated, what alternatives are available? What

FIGURE 11.2 Winter storm damage on East Beach, Point Pelee National Park, 3 May 1986. The high water levels in Lake Erie, combined with winter storms, resulted in severe damage to the sand-based forests of Point Pelee. *Photo: P. Dearden.*

is the probability of failure or of unanticipated consequences for each possible management action?

What was done at Pelee? The managers stuck to the non-interference philosophy as much as they deemed good. However, some action was taken to reduce erosion. Various mechanical means were employed, including rock rip-rap, offshore pilings, and concrete structures embedded offshore. These would trap moving sand and create shoreline deposition. However, the shoreline erosion on the eastern shore increased in scope. Several damaged structures were removed and replaced with buildings in an area out of harm's way.

During the same period the US Army Corps of Engineers took a very active intervention approach towards reducing the erosion at Presquile State Park in Pennsylvania on the south shore of Lake Erie. This park is also a forest sand spit projecting out into the lake. The high water level affected this park similarly to Point Pelee. The Corps dumped millions of tonnes of sand onto the exposed beaches and let the currents move the deposit along the sand spit. This new sand beach acted as a buffer from the action of the waves. The approach at Presquile State Park was much more interventionist than was the approach taken at Point Pelee National Park.

In 1988 and again in 1999 the lake levels started to drop dramatically, thereby suspending much of the erosion problem. If the lake level had stayed high, would the park managers at Pelee have allowed the forests to be destroyed? Even if the managers decided to interfere would they have been able to find the money to engineer on a big scale? The Pelee and Presquile examples show that many managers feel that given the vagaries of nature and the omnipresent effects of humans that active intervention in parks is inevitable if they are to survive.

VISUAL MANAGEMENT:
RONDEAU PROVINCIAL PARK CASE STUDY

The stewardship philosophy holds that it is 'humans' duty to manage nature', that man was given domination over the earth and has the right and indeed the obligation to manage nature. It is a belief that may be interpreted two ways: from the purist standpoint, humans should approach interference with the greatest caution. Others take the stance, 'If it's there, use it.' This latter view is very widely held in resource extraction communities and it extends to the attitude of many in parks management in Canada. During the depression years of the 1930s, the government made jobs for many people, and some of those jobs were in parks. After World War II, many jobs in the parks were created for the returning veterans. The construction of the Banff-Jasper Highway, now called the Icefields Parkway, was one such government make-work project.

Rondeau Provincial Park is on the north shore of Lake Erie, half way between Windsor and Niagara Falls. This park contains 2,500 hectares of mature, southern forest of a type found in Canada only in southwestern Ontario. The forest has never been cleared. Early in the 1800s the British military took large quantities of white pine and some oaks of which the amount is not known (Woodliffe, n.d.). Outside the park, the Carolinian forests virtually ceased to exist due to the clearing for agriculture.

During the 1930s crews of men were sent into the parks on make-work projects. This was a fairly common activity during the Depression. They set about cleaning up the parks. They removed dead trees and brush. They removed some massive trees because they were not perfect. They removed a tulip tree that was three metres in diameter because it was hollow (North, n.d.). They appeared to have this image that nature as it existed was imperfect and that it was their duty to make it more civilized.

Similar management regimes existed in most older parks in Canada at some time in the past. The goal was often aesthetic management—the removal of ground shrubbery, the sweeping of trails and the opening of the forest. This active interference with the natural environment of a park, based upon some fussy concept of people cleaning up, civilizing, or beautifying nature is still practised in some parks. It is most frequent in municipal parks, especially so when the management is operated from a horticultural perspective.

FIRE MANAGEMENT:
BANFF NATIONAL PARK CASE STUDY

Banff National Park was one of the pioneers in the development of a fire management policy in Canada. In 1979 the planning for the use of fire in ecologically-based management was begun in this park. These early explorations have now spread across the entire Canadian national parks system and are now enshrined in National Park Policy (1994).

In the not-too-distant past, fire was viewed as 'damage' to park landscapes, in much the same way as foresters tend to view fire as destructive for commercial forests. Those who value wood products from forests often see fire as a negative influence because of the change of the organic matter into other forms. A forester wants a log and has little use for the tree once it has changed into ash. And of course fire is dangerous to people. Its impact is often dramatic and easily observable. An attitude grew that fire within a natural ecosystem is bad. A lot of effort was expended in fire suppression. These attitudes found their way into park management and fire suppression became a common management action.

In recent decades, ecologists recognized that fire is a natural component of most terrestrial ecosystems. It was discovered that some species are dependent upon fire, to a degree. For example, the cone of the Jack Pine does not open to release its seed until heated by a fire. Such an adaptation is advantageous to a species frequently exposed to fire. It is now recognized that the boreal forest in Canada of which Jack Pine is an important part, is a fire-adapted ecosystem. These forests burn at intervals and have done so for millennia. Since this species requires fire to propagate, fire suppression in the boreal forest can have a negative impact on Jack Pine regeneration.

It is now recognized that many species of plants and wildlife have evolved within an environment that includes fire as a normal influence. A fire frequency of 40, 60, or 100 years will occur in different areas under varying rainfall, temperature, and growth regimes. It is only in the wettest forests that fire is a minor influence. It is now also recognized that the artificial suppression of fire can cause unanticipated results. The suppression of fire results in the building of a large fuel inventory. In a forest a deep layer of leaves, branches, and other organic litter accumulates on the ground. The trees attain a large size. When a fire occurs it may be very large and very hot. As a result the impacts may be large, and possibly stronger than the ecosystem normally encounters. The massive fires in the forest of Yellowstone National Park in the summer of 1989 may be an example. Almost one-half of the park's forest burned in one short period of intense fire (Jeffery 1989). This fire occurred during a very dry period and fed on fuel created by decades of low fire occurrence.

Fire suppression mediates to the detriment of those species that are adapted to those conditions that occur in a normal fire regime. For example, open areas, such as small clearings, in a closed forest are important to species of birds that require such openings. In a normal fire forest regime such openings occur at frequent enough intervals to allow adapted species to find them and to survive. Fire suppression may result in a large, closed forest without such openings. Then, when the inevitable fire does result, the created openings may be huge—much larger than normal.

Throughout North America the standard policy in the past was to suppress fire whenever possible. A recognition of the role of fire resulted in a re-evaluation of that policy. As a result, many parks developed fire policies (Canadian Parks Service, 1986), with, however, many years of fire suppression as a precursor. Once it was recognized that fire was a natural process in an ecosystem, a problem had to be faced. Past fire suppression by park managers had created a situation that was both unnatural and dangerous. The forests were mature, the fuel load was high, many forests were ready to burn. This was the situation in Banff in the early 1980s.

In Banff the decision was made to concentrate the early planning in the lower Bow River Valley. The forests in this area are prone to fire. This area contains the Town of Banff and is one of the most heavily-used portions of any Canadian national park. Fire had been suppressed for a long time. Any fire planning here had to deal with a complicated and challenging situation.

One of the first jobs was to try to discover the past periodicity of forest fire. This was done by looking at fire scars on old trees and at information from other, similar locations. The size and intensity of past fires had to be estimated. Out of this came a simulation of past forest fire behaviour, without fire suppression (Lopoukhine and White, 1985). The planners then had to develop a vegetation plan, outlining what kind of vegetation communities the Bow Valley should have. The valley vegetation was mapped into vegetation 'ignition units'. A time for the burning of each unit was chosen randomly. A plan was put into place for the burning of the various units at different times up to the year 2035 (Lopoukhine and White, 1985). This burning program has been started.

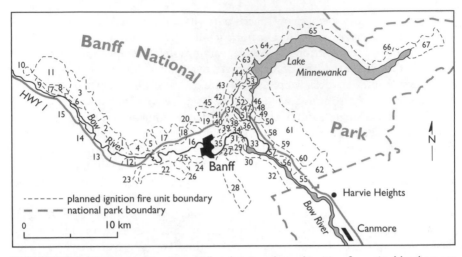

FIGURE 11.3 The Lower Bow River Valley showing planned ignition fire units. Numbers are keyed to Table 11.1.

TABLE 11.1 Examples of the Lower Bow Valley River Planned Ignition Burn Units 1 to 15, With a Simulated Random Burning Schedule.

Map	Area (ha)	Last Fire Year	Fire Cycle	Simulated Burn Years (1986–2035)
1	112	1891	40	1987
2	362	1904	40	2008
3	900	1801	40	
4	375	1891	40	2035
5	281	1903	40	1991, 1992, 1993
6	69	1930	20	2011
7	82	1861	40	2035
8	84	1801	40	1998, 2032
9	56	1881	40	1998, 2032
10	81	1881	40	
11	937	1881	40	
12	125	1881	60	1996
13	80	1891	60	
14	62	1891	40	2019, 2026
15	100	1925	40	2030

The Banff experience has been recognized as 'an outstanding effort to design and implement an integrated resource management plan using fire' (REMS Research, 1988). Although fire management is now a concept accepted by most ecologists, the Smokey the Bear anti-fire campaign of the US Forest Service and similar efforts in Canada have made their impact on public opinion across North America. Many members of the public are against the burning of forests, for any purpose. This can be a stumbling block to the purposeful introduction of fire. Many managers are finding that they can overcome this reticence with a carefully conceived public consultation program before any fire introduction program starts. For example, at Yellowstone National Park in the US, a natural fire in the late 1980s was allowed to burn, consistent with national park policies. Pubic reaction was strongly opposed to this management response, to the point that the fire management policy was threatened. As a result, a research project was undertaken to determine the attitudes, values, and perceptions of the general public regarding fire management in parks. What emerged from the study was a strategy for educating the public to make people better informed about the positive values associated with the role of fire in natural ecosystems (Bright et al., 1993).

In addition to public opposition to fires in parks, another challenge exists for park managers who have 'island' parks. The use and management of fire in a park surrounded by private lands and buildings is also a significant problem due to the concern that fire allowed to burn within a park may spread outside of the park and damage private property. Unfortunately, most Canadian parks are becoming islands of green in a sea of logged, farmed, mined, or residential lands.

VEGETATION MANAGEMENT:
OJIBWAY PROVINCIAL PARK CASE STUDY

A prairie is an open landscape dominated by herbaceous plants and with few trees. This community type is rare in Ontario, but a few significant remnants have survived agricultural clearance in southwestern Ontario. One of these occurs within Windsor. When the rarity of the vegetation in this area became recognized, suggestions were made for the establishment of a park. In 1957 Windsor acquired 44 hectares of oak woods and oak savannah. This was named the Ojibway Park. Facilities such as a picnic area, two parking lots, a nature interpretation centre and many trails were constructed. In 1989 the city purchased an additional 52 hectares of an area known as the Black Oak Woods.

As more information was collected on the prairie communities in the area, the Ontario Ministry of Natural Resources became involved. In 1971 the Ministry started an active land purchase program that has continued until the present time. Much of the land purchase was assisted with funds from the Nature Conservancy of Canada. As of 1990, 81 hectares have been bought for the Ojibway Prairie Provincial Nature Reserve and an additional 25 hectares were under active negotiation (Woodliffe, n.d.). In total, the city and the Ministry have preserved 187 hectares of the prairie as parkland.

This type of prairie once covered an estimated 1,000,000 sq. km of North America (ibid.). Even though the long-grass prairie was once widespread in the central parts of the continent, clearance for agriculture has reduced it considerably. Now only 0.16 per cent of the original area is officially protected, and there are vigorous efforts to protect prairie remnants throughout the US Midwest (ibid.).

FIGURE 11.4 Long-grass prairie in the Ojibway Prairie Provincial Park (Nature Reserve Class).

The Ojibway Prairie is of national and international significance. These two small parks (Ojibway Park, and Ojibway Prairie Nature Reserve) in Windsor contain half of all the prairie plants known to occur in Ontario. A total of 533 species of plants occur in the area, which is approximately 13 per cent of the flora of Canada (Pratt, 1979).

The development of management policies for such a unique and interesting area is a considerable challenge. The Ministry of Natural Resources, with the co-operation of the Parks and Recreation Department of the City of Windsor, undertook a detailed investigation of the site. This included: tracing the history of prairie development in Ontario, vegetation community mapping on the site, and detailed inventories of the plants, birds, mammals, reptiles, and amphibians. Once the state of the environment had been determined, policy development could take place. Detailed recommendations were made for the long-term maintenance and restoration of the prairie (Pratt, 1979). This was followed by a resource management plan (Ministry of Natural Resources, 1991).

Several important issues were outlined in the plan. One of the more significant issues dealt with vegetation management, which emphasized the use of active management to remove and keep in check undesirable woody and herbaceous plants. A number of approaches for vegetation control are used. These include: natural fire, woody stem cutting, artificial fuel, herbicides, and mowing. Prairies are typically fire succession communities, in which fire periodically burned across the grasslands killing most trees and shrubs. The more recent lack of fire has allowed the woody vegetation to invade and subsequently shade out the herbaceous open-ground dwelling plants.

Fire is essential to the long-term maintenance of the prairie. The removal of the woody vegetation by fire is necessary for the growth of the prairie grasses and herbs, but the implementation of a burn policy is difficult because the prairie is now an urban park surrounded by home owners who are not sympathetic to the thought of a forest fire being encouraged nearby.

Provincial parks policy suggests using very small burns under rigorous control, with lots of fire suppression capability near at hand (Pratt, 1979). After 1982, the MNR has been able to carry out successful prescribed burns in five different years. Approximately 80 per cent of the reserve was treated in this way, including area under the power lines. The public opposition lessened as the local residents saw the results and the professional manner in which it is conducted. Mowing and herbicides were not used, but herbicides were being considered on persistent foreign species such as Black Locust. Some cutting was done in areas where the woody thickets are too dense for proper fire action (Woodliffe, n.d.).

The prairie is now the site of an environmental education program for school children and for the public. Emphasis is placed upon prairie ecology in the programs. The goal is to create a local community knowledgeable about the value of this site and its ecological features.

The Ojibway Prairie complex is a good example of the role of parklands in protecting endangered species and their habitats. The site is also a fine example of municipal and provincial park agencies' co-operation on a joint conservation and environmental education goal. The environmental education program is noteworthy in its aim of fostering a community appreciation for this prairie ecosystem. The role of detailed and thorough research in the development of management policy is critical. All management activities in this prairie are based on the best scientific information available. The prairie also shows that even small parks in an urban area can have significant conservation roles.

BEAR MANAGEMENT:
ALGONQUIN PROVINCIAL PARK CASE STUDY

Canada is fortunate in having one of the lowest human population densities of any country in the world. This provides the opportunity to preserve very large pieces of landscape in the form of parks and reserves needed by large species of wildlife. For example, the grizzly, the wolverine, and the wolf are upper trophic level predators that need large territories. Some of the Canadian parks protect sufficiently large areas that these species can fulfil all of their life cycle requirements without leaving the parks. In addition, many of the parks are remote with acceptable habitat in areas adjacent to the parks.

In recent decades parks have become the only safe refuge for many large animals. For example, in the United States the grizzly bear and the wolf are almost extinct from the lower 48 states. The grizzly is only found in the Yellowstone National Park ecosystem and in Glacier National Park. The wolf is largely eliminated from the lower 48 states of the USA. The largest, non-endangered population of wolves is in Minnesota with additional breeding populations in Washington, Montana, Wisconsin, and Michigan, according to Thiel and Ream (1992). Unfortunately all of the few remaining animals are under constant hunting attack. To help reduce this problem, the wolf was successfully reintroduced to the Yellowstone National Park ecosystem, but not without considerable controversy and many legal challenges.

Parks play an important role in the conservation of all native wildlife species, whether large or small. However, the land use around the park is critical to the survival of the wildlife in the park. Most wildlife moves in and out of the park during certain times of the year. When a park becomes a green island in a sea of 'hostile' habitat, such as an urban park surrounded by houses, some species are unable to cope.

Those parks that do not allow hunting are particularly important. Only here can wildlife research be done on populations that are subject to relatively natural ecological forces. The lack of hunting is critically important to wildlife viewing as the animals are free of fear of man and therefore relatively easy to observe.

It must be remembered that the lack of hunting and the associated interference with natural population process does not ensure a pristine condition. Most wildlife populations are exposed to hunting and other influences in the parts of their life cycle that take them out of the parks. In recent decades Aboriginal land claims and political activity has resulted in many parks being opened to Aboriginal subsistence hunting. This hunting is often poorly monitored and regulated.

The Black Bear is a common inhabitant of the forests of central Canada. They are hunted everywhere in Canada and, as a result, they are wary of contact with people. However, in a park as large as Algonquin it is possible for the majority of the bears to live their lives without being subjected to hunting. As a result, the animals have little fear of people. Algonquin Provincial Park in Ontario has a robust population of these animals, and the chance of seeing a Black Bear is of importance to many of the visitors to this park. However, Black Bears are large and potentially dangerous animals. They are omnivorous animals, eating copious amounts of berries and seeds, but are quite willing to take a meat meal if presented with the opportunity.

Algonquin has many canoe campers each year. These visitors travel through the park by canoe, carrying their necessary food and supplies as they go. Some bears have learned that campers carry food that is usually quite easy to get. As a result a bear 'problem' has developed as the campers' food is stolen, often with equipment damage during the theft.

Typically, the bears do not bother the people directly, as long as the people stay out of the bears' way. Atypically, Black Bears attack people. Herrero (1985) documented the death of 26 people caused by Black Bears in North America from 1900 to 1983. More have occurred since then. On 13 May 1978 three teen-aged boys on a fishing trip in Algonquin were killed. One other boy survived and provided details. A large male bear was later shot and positively linked to the boys' deaths. Herrero (1985) concluded that this bear killed the boys as food. There was no evidence that the bear was old or diseased, two factors often thought to drive bears to attack people. It was a healthy male that decided to stalk human prey. A few years later a man and a woman were killed by a bear while camping on an island in the park. In 1998 a canoe-trip leader beat off a bear with a paddle as it was dragging a young boy into woods after pulling him out of his tent at night.

The management of the interactions between park visitors and dangerous animals is an important concern. The management of the park has several options. Bears that develop dangerous habits may be killed to avoid the possibility of repetition. This approach has become less acceptable in recent years as the concept that the wild animal also has a right to exist became more prevalent. The practice now is to kill only those specific animals that pose a strong threat. This might apply to aggressive, injured, or diseased animals. Animals that actually injure or kill people are usually killed.

The public is informed, through the interpretive program of the park, of the danger of bears. Appropriate camping procedures are encouraged to lessen the potential of attracting bears to a campsite. The education of the visitor about the danger and the means of minimizing the danger has become widespread. However, this is expensive. The actual implementation of education is usually a hit-and-miss proposition, with many of the visitors missed.

The restriction of visitor activities is becoming more common and accepted. In some parks, the visitors are not allowed to enter certain areas when grizzly sows with cubs are present. In other parks, visitors must be accompanied by guards when they visit locales that have dangerous animals. In some parks where visitors travel by vehicle, no egress from the vehicle is allowed.

It is now generally accepted that in parks the park visitors have to learn to live with the environment as it is, bears and all. They must learn to adapt to the ways of nature, and not to have nature changed for their needs. Not all visitors agree that they should take the environment as they find it. Some feel that all dangerous animals should be removed. Others feel that the park management has a duty to protect the visitor from any harm that might come their way from such animals.

BOX 11.1 Banff National Park: ELK OUT OF BOUNDS ON GOLF COURSE

For decades, elk at the Banff Springs Golf Club have freely puttered around greens, munched on manicured fairways and drunk from pristine ponds. But the free range is coming to an end—Parks Canada is running about 200 lollgagging elk off the 27-hole golf course into the wild. 'Next summer we are going to try to keep the golf course elk-free', says park warden David Norcross. 'then we don't have to worry about golfers getting ambushed.'

Removing the elk is the latest in a long running-battle between commercial developers and environmentalists over wildlife in federal parks. In Banff, it's a fight that has seen wardens and locals use slingshots, rubber bullets and border collies to run the elk out of town. Parks Canada and many of the 8000 Banff townsite residents want the elk removed because of vicious attacks and, they say, it just isn't natural for such animals to live on pavement. But wildlife protectors say the elk have a right to live wherever they choose in federal parks. 'That's their habitat and we are taking it away' said Liz White of Animal Alliance of Canada. 'You have to ask the government every time you build another recreational golf course or hotel in the park and the animals intrude on the territory, is the end result going to be trapping and moving?'

Parks Canada moved 150 elk from the centre of town last year because officials said it was too dangerous for them there. The number of aggressive elk cases in Banff soared to 109 in 1999 from 42 in 1993. Each year the habituated beasts hurt several people—locals and tourists who often require stitches. Many tourists believe the elk are cute, docile animals; some feed the animals in town and take pictures. But the wild animals can be unpredictable, particularly when their hormones are raging and parenting instincts kick in. Bulls get into a flap in October during rutting season; cows become protective of their little ones after calving in April and May.

Earlier this year Parks Canada officials and locals ran hundreds of urban elk out of town by harassing them with loud pistol shots and stinging them with rocks from rubber bullets from shotguns. Then they brought in more effective artillery— two border collies. The little black and white dogs, bred for herding sheep, were dispatched to nudge and push the elks' hooves to the town limits.

The golf course wasn't a priority last year for clearing the four-legged beasts from town.

'It's more open, most people are using carts and you don't have children playing and getting ambushed' said Norcross. Besides, he noted, golfers carry weapons—a bag full of clubs.'

Park wardens plan to trap elk in pens on the golf course, using alfalfa as bait, then truck the animals beyond park boundaries. White calls that cruel. 'They are all of a sudden being displaced into a territory that has already been established and a pecking order has to reoccur.'

But all elk may not have to be transported. A pack of eight wolves, living three kilometers away from the golf course, is expected to consume one elk every 10 days. In hopes of encouraging more predators to the golf course to eat stray elk, the area is closed this winter to cross-country skiers and snowshoers, said chief park warden Ian Syme. 'This pack of wolves, we expect, will be very active in there this winter,' Syme said.
—*Victoria Times Colonist*, 11 December 2000.

Unfortunately there is a sequel to this story. In early January a fatal attack occurred on a woman cross country skiing near Banff by a cougar that was in apparent good health. The cougar was destroyed. However, several other cougars were also involved in close and threatening encounters with Banff residents around the same time. Park officials suggest that the cougar are being drawn into Banff by their main source of food, elk. In response to the danger, officials decided to relocate several cougars to more remote areas of the park. Obviously this is not a permanent solution to a problem caused by ecosystem imbalances and human intrusion.

FISHERIES MANAGEMENT:
FUNDY NATIONAL PARK CASE STUDY

Fundy National Park is located in New Brunswick on the shore of the Bay of Fundy. The park contains clear, freshwater streams that attract spawning Atlantic Salmon each spring. Salmon spend three years of their life in the streams. They then go to the sea for one or two years. When the salmon reach breeding age, they migrate back to their ancestral river to spawn.

National park policies recognize the significance of the park's streams to the salmon, and Parks Canada tries to maintain the water quality to the highest possible standard. Parks Canada has a research program aimed at measuring the number of spawning salmon and the survival rates of the young. In recent years the park officials have found a decrease in the numbers of spawning salmon and so the park has instituted a release program to increase the salmon population.

In 1986, Atlantic Salmon returned to the Point Wolf River in Fundy National Park for the first time in more than 100 years. A logging dam that had prevented salmon from entering the river was then removed. For three years prior, the river had been stocked with juvenile salmon obtained from adjacent rivers. The juveniles were able to go downstream, over the dam. After one year in salt water, the first grilse salmon returned to attempt to spawn in the river (Woodley, n.d.). This reintroduction program was successful, but the rate of return was much lower than anticipated (ibid.). The reasons are unclear but the low return rate occurs in all local rivers, not just the Point Wolf. It is possible that survival at sea is low due to overfishing, or other, unknown factors.

The case of these Atlantic Salmon demonstrates an important ecological fact— parks are connected with the environment around them. Fundy provides critical spawning habitat. However, this is not sufficient to protect the salmon populations. The fish population is being heavily exploited in the open ocean and therefore has a reduced opportunity to renew itself.

PALEONTOLOGICAL RESOURCE MANAGEMENT:
DINOSAUR PROVINCIAL PARK CASE STUDY

Parks often have significant abiotic resources. Mountains, rivers, rocks, and fossils are examples of non-living resources that occur in parks and require special consideration. Fossils are special because they are of sometimes very high scientific value, and are non-renewable. Canada has important fossil deposits in some parks. For example, the fossils found in the Burgess Shales of Yoho National Park are a World Heritage Site. These shales contain the most significant early Cambrian fossils found anywhere in the world. Their analysis has fundamentally altered our understanding of the earliest evolution of soft bodied animals (Gould, 1990).

The collection of fossils may be important to the science of palaeontology. In addition, the private collector is often willing to pay quite large sums for prize fossil specimens. The methods of determining who can collect fossils and under what conditions

FIGURE 11.5 Dinosaur Provincial Park, Alberta. The constant erosion exposes new dinosaur skeletons each year.

is another challenging responsibility of management. The methods used to collect the fossils can be destructive of the remaining resources in the park. Some early scientific collection practises at the Burgess shales were very destructive to the fossils collected and to the surrounding landscape.

Since fossils often come to light due to natural erosion of geological strata, these same forces will destroy the specimen in time. Hence, the protection and management of paleontological resources is a complex undertaking. Within Canada, several parks have been established for the specific purpose of conserving and interpreting fossil resources. Specimen collection, as well as overt vandalism, is a constant threat to the fossils. Parks provide a means of assuring constant protection of the fossil resources. Further, the interpretation of the significance of the fossils to the public is an important facet of park operation, and the provision of a site for long-term scientific research and collection is a critical role of many parks.

The badlands of southern Alberta contain a spectacular series of valleys and hills. They were created over the centuries by water erosion of dry soils. The rainfall and the rivers have carved deep into ancient fossil strata. The resultant exposure of the fossil specimens has created a situation of relatively easy access to the buried specimens. Dinosaur Provincial Park in Alberta was created for the specific purpose of protecting a large tract of badlands. These areas contain many rare species preserved in the semi-desert environment. Furthermore, Native peoples have used the area for millennia. Finally, the badlands contain one of the world's most significant deposits of fossilized bone. The fossils frequently are found to be well-preserved specimens of dinosaurs from the upper Cretaceous period. The park contains areas with a very high occurrence of bones. In some places, fully articulated dinosaur skeletons have been discovered. Other sites contain isolated bones, petrified wood, clam beds, marine fossils, fossil pollen, leaf imprints, and amber. One fossil footprint has been found (Alberta Provincial Parks Service, n.d.).

The park staff monitor all activities and ensure that no unlicensed fossil collection takes place. In addition, the most important fossils are protected from natural degradation caused by weather until the time they can be studied or removed for museum conservation. In addition to this protection function, the park plays an important scientific function. More than 300 complete and nearly complete dinosaur skeletons have been found and removed from the general area in the last 80 years. These specimens are displayed in major museums around the world. Prospecting continues and during an active summer an average of six new skeletons will be found, of which 30 per cent are good specimens. Thirty-five different dinosaur species have been found within the park. The bones of hadrosaurs are particularly abundant (Alberta Provincial Parks Service, n.d.). Excavations of important fossil assemblages are constantly underway, in co-operation with the Tyrell Museum of Palaeontology.

The park plays an important educational role. Dinosaur Provincial Park is the best place in Canada for a member of the public to observe fossils in situ and to see fossil excavations underway. In addition, interpreters with special paleontological training provide enriching educational programs. In order to restrict and control access to the

BOX 11.2 Yoho National Park:
SCIENTISTS SMUGGLE PRICELESS FOSSILS

Last summer, Parks Canada stepped up security in a small area high in the mountains of Yoho National Park with surveillance cameras and added manpower. For buried in a rubble of rock on this remote, wind-swept precipice near the Alberta-British Columbia border are weird and wonderful fossils.

These fossils are so priceless, many scientists believe they surpass even the dinosaurs for what they can tell us about how multi-celled animals first burst onto the scene a half billion years ago. But the temptation to smuggle some of these so-called 'oddballs of nature' out, however, was apparently too great for some people, including one British scientist who hiked up to the fossil beds last summer. Those people were caught in four separate incidents, charged with entering a restricted area, and will appear in court this fall. 'It may be the tip of the iceberg' says Brad Bischoff, of Parks Canada, on the possibility of widespread smuggling. 'Given the importance of these fossil beds, we plan on taking these acts very seriously in the future.

Designated a United Nations World Heritage Site in 1984, the fossils of the Burgess Shale are considered to be the most important in the world. The animals that once lived here are so bizarrely put together that scientists have trouble placing them within any known living group of animals.
—*Victoria Times Colonist*, 24 October 2000.

most important fossil areas, one-third of the park has been zoned as a 'Natural Preserve'. Access is allowed only for specialized uses such as: scientific research and collection, guided interpretive tours, and approved photographic work (Thesen, 1990). The enforcement of the restrictions in the Natural Preserve Zone is not as complete as the Parks Service would like. [There is a suspicion that illegal collection may be occurring because of a lack of staff to maintain a sufficient level of field patrol through the more remote back country areas of the park (Alberta Provincial Parks Service, n.d.). Thesen (1990) maintains that there is:

> a split in job functions and responsibilities between providing service, enforcement and public safety to the general public in the core area of the park and providing an effective level of backcountry patrols in the outer more inaccessible areas of the park. In addition, the effectiveness of backcountry patrols is limited due to the inaccessibility of areas of the park to vehicle traffic and the nature of the badland terrain which because of its erosional formation, makes it difficult to observe activities other than those taking place within the immediate area.

This type of problem occurs in almost all parks particularly in the larger parks where the enforcement staff are few in number and the wilderness nature of the land makes access time-consuming and difficult.

Dinosaur Provincial Park is an example of a highly specialized environmental management operation. The resource management functions in this park include resource protection, scientific research, and public education. These functions are not unique to Dinosaur Park. Similar functions occur in all parks. What is unique, is the rarity of the paleontological subject matter. The significance of the fossil resources were fully recognized when UNESCO placed the park on the World Heritage List in 1979. A World Heritage Site is of such a high level of importance that it is considered to be of value to all of human kind.

INFORMATION FOR MANAGEMENT

In site management there is a critical need for information. Baseline information is needed on the characteristics of the environment. Before any environmental feature can be assessed, the following questions must be answered:

- How much is there?
- Where is it?
- How has it changed over time?
- How does it relate to other aspects of the environment?
- What types of information should be collected?
- How much information is necessary to solve the problem at hand?

Once sufficient information is available to provide a level of confidence in the manager that the questions have been answered, then the problem can be properly stated. Under the environmental assessment policy or legislation that is found in many jurisdictions in Canada the manager must look at various alternatives for solving the problem. These alternatives must be assessed against each other to find a solution that is the most environmentally suitable. Once a course of action is decided upon, an intervention takes place. It is critically important that the impact of this intervention be measured and monitored down through time.

Eagles (1987) studied the use of natural resource information in the planning and management in the national parks of Canada. The research found that Parks Canada has an information base adequate for the demands placed upon it, and that it is well used. This information was transferred to computer data base storage and linked to the impressive manipulation and display capabilities of geographical information systems. This technology allows for the rapid analysis and presentation of mapped information by a computer and has become very useful for the manager who translates raw, field data into useful information on trends.

Thorsell (1990) suggested that a manager needs accurate biophysical information on five different areas before management decisions can be made. These five areas are basic inventory, species needs, ecological relationships, monitoring and dynamics of change, and predictive manipulation of ecosystems.

The basic inventory provides estimates of the most important natural features of a park—the plants, animals, soils, and geological phenomenon. The inventory should estimate numbers and indicate spatial density. Any threats to the natural environment should be identified. So should the needs of those species that are of special significance, including rare species and those of particular cultural significance. Also required is information on the ecological relationships of key species, and species with particular importance in the food chain.

Possibly the ecosystem is in flux; if so, the changes must be monitored. New species may be invading. Erosion may be underway. Water levels may be changing. Such changes may have profound impact on the ecosystem and must be tracked with care.

Once enough information has been collected so that the six questions can be answered confidently, the problem, whatever it is, can be stated definitively and solutions can be sought. Environmental assessment policies or legislation, where these exist, require managers to look at alternative solutions, which must be assessed and compared to determine which is most environmentally suitable, and acceptable for those people or groups involved in making management decisions. Management decisions are made on the basis of value systems as well as scientific evidence. Once a course of action is decided upon, it can be set in motion. Again, monitoring the effect of intervention is essential and should be undertaken over the long-term.

Park Management Plans

Starting about 1970, park managers in Canada began to develop management plans for each park. The purpose of these management plans was to state the park level policies that will guide development and management activities for a given period of time, typically for five or 10 years. Management plans vary somewhat from agency to agency but each park management plan is written to reflect the existing legislation and various policies unique to each agency. These laws and polices were designed to provide a level of system-wide consistency across all parks within an agency.

A park management plan provides background to the park and to the park agency. A basic description of the legal, cultural, environmental, and historic features of the park provides a reader with the context of the plan. Usually the plan describes the timing and the planning procedures used in plan development. The most important part of the plan is the policy section. This describes park policy for all major programs and activities, including land acquisition, resource protection, resource exploitation, public use, recreation use, tourism, historic sites, community development, land uses, interpretation, environmental education, and research.

The plan contains maps, including those outlining resource and use zones. Park plans typically use zoning as a means of outlining resource and cultural areas and their associated uses. Many approaches to park zoning resemble the ROS system described in Chapter 7.

Park management plans are implemented by park staff, so require appropriate levels of expertise and numbers of staff. Therefore, management plans often include a section that outlines park staff requirements. In a few cases park staff are assisted by advisory committees or groups of local volunteers. Although park staff have the responsibility to follow the guidelines set out in management plans, the management plans are not usually legal documents, they are policy statements. This means that there is no legal requirement that the plan be implemented as written. A park employee who does not follow the plan will bring disrepute to himself or herself and to the agency, but cannot be penalized in a court of law.

Park management also requires suitable levels of finance. Unfortunately, most governments are loath to tie themselves in writing to a long-term financial commitment, so most management plans do not contain details of park finance. This is often a problem as many park management plans fail to be fully implemented due to weak financial commitments from government.

The development of park management plans in Canada typically involves substantial levels of public involvement. All individuals and groups that are interested in becoming involved in developing a management plan may be given an opportunity, as described earlier in this chapter (who determines 'value'). In Canada, the final say on the contents of a management plan comes from parks staff and from ministers responsible for parks. Typically, no independent bodies are involved, no appeals to the courts are allowed, and no administrative tribunal review occurs. This is very different from other forms of planning in Canada, such as city plans, where it is common to have planning disputes referred to independent courts established for this purpose.

The park management plan is a foundation policy document. It is a statement of government and agency intent for a park, providing the public with details of all major policies governing protection and use of a park. Although most national and provincial park agencies in Canada have declared a policy to provide a management plan for each park, financial limitations have meant that very many parks do not have such plans, and many more have plans that are out of date. It is to be hoped that in the future all parks in Canada will have up-to-date management plans.

SUMMARY

The management of the natural and cultural resources of a park is a fundamental aspect of park administration. Whether the resources are living creatures, abiotic elements, or fossil artifacts their management entails several critical components.

- First, the human, cultural, and environmental resources must be known and understood. Research is a vital aspect of all resource management policy-making.
- Second, the values placed upon the resources must be known and understood. These values will determine the types of options that will be available for the management regime.
- Third, the methods used to elicit value determinations from the decision-making constituencies will largely determine the types of policies that will result.
- Fourth, the vast majority of environmental management is really people management; this is the largest issue to be tackled.
- Fifth, management is undertaken with less than complete knowledge, and outcomes are not always as expected.

Park management must also consider what occurs outside their bailiwicks. Outside land or sea practices may have serious consequences for park species that depend on a larger area.

Parks play a major role in the long-term protection of the world's genetic diversity and in providing outdoor recreation opportunities for many people, but parks are under constant pressure from use within and from nearby influences that degrade environmental quality. This makes for tremendous challenges for those who manage our parks.

ACKNOWLEDGEMENTS

Special thanks to the many professional environmental managers who provided information and advice during the preparation of this chapter. Allen Woodliffe, District Ecologist for the Chatham District of the Ontario Ministry of Natural Resources, provided information on the management of the Ojibway Prairie Nature Reserve. Tom Beechey, Life Science Specialist for the Ontario Ministry of Natural Resources gave assistance on many policy issues dealing with the provincial parks management. Cliff White, formerly Park Warden of Banff National Park has been instrumental in developing the fire management strategy for Banff National Park; his advice was very much appreciated on this topic. Jim Boissonneault, formerly Chief Park Warden of St Lawrence Islands National Park, commented on the text from his experience in applying resource management plans in several Canadian national parks. Marilyn Watson, Chief Planner, Ontario Region of Parks Canada gave advice based upon her extensive experience in parks planning in Canada. Dr Steven Woodley, former Park Ecologist for Fundy National Park, advised on the Atlantic Salmon management issues. Christopher Wilkinson a graduate student at the University of Waterloo read and commented on the paper. While grateful for their advice, I would add that any errors, omissions, or opinions are, of course, those of the author. I would like to acknowledge the influence of the late George North of Burlington who was a interested visitor to Rondeau throughout the early part of the twentieth century. Finally, special thanks to the World Commission on Protected Areas that provides the author with the opportunity to study park management worldwide.

REFERENCES

Alberta Provincial Parks Service. n.d. *Dinosaur Provincial Park Resource Management Plan.* Edmonton: Alberta Recreation and Parks.

Bright, A.D., M.J. Manfredo, M. Fishbein, and A. Bath. 1993. 'Application of the theory of reasoned action to the National Park Service's controlled burn policy', *Journal of Leisure Research* 25, 3: 263-80.

Canadian Parks Service. 1986. *Fire Management.* Management Directive 2.4.4. Ottawa: Natural Resources Branch.

Dorney, R.S. 1989. *The Professional Practice of Environmental Management.* New York: Springer-Verlag.

Eagles, Paul F. J., Daniel McLean, and Mike J. Stabler. 2000. 'Estimating the Tourism Volume and Value in Parks and Protected Areas in Canada and the USA', *George Wright Forum* 17, 3: 62-76.

Eagles, P.F.J. 1987. *The Use of Biophysical Inventories in Park Planning and Management in National Parks in Canada.* Occasional Paper Number 9, Department of Recreation and Leisure Studies, University of Waterloo, Waterloo, Ont.

Godfrey, W.E. 1986. *The Birds of Canada.* Ottawa: National Museum of Natural Sciences.

Gould, S.J. 1990. *Wonderful Life: The Burgess Shale and the Nature of History.* New York: W.W. Norton & Company.

Herrero, S. 1985. *Bear Attacks—Their Causes and Avoidance.* New York: Lyons and Burford.

Jeffery, D. 1989. 'Yellowstone—The Great Fires of 1988', *National Geographic* 175, 2: 255-73.

Lopoukhine, N., and C. White. 1985. 'Fire Management Options in Canada's National Parks', in D.E. Dube, ed., *Proceedings of the Intermountain Fire Council 1983 Fire Management Workshop.* Edmonton, Alta: Northern Forest Research Centre, Canadian Forestry Service, Information Report NOR–X–271, 59–68.

Ministry of Natural Resources. 1991. *Draft Resource Management Plan for Ojibway Prairie Provincial Nature Reserve 1991-1996.* Chatham, Ont.: Chatham District Office.

North, G. n.d. Hamilton Naturalists Club, Hamilton, Ont., personal communication.

Pratt, P.D. 1979. *A Preliminary Life Science Inventory of The Ojibway Prairie Complex and Surrounding Area.* City of Windsor and Ontario Ministry of Natural Resources.

REMS Research Ltd. 1988. *Fire Management in the Canadian Parks Service: Evaluation and Recommendations.* Ottawa: Canadian Parks Service, Department of the Environment.

Thesen, C. 1990. Letter dated 12 Oct. 1990. Acting District Manager, Badlands District, Provincial Parks Service, Alberta Recreation and Parks, Patricia, Alberta.

Thiel, Richard, and R. Ream. 1995. 'Status of the Gray Wolf in the Lower 48 United States to 1992', in L.N. Carbyn, S.H. Fritts, and D.R. Seip, eds, *Ecology and Conservation of Wolves in a Changing World.* Edmonton, Alta.: Canadian Circumpolar Institute, Occasional Publication No. 35.

Thorsell, J.W. 1990. 'Research in Tropical Protected Areas: Some Guidelines for Managers', *Environmental Conservation* 17, 1: 14-18.

Woodley, S. n.d. Park Ecologist, Fundy National Park, Canadian Parks Service, personal communication.

Woodliffe, A. n.d. District Ecologist, Chatham District, Ontario Ministry of Natural Resources, personal communication.

KEY WORDS/CONCEPTS

park values
management
natural resource management
environmental management
market point of view
ecological point of view
process management
non-interference
Spotted Owl controversy
historic parks
recreation management
visual management
fire management
vegetation management
paleontological resource management

STUDY QUESTIONS

1. Compare the concepts of 'natural resource management' and 'environmental management.'
2. Outline advantages and disadvantages of the 'non-interference' approach.
3. List the types of 'constituents' or stakeholders that could be consulted when resolving 'values' to guide the management of a park. For each type of stakeholder, list specific advantages and disadvantages of consulting such a group.
4. Discuss how the Spotted Owl controversy in the US represents a clash between market values and environmental values.
5. The Point Pelee case study illustrates the challenge of addressing an environmental issue such as beach erosion when the causes are uncertain. Compare the actions taken at Point Pelee with those taken at Presquile. Which approach is more appropriate and why?
6. Present arguments for and against the approach to visual management used in Rondeau Provincial Park.
7. Present arguments for and against fire suppression in parks.
8. Discuss why 'planned burns' in parks are controversial.
9. Present arguments for and against limited hunting in parks by First Nations.
10. Bear-human interactions are of concern in many Canadian parks, such as Algonquin Provincial Park. Discuss options for dealing with this issue, assessing advantages and disadvantages of each approach.
11. The salmon recovery plan in Fundy National Park was only partially successful. Discuss why this was the case.
12. Outline the unique challenges of protecting fossil resources, such as those found in Dinosaur Provincial Park or Yoho National Park.
13. Why is elk management at Banff Springs Golf Club controversial?

CHAPTER 12

Protected Areas and Ecosystem-Based Management

D. Scott Slocombe & Philip Dearden

INTRODUCTION

Earlier chapters have highlighted the ways in which protected areas are linked to their surroundings physically, ecologically, economically, and culturally. During the past 30 years, but particularly the last 15, the interaction between protected areas and their surroundings has been increasingly recognized. Managing protected areas without recognizing these linkages can lead to many problems, such as population increases in some wildlife species and decreases in others; ignorance of pollution originating outside the protected area; lack of support from local residents and failure to learn from their experiences; and institutional conflict and competition. As the title of Dan Janzen's (1983) influential article observed, 'No park is an island'.

As managers and conservationists have come to understand the challenges facing protected areas, particularly those related to the reduction of undisturbed ecosystems surrounding them, the need for a more regional, multi-stakeholder, science-based, and co-operative approach has become widely recognized. Threats originating outside parks (see, for example, Machlis and Tichnell, 1985, 1987; Dearden and Doyle, 1997; Parks Canada, 1998), the application of gap analyses to identify critical unprotected areas (Grumbine, 1990), the need for inter-agency co-operation to facilitate networks of protected areas for biodiversity (see, for example, Sax and Keiter, 1987), and under-standing of the significance of local support for the long-term effectiveness of pro-tected areas (e.g., Batisse, 1982) all have fostered the development of more regionally integrated approaches to protected areas management.

These concerns are not limited to protected areas' management; they influence and are influenced by similar changes in resource and environmental management. Multiple-use management, integrated resource management, watershed manage-ment, and comprehensive regional land-use planning have converged during the past decade to become known as ecosystem, or ecosystem-based, management. Although various definitions for the particular approaches exist, most share the con-cept of a regional 'greater ecosystem' for management based on biophysical rather than on administrative boundaries. Common themes include stress on the role of scientific knowledge as a basis for management, a co-operative and participatory process, and explicit definition of such complex management goals as ecological integrity, biodiversity maintenance, and sustainability.

Such approaches have developed over a number of years in Canada. By the early 1970s there was much work on ecosystem approaches in the context of problems of the North American Great Lakes (Caldwell, 1970; Francis et al., 1985; Vallentyne and Beeton, 1988). The concept and implications of the ecosystem approach were ultimately reflected in the Great Lakes Water Quality Agreement and the Remedial Action Plan process for Areas of Concern in the Great Lakes Basin (e.g., Hartig, et al., 1998; MacKenzie, 1996). These efforts had wide influence in the development of regional-scale environmental management over many years. The earliest parks-related interest in Canada probably was catalyzed by biosphere reserves, especially Waterton Lakes National Park Biosphere Reserve in Alberta. Parks Canada and the US National Parks Service co-sponsored a workshop in June 1982 on the theme 'Towards the Biosphere Reserve: Exploring Relationships between Parks and Adjacent Lands'. By the mid-1980s Parks Canada was exploring the 'regional integration' of parks. This had strong economic and political dimensions, but was also concerned with ecological issues, such as resource and tourism development around parks (Community and Municipal Affairs, 1985). Several case studies were completed in the later 1980s, including one on Waterton.

The first book to explicitly link ecosystem management and protected areas appeared in 1988 (Agee and Johnson, 1988). Its authors were American, as were its examples—including Montana's Yellowstone National Park, a recurring American example in the history of ecosystem management. The contributors to the book stressed many of the

FIGURE 12.1 International boundary between Canada and the US linking Waterton and Glacier National Parks. Political boundaries, even international ones, hold little significance for ecological processes. *Photo: P. Dearden.*

themes highlighted above: external threats; the need for interagency co-operation; new scientific understanding of diversity, disturbance, and ecosystems;, and a better appreciation for the human dimension of management. By this time research in Canada was growing on similar topics, most notably on environmental monitoring and ecosystem integrity. A workshop in Waterloo, Ontario focused on ecological integrity and ecosystem management in parks, and resulted in several influential publications (for example, Woodley, 1993). In 1988 the National Parks Act was amended to require maintenance of ecological integrity as the top priority, (Chapter 3). Perhaps not coincidentally, Canadian approaches to ecosystem-based management have tended to be strongly based in science and ecological integrity, and are arguably less participatory and process-oriented than those developed in the US and elsewhere.

Today, ecosystem-based management approaches are widely endorsed and increasingly implemented. For example, the 1994 Parks Canada Policy (Parks Canada, 1994) recognized ecosystem management and that it must be broad in scope, and based on wide support in terms of regional co-operation and integration of the park into the surrounding region (section 2.1.7). A similar approach is implicit in the National Marine Conservation Areas system plan as discussed in Chapter 14 (Parks Canada, 1995). More recently, the report of the Panel on the Ecological Integrity of Canada's national parks made management of whole ecosystems using the best scientific knowledge and involving local people and their concerns as a key part of its recommendations (Parks Canada Agency, 2000). Recent analyses of the minimum critical area for large carnivores in the national parks (Gurd and Nudds, 1999; Landry et al., 2001) have shown clearly that most parks are too small to sustain minimum viable populations of these species without the use of appropriate habitat outside the parks. Ecosystem management for parks is now a necessity for their survival and not an optional management fad.

The remainder of this chapter introduces the principles, tools, and methods of ecosystem-based park planning, and provides examples of its application.

THE ELEMENTS OF ECOSYSTEM-BASED PARKS MANAGEMENT

Ecosystem-based management has diverse roots. It draws on social and natural science, theory and practice, and protected and non-protected area examples. It is a new approach but with a long history. It has supporters as well as critics. In this section we will highlight different perspectives on the central ideas and elements of ecosystem-based management, moving towards a synthesis for protected-areas management.

Agee and Johnson (1988) stress nine principles that remain important today:

- co-operation and open negotiation are fundamental to success;
- individual agencies and stakeholders have different mandates, objectives, and constituencies;
- success should be measured by results;
- threshold management goals are stated by the park and wilderness legislation;
- problems defined clearly have a better chance of being resolved;
- over the long term, ecosystem management must accommodate multiple uses at

a regional scale and dominant or restricted uses at the unit or site scale;
- high-quality information is necessary to identify trends and respond to them intelligently;
- social, political, and environmental issues must be viewed in a system context, not as individual issues;
- all management is a long-term experiment and decisions are always made with incomplete information.

Agee and Johnson's perspective is rooted in that of the professional park manager, and is particularly concerned with agencies, information, land management units, and satisfying the often conflicting demands of legislation, the public, and conservation.

Much of the discussion of ecosystem management is focused on public, government-owned land: Crown land in Canada, federal and state lands in the US. Hence, ecosystem management literature often takes the perspective of government land managers. This perspective tends to stress inter-agency co-operation and legislative foundations for management, and, (especially for multiple uses) public consultation (perhaps instead of real public participation), and ways to link science and public policy to produce better outcomes (see, for example, Keiter, 1994). In most of the US and in the more populated regions of Canada, incorporating privately owned lands into ecosystem-based management is a challenge for protected-area managers. It is of particular concern when private lands surround the protected area. (Box 12.1). This is part of the general challenge of including private lands into an integrated land and resource management framework. Possible approaches to this problem include improved understanding of the linkages between public and private lands, clarifying the space and time dimensions needed to ensure ecological integrity and resilience, co-operative efforts to diversify the local economic base, and consensual development of law and policy that can be used to promote ecological and economic sustainability (Keiter, 1998).

BOX 12.1 Bruce Peninsula National Park and Private Lands

Contrary to common belief, Bruce Peninsula in Ontario is not a national park. It is a national park reserve, which means that it is not yet protected under the National Parks Act and its boundaries are not legislated. A timber company has purchased 486 ha of white cedar forest adjacent to the park. The forest, originally included in the park study area, is part of the largest winter deer yard on the northern Bruce Peninsula and contains important wetlands. The company wishes to re-open a road allowance owned by the Municipality of the Northern Bruce Peninsula, which passes through lands to be included in the park. Since the park boundaries have yet to be legislated, the Township has given preliminary approval to open the road. Parks Canada has offered to buy the portion of the land within the park study area, but the offer has not been accepted. In response, the Canadian Parks and Wilderness Society in joint action with the Chippewas of Nawash and Saugeen

First Nations were successful in obtaining a court order to delay road construction until a full enviromental assessment could be undertaken.

Forest harvesting activities on adjacent lands are a major threat to many parks throughout Canada. The 1997 *State of the Parks Report* (Parks Canada, 1998) cites forestry as the most common threat to park values originating solely outside park boundaries (Figure 12.6). The Forestry Guidelines developed at Fundy National Park, and outlined in this chapter, and similar initiatives at Pacific Rim National Park Reserve point the way forward to a more ecosystem-based approach to forestry surrounding protected areas.

In contrast to the perspective outlined above, other writers have approached the issue from a more ecological point of view. Grumbine (1994) traced the origins of ecosystem management through Aldo Leopold's research and writing on wildlife, land, and ecosystems (1920s to the 1940s); to early research on wildlife in the US national parks by George Wright and others(1930s and 1940s); through to the Craigheads' bear research in Yellowstone National Park beginning in the 1960s. Ecological work, along with a great deal of experience in national park and national forest management has uncovered the complexity of natural ecosystems and the need for large, intact areas to maintain diverse wildlife populations (Box 12.2).

BOX 12.2 Woodland Caribou and Nahanni National Park Reserve

Often parks are created with one major threat to a particular resource in mind, and boundaries are drawn to reflect this. Nahanni National Park Reserve, on the border between the Yukon and Northwest Territories, is one such example. The boundaries of the reserve were delimited to protect the river from hydro-electric development and resulted in a linear corridor centred on the South Nahanni and Flat Rivers. Important mammal populations, including the South Nahanni Woodland Caribou Herd (SNH), composed of the COSEWIC vulnerable-listed, western woodland caribou (*Rangifer tarandus caribou*), are not well protected by this configuration.

In response, Parks Canada sponsored a three-year study in co-operation with territorial governments and First Nations to learn more about the range of the SNH and the degree of protection offered by the reserve. At the outset of the study virtually nothing was known of the herd size, composition, and seasonal distribution. Results indicate that only a small proportion of the caribou's 4,000-km range is protected within the reserve, with the remainder in mineral-rich lands accessible by the Nahanni Range Road (see Gullickson, 1998). As a result, the Nunavut government has stepped forward to take a lead role in conducting further studies to protect the herd. The initiative illustrates the importance of ecosystem-based management principles—such as thinking beyond park administrative boundaries, undertaking solid scientific research, and building partnerships with local stakeholders.

Based on an extensive review of the literature, Grumbine (1994: 31) identified 10 themes for ecosystem management: hierarchical context, ecological boundaries, ecological integrity, data collection, monitoring, adaptive management, interagency cooperation, organizational change, humans embedded in nature, and values. His definition— 'ecosystem management integrates scientific knowledge of ecological relationships within a complex sociopolitical and values framework toward the general goal of protecting native ecosystem integrity over the long term'—(ibid.: 31) is widely cited, as is his list of goals:

- maintain viable populations of all native species in situ,
- represent native ecosystem types across natural range of variation,
- maintain evolutionary and ecological processes,
- manage over long enough periods of time to maintain the evolutionary potential of species and ecosystems,
- accommodate human use and occupancy within these constraints.

Grumbine presents an ecological view of ecosystem-based management. Many ecologists and other natural scientists, who may not even agree with the use of 'ecosystem' in such a broad context or who dislike the vagueness of 'ecosystem management', are relatively content with species conservation as the basis for ecosystem management coupled with its scientific, rational character (for example, Wilcove, 1995). This approach can be strengthened by placing greater emphasis on the contributions of conservation biology, landscape ecology, and systems ecology to land management, resulting in an approach based on integrated ecological assessment and adaptive management (Jensen et al., 1996). Of course, a scientific (ecological or otherwise) basis for ecosystem management is not only intellectually desirable, but is essential. In a litigious system, such as that of the US, such a foundation enables managers to defend decisions against those who do not approve. Clearly, ecosystem management has received much attention for both scientific and political reasons (cf. Ecological Society of America, 1995).

Slocombe (1993a, 1993b) addressed ecosystem-based management with a greater degree of social context. He drew particularly on experience with large, wilderness, protected areas and their surrounding regions, on comprehensive regional planning, and on the Great Lakes Basin experience to develop a characterization of an ecosystem approach (Table 12.1). Based on this characterization, Slocombe highlighted three dimensions of ecosystem-based management: defining management units, developing understanding, and creating planning and management frameworks. Overall, this approach tried to balance ecological and scientific dimensions with social and process-oriented ones.

The Great Lakes Basin Remedial Action Plan (RAP) process has provided fruitful lessons developed from locally-run programs for relatively small sites, albeit ones of considerable significance. After reviewing and analysing the RAP experience, Hartig and others (1998) developed eight principles and elements for effective ecosystem management:

- broad-based stakeholder involvement,
- commitment of top leaders,

TABLE 12.1 Characteristics of Ecosystem Management

- Describe parts, systems, environments and their interactions.
- Be holistic, comprehensive, trans-disciplinary.
- Include people and their activities in the ecosystem.
- Describe system dynamics, e.g., with concepts of homeostasis, feedbacks, cause-and-effect relationships, self-organization, etc.
- Define the ecosystem naturally, i.e., bioregionally, instead of arbitrarily.
- Consider different levels/scales of system structure, process, and function.
- Recognize goals and take an active management orientation.Include actor-system dynamics and institutional factors in the analysis.Use an anticipatory, flexible, research and planning process. Enact implicit or explicit ethics of quality, well-being, and integrity
- Recognize systemic limits to action.
- Define and seek sustainability

After Slocombe (1993a, 1993b).

- agreement on information needs and interpretation,
- action planning within a strategic framework,
- human resource development,
- results and indicators to measure progress,
- systematic review and feedback,
- stakeholder satisfaction.

In addition, government agencies were asked to change their traditional, top-down regulatory structure to one that is more co-operative, values-driven, and supportive. The authors identified central concepts to help guide public and private efforts, many of which are familiar from other ecosystem management writings. These included, among others: the watershed/bioregion as the management unit, partnerships, long-term vision, the defining of principles to guide the process, GIS and decision support systems, data compilation, incentives, and utilizing of market forces.

Clearly many of these perspectives are related: some are complementary, some include or are included in others. Steven Yaffee (1999) has suggested that there is a continuum of ideas and concerns related to management and stressed three points of view or approaches for ecosystem management:

- environmentally sensitive multiple use (anthropocentric; human use subject to constraints that are usually beyond those in traditional resource management);
- ecosystem approach to resource management (biocentric; ecosystem implies holistic thinking, dynamics, scale, complexity and cross-boundary management, problem-orientation);
- eco-regional management (ecocentric; managing landscape ecosystems in specific places, emphasizing ecosystem processes rather than biota; an integrated spatial unit).

Though ecosystem management approaches and theory enclose a common core of concerns and concepts, the complexity and diversity of protected areas implies the need for a multiplicity of approaches, methods, and techniques. The next section reviews various tools and methods used in ecosystem management

TOOLS AND METHODS

This section will review several of the tools and methods of ecosystem-based management, including systems approaches, conservation biology and landscape ecology, reserve design, adaptive management, GIS and EIS, and participatory and collaborative approaches. However, in an ecosystem approach it is not so much the specific tools used that are important, but rather the way they are combined and integrated into an overall process.

A systems approach is integral to ecosystem-based management and, indeed, many environmental analyses foster connections within and between systems, and the dynamic nature of systems. This approach may be more or less quantitative and provides a framework for the analysis, description, and integration of different kinds of information (Slocombe, 2001). When we think of systems it is often natural systems that come to mind. Many people are familiar, for example, with the connectivity of the hydrological cycle. Social systems are equally interconnected and complex. Within protected areas there may be different but related human populations, such as residents, employees, and visitors. At the bioregional scale, these relate to local communities and economies, at the national scale they relate to legislation, policies, the media, and so on, up to international treaties and conventions. Natural and social systems are intimately connected through all these different scales. And they all permeate what we, at one time, considered to be the inviolate boundaries of the protected area. Knight and Landres (1998) provide a useful collection of papers on the challenges of 'stewardship across boundaries'.

A fundamental premise of ecosystem management is to turn protected area managers from 'boundary thinking'—that dominated plans and actions for virtually the first century of the national parks movement—to an understanding of the spheres of influence that affect parks beyond the administrative boundary (Figure 12.2). The difficulty of effecting this change should not be underestimated in terms of either theory or practice. This new 'thought boundary' may be extremely large, and will vary in size according to the particular threat being faced or resource being protected. Ecosystem-based boundaries are often bound to natural units, particularly the home ranges of key species (Beazley, 1999), or to watersheds (see, for example, Mayhood, 1998), or to a combination of factors (Ruel, 1998). However, other dimensions of park values are also important and may not be supported by imposing another rigid boundary. Aesthetic threats, for example, may be defined in terms of the viewshed from the park (Dearden, 1988). Park managers may also be able to wield powers of persuasion with neighbouring land users where legislative powers do not exist. In other cases, however, where ecological values are being degraded, as, for example, by air pollution the determining of the 'thought boundary' may be much more difficult for the manager who must address the problem (Welch, 1998).

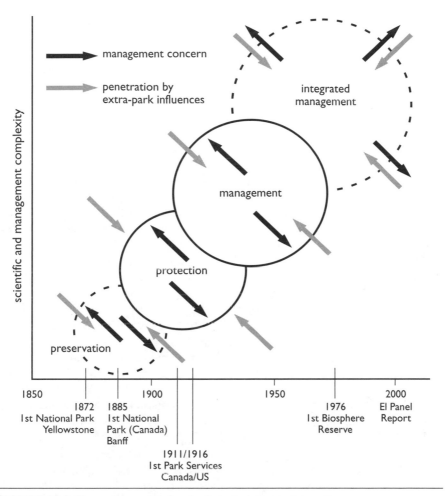

FIGURE 12.2 The evolving role of parks, from isolation to integration.

Between these extremes of difficulty arise intermediate problems that park managers may be able to address in more innovative ways. Stresses on ecological integrity caused by visitor activities, where the social systems impact on the natural systems, provide numerous challenges. Since it has proven inadequate simply to deal with these social systems as 'visitors' when people are in the park, outreach beyond the park boundaries to relevant 'visitorsheds', or where the people originate, seems a solution. Such attempts raise awareness among potential visitors about the purposes of national parks, about appropriate and inappropriate activities, and how visitors can reduce their impacts on the environment (Promaine, 1998).

Conservation biology and landscape ecology have been discussed in Chapters 4 and 5. Together with newer ideas, such as Peterson and Parker's work on hierarchy and scale (1998), and with growing understanding of systems ecology and ecosystem function and processes the rationale for, and the analytic tools of, ecosystem-based management are developing well. This evolution can be traced in many papers in Samson and Knopff's *Ecological Management: Selected Readings* (1996). These theories underly our perspectives on the effects of the size and spatial relationship of protected areas, and our decisions about which areas ought to be protected and how they should be connected. Schwartz (1999: 100) summarized the development of reserve choice criteria, from fine-filter (genes, species, populations) to coarse-filter (communities, habitats, ecosystems, landscapes) over the last 10 years. He suggests that embracing ecosystem-based management does not mean restricting conservation to large reserves; the key is 'focusing efforts on conserving interactions among species and processes within ecosystems'. However, holistic reserve design that integrates across scales is the desirable modus operandi.

Adaptive management is not a new idea (Holling, 1978) but has recently been invigorated through ecosystem management initiatives and assessments of various resource management failures (Ludwig et al., 1993). Adaptive management is essentially management that adopts a systems approach, recognizes ubiquitous change, uncertainty, and complexity in natural and human systems, and accepts the necessity of learning by doing. It calls for the use of science and modeling in determining management actions, experimental management that is carefully monitored to provide feedback, and regular evaluation and revision of management based on what is learned. It can be a challenge to people and institutions who are used to certainty, who want to make a decision and move on without monitoring and re-evaluating. And it can be expensive. Still, its iterative process of establishing goals and objectives, developing hypotheses, making decisions and implementing them, and subsequently learning, monitoring, and evaluating is highly suited to ecosystem management and protected areas (Lessard, 1998).

Geographic information systems (GIS) have been a park management tool for the past two decades. However, in many protected areas they have become available only recently. This reflects changes in hardware and software costs, as well as better and wider understanding of how to use them. Used co-operatively across disciplines, GIS can be a powerful means of organizing, presenting, and integrating information about a park and its surroundings. For example, Barnes and Ayles (1998) used GIS to develop a system for identifying and ranking ecosystem stressors at Prince Edward Island National Park. GIS was also used as a powerful tool in a study to document landscape change at six of Canada's biosphere reserves (Canada MAB, 2000).

If a GIS is too expensive to use, data is inadequate, or the process and results of its use are not made public, then GIS benefits will be few or potentially negative, especially if stakeholders feel that the technology is being used to hide information or support unpopular conclusions. Environmental information systems are more comprehensive systems of spatial and non-spatial information, often with a decision-support capability. Petersen (1998) provides an interesting example of a GIS/decision-support model for

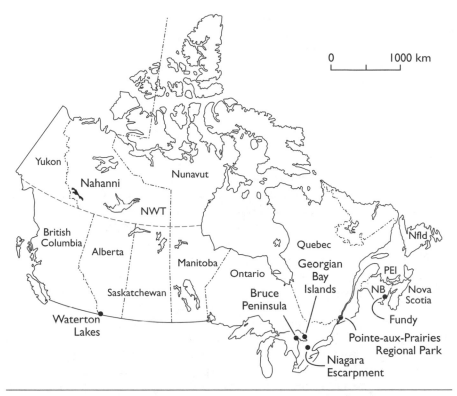

FIGURE 12.3 Sites of ecosystem-based management mentioned in text.

allocating land resources between grizzly bears and humans in Yoho National Park. However, there are relatively few examples of GIS application in protected areas management, although initiatives around Yellowstone National Park and Waterton National Park have received some attention (see the comparison in Danby, 1998). Slocombe (2001) addresses information management and integration in more detail.

Participatory and collaborative approaches are increasingly stressed as the solution for making ecosystem-based management work. This may be especially true for protected-area-centred and -led initiatives where the public and co-workers may be suspicious of the purposes of the leaders of the exercise. Local landowners, for example, may perceive collaboration as simple coercion by government agencies to gain greater control over their land. Participatory methods and strategies encompass a wide range, from simply informing the public to actively delegating decision-making to its members. Commonly-used tools include public meetings, public submission of comments on draft plans, workshops to develop information products for a common base of understanding, facilitated discourse, and discussion. Drawing on the Yellowstone experience, Varley and Schullery (1996) highlight multiple dimensions and complexities of public involvement in ecosystem management, including identifying the public, producing credible information to support public understanding, and developing effective, targeted communication devices.

Daniels and Walker (1996) provide a detailed case study and evaluation of collaborative learning in the US Oregon Dunes National Recreation Area (ODNRA) planning process. Collaborative learning emphasizes experiential learning, systemic improvement, and constructive discourse more than one would find in typical public participation programs. The process in ODNRA had three stages: (1) inform stakeholder groups and involve them in process design; (2) provide a common knowledge base about dunes issues, identify concerns about ODNRA management and generate suggested improvements; (3) organize improvements based on different strategic visions for the ODNRA and then debate improvement sets. Workshops involved four main activities: issue presentations, panel discussion, best and worst views and situation mapping, and individual and small group tasks. The program was quantitatively assessed and found to have improved dialogue among diverse communities, to have integrated scientific and public knowledge, and to have increased rapport, respect, and trust.

In some places collaboration and participation have moved beyond communicating information and participation in meetings. In much of Canada's North, park management is increasingly a matter of co-management between Federal, First Nations, Territorial, and sometimes other local interests, brokered through Boards established directly or indirectly via comprehensive land claims settlements (Chapter 13). Few such Boards have been in operation for more than a few years, so it is too early to attempt any conclusive assessment. They are, however, changing management and planning methods, particularly to include more consultation and local knowledge in many instances.

ECOSYSTEM-BASED MANAGEMENT IN PRACTICE

Ecosystem-based management programs have been implemented, if not always under that name, at many protected areas. It is arguable that the theory and practice have been more popular in the US than in Canada, but even if true in the past, this is changing. Here we briefly discuss a number of ecosystem-based park management examples to illustrate the points made above, as well as the practical means and difficulties of implementing such programs. Ecosystem-based management is often much simpler in plan, and more complex in execution, than the theory would suggest.

Waterton Lakes National Park in Alberta and Glacier National Park in Montana (Figure 12.1), and surrounding areas in Alberta, British Columbia, Montana, and Idaho (often referred to as the Crown of the Continent as it is the meeting place of the Atlantic, Pacific, and Arctic drainages) are among the most discussed examples of biosphere reserves, regional integration, or ecosystem management. The two national parks were jointly commemorated in 1932 as the Waterton-Glacier International Peace Park and received World Heritage designation in 1995. The area boasts an exceptional diversity of flora and fauna due to its varied topography where the prairie meets the mountains. Both geologically and ecologically it is distinct from the larger mountain park block (Banff, Yoho, Kootenay, and Jasper) to the north. There is a strong influence from Pacific Maritime weather systems, as this is the narrowest point of the Rockies, and elements of biota from the Pacific Northwest mingle with those from the interior plains and montane regions.

The complex mix of public and private ownerships and resource development activities surrounding the park matches this biophysical diversity. Alberta and British Columbia manage surrounding lands for multiple use including extensive gas, oil, forestry, and ranching use. To the north and east of the park much land is in private ownership, predominantly used for ranching, although small recreational holdings are increasing rapidly. There are also important multiple-use lands administered by the Blood Tribe. The international border across the middle allows for interesting comparisons between American and Canadian experiences. Waterton and Glacier were designated as a Biosphere Reserve by UNESCO in 1979. Although undefined, the zone of co-operation extends about 20 km to the east and north of the national park. This region is mostly privately owned or provincial Crown lease. The Waterton Biosphere Association is comprised of local ranchers, business people, and three park staff. Membership is open to anyone interested. An annual contribution from Parks Canada of $5,000 further helps to support general administrative costs.

Zinkan (1992) described the characteristics and success of the Waterton National Park Biosphere Reserve and the origins of the Crown of the Continent initiative through the 1980s. Critical factors included early development of a vision statement and guidelines and identification of elements that would lead to a sustainable strategy. These included local initiative, involvement of all sectors, regional integration rather than reaction to threats, strategies based on sound vision and guidelines, educational activities, information made readily available in an integrated form, a clear research strategy and support, and realigning traditional government organization and scientific specialization. It was felt that in the long run political leadership in the form of legislation would be required, and that sustainable development models would become increasingly complex. While the latter is certainly true, there is no legislation or regulations governing overall management of the zone of co-operation.

Waterton has recently been identified (Parks Canada Agency, 2000) as among the best examples of co-operation among diverse groups benefiting national parks: hunters, ranchers, environmentalists, conservationists, and park staff. NGOs with such diverse mandates as the Nature Conservancy of Canada and the Rocky Mountain Elk Foundation have worked with park staff and nearby landowners to address conservation, rancher, land development, and other issues. Throughout the 1980s and 1990s, Waterton has illustrated the role of particular people and personalities in making diverse groups work together. It also illustrates the park's organizational need to encourage staff and their ecosystem management activities, to ensure that they could become comfortable in senior administration positions, thus ensuring the continuation of such approaches to management. Despite these indicators of success, studies of landscape change in the Greater Waterton Ecosystem graphically illustrate the scale of the ongoing challenge in maintaining ecological integrity (Stewart et al., 2000).

The year was 1895. The efforts of local people were finally rewarded. Waterton Lakes National Park was established to protect the water, mineral and timber resources of the mountain panorama before you. This role was later expanded to include preservation of wildlife and the total park environment of spectacular lakes, mountains, forests and prairies. Recently, the park gained an additional role, serving as the core area of the Waterton Biosphere Reserve.

Here you will find one of the highest concentrations of prehistoric archaeological sites in Alberta. Wind and water are two of the most distinctive features of the park. The deepest lake in the Canadian Rockies, Upper Waterton Lake, is sometimes kept ice-free through much of the winter by the warm chinook winds that originate over the Pacific and rush down the eastern front of the Rockies. Welcome to this special corner of Alberta.

FIGURE 12.4 Waterton Lakes Biosphere Reserve. Some people might question whether an interpretive sign entitled 'A National Park', should contain as its only picture a modern industrial complex, even if the sign was paid for by Shell. *Photo: P. Dearden.*

BOX 12.3 Biosphere Reserves

The Biosphere Reserve Programme was started by the United Nations Educational, Scientific and Cultural Organisation (UNESCO) as part of the Man and the Biosphere (MAB) Programme in 1968 as an aid to achieving MAB's objective of striking a balance between conserving biodiversity, encouraging economic and social development, and preserving cultural values. Biosphere reserves are areas of terrestrial and coastal/marine ecosystems where, through appropriate zoning patterns and management mechanisms, the conservation of ecosystems and their biodiversity is ensured. Each biosphere reserve has a conservation function: to contribute to the conservation of landscapes, ecosystems, species and genetic variation; a development function: to foster economic and human development that is socially and ecologically sustainable; and a logistic function: to provide support for research, monitoring, education, and information exchange related to local, national, and global issues of conservation and development.

Typically, reserves should be divided into three zones:
- a core zone: strictly protected areas with very little human influence, which are used to monitor natural changes in representative ecosystems and serve as conservation areas for biodiversity;
- a buffer zone: areas surrounding the core zone where only low-impact activities are allowed, such as research, environmental education, and recreation; and
- a transition zone: the outer zone where sustainable use of resources by local communities is encouraged and these impacts can be compared to zones of greater protection.

How these zones are delimited is a national affair and the UNESCO designation does not add any legislative requirements, although some countries, such as Mexico, have enacted their own legislation to try to make the reserves more effective. There are now some 365 biosphere reserves distributed throughout the world. However, it is a challenging task to find one that successfully implements all aspects of the program. In Canada there are six reserves, located at Clayoquot Sound, BC, Waterton, Alberta, Redberry Hills, Saskatchewan, Riding Mountain, Manitoba), Niagara Escarpment, Ontario, Long Point, Ontario, Charlevoix, Quebec, and Mont St Hilaire, Quebec. A seventh on the east coast of Vancouver Island, the Arrowsmith Reserve, was announced in November, 2000.

Georgian Bay Islands National Park in Ontario has started an ecosystem management program and has followed a path that incorporates the Waterton lessons. A symposium in 1994 led to an informal working group, a vision, and terms of reference for ecosystem-based management for the park. This initiative supported boundary definition, visioning for park planning, and 1:250,000 mapping to identify core wildlife habitats and corridors connecting them. In 1996 a regional ecosystem symposium was held, and work started on a monitoring program (Walton, 1998).

Another protected area that has stressed monitoring programs, and built on its biosphere reserve status, is the Niagara Escarpment Planning Area, also in southern Ontario. Its approach to improving management in the greater ecosystem has stressed a monitoring program tied to regional planning along the escarpment, developing stewardship, trust, and research programs, and creating new organizational initiatives involving communities and stakeholders (Ramsay and Whitelaw, 1998).

While many ecosystem-based management programs are for large wilderness parks and regions, this need not be the case. Lajeunesse and others (1995) present an ecosystem management approach for small, protected natural areas subject to intense user pressures, in both urban and suburban locations. Stages in the approach include initial ecological evaluation, followed by management interventions, which builds on a sensitivity map created during the ecological evaluation stage, definition of ecological and social objectives and consultation, largely related to vegetation succession; and a follow-up monitoring scheme. They have applied the approach to Pointe-aux-Prairies regional park in Montreal, Quebec. This is an active, science-based management approach that with consultation and monitoring could lead to adaptive management.

Ecosystem-based management has also been assessed at larger scales. Burroughs and Clark (1995) compared ecosystem management in Greater Yellowstone and Georges Bank off the northeastern coast of North America. They observed that although the two areas have different histories, they have converging patterns of similarly changing uses. This is true of most large regions: they face complex challenges due to multiple (traditional and new) extractive resource development. They are also

FIGURE 12.5 Ecosystem-based management: the reality. Logging on the borders of Pacific Rim National Park Reserve. The reality is that managers often have little leverage to influence activities outside the administrative boundaries of the protected area. *Photo: P. Dearden.*

The Coarse-Filter Approach	The Fine-Filter Approach
ecological land classification + natural disturbance regime + 12% in mature-overmature patches + connectivity + silviculture by disturbance + protected areas = coarse-filter scale biodiversity	special status species (rare, keystone, economic) + snag and cavity tree retention + coarse woody debris = fine-filter scale biodiversity

FIGURE 12.6 Coarse- and Fine-Filter approaches to establishing forest management guidelines to protect biodiversity conservation in the Greater Fundy Ecosystem. SOURCE: Woodley and Forbes (1995).

institutionally complex and concern for endangered species is rising. Common challenges include the public's attachment to symbolic species and activities, the ambiguities of ecosystem management, the availability and use of information, and the administrative setting including organizational learning capabilities.

A strong scientific background is essential to provide accurate advice for ecosystem-based initiatives. The Greater Fundy Ecosystem Group has provided what is perhaps the strongest scientific research base in Canada. The group includes over 30 researchers from several universities, government departments, and industry. Although pre-dating the Fundy Model Forest (FMF), the group now works closely with the FMF and seeks to provide the ecological background for sustainable forestry practices. This is especially relevant as the FMF is adjacent to Fundy National Park and a main goal is to complement the biodiversity conservation objectives of the park (Woodley and Forbes, 1995). In particular, research aims to:

- identify strategies to maintain viable populations of native species;
- quantify species-habitat relationships;
- examine ecological stressors; and
- identify operational management options.

The Group has initiated numerous studies within this context, many of which are on-going. They have, however, been able to distill some of their findings to produce a series of forest management guidelines for protecting native biodiversity. In so doing they used a combined top-down/coarse-filter approach and a bottom-up/fine-filter approach (Figure 12.6). The coarse-filter approach facilitates planning of larger arrangements of communities, taking into account factors such as composition, size, adjacency, and age-class distribution. The needs of specific species and species groups of interest can be taken into account in more detail by the operation of the fine filter approach. This combination has resulted in some very specific management prescriptions that should aid considerably in biodiversity conservation in the Greater Fundy Ecosystem (Forbes et al., 1999)— a good example of the application of a science-based approach to ecosystem-based management to further protected area goals.

CONCLUSIONS

The late 1990s saw several efforts to learn from the previous decade's experience with ecosystem management. Some of this reflection has addressed the fundamental ideas and principles of ecosystem management. Stanley (1995), for example, has argued that ecosystem management symbolizes the arrogance of humanism, and the doctrine of final causes, i.e., that nature is there primarily for human benefit. This is one reason why some authors have been careful to use the term 'ecosystem-based management' to make the point that we are managing human activities, not the natural environment. Stanley's other point is that ecosystem management cannot deliver what it promises due to issues of complexity, uncertainty, and control. This is where most authors see the need for adaptive, precautionary management.

BOX 12.4 Ecosystem-Based Management: The Reality

Ecosystem-based management makes so much sense it is difficult to find anyone who would argue against it as a means to improve the protection of parks and similar reserves. If this is the case, why are there so few examples of comprehensive ecosystem-based management actually in operation? One of the main impediments, especially in Canada, is that National Parks, a federal jurisdiction, usually have limited influence on the provincial land bases surrounding the parks. And provincial parks, generally with a much weaker protection mandate and more limited resources, are rarely in a position to undertake ecosystem-management exercises. A major challenge for protected-area managers, therefore, is to gain greater influence over areas over which they have little, if any, jurisdiction. There are several ways to extend influence. For example:

1. PA managers should understand the political decision-making system on lands outside their jurisdiction, so they will know where, when, and how they can formally intercede to protect park values. Parks Canada staff should routinely participate in local and regional planning initiatives with agencies that have jurisdiction in greater park ecosystems. Furthermore, it should not be forgotten that the federal government has jurisdiction over fisheries, endangered species, migratory birds, long-range air pollution, navigable waters, and related environmental impact assessments. All these existing powers should be mobilized to support ecosystem-based park management.

2. It is important to build formal and informal links with outside agencies, industry, local communities, First Nations, and NGOs.
3. Good communications skills are essential to inform other stakeholders of park concerns. Of special importance is the on-going challenge of raising park literacy among the general public through interpretation programs so that people are aware of the roles that parks play in the landscape (Chapter 8).
4. Canadians love their parks. There is a huge resource of public goodwill directed towards parks. Sometimes this goodwill capital has to be drawn on when the formal and informal contacts mentioned above are inadequate to ensure ecological integrity through ecosystem-based management. The willingness of over 800 Canadian citizens to be arrested in defence of a more ecosystem-based approach to the management of Clayoquot Sound adjacent to Pacific Rim National Park Reserve in the early 1990s is testament to the strength of this feeling for parks.

Other authors have argued that ecosystem management is not a panacea for successful conservation, that scientific information is just one part, and perhaps not the most important part, of what is needed for good land and resource management. Terms like sustainability and integrity are variable and must be well-defined, and management cannot escape being location-specific. The lesson here is that consultation, participation, and consideration of local people and their interests must also be a major part of management (Lackey, 1998). In a similar vein, Brunner and Clark (1997) sought to address the problem of ecosystem management principles being unsatisfactory for practical purposes. Three major approaches were evaluated: clearer ecosystem management goals, a better scientific foundation for management decisions, and comparative appraisal of current practices. They argued the first two were not enough as the problem is not a primarily technical one. Instead, they advocate and describe a practice-based approach, drawing on adaptive management, prototyping, and a process for inventorying and appraising and learning from decisions nationally.

Slocombe (1998a) sought to draw practical lessons from experience with ecosystem management and related programs in Canada and Australia, revisiting his 1993 articles (Table 12.2). Building on that article Slocombe (1998b) presented a theoretical discussion of the nature of goals for ecosystem-based management, both substantive (what we seek to achieve) and procedural (how we seek to get there). The challenges of identifying goals for ecosystem management were noted in several places above. In practice, most planners and managers of both ecosystems and economies continue to pursue traditional goals and targets, which miss many desirable characteristics of ecosystem-based management goals. Substantive goals can be grouped according to their relationship to system structure, organization, and process/dynamics, and their disciplinary or subsystemic breadth (see Table 12.3 for examples).

Procedural goals discussed include four high-level goals: develop consensus, develop understanding of the system, implement a framework for planning and management, and do specific things that make a difference. A parallel, linked system of substantive and procedural goals at different levels of complexity and disciplinarity ideally would be needed to facilitate ecosystem-based management.

Grumbine (1997) also revisited his earlier article to address the question of why ecosystem management is still vague or difficult. He identified several issues: the politics

TABLE 12.2 Practical Lessons for Making Ecosystem-Based Management Work

Defining Management Units	Developing Understanding	Creating Planning & Management Frameworks
Use meaningful units	Describing and interpreting many dimensions of the ecosystem	Keep it simple, try not to layer new levels and organizations onto existing ones
Be flexible; use multiple ways of defining units	Make information available within and outside ecosystem	Get top-level commitment and leadership
Build on, but don't be constrained by existing units	Use local and traditional knowledge	Implement close to the ground and ensure there are some immediate, visible benefits and products
Ensure it is an operational unit, in at least some way	Be practical; when resources are limited focus on understanding, that would make a difference	Focus on management processes information flow, and planning and target-setting.
Maintain higher admini-strative levels' interest in lower and newer units by communication, involvement	When you've got information, use it: analyze, map, simulate, discuss	Maintain flexibility, and ensure reviews to foster adaptation

SOURCE: After Slocombe (1998a)

TABLE 12.3 Substantive Goals and Objectives for Ecosystem-Based Management

	Structure	Organization	Process
Biophysical environment	Areas, amounts, patterns, including biodiversity	Ecological linkages, flows	Sustainability
Community & society	Demographic, economic, social amounts, patterns	Human, societal economic linkages	Quality of life, Sustainability
Whole ecosystem	Health	Integrity	Evolutionary complexity

of definition—who? and why?; changing goals from resource extraction to ecosystem protection; the need for contextual thinking; and the lack of problem-definition skills. He felt his 10 themes, outlined above in this chapter, were still accurate and relevant. Grumbine also drew on the organizational change literature (e.g., Westley, 1995) to call attention to the sort of institutional changes that are needed to foster ecosystem management, and which other writers are also increasingly stressing: e.g., re-organization on ecosystem-based management themes, staff training in ecosystem-based management, teamwork, communication, consensus-building, employee incentives, staff training across disciplines, stewardship programs, independent audit and evaluation. He also stressed adaptive management topics more, such as prototyping, monitoring, dealing with complex problems and multiple causes, and recognizing that there is no simple fix.

There has been relatively little systematic assessment of ecosystem management programs. An assessment of relatively new ecosystem management programs in Mount Revelstoke and Glacier National Parks reached some initial conclusions (Feick, 1998). The program's basis is a two-way flow of scientific information between the parks and surrounding land and resource management agencies. The ecosystem management program has grown from trying to get a seat at the table for the parks, to becoming an invited partner in large, expensive multi-agency programs. The preliminary results of the evaluation suggest staff are satisfied with results but concerned over organizational impediments.

Stephenson and Zorn (1997) reported on evaluation of the ecosystem management program in the Ontario region of Parks Canada. Evaluation was based on eleven components: Ecosystem Conservation Plan, greater park ecosystem inventory and analysis, greater park ecosystem, area of co-operation, ecological integrity indicators, scientific research program, ecological indicators, information network, stakeholder analysis, partnership group management guidelines, ecological integrity monitoring program, and a communication strategy.

The report stressed how this program was successfully implemented through restructuring in-park conservation programs and a bottom-up change in philosophies and approaches that complemented top-down Parks Canada policies and programs (see also, Zorn et al., 2001).

If one can conclude anything about ecosystem-based management at this point, it might be that although science and information are critical foundations for good management, making ecosystem management effective and durable requires additional effort. Much greater attention to local and distant benefits, to inter- and intra-organizational issues, and to developing real collaboration with stakeholder groups are required.

It is also true, of course, that park and regional and resource management will continue to evolve, other approaches will influence and perhaps eventually subsume ecosystem-based management. One such trend may well be bioregional approaches, which emphasize even larger regions, longer time scales, complex protected area networks, and stronger socio-cultural content (Chapter 15). Miller and Hamilton (1999) provide a global summary in a recent special issue of Parks magazine of bioregional approaches. Brunckhorst (2000) provides a more extended treatment with a strong emphasis on case-studies on biosphere reserves and other protected areas. Nelson and Sportza (2000) highlight a range of trends in protected areas, including funding, cultures and values, changes in science, scale, changing government and other actor roles, stewardship, and planning. In a related paper Sportza (1999) reviews 'regional' approaches to protected areas, and develops some useful criteria for regional approaches; indeed, her paper introduces a special issue of the journal *Environments* on regional approaches to protected areas in North America.

Over a decade ago Agee and Johnson (1988) identified four critical questions:

- What are the important research needs associated with ecosystem management?
- What are the important general management, planning, and communication issues associated with them?
- What are the important challenges to ecosystem management in the areas of conflict resolution and co-operation? and
- What are the important limits and constraints to ecosystem management?

These questions remain valid. We have some answers to these questions, and hopefully this chapter has illustrated them, but there is no doubt that much more experience, practice, and analysis is required before we can begin to think we have fairly complete answers to the assaults on our ecosytems.

REFERENCES

Agee, J.K., and D.R. Johnson, eds. 1988. *Ecosystem Management for Parks and Wilderness.* Seattle: University of Washington Press.

Batisse, M. 1982. 'The Biosphere Reserve: A Tool for Environmental Conservation and Management', *Environmental Conservation* 9: 101-11.

Barnes, S., and P. Ayles. 1998. 'GIS as a Decision-Making Tool in the Ecosystem Conservation Planning Process', in Munro and Willison (1998: 705-11).

Beazley K. 1999. 'Permeable Boundaries: Indicator Species for Trans-Boundary Monitoring at Kejimkujik National Park', in *Protected Areas and the Bottom Line*, Proceedings of the 1997 Conference of the Canadian Council on Ecological Areas. Information Report MX 205E/F. Ottawa: Canadian Forest Service, 119-35.

Brunner, R.D., and T.W. Clark. 1997. 'A Practice-Based Approach to Ecosystem Management', *Conservation Biology* 11, 1: 48-58.

Brunckhorst, D.J. 2000. *Bioregional Planning: Resource Management Beyond the New Millennium.* Amsterdam: Harwood Academic Publishers.

Burroughs, R.H., and T.W. Clark. 1995. 'Ecosystem Management: A Comparison of Greater Yellowstone and Georges Bank', *Environmental Management* 19, 5: 649-63.

Canada MAB (Man and the Biosphere Committee). 2000. *Landscape Changes at Canada's Biosphere Reserves.* Toronto: Environment Canada.

Caldwell, L.K. 1970. 'The Ecosystem as a Criterion for Public Land Policy', *Natural Resources Journal* 10: 203-21.

Community and Municipal Affairs, National Parks Branch. 1985. *Regional Integration of National Parks.* Ottawa, Dec.

Danby, R.K. 1998. 'Regional Ecology of the St. Elias Mountain Parks: A Synthesis with Management Implications', MES thesis, Wilfrid Laurier University.

Daniels, S.E., and G.B. Walker. 1996. 'Collaborative Learning: Improving Public Deliberation in Ecosystem-Based Management', *EIA Review* 16: 71-102.

Dearden, P. 1988. 'Protected Areas and the Boundary Model: Meares Island and Pacific Rim National Park', *Canadian Geographer* 32: 256-65.

———— and S. Doyle. 1997. 'External Threats to Pacific Rim National Park Reserve, BC', in C. Stadel, ed., *Themes and Issues of Canadian Geography II*. Salzburg, Austria: *Salzburger Geographische Arbeiten*, 121-36.

Ecological Society of America. 1995. *The Scientific Basis for Ecosystem Management: An Assessment*. Washington: ESA.

Feick, J. 1998. 'Does "Good" Information Equal "Better" Decisions? A Study in Progress to Evaluate Parks Canada's Ecosystem Management Efforts in the Columbia Mountains of B.C.', in Munro and Willison (1998: 790-7).

Forbes, G., S. Woodley, and B. Freedman. 1999. 'Making Ecosystem-Based Science into Guidelines for Ecosystem-based Management: The Greater Fundy Ecosystem Experience', *Environments* 27, 3: 15-23.

Francis, G.R., A.P.L. Grima, H.A. Regier, and T.H. Whillans. 1985. *A Prospectus for the Management of the Long Point Ecosystem*. Ann Arbor, Mich.: Great Lakes Fishery Commission Technical Report 43.

Grumbine, R.E. 1990. 'Protecting Biological Diversity through the Greater Ecosystem Concept', *Natural Areas Journal* 10, 3: 114-20.

————. 1994. 'What is Ecosystem Management?', *Conservation Biology* 8, 1: 27-38.

————.1997. 'Reflections on "What is Ecosystem Management?"', *Conservation Biology* 11, 1: 41-7.

Gullickson, D. 1998. 'Beyond Boundaries: South Nahanni Woodland Caribou', *Research Links* 6, 4: 10-11.

Gurd, D.B., and T.D. Nudds. 1999. 'Insular Biogeography of Mammals in Canadian Parks: A Re-Analysis', *Journal of Biogeography* 26: 973-82.

Hartig, J.H., M.A. Zarull, T.M. Heidtke, and H. Shah. 1998. 'Implementing Ecosystem-Based Management: Lessons from the Great Lakes', *Journal of Environmental Planning & Management* 41, 1: 45-75.

Holling, C.S., ed. 1978. *Adaptive Environmental Assessment and Management*. Chichester: Wiley.

Janzen D.H. 1983. 'No Park Is an Island: Increase in Interference from Outside as Park Size Decreases', *Oikos* 41: 402-10.

Jensen, M.E., P. Bourgeron, R. Everett, and I. Goodman. 1996. 'Ecosystem Management: A Landscape Ecology Perspective', *Water Resources Bulletin* 32, 2: 1-14.

Keiter, R.B. 1994. 'Beyond the Boundary Line: Constructing a Law of Ecosystem Management', *University of Colorado Law Review* 65: 293-333.

————. 1998. 'Ecosystems and the Law: Toward an Integrated Approach', *Ecological Applications* 8, 2: 332-41.

Knight, R.L., and P.B. Landres. 1998. *Stewardship Across Boundaries*. Washington: Island Press.

Lackey, R.T. 1998. 'Seven Pillars of Ecosystem Management', *Landscape and Urban Planning* 40: 21-30.

LaJeunesse, D., G. Domon, P. Drapeau, A. Cogliastro, and A. Bouchard. 1995. 'Development and Application of an Ecosystem Management Approach for Protected Natural Areas', *Environmental Management* 19, 4: 481-95.

Landry, M., V.G. Thomas, and T.D. Nudds. 2001. 'Sizes of Canadian National Parks and the Viability of Large Mammal Populations: Policy Implications', *George Wright Forum*: 18: 13-23.

Lessard, G. 1998. 'An Adaptive Approach to Planning and Decision-Making', *Landscape and Urban Planning* 40: 81-7.

Ludwig, D., R. Hilborn, and C. Walters. 1993. 'Uncertainty, Resource Exploitation, and Conservation: Lessons from History', *Science* 260: 17, 36.

Machlis, G.E., and D.L. Tichnell. 1985. *The State of the World's Parks*. Boulder, Colo.: Westview Press.

———— and ————. 1987. 'Economic Development and Threats to National Park: A Preliminary Analysis', *Environmental Conservation* 15: 151-6.

MacKenzie, S.H. 1996. *Integrated Resource Planning and Management: The Ecosystem Approach in the Great Lakes Basin*. Washington: Island Press.

Mayhood, D.W. 1998. 'Is the Greater Ecosystem Concept Relevant for Conserving the Integrity of Aquatic Ecosystem in the Canadian Rocky Mountains?', in Munro and Willison (1998: 772-80).

Miller, K.R., and L.S. Hamilton. 1999. 'Editorial', *Parks* 9, 3: 1-6.

Munro, N.W.P., and J.H.M. Willison. 1998. *Linking Protected Areas with Working Landscapes*, Proceedings of the Third International Conference on Science and Management of Protected Areas, Wolfville, NS.

Nelson, J.G., and L.M. Sportza. 2000. 'Evolving Protected Area Thought and Practice', *George Wright Forum* 17, 2: 59-69.

Parks Canada. 1994. *Guiding Principles and Operational Policies*. Ottawa: Supply and Services Canada.

Parks Canada. 1995. *Sea to Sea to Sea: Canada's National Marine Conservation Areas System Plan*. Ottawa: Canadian Heritage.

————. 1998. *State of the Parks 1997*. Ottawa: Minister of Public Works and Government Services Canada

Parks Canada Agency. 2000. *Unimpaired for Future Generations? Protecting Ecological Integrity with Canada's National Parks*, vol. 1: *A Call to Action*; vol. 2: *Setting a New Direction for Canada's National Parks*. Report of the Panel on the Ecological Integrity of Canada's National Parks. Ottawa.

Petersen, D. 1998. 'Allocation of Land Resources between Competing Species—Human and Grizzly Bears in the Lake O'Hara Area of Yoho National Park', in Munro and Willison (1998: 478-91).

Peterson, D.L., and V.T. Parker, eds. 1998. *Ecological Scale: Theory and Applications*. New York: Columbia University Press.

Promaine, R.H. 1998. 'Applying Ecosystem Management Principles to Public Education: A Case Study of Pukaskwa National Park', in Munro and Willison (1998: 633-42).

Ramsay, D., and G. Whitelaw. 1998. 'Biosphere Reserves and Ecological Monitoring as Part of Working Landscapes: The Niagara Escarpment Biosphere Reserve Experience', in Munro and Willison (1998: 295-307).

Ruel, M. 1998. 'The Greater Kouchibouguac Ecosystem Project', in *Protected Areas and the Bottom Line*. Proceedings of the 1997 Conference of the Canadian Council on Ecological Areas. Information Report MX 205E/F. Ottawa: Canadian Forest Service, 136-9.

Samson, F.B., and F.L. Knopf, eds. 1996. *Ecosystem Management: Selected Readings*. New York: Springer-Verlag.

Sax, J.L., and R.B. Keiter. 1987. 'Glacier National Park and Its Neighbours: A Study of Federal Interagency Relations', *Ecology Law Quarterly* 14, 2: 207-63.

Schwartz, M.W. 1999. 'Choosing the Appropriate Scale of Reserves for Conservation', *Annual Review of Ecological Systems* 30: 83-108.

Slocombe, D.S. 1993a. 'Environmental Planning, Ecosystem Science, and Ecosystem Approaches for Integrating Environment and Development', *Environmental Management* 17, 3: 289-303.

―――.1993b. 'Implementing Ecosystem-Based Management', *BioScience* 43, 9: 612-22.

―――.1998a. 'Lessons from Experience with Ecosystem Management', *Landscape and Urban Planning* 40, 1-3: 31-9.

―――. 1998b. 'Defining Goals and Criteria for Ecosystem-Based Management', *Environmental Management* 22, 4: 483-93.

―――. 2001. 'Integration of Biological, Physical, and Socio-Economic Information', in M. Jensen and P. Bourgeron, eds, *A Guidebook for Integrated Ecological Assessment Protocols Guidebook*. New York: Springer-Verlag, 119-32.

Sportza, L.M. 1999. 'Regional Approaches to Planning for Protected Areas and Conservation', *Environments* 27, 3: 1-14.

Stanley, T.R., Jr. 1995. 'Ecosystem Management and the Arrogance of Humanism', *Conservation Biology* 9, 2: 255-62.

Stephenson, W.R., and P. Zorn. 1997. 'Assessing the Ecosystem Management Program of St. Lawrence Islands National Park, Ontario, Canada', *George Wright Forum* 14, 4: 51-64.

Stewart, A., A. Harries, and C. Stewart. 2000. 'Waterton Biosphere Reserve Landscape Change Study', in Canada MAB (2000: 13-20).

Vallentyne, J.R., and A.M. Beeton. 1988. 'The "Ecosystem" Approach to Managing Human Uses and Abuses of Natural Resources in the Great Lakes Basin', *Environmental Conservation* 15, 1: 58-62.

Varley, J.D., and P. Schullery. 1996. 'Reaching the Real Public in the Public Involvement Process: Practical Lessons in Ecosystem Management', *George Wright Forum* 13, 4: 68-75.

Walton, M. 1998. 'Ecosystem Planning within Georgian Bay Islands National Park—A Multi-Jurisdictional Approach', in Munro and Willison (1998: 552-8).

Welch, D. 1998. 'Air Quality Issues, Monitoring and Management in Canadian National Parks', in Munro and Willison (1998: 336-77).

Westley, F. 1995. 'Governing Design: The Management of Social Systems and Ecosystems Management', in L.H. Gunderson et al., eds, *Barriers and Bridges to the Renewal of Ecosystems and Institutions*. New York: Columbia University Press, 391-427.

Wilcove, D.S., and R.B. Blair. 1995. 'The Ecosystem Management Bandwagon', *TREE* 10, 8: 345.

Woodley, S. 1993. 'Monitoring and Measuring Ecosystem Integrity in Canada's National Parks', in S. Woodley, J. Kay, and G. Francis, eds, *Ecological Integrity and Management of Ecosystems*. St Lucie Press, 155-76.

――― and G. Forbes. 1995. 'Ecosystem Management and Protected Areas', in T.B. Herman,

S. Bondrup-Nielsen, J.H.M. Willison, and N.W.P Munro, eds, *Ecosystem Monitoring and Protected Areas*. Amsterdam: Elsevier, 50-8.

Yaffee, S.L. 1999. 'Three Faces of Ecosystem Management', *Conservation Biology* 13, 4: 713-25.

Zinkan, C. 1992. 'Waterton Lakes National Park Moving towards Ecosystem Management', in J.H.M. Willison, ed., *Science and the Management of Protected Areas*. Amsterdam: Elsevier, 229-32.

Zorn, P., W. Stephenson, and P. Grigoriew. 2001. 'Ontario National Parks Ecosystem Management Program and Assessment Process for Ontario National Parks', *Conservation Biology* 15, 2: 353-62.

KEY WORDS/CONCEPTS

multiple use
integrated resource management
watershed management
regional land use plan
ecosystem
ecosystem management
ecological integrity
biosphere reserve
systems approach
watershed

visitorshed
boundary thinking
conservation biology
landscape ecology
adaptive management
Geographic Information Systems (GIS)
co-management
anthropocentric
biocentric
ecocentric

STUDY QUESTIONS

1. Discuss each of Agee and Johnson's (1988) principles of ecosystem management. Speculate what difficulties may be encountered with the implementation of each principle.
2. Why is ecosystem management important?
3. Why are linkages between different management agencies important?
4. Why are linkages between parks and private landowners important?
5. What is significant about ecosystem management in Nahanni National Park?
6. What methods have been developed for participation and collaboration?
7. Examine a park in your area for evidence of 'boundary thinking', 'adaptive management', and co-operation with adjacent landowners.
8. Why is ecosystem management not more widely used?
9. What can park managers do to improve the use of ecosystem management?
10. Discuss how the Bruce Peninsula national park issue can be understood through an understanding of ecosystem planning.
11. What is the significance to ecosystem management of outreach programs?
12. Review a management plan from one of Canada's northern national parks for evidence of co-management.
13. Discuss how ecosystem management has been used in the Waterton Biosphere Reserve.

PART V

Thematic Issues

This section expands on major challenges mentioned in previous chapters that deserve more in-depth consideration. Students are encouraged to identify other issues as they emerge or become more important. Themes that have been addressed in the past include 'rails to trails', heritage rivers, and international co-operation.

The significance of adjacent communities has been raised within the context of ecosystem management, the management of Banff, and as one aspect of social considerations. Adjacent communities may benefit, but at times are negatively impacted by parks and protected areas. Negative impacts may occur as a result of undesirable tourism developments or activities, or through the loss of access or use of an area when a new park is created. Another form of damage occurs when wildlife stray across park boundaries onto private land, such as the damage caused when elk, bears, and wolves enter private land from Riding Mountain National Park. Aboriginal communities are a particularly important component of this interaction between parks and adjacent communities. Aboriginal peoples have a stake in park development and management for a number of reasons. Parks contain important resources for many Aboriginal cultures—as places for traditional activities such as hunting, trapping, and fishing, as well as for the spiritual and cultural values Aboriginal cultures derive from park settings. The nature of Aboriginal involvement in the creation and management of parks and protected areas has been an important, but challenging and sometimes controversial process, as outlined in Chapter 13.

The second theme developed in this section deals with the frustrations surrounding attempts to create marine protected areas in Canada. Chapter 14 outlines the need to protect the biodiversity found in marine environments, and describes the role of marine protected areas as part of a marine conservation strategy. Difficulties in moving ahead with this initiative in Canada are described, as well as a number of issues related to the management of marine protected areas.

Stewardship is the third theme of this section. Here we examine conservation developments that take place outside traditional parks managed by government agencies. This includes private or private-public collaboration to achieve stewardship objectives. These initiatives are particularly important in light of the growing evidence that the conservation of biodiversity cannot be achieved entirely within park boundaries, and must involve conservation strategies in landscapes outside of parks. Hence, the work of such private non-governmental organizations as Ducks Unlimited and the Nature Conservancy of Canada have become very significant. Chapter 15 describes a number of conservation strategies, successes, and challenges experienced by these organizations.

CHAPTER 13

The Role of Aboriginal Peoples

Juri Peepre & Philip Dearden

INTRODUCTION

Modern concepts about protected areas and wilderness have evolved from ancient cultural and religious ideas related to spirituality and primeval nature. Although the notions of parks and wilderness are foreign to most Aboriginal languages that reflect the place of humans as an integral part of nature, many cultures have embraced the idea of sacred places (Peepre and Jickling, 1994). However, national parks, as we understand them today, originated in the United States. Nash (1970) asserts that the origins of the national park idea can be traced to the year 1832. At that time, he observes, the artist-explorer George Catlin called for the creation of a 'nation's park' to protect the Indians and the wild animals of the American plains. The institution proposed by Catlin differs very little from the essentials of the national park idea as it exists today. Perhaps ironically, the one significant difference was Catlin's proposal that Indian people be part of '. . . the [life] in the preserve' (Nash, 1970: 730).

On 1 March 1872 over 810,000 ha of north-western Wyoming were designated as the world's first national park—Yellowstone. The park was set aside during an effort to subdue plains Indian tribes, and the traditional inhabitants of the park moved to reservations or were forced out by the United States Army. In 1885, Banff National Park was established in Alberta, seven years after the Siksika (Blackfoot) and Nakoda (Stoney) tribes ceded much of southwestern Alberta to the Crown. The treaty allowed the tribes to continue hunting in the region, but the federal government decided these rights would not apply to Banff National Park (Morrison, 1995). Since the establishment of these early national parks, thousands of new protected areas have been created world-wide. Many of these protected areas have been designated on lands traditionally used by Aboriginal peoples. Often, they have been established without the participation of Aboriginal peoples living in the regions affected. In many instances, the Aboriginal people have been forcibly removed from regions in which protected areas were established.

The policy of establishing protected areas without regard for the needs of Aboriginal people has sometimes adversely affected both Aboriginal societies and protected area conservation initiatives. In effect, 'indigenous people have borne the costs of protecting natural areas, through the loss of access for hunting, trapping or other harvesting activities' (Morrison, 1995: 12). Displacement of Aboriginal people often disrupts traditional social and economic systems and results in serious social problems such as malnutrition and loss of cultural identity (Dasmann, 1976; Mishra, 1982; Nowicki, 1985). At the very least, such negative impacts may reduce popular support among Aboriginal peoples for protected areas. Consequently, the effectiveness of protected-area conservation has been compromised because of poaching, clandestine exploitation of resources, or other forms of non-compliance with protected area regulations (see, for example, Dearden et al., 1996; Terborgh, 2000).

In response to these problems, it became clear there was a need to involve Aboriginal peoples in protected-area planning and management, and further to allow exploitation of protected-area resources for subsistence purposes. The role of Aboriginal people in national parks has become an important area of concern for Aboriginal organizations as well as protected-area managers and social scientists world-wide. In the last 20 years, the relationship between Aboriginal people and national parks in Canada has changed fundamentally, although these changes are uneven across the country. Aboriginal peoples in northern Canada have played a significant role in national park planning and development, while in southern Canada their role has varied from park to park. Aboriginal people have little or no involvement in some national parks, while initial steps towards co-operation have taken place in others. Northern national parks have been established in conjunction with Aboriginal land-claim settlements, while park reserves await claims settlement before attaining full park status. Overall, more than 50 per cent of the land area in Canada's national park system has been protected as a result of Aboriginal peoples' support for conservation of their lands (Parks Canada Agency, 2000), and Dearden and Berg (1993) suggest that First Nations have emerged as the most dominant force influencing the establishment of national parks in Canada over the last decade.

This chapter provides an overview of the past and present role of Aboriginal people in national park designation, planning, and management in Canada. An introduction to the changing social and legal status of Aboriginal people in Canada sets the historical context as it pertains to conservation and protected areas. This is followed by a discussion of Parks Canada's evolving policy, regulations, and legislation as it relates to Aboriginal peoples. Using examples from several parks in the Canadian north, the next section illustrates Aboriginal peoples' involvement in national park management where land claims agreements are in place. The contrasting situation in southern Canada is then outlined, with several examples of Aboriginal peoples' role in national park management. Finally, some recent trends and advances by Parks Canada, as well as a discussion of future directions are presented.

ABORIGINAL PEOPLES IN CANADA

Definition

In Canada one million people can claim at least partial Aboriginal ancestry (McMillan, 1988). The Constitution Act, 1982 defines three categories of 'aboriginal peoples': Indian, Inuit, and Métis. However, these three categories of Aboriginal people are not homogeneous cultural groups, but contain a great variety of peoples with differing histories, languages, and cultures. Accordingly, the name 'First Nations', has been adopted by many Aboriginal peoples when referring to themselves, to reflect their perception of their status as separate, and sovereign, entities.

Aboriginal Treaties in Canada

Southern Canada, with the exception of the Atlantic provinces, and most of Quebec and British Columbia, is covered by Indian treaties that lay out certain legal obligations of the Crown towards Aboriginal peoples. Between 1780 and 1850, a number of small treaties were negotiated with the Indians in what is now southern Ontario. These treaties usually involved small, lump-sum payments in return for extinguishing Aboriginal title. On rare occasions, fishing and hunting rights were guaranteed, and reserves were granted. In 1850, the Robinson-Superior and Robinson-Huron Treaties were negotiated with Indians of the upper Great Lakes region. In return for surrender of large areas of land, Indian people received lump-sum cash payments, annual payments to each person, and promises of continued hunting and fishing on unoccupied Crown land (Cumming and Mickenberg, 1972).

Robinson's 1850 treaties became the model for subsequent 'numbered' treaties that encompass much of Ontario, all of Manitoba, Saskatchewan, and Alberta, as well as portions of British Columbia and the Yukon and Northwest Territories. These treaties, numbered 1 to 11, were completed between 1871 and 1929 by federal government representatives. The Williams treaties, completed in 1923 by the federal government, purportedly extinguished Aboriginal title to lands in southern Ontario. With some minor differences, treaties negotiated by the federal government are all similar. In return for cessation of their title, Aboriginal peoples received reserves, small cash payments, hunting and fishing gear, annual payments to each member of the signatory group, and promises of continued hunting and fishing rights.

About the same time as Robinson completed his treaties, James Douglas, as Chief Factor of the Hudson's Bay Company and later Governor of the Colony of Vancouver Island, began treaty-making with a number of Island Tribes. Between 1850 and 1854, Douglas completed 14 treaties, extinguishing Aboriginal title to lands around Victoria, Nanaimo, and Fort Rupert (present-day Port Hardy). In return for surrender of their lands, Aboriginal people maintained possession of their village sites and fields, and were guaranteed the right 'to hunt on unoccupied lands, and to carry on [their] fisheries as formerly' (British Columbia, 1875: 5–11).

Aboriginal Rights in Canada

Most of the Yukon, Northwest Territories, British Columbia, Quebec, and the Atlantic provinces are free of the nineteenth-century treaties. Aboriginal peoples living in the areas where modern land claims treaties have not yet been settled have not ceded their Aboriginal title by treaty, nor have they been conquered by overt act of war. Nonetheless, they have been denied their Aboriginal rights and title, and they have been 'colonized' and marginalized over the last 100 years. In spite of this, Aboriginal people in Canada have never stopped pressing government for recognition of their Aboriginal rights (Frideres, 1988). Until relatively recently, however, such efforts were largely unsuccessful. This situation is gradually changing following several important legal rulings, and amendments to Canada's constitution.

The Calder Case

In 1967, the Nisga'a initiated a suit before the Supreme Court of British Columbia, asking the court for a declaration that their Aboriginal title had never been extinguished (Sanders, 1973; Berger, 1982; Raunet, 1984). The trial, which came to be known as the 'Calder Case', opened in the Supreme Court of British Columbia, which ruled against the Nisga'a, asserting that their Aboriginal rights were extinguished by overt acts of the Crown (*Calder v Attorney General of British Columbia*, 1969). The Nisga'a appealed, but the British Columbia Court of Appeal (*Calder v Attorney General of British Columbia*, 1970) upheld the lower court ruling. The Nisga'a then appealed to the Supreme Court of Canada (*Calder v Attorney General of British Columbia*, 1973), and although they lost, three out of seven judges agreed with their position. Three judges ruled that the Nisga'a had Aboriginal title and, further, that this title was recognized under English law.

The Calder case had important repercussions for Aboriginal policy and law. For the first time, the Supreme Court of Canada recognized that Aboriginal title existed at the time of colonization as a legal right derived from the Aboriginal peoples' historical occupation and possession of the land, independent of any proclamation, legislative act, or treaty. Following this judgement, the federal government was willing to negotiate 'comprehensive' land-claim settlements in British Columbia, Quebec, and the two northern territories (Canada, 1981; Sanders, 1983; Task Force to Review Comprehensive Claims Policy, 1985; Canada, 1987).

Constitution Act, 1982

After intense lobbying by Aboriginal groups, the Constitution Act, 1982, was enacted containing two sections protecting Aboriginal rights. Section 25 protects Aboriginal, treaty, or other rights from infringement by other guarantees in the Charter. Section 35, entitled Rights of the Aboriginal Peoples of Canada, entrenches Aboriginal rights in the Constitution and also adopts and confirms the large body of common law, which has come to be known as the 'common law doctrine of Aboriginal rights'. This doctrine holds that the property rights, customary laws, and governmental institutions of Aboriginal peoples were assumed to survive the Crown's acquisition of North American territories.

FIGURE 13.1 Vuntut National Park reserve in the NW Yukon was created as part of the Inuvialuit Final Agreement. *Photo: P. Dearden.*

The Constitution Act 'set the consideration of native law in a new context' (Elias, 1989: 4), which appears to be more favourable to the aspirations of Aboriginal people in Canada. This 'new context' is evident in the Supreme Court of Canada ruling in *Sparrow v. The Queen et al.*, (1990) described below.

A new era in the relationship between Native peoples and the Government of Canada was ushered in during the 1990s. The federal policy on land claims recognizes the inherent right to self-government of Aboriginal peoples, a policy that has had significant ramifications for protected areas and conservation in Canada.

The Sparrow Case

In May, 1990, the Supreme Court of Canada handed down its landmark judgement in the case of *Sparrow v. The Queen et al.*, (1990; hereafter cited as Sparrow, 1990). Ronald Edward Sparrow, a Musqueam Indian (from British Columbia), was charged in 1984 under the Fisheries Act with using a drift net longer than that permitted by the terms of his Band's Indian food fishing licence. Sparrow admitted that the Crown's allegations were correct, but he defended his actions on the grounds that he was exercising an existing Aboriginal right to fish, protected under s. 35(1) of the *Constitution Act*.

The Provincial Court held that the Musqueam did not have an Aboriginal right to fish. Sparrow appealed to County Court (*Sparrow v. The Queen*, 1986a) and the case was dismissed for similar reasons. The case was then appealed to the British Columbia Court of Appeal (*Sparrow v. The Queen*, 1986b), which held that the lower Courts had erred in ruling that the Musqueam had no Aboriginal fishing rights. The Appeal Court also ruled that the Aboriginal right to fish existed at the time of enactment of the Constitution Act, and was therefore a constitutionally protected right that could no longer be extinguished by unilateral action of the Crown. The Court also held, however, that the trial judge's findings of facts were insufficient to lead to an acquittal. The ruling was appealed by Sparrow and argued before the Supreme Court of Canada in 1987.

In a unanimous ruling, the Supreme Court of Canada held that there was insufficient evidence on which to decide the guilt or innocence of Mr Sparrow. More importantly, however, the Court affirmed that the Musqueam people have an unextinguished Aboriginal right to fish. It also set forth a framework for defining the existence and scope of Aboriginal rights in Canada. In this regard, the Court (*Sparrow*, 1990: 16) held that prior to 1982 Aboriginal rights continued to exist unless they had been extinguished by an action of the Crown that was clearly intended to do so. Therefore, contrary to arguments made by the government of British Columbia, legislative action that is merely inconsistent with the concept of Aboriginal title cannot be construed as extinguishing such title. Following enactment of the *Constitution Act*, Aboriginal rights could no longer be extinguished by the Crown. The Supreme Court (*Sparrow*, 1990: 26) further defined the nature of constitutional protection of Aboriginal rights:

> the constitutional recognition afforded by the provision [s. 35(1)] therefore gives a measure of control over government conduct and a strong check on legislative power. While it does not promise immunity from government regulation in a society that, in the twentieth century, is increasingly more complex, interdependent, and sophisticated, and where exhaustible resources need protection and management, it does hold the Crown to a substantial promise. The government is required to bear the burden of justifying any legislation that has some negative effect on any Aboriginal right protected under s. 35(1).

In the eyes of the Court, both 'conservation' and 'resource management' constitute justifiable grounds for legislation that may have a negative effect on Aboriginal rights. However, even when such measures must be implemented, the Court held that Aboriginal people must be consulted so as to mitigate any impact upon their rights.

The Sparrow case directed the government to include Aboriginal people in co-operative management of natural resources. With respect to parks, it is clear that the ruling reinforced Aboriginal beliefs that they deserve special recognition with respect to management when their traditional territories coincide with park lands.

Delgum'uukw

The *Delgum'uukw v. Auditor General of British Columbia* (1997) case, seven years after the Sparrow decision, ruled on Aboriginal title. Since Aboriginal title is an interest in land within the British common law system, the relevant date for a court to examine whether Aboriginal title exists is the date of the assertion of British Crown sovereignty in an area. The case also affirmed that both Canadian law and the laws of the Aboriginal nations involved must be considered in providing definition to Aboriginal rights and title (Parks Canada Agency, 2000). This ruling could affect government resource dispositions on traditional lands as well as Aboriginal claims for title inside some national parks. In 1999, *Marshall v. The Queen* confirmed that oral tradition that can provide a context for a transaction is admissible to help a court interpret a treaty (Parks Canada Agency, 2000).

Comprehensive Land Claim Policy

Following the Calder case, the federal government released a policy statement announcing its willingness to negotiate the settlement of comprehensive land claims, and the objectives to guide its involvement in such negotiations (Canada, 1981). After the recommendations of the 1985 Task Force to Review Comprehensive Claims Policy, a substantially modified land claim policy was unveiled by the federal government late in 1986 (Canada, 1987). Notwithstanding the Sparrow judgement (*Sparrow*, 1990)— and additional Aboriginal rights cases heard since then—the Minister of Indian Affairs and Northern Development has stated that the 'basic principles' of the current comprehensive land claim policy are not likely to change.

The current comprehensive land claim policy requires Aboriginal peoples to sur- render to the Crown their rights, interests, and 'Aboriginal' title in and to the land, water, and natural resources, in exchange for which they are to receive constitution- ally protected rights, benefits, and privileges defined in land claim settlements. The Comprehensive Land Claim Policy does not deal explicitly with national parks or other forms of protected areas. This is not too surprising, for the intent of the policy and of government's strategy in entertaining land claim negotiations is quite specific: that is, to clear the ill-defined Aboriginal title from the land in question. Whether national parks are included in the rights and benefits Aboriginal peoples obtain in return, depends upon the policy and strategy of Aboriginal peoples as well as the intent of government. It is clear, however, that comprehensive land claim settlements concluded under the existing (Canada, 1987) and the preceding policy (Canada, 1981) stress environmental conservation and protection of wildlife habitat. Moreover, many final agreements in the territorial north deal with national parks.

PARKS CANADA POLICY, REGULATIONS, AND LEGISLATION RELATING TO ABORIGINAL PEOPLES

Many of Canada's national parks were designated at a time when both the federal and provincial governments did not acknowledge Aboriginal rights and title. Aboriginal peoples utilizing traditional lands or occupying reserves encompassed by newly des- ignated parks were given little, if any, input in park planning and management. Indeed, when Riding Mountain National Park was established in 1933, the Keeseekoowenen Band was evicted and their houses burned (Morrison, 1995). Aboriginal people with reserves in proposed park areas were encouraged by Parks Canada to sell or trade their reserves for lands outside proposed parks, and were prevented from hunting and trap- ping within them. There was little appreciation within government that parks could be used to support and maintain the land uses of Aboriginal peoples, and hence pro-tect their land-based cultures. Instead Parks Canada stressed the need for the parks sys-tem to 'represent' biophysically defined natural areas. Adherence to the natural areas framework may have contributed to the estrangement of parks from Aboriginal peo-ples. Parks identified through the framework might have been excellent choices to represent natural areas, but were sometimes irrelevant to protecting vital wildlife habi-tat, the element of parks legislation that interested many Aboriginal groups. To Aboriginal peoples dependent on hunting, fishing, and trapping, the location of a park was the key to its utility and political acceptability.

The attitude of Parks Canada began to change in the 1970s as the values and aspi-rations of Aboriginal peoples seeped into the Canadian body politic. This process was aided by public hearings into oil and gas 'megaprojects', which brought representatives of Aboriginal peoples and environmental and other groups into the same camp. The Berger inquiry into a proposed gas pipeline from the Mackenzie Delta and northern Alaska, for example, noted the need for parks and conservation areas to be planned simultaneously with non-renewable resource development (Berger, 1977). In addi-tion, Justice Berger proposed a new type of park, a 'wilderness park', to preserve wildlife, wildlife habitat, and natural landscapes in the northern Yukon, and to under-pin the still-vibrant renewable resource economy of Inuvialuit and Dene. This rec-ommendation is now an acknowledged milestone in the debate that connects Aboriginal peoples with national parks.

The 1979 Parks Canada Policy tried to respond to Aboriginal issues and Justice Berger's path-breaking report. The policy contained a number of sections that defined a new relationship between local people and potential national parks. In this regard, Section 1.3.5 of the *National Parks Policy* (Parks Canada, 1979: 39) stated that Parks Canada 'will contribute toward the cost of special provisions to reduce the impact of park establishment on occupants or other users of lands acquired for a national park.' While not directed specifically at Aboriginal people, this section indicated a willing-ness on the part of Parks Canada to be more sensitive to impacts upon local people, including Aboriginal peoples, when establishing national parks. Consistent with the federal government's 1973 policy stating its intent to negotiate land claims in Quebec, British Columbia, and the Territories, the 1979 parks policy also recognized the poten-tial existence of certain Aboriginal rights in Section 1.3.13 (Parks Canada 1979, 40). Thus the 1979 *Parks Canada Policy* embraced the concept of joint management by government and Aboriginal people eight years before this same concept was endorsed and adopted in the land claims policy.

In 1994, Parks Canada revised its policies, with a new and strong emphasis on eco-logical integrity, improved regional integration through co-operation with other juris-dictions, and a more comprehensive approach to working with Aboriginal peoples (Parks Canada, 1994). The 1994 Guiding Principles and Operational Policies sets out several polices with respect to Aboriginal interests:

- negotiation of comprehensive claims based on traditional uses and occupancy of land;

- rights and benefits in relation to wildlife management and the use of water and land, and the opportunity for participation on advisory or public government bodies;
- respect for the principles set out in court decisions, such as Regina v. Sparrow, where existing Aboriginal or treaty rights occur within protected areas;
- at the time of new park establishment, respect for Canada's legal and policy framework regarding Aboriginal rights as affirmed by Section 35 of the Constitution Act, and consultation with affected Aboriginal communities.

Of particular note, the policy also recognizes 'local knowledge' as valuable to management of heritage areas, although there is no explicit reference to Aboriginal ecological knowledge (Parks Canada, 1994: 18). Guiding principles make reference to collaboration and co-operation with '. . . Aboriginal interests to achieve mutually compatible goals and objectives. These relationships support regional integration, partnerships, co-operative arrangements, formal agreements, and open dialogue with other interested parties, including adjacent or surrounding districts and communities' (Parks Canada, 1994: 19). This policy set out a new approach directing park managers to work with a broad range of partners both inside and outside the national parks. Finally, in reference to National Park Agreements, the policy has provisions for 'continuation of renewable resource harvesting activities, and the nature and extent of Aboriginal peoples' involvement in park planning and management', and 'establishment pursuant to agreements with Aboriginal organizations' (Parks Canada, 1994: 28, 51).

While the 1994 Parks Canada policy made significant progress on the role of Aboriginal peoples in national park establishment and management, the policy stops short of advocating true partnerships with shared authority and resources, and it does not ensure genuine joint or co-operative decision-making, even where the park is established through land claim agreements. Some park planners and managers feel that this policy guarantees Aboriginal people only a right to 'participate' in decision-making, and does not convey to them a veto over decisions. The Panel on the Ecological Integrity of Canada's national parks found that 'consistent with the overall Government of Canada approach to the resolution of issues respecting Aboriginal peoples, Parks Canada has traditionally adopted a legalistic approach and position in dealing with Aboriginal issues—which are often referred to as "problems"' (Parks Canada Agency, 2000).

The most recent National Parks System Plan reflects implementation of Parks Canada's policies with respect to Aboriginal people when it endorses, 'a new type of national park where traditional subsistence resource harvesting by Aboriginal people . . . continues and where co-operative management approaches are designed to reflect Aboriginal rights and regional circumstances' (Parks Canada, 1997).

Amendments to the National Parks Act in 1988 and 2000 also recognize the importance of traditional resource harvesting to Aboriginal peoples. The 1988 amendments allowed specific indigenous people to carry out such harvesting in certain parks. It also extended traditional renewable resource harvesting rights in wilderness areas of national parks to Aboriginal peoples with land claim settlements at the Minister's discretion. The amendments also allowed for regulation of traditional renewable resource harvesting in national parks by Order-in-Council.

The 2000 amendments to the Canada National Parks Act (Bill C-27) extend harvesting rights to a larger number of parks including all those established by agreement. Section 10 (1) of the Act also supports co-operative agreements with a wide range of organizations, including Aboriginal governments, for carrying out the purposes of the Act. The Act specifies that the Governor in Council may 'make regulations respecting the exercise of traditional renewable resource harvesting activities' in Wood Buffalo, Wapusk, and Gros Morne National Parks, any park established in the District of Thunder Bay in the Province of Ontario; and 'any park established in an area where the continuation of such activities is provided for by an agreement between the Government of Canada and the government of a province respecting the establishment of the park' (Bill C-27: 17 (1)). For the first time, the National Parks Act also makes provisions for the removal of non-renewable resources in the form of carving stone, in order to support traditional economies. Current harvesting activities are summarized in Table 13.1; however, no trend data are currently available.

Limits to Aboriginal harvesting are specified by regulations under the Act that may:

- specify what are traditional renewable resource harvesting activities;
- designate classes of persons authorized to engage in those activities and prescribe the conditions under which they may engage in them;
- prohibit the use of renewable resources harvested in parks for other than traditional purposes;
- control traditional renewable resource harvesting activities;
- authorize the superintendent of a park to close areas of the park to traditional renewable resource harvesting activities for purposes of park management, public safety, or the conservation of natural resources;
- authorize the superintendent of a park to establish limits on the renewable resources that may be harvested in any period, or to vary any such limits established by the regulations, for purposes of conservation; and
- authorize the superintendent of a park to prohibit or restrict the use of equipment in the park for the purpose of protecting natural resources.

The new National Parks Act does not guarantee joint management for Aboriginal peoples whose traditional lands fall within national parks. Such joint management regimes are only specified in the policy, and only then for Aboriginal groups who have successfully completed land claims settlements. Accordingly, a number of Aboriginal peoples whose traditional lands are affected by national park initiatives, but who have not concluded land claim settlements with the government—including the Nuu-chah-nulth in British Columbia, and the Inuit of northern Labrador—may or may not have an opportunity for joint management. In the case of Gwaii Haanas, the National Parks Act specifies in Section 41 (1), that, 'the Governor in Council may authorize the Minister to enter into an agreement with the Council of the Haida Nation respecting the management and operation of Gwaii Haanas National Park Reserve of Canada.' Section 41 (2), further allows for 'regulations, applicable in the

TABLE 13.1 Aboriginal Harvest in National Park System

Park	None	Very Limited	Limited	Comment
Aulavik National Park		×		fish, fox
Auyuittuq National Park			×	caribou, ptarmigan, hare, seals
Bruce Peninsula/ Fathom Five National Park	×			
Grasslands National Park	×			
Gros Morne National Park	×			
Gwaii Haanas National Park Reserve			×	deer
Ivvavik National Park			×	char, caribou, wolves, waterfowl. Limit of 3 grizzly bears has never been taken
Kluane National Park Reserve		×		Rights exist but hunting is better elsewhere
Mingan Archipelago National Park Reserve			×	ducks
Nahanni National Park Reserve			×	moose, sheep, fur bearers, fish
Pacific Rim National Park Reserve			×	fish, plants, mushrooms
Pukaskwa			×	fish
Quttinirpaaq National Park	×			
Sirmilik National Park Reserve			×	geese, seals, no formal records
Tuktut Nogait National Park		×		caribou, musk-ox, fish
Vuntut National Park			×	muskrat, wolverine, caribou, moose
Wapusk National Park	×			Rights exist but hunting is better elsewhere
Banff National Park	×			
Cape Breton Highlands National Park	×			
Elk Island National Park	×			
Forillon National Park	×			
Fundy National Park	×			
Georgian Bay Islands National Park	×			
Jasper National Park	×			
Kejimkujik National Park	×			
Kootenay National Park	×			
Kouchibouguac National Park	×			
La Maurice National Park	×			
Mt Revelstoke/Glacier National Park	×			
Point Pelee National Park	×			

TABLE 13.1 Aboriginal Harvest in National Park System (continued)

Park	None	Very Limited	Limited	Comment
Prince Edward Island National Park	×			
Riding Mountain National Park		×		fish
St Lawrence Islands National Park	×			
Terra Nova National Park	×			
Waterton National Park	×			
Yoho National Park	×			
Wood Buffalo National Park			×	moose, muskrat & other fur-bearers

SOURCE: Aboriginal Secretariat, Parks Canada, May, 2001.

Gwaii Haanas National Park Reserve of Canada, respecting the continuance of traditional renewable resource harvesting activities and Haida cultural activities by people of the Haida Nation to whom subsection 35(1) of the *Constitution Act*, 1982 applies.'

Perhaps the most important accommodation the National Parks Act makes to Aboriginal peoples lies in the term 'National Park Reserve' introduced into the protected-areas lexicon through amendment to the statute in 1972. This designation applies, for example, to the Kluane, Nahanni, and Mingan Archipelago regions, which are to become full National Parks upon settlement of comprehensive land claims. The 'reserve' designation allowed Parks Canada to treat and manage the areas in question as national parkland, but did not extinguish any Aboriginal rights or title to the areas. Importantly, this designation does not prejudice the ability of Aboriginal peoples to select parkland in the course of land claim negotiations.

Canadian legislators seem to have chosen an ad hoc approach to accommodating the needs of Aboriginal peoples in national parks. Wood Buffalo National Park and Auyuittuq National Park Reserve provide examples of this *ad hoc* approach. The area around Wood Buffalo National Park was a favoured hunting ground of Aboriginal people for many years prior to its establishment as a park in 1922 (Lothian, 1976). When the park was established, Aboriginal people who had previously hunted and trapped in the area continued these activities under permit. In 1949, special district game regulations for Wood Buffalo National Park were instituted, which superseded the National Parks Game Regulations and which allowed for traditional hunting, trapping, and fishing by Aboriginal people (Lothian, 1976). The National Parks Act also enables the appointment of a Wildlife Advisory Board for the traditional hunting grounds of Wood Buffalo National Park, and this Board has a role, for example in bison management and hunting, fishing, and trapping regulations (Canada National Parks Act: 37). Auyuittuq National Park Reserve, located on Baffin Island, was established in 1972 long before the Nunavut Agreement. Public park planning meetings in the early 1970s resolved that the Inuit, who had inhabited the region for almost 4,000 years, would retain traditional resource extraction rights within the park. In addition, the Inuit participated in management through membership on a local park advisory committee, but their role was in an advisory capacity to the park superintendent and real decision-making powers were limited (Lawson, 1985).

The interaction between Aboriginal peoples and National Parks in Canada is not as clear as might be suggested by National Park Policy and legislation. Rather than work within a nation-wide comprehensive policy regarding Aboriginal peoples, Parks Canada has tended to follow an ad hoc approach. Land claim settlements themselves, rather than National Park Policy or legislation determine the role of Aboriginal peoples in planning for, and managing, national parks. This has given rise to subtly different kinds of parks in northern and southern Canada, for a significant park planning and management role is accorded Aboriginal peoples in northern Canada where parks are tied to settlement of land claims. Land claims in northern Canada will likely be completed sooner than those in southern Canada. In addition, many Aboriginal peoples in the south must look to old treaties and the National Parks Act and policy, rather than to comprehensive land claim settlements, to protect their interests.

In response to this variation in approaches to working with Aboriginal organizations, the Panel on the Ecological Integrity of Canada's National Parks recommended that, 'Parks Canada adopt clear policies to encourage and support the development and maintenance of genuine partnerships with Aboriginal peoples in Canada' (Parks Canada Agency, 2000: 7-8). The Panel also outlined key steps to foster trust and respect between Parks Canada and Aboriginal peoples, such as initiating a process of healing; providing adequate resources to maintain genuine partnerships; integrating Aboriginal culture, knowledge, and experience into education and interpretation programs; and ensuring protection of cultural sites, sacred areas, and artifacts. In an effort to move beyond the constraints of strict government legal positions, Parks Canada established an Aboriginal Secretariat in 1999, with the task of improving relationships with Aboriginal organizations throughout the national park system.

The following case studies describe current approaches to involvement of Aboriginal peoples in national park designation, planning, and management in both northern and southern Canada.

THE ROLE OF ABORIGINAL PEOPLES IN NATIONAL PARKS: NORTHERN CANADA LAND CLAIMS AGREEMENTS

The Inuvialuit Final Agreement

Inuvialuit of the Beaufort Sea region began land claim negotiations with the federal government in the mid-1970s and reached a Final Agreement in 1984 (Canada, 1984). Legislation to approve the final agreement and to amend the National Parks Act in consequence was passed in 1984. The Inuvialuit Final Agreement (IFA) requires the federal government to establish the western portion of the northern Yukon as a national park, subsequently named Ivvavik (Figure 13.2). In line with Justice Berger's recommendations (Berger, 1977), the IFA characterizes Ivvavik as 'wilderness oriented', and requires that the planning for the park: 'Maintain its present undeveloped state to the greatest extent possible' (Canada, 1984: 18). Moreover, a central aim of the park is 'to protect and manage the wildlife populations and the wildlife habitat within the area'. This objective reflects the national and international importance of the calving grounds of the Porcupine caribou herd, which are partially within the park. Not only did the IFA commit government to establish the park, define its boundaries, and specify its purposes and objectives, it mandated a Wildlife Management Advisory Council, composed of an equal number of government and Aboriginal members, to 'recommend a management plan for the National Park' (Canada, 1984: 18).

The 1978 Agreement-in-Principle promised that all of the Yukon north slope from the Alaskan border in the west to the NWT border in the east would be established as a national park. Due to the objections of the Yukon government and the oil and gas industry, the park boundaries defined in the final agreement were altered to divide the north slope into two zones (Fenge et al., 1986). The western portion, west of the Babbage River, was confirmed as a national park, but the eastern portion was excised from the proposed park to allow for the development of a transportation corridor. Nevertheless, this area was still to be subject to a 'special conservation regime whose dominant purpose is the conservation of wildlife, habitat and traditional native use' (Canada, 1984: 18). The Wildlife Management Advisory Council has responsibility for both the eastern and western portions of the north slope. This arrangement and the operations of the Porcupine Caribou Management Board link the national park to broader regional wildlife management and environmental conservation objectives. The IFA makes it very clear that Inuvialuit have the right to harvest wildlife for subsistence purposes throughout the north slope, and an exclusive right to do so in the national park. The door was left open, however, for Aboriginal peoples represented by the Council for Yukon First Nations to acquire harvesting rights in the park through their own land claim settlement.

In the case of Ivvavik National Park, it was the land claim settlement rather than the intra-governmental work of Parks Canada that resulted in the establishment of this national park. Two additional National Parks have been established in the Inuvialuit settlement region since 1984, Aulavik on Banks Island and Tuktut Nogait on the Arctic coast (Figure 13.2).

Yukon First Nations

The Umbrella Final Agreement (UFA) with the majority of Yukon's First Nations was ratified in 1994, enabling a wide range of co-operative conservation initiatives in the territory, including national parks. Chapter 10 of the UFA sets out the conditions for Special Management Areas (SMA), a unique tool that allows First Nations to negotiate government-to-government arrangements for habitat protection, watershed protection, national wildlife management areas, parks, or other types of management agreements.

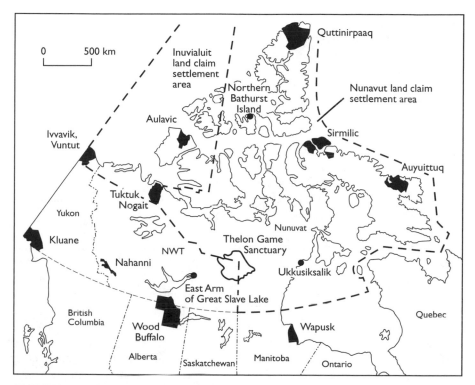

FIGURE 13.2 Existing and proposed parks in northern Canada.

Vuntut National Park was established in 1993 through the Vuntut Gwitchin Final Agreement and was linked to a regional conservation package that included the Old Crow Flats SMA. Lands within Vuntut National Park are managed according to the National Parks Act and the Final Agreement, while the Final Agreement and a locally produced plan guides management of the SMA. Of interest were the different, and complementary, perspectives on park establishment held by Vuntut Gwitchin and Parks Canada. Gwitchin primarily viewed the park as a way to protect their traditional lands for harvesting and other cultural values, while Parks Canada saw the park as improving representation of the natural region (Njootli, 1994; Johnson, 1994). The objectives of the park agreement include recognition and protection of the traditional and current use of the Park by Vuntut Gwitchin in the development and management of the Park (Canada, 1993: Schedule A, 105). The agreement provides economic and employment opportunities, recognizes oral history as a valid form of research, and gives Vuntut Gwitchin the exclusive right to harvest for subsistence at all times and for all species. Commercial trapping is also supported. Park management is based on a co-operative working arrangement between a local Renewable Resources Council that may make recommendations to the Minister on all matters pertaining to the management of the park, and Parks Canada is directed to implement the recommendations of the Council that are accepted by the Minister. The Vuntut Gwitchin First Nation also maintains a central role in park management, as shown by the Interim Management Guidelines (Parks Canada, 1999). The IMG were created in partnership with the Gwitchin, Parks Canada, and the Renewable Resources Council, whereby the park vision statement strongly reflects First Nation values. A complementary Co-operation Agreement was signed in 1998, which sets out clear roles and responsibilities in the park. Parks Canada retains overall responsibility for management and operations of the park.

Kluane National Park Reserve was established in 1972, followed two decades later by a new negotiated management arrangement through the Champagne and Aishihik First Nations Final Agreement for the southern part of the park. The Kluane First Nation, with traditional lands in the northern part of the park, had not settled their Final Agreement as of Spring 2001, although it is anticipated they will also enter a management agreement with Parks Canada. Unlike Vuntut National Park, the Kluane Park agreement establishes a management board consisting of First Nations and community representatives and an ex officio member from Parks Canada. Although the agreement has enhanced local co-operation, and the Board provides advice to the Minister through the Park Management Plan, the agreement does not appear to meet the test of a true joint management regime where decisions and resources are shared equally.

In 1999, the Champagne and Aishihik First Nations proposed six goals for management of the park including: renewing cultural ties to the park, learning and teaching cultural heritage, keeping plants and animals healthy for the future, creating training and employment opportunities, participating in tourism, and *sharing responsibility for the park, by working towards First Nation members becoming full co-managers of the park* [emphasis added] (Parks Canada, 2000).

The Inuit Land Claim

A key step in the political and social evolution of the Eastern Arctic took place in 1993, with the signing of the Agreement Between the Inuit of the Nunavut Settlement Area and Canada. This agreement commits Parks Canada to work with regional Inuit communities and designated Inuit organizations in the development of co-management structures for the parks as well as the broader implementation of the Nunavut Land Claim Agreement (Parks Canada, 1999).

During the last two decades, Inuit generally have viewed national parks as 'friendly' land use designations. In 1983, for example, the Nunavut Constitutional Forum (NCF), which represented Inuit in constitutional discussions within the NWT, proposed that approximately 25 per cent of the Arctic be set aside for park purposes (Doering, 1983). This proposal was not viewed favourably, hence the final agreement contains less dramatic and less far-reaching provisions on parks. The Inuit strategy during formal negotiations was later quite clear: parks were to be used to protect key wildlife habitat allowing negotiators to concentrate land ownership selections elsewhere.

While the IFA dealt with one park, the Nunavut Agreement does not commit government to establish any specified areas as national parks. Since the agreement was signed, significant progress has been made on new national park designations.

BOX 13.1 The Nunavut Agreement

The Nunavut Agreement is a land claim agreement as defined in Section 35 of Canada's Constitution. It forms a modern treaty between the Inuit of the Nunavut Settlement Area, who were represented in negotiations by the Tungavik Federation of Nunavut (TFN), and the federal government. The agreement defines an exchange between Inuit and the federal government. Inuit agree to give to the government their Aboriginal title to land, water, and the offshore. In exchange, Inuit are to enjoy the rights and benefits defined in the agreement. These rights and benefits, which are 'guaranteed' under Canada' s constitution, include:

- title to approximately 350 000 sq. km of land, of which approximately 36,000 sq. km will include mineral rights;
- the right to harvest wildlife on lands and waters throughout the Nunavut Settlement Area;
- a guarantee of the establishment of (at least) three national parks in the Nunavut Settlement Area;
- equal membership with government on new institutions of public government (established through the agreement) to manage the land, water, offshore, and wildlife of the Nunavut Settlement Area and to assess and evaluate the impact of development projects on the environment. These public institutions include the Nunavut Wildlife Management Board (NWMB), the Nunavut Water Board (NWB), the Nunavut Impact Review Board (NIRB), and the Nunavut Planning Commission (NPC).

SOURCE: Canadian Arctic Resources Committee 1993, *Northern Perspectives* 21: 3.

TABLE 13.2 Progress on National Park Establishment in Nunavut

Park Name	Historic milestones	Status in early 2000
Auyuittuq	Park Reserve established in 1976	Agreement in 1999
Sirmilik	Negotiations Began 1987	Agreement in 1999
Quttinirpaaq	Park Reserve established in 1988	Agreement in 1999
Wager Bay	Land withdrawal announced in 1996	Final Boundary Negotiations in 2000
Tuktut Nogait	Inuvialuit portion designated in 1998	Negotiations on Nunavut portion underway

SOURCE: Aboriginal Secretariat, Parks Canada, May, 2001

The park management provisions in the Nunavut Agreement are similar to those in the IFA. For each park, Inuit and government are to negotiate an Inuit Impact and Benefits Agreement (IIBA) to channel economic and social benefits from the park to local Inuit. As part of an IIBA, a joint Inuit/government parks planning and management committee can be set up to advise 'on all matters related to park management'

(Tungavik Federation of Nunavut, 1990: 119). Management plans developed by Parks Canada will be based on the recommendations of the committee. Such plans have to be approved by the Minister responsible for national parks. In conducting negotiations, TFN tried to persuade the federal government to adopt the term 'joint management regime' as used in the 1979 Parks Canada Policy, and to have this term enshrined in the final agreement. The federal government refused, saying that this concept was vague and open to misinterpretation.

The Nunavut Agreement also followed the lead of the IFA in characterizing National Parks in the Arctic as 'wilderness oriented'. The Agreement stipulates that: 'each National Park in the Nunavut Settlement Area shall contain a predominant proportion of Zones I and II, as such zones are defined in the Parks Canada Policy'. Inuit also hope National Parks will be tools for economic development. Very few 'outsiders' currently visit national parks in the Arctic, for example less than 1,000 people visit the remote Auyuittuq National Park Reserve every year. Nevertheless, Inuit hope to use money from the land claim settlement to provide tourist and recreational facilities in communities adjacent to parks, to attract more visitors to these places.

THE ROLE OF ABORIGINAL PEOPLES IN NATIONAL PARKS: EXAMPLES FROM SOUTHERN CANADA

Parks Canada has a wide spectrum of arrangements with Aboriginal peoples in park designation, planning, and management in southern Canada. Both Pacific Rim and Gwaii Haanas, for example, are designated as National Park Reserves, pending settlement of Aboriginal land claims encompassing the park areas. They differ, however, in the level of Aboriginal involvement in park designation, management, and planning; historically, Aboriginal people have had little involvement at Pacific Rim, while they enjoy significant involvement at Gwaii Haanas. This contrasting situation reflects the variability of many other national parks across the country, such as Pukaskwa in Ontario compared to Fundy in New Brunswick, or Riding Mountain compared to Wapusk in Manitoba. The continuum of Aboriginal involvement extends from virtually complete exclusion to co-operative management. Overall, however, the level of communication and co-operation between Parks Canada and Aboriginal peoples has increased dramatically during the last decade.

Pacific Rim National Park Reserve

Pacific Rim National Park Reserve is located on the west coast of Vancouver Island, and is divided into three distinct geographic units. The southerly West Coast Trail Unit of the Park Reserve traverses reserve lands of the Nuu-chah-nulth Indian people; these people also have enclave reserves contained in the Long Beach and Broken Group Islands units of the park (Figure 13.3). In total, there are 28 Indian reserves belonging to seven different bands, either adjacent to the park or enclosed within its boundaries. There are also 289 recorded archaeological sites 'that relate to the native history within Pacific Rim National Park' (Inglis and Haggarty, 1986: 256). The park

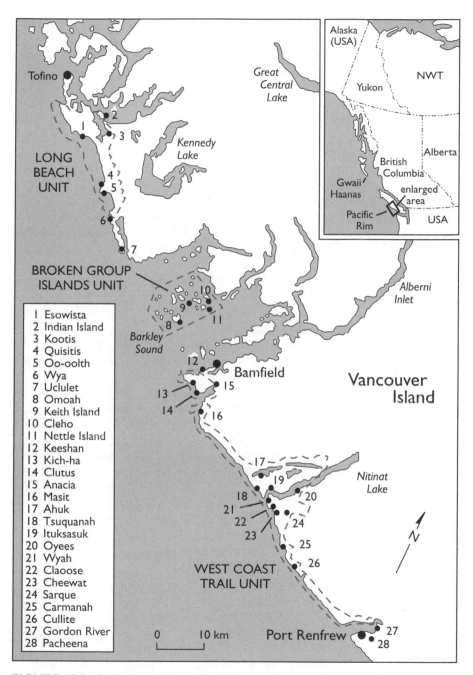

FIGURE 13.3 Pacific Rim National Park Reserve showing the three different units and principal Native reserves.

reserve is part of a larger area occupied by the Nuu-chah-nulth people for approximately 4000 years (Dewhirst, 1978). The Nuu-chah-nulth have never been conquered by Europeans, nor have they ceded this territory by treaty (with the exception of one small, and illegal, treaty). As a result, they are now part of the British Columbia Treaty Process, and negotiations cover a large portion of the west coast of Vancouver Island, fully encompassing the national park reserve. Two Nuu-chah-nulth Tribal Council First Nations, the Ditidaht and the Pacheedaht, are pursuing a separate treaty claim apart from the comprehensive treaty negotiations.

In spite of the fact that the Nuu-chah-nulth people have a significant interest in the park area, a comprehensive land claim that fully encompasses the park, and unextinguished Aboriginal rights to hunt and fish in the park region, they had little say in the designation, planning, or management of the park. Nuu-chah-nulth people enjoy some special privileges within the park reserve, as they are allowed to continue harvesting park resources for subsistence purposes. However, subsistence gathering of seafoods and other ocean resources has been curtailed by the Department of Fisheries and Oceans (DFO), which maintained management jurisdiction over fishery resources within the park before it was gazetted under the National Parks Act. Over the years, Nuu-chah-nulth people have complained of poor communication between themselves and park managers. Prior to park designation, Parks Canada told the Nuu-chah-nulth that the park would bring jobs to the area, but the Nuu-chah-nulth assert that while park designation has resulted in increased local jobs, both directly and indirectly through tourism, in most cases their people have not been the recipients of these jobs. The Nuu-chah-nulth have also observed that the large numbers of park visitors are having a negative impact on their traditional lands and reserves encompassed by the park. Since 1990, co-operation between the Nuu-chah-nulth and Parks Canada has increased and there are now several new initiatives (Box 13.2).

BOX 13.2 Pacific National Park Reserve First Nation Initiatives

Pacific Rim has made many initiatives to improve relationships with surrounding First Nations peoples over the last decade. Some of these include:
* allowance of traditional activities, such as the harvesting of medicinal and sacred plants and the documentation and protection of important harvesting sites;
* development of common conservation goals and the incorporation of traditional knowledge;
* developing expanded targets for First Nation's employment;
* developing training and mentoring programs;
* promoting Aboriginal tourism, including guiding, and outfitting opportunities;
* establishing an agreement for enhanced First Nations presence on the West Coast Trail to provide for cultural resource protection, interpretation and maintenance;
* developing cultural interpretation programs;
* establishing joint archaeological projects;

- respecting and using First Nation's place names in signs and brochures;
- developing a Co-operative Management Board to deal with management planning, relevant operational issues, training and employment, cultural interpretation, harvesting activities, and joint research.

Gwaii Haanas National Park Reserve

Gwaii Haanas (formerly known as South Moresby), is located in the southern portion of the Haida Gwaii archipelago, 170 km off-shore from Prince Rupert. In 1985, under the authority of the Haida Constitution, Gwaii Haanas was designated a Haida Heritage Site. On 11 July 1987, a Memorandum of Understanding to negotiate a National Park Reserve and National Marine Park in South Moresby was signed by the Prime Minister of Canada and the Premier of British Columbia (Sewell et al., 1989). This was followed in 1988, by the South Moresby Agreement, formally designating the area as a National Park Reserve. In 1993 the Gwaii Haanas Agreement was signed, setting out the terms of co-management between the Haida Nation and the Government of Canada and stipulating that:

> Gwaii Haanas will be maintained and made use of so as to leave it unimpaired for the benefit, education and enjoyment of future generations. More specifically, all actions related to the planning, operation and management of Gwaii Haanas will respect the protection and preservation of the environment, the Haida culture, and the maintenance of a benchmark for science and understanding.

Gwaii Hanaas lies within a region inhabited by the Haida people for thousands of years (McMillan, 1988), and it is fully encompassed by the comprehensive land claim

---

BOX 13.3 Haida Gwaii Watchmen

The Haida people, in recognizing that natural and cultural elements cannot be separated and that the protection of the Gwaii Haanas is essential to sustaining Haida culture, initiated the Watchmen Program to protect culturally significant sites in the South Moresby region, now known as Gwaii Haanas. Since the co-management of Gwaii Haanas, key elements of the Haida Gwaii Watchmen program remain unchanged, with Watchmen posted at all the previous sites with the exception of Burnaby Narrows. The mandate of the program continues to be, first and foremost, the safeguarding of Gwaii Haanas. The presence of the Watchmen plays an important role in the protection of the sensitive sites, accomplished largely by educating visitors about the natural and cultural heritage of Gwaii Haanas and ensuring that visitors know how to travel without leaving a trace of their passage. General information about safety and the latest marine forecasts that come in by radio are also provided. SOURCE: Parks Canada (1999).

FIGURE 13.4 Totem poles at Ninstints, the World Heritage Site on South Moresby/Gwaii Haanas National Park Reserve. *Photo: P. Dearden.*

of the Haida Nation. One Haida group, the Skidegate Indian Band, has reserve lands adjacent to, and within the proposed park boundaries. Numerous Aboriginal heritage sites, including the Haida village of Ninstints—a UNESCO World Heritage Site—are situated within the park reserve. The Haida Nation has indicated that they will seek title to Gwaii Haanas Park in any land claims settlement, which may oblige Canada to reconsider its policy of allowing only Crown ownership of national park lands.

The level of Aboriginal involvement in park management at Gwaii Haanas is much greater than that at Pacific Rim. The Government of Canada and the Haida Nation negotiated an interim 'Archipelago Management Board' (AMB) comprised of two representatives each from the Haida Nation and the Government of Canada (Canada, 1990). The interim AMB examines all initiatives relating to the management of the Gwaii Haanas archipelago. Once the national park reserve is gazetted under the National Parks Act, a permanent AMB will be constituted under an agreement between the Haida and the Government of Canada, and it will be responsible for reviewing all aspects of park operation and management, including Park Management Plans and Annual Work Plans. Haida people will also be guaranteed continued access to Gwaii Haanas for a host of traditional activities, including: gathering of traditional Haida foods, gathering of plants for medicinal or ceremonial purposes, cutting trees for ceremonial or artistic purposes, hunting, fishing, trapping, conducting ceremonies of traditional, spiritual, or religious significance, and seeking cultural and spiritual inspiration.

The AMB is empowered to examine the scope and intent of all Haida subsistence and traditional activities in the proposed park reserve, and to ensure that such activities are not contrary to national park purposes (Canada, 1990). Finally, the government of Canada provides training to assist Haida people to qualify for park employment, and the Haida participate in the selection of park employees.

BOX 13.4 A First Nations Perspective on Parks Management

Tribal peoples in Canada have been managing their lands for eons before the arrival of settler populations, often in a state that resembles the present lands now protected as parks. Many government land managers are, in fact, examining indigenous practices in their continued efforts to return lands to the conditions that settlers found, and which shaped their ideas of wilderness. At the same time, tribal peoples themselves are regaining jurisdiction over portions of their traditional territories and in some cases are co-managing some parks or protected areas.

It is important to note that territories called wilderness by settlers or modern park managers are thought of as homelands by First Nations people. These lands are full of evidence of long-standing continuous relationships between the tribe and the environment. A short walk from any beach on Haida or Nuu-chah-nulth territory, one encounters culturally modified trees, often centuries old. The Salish-Kootenai land still bears vegetative patterns reflective of centuries of controlled burns. In each case, their lands are far from untrammeled in tribal eyes and humans certainly are not intruders into nature. The following discussion reflects the views of protected-area management that have been developed by the Confederated Salish-Kootenai First Nations in British Columbia for the Mission Mountain Tribal Wilderness.

When tribal land managers speak of their stewardship role, a notion of both physical and spiritual protection emerges. While the physical protection of places is common to all land managers, spiritual protection is of special importance to tribal managers. Tribal societies have always believed that spiritual obligation to the land is as important as physical protection. This obligation may take the form of ritual observance on the land at sacred sites, of traditional practices associated with the hunting of game species, and of the return to the land of the remains of plant or animal harvest after human use. These centuries-old practices are considered vital by tribal communities for continued health of the land and of the people. A major factor in establishing the Mission Mountains Tribal Wilderness (MMTW) was the importance of the Mission Mountains to the spiritual well-being of the Salish-Kootenai people. The religious practices of the Salish-Kootenai people—conducting vision quests, hunting and gathering medicinal roots and herbs—continue today in the wilderness, and these practices are being passed on to the next generation.

Tribal land managers, often trained in Western resource management schools, also speak of the need to respect traditional land management and tenure systems. Many of these land tenure systems are organized around certain families, who have delegated certain responsibility to care for particular hunting areas or sacred sites. In most cases, their land management roles coexisted with their role as harvesters, unlike the Western system, which separates these functions. This integrated system, where hunters monitored their own areas, depended not on career managers but on family responsibility to the larger community.

The collective emphasis rather than individualistic emphasis of most non-tribal communities also influences tribal land management. Tribal communities have always had decision mechanisms that focus on the collective, but this search for collective consent is increasingly difficult in a modern context. The unity of perspective gained by shared experiences of education, spiritual practice, and pursuits on the land is no longer evident. Communities now reflect some of the diversities that challenge decision-makers in the larger, dominant society, but communities show a continued desire to make the majority of decisions collectively, rather than leaving them to individuals.

Since many tribal communities are also impoverished ones, there is also considerable pressure on land managers to ensure that wilderness areas provide direct economic benefits to the community. Most tribal communities want to continue hunting, fishing, agriculture, and gathering on wilderness lands, even if they deny such opportunity to non-members of their community. In many Canadian tribal communities 'country food' continues to account for a majority of the people's diet.

Many communities also want a large stake in the tourist economy that often results from the designation of a park or protected area. For example, some tribes have been attracted by the potential for sport hunting and fishing as a source of income from their traditional lands. However, some of these communities have serious ethical concerns about the very notion of hunting for sport, yet they recognize the growing impact of nature-based tourism. The issue for tribal land managers is how to accommodate this desire from the non-Aboriginal community without compromising either the needs of tribal members or the beliefs that underpin the tribal approach to land management.

Tribal land managers are also charged with cultural interpretation of both their lands and the people who live on them. Many non-tribal visitors to areas perceived as 'primitive' expect 'authentic' tribal culture to be part of that experience and their notion of authenticity is usually rooted in settler reports of early contacts. Tribal communities are modern communities and do not wish to be held up to a standard of modernity that differs from other cultures. So the issue becomes one of how to portray relationship to the land in a way that does not make culture a commodity or portray it as a frozen artifact.

Another issue raised by tribal wilderness managers is the need to preserve knowledge about the land that is presently held by the elders of the community. To pass this knowledge on to the next generation, there is a need for younger tribal members to accompany elders onto the land. The elders, in turn, need to find a land that continues to resemble the one they know, so that they can pass on knowledge of animal behaviour or plant habitat. At the same time, as Western science and land management becomes more interested in traditional ecological knowledge, there is real concern in tribal communities about protection of the intellectual property rights of this community-held knowledge. Tribal land managers have to deal with who owns knowledge, and who can consent to its being shared, as well as identify who it will be passed on to and thus who they will consult in the future.

SOURCE: Abstracted from McDonald et al. (2000).

Southern and Eastern Canadian National Parks

The role of Aboriginal peoples in national park management in the rest of Canada varies according to the status of treaties, the date of park establishment, the historic relationship between Parks Canada and local First Nations, the size of the park, and the proximity of Aboriginal communities to the park. In the mountain parks, Aboriginal people historically have had a very limited role in park management, although in recent years increased communication and co-operation is the trend. In Waterton Lakes National Park, for example, the Blood Tribe are co-operating with Parks Canada on a 'good neighbour' basis within their traditional territory, even though they do not have direct jurisdiction in the park.

After a long history of exclusion of Aboriginal people at Riding Mountain, communications have increased in recent years, even though local Aboriginal people are still absent from a formal management role. A 'Senior Officials Forum' with First Nations participation has been established to discuss park management issues, and a historic use study has been completed in co-operation with Aboriginal people. Many Aboriginal people remain frustrated over their exclusion from hunting or ceremonial activities in the park, and there still are unsettled land claims and grievances from earlier land expropriations.

At St Lawrence Islands a working group on historic site management has been established with the Akwesasne. At Fundy National Park, historically there has been little communication between the Micmac and Parks Canada, although the First Nation is now a partner in the Fundy Model Forest.

Pukaskwa National Park has a progressive co-operative arrangement with the Ojibways of Pic River. In fact, the Pukaskwa situation is unique among those national parks in treaty areas, since harvesting activities described in the National Parks Act are allowed (Morrison, 1995: 19). According to Parks Canada, 'the Robinson-Superior Treaty Group (RSTG) will play a significant role in helping to achieve this [the park's] mission since the park is located within that portion of Ontario subject to the Robinson-Superior Treaty of 1850' (Parks Canada, 1999). The Park Management Plan advocates strengthening the relationship with First Nations towards a common vision for the park; and further indicates that a joint wildlife management strategy for renewable resource harvesting will be developed in conjunction with representatives of the Robinson—Superior Treaty Group, in order to meet the commitment to allow native harvesting and traditional use activities within the park.

In sum, the progress towards co-operative management with Aboriginal people in southern parks has been steady and widespread although not yet on a par with the constitutionally mandated arrangements with First Nations where land claims have been settled, or where formal interim arrangements have been negotiated, such as at Gwaii Haanas.

DISCUSSION AND CONCLUSION

Prior to the late 1970's, Canadian national parks were designated with little consideration for Aboriginal peoples. However, following Berger's (1977) ground-breaking northern pipeline enquiry, Parks Canada became more sensitive to Aboriginal people's concerns. In fact, the 1979 Parks Canada Policy embraced the concept of joint management of parks by government and Aboriginal people fully eight years before this same concept was adopted in Canada's land claims policy.

Land claim settlements and Aboriginal treaty rights now play as great a part as National Park Policy or legislation in determining the role of Aboriginal peoples in planning for and managing national parks. Diverse approaches to settlement of land claims, as well as varying treaty rights, result in differing relationships between Aboriginal people and national parks throughout Canada. For example, a significant park planning and management role is accorded Aboriginal peoples in northern Canada where parks are tied to settlement of land claims. Similar situations have evolved in southern Canada, now that Aboriginal and treaty rights have been given greater recognition by the courts. However, significant disparities still exist in the relations that various Aboriginal groups have with Parks Canada.

Parks Canada may have exacerbated this situation through their ad hoc approach to relations with Aboriginal peoples. On the one hand, such an approach affords a level of flexibility, allowing park managers to respond to the exigencies of individual situations. On the other hand, without clearly defined parameters for relations with Aboriginal people, other challenges are likely to emerge as all Aboriginal groups strive to achieve the highest possible standard of participation in park management. Other complex issues are likely to arise as Aboriginal and treaty rights continue to be defined. The questions of Aboriginal and treaty rights to hunting and fishing have yet to be definitively dealt with by Parks Canada. With regard to the former, the courts are giving increasing recognition to Aboriginal rights to hunt and fish. These court rulings have a direct impact on management of national parks situated in regions traditionally utilized by Aboriginal people, or for the future planning of parks proposed for such regions.

Similar questions emerge concerning Aboriginal treaty rights to hunt and fish. As part of most treaties in Canada, Aboriginal groups were promised continued rights to hunt and fish on 'unoccupied Crown land'. In this context, a question arises: 'Can National Parks be considered unoccupied Crown land?' To our knowledge, this question has yet to be definitively answered. Nonetheless, it will certainly become important as Aboriginal groups further test the limits of treaty rights that are being re-invigorated as a result of the sympathetic stance towards such rights in Canadian courts. As in the case of Aboriginal rights, how Parks Canada will respond to the treaty rights issue is not apparent.

What is clear, however, is that Parks Canada has changed its approach to managing existing national parks and to planning for, and designating, new ones that fall within lands traditionally used by Aboriginal peoples. A majority of national parks and unrepresented National Park Terrestrial Natural Regions fall within territory traditionally used by Aboriginal peoples. Aboriginal and treaty rights are thus likely to have a con-

BOX 13.5 Park Conflicts and First Nations

Although First Nations peoples have been responsible for advancing the amount of land that has been available and included in park systems in Canada, there are also conflicts between First Nations aspirations and parks regarding specific locations and issues. At the national park level, for example, the Siksika Nation of southern Alberta are threatening to occupy a well-known landmark in the middle of Banff National Park, Castle Mountain, between the communities of Banff and Lake Louise. The Band wants the land for housing, elk and buffalo ranches, a sweat lodge, and to participate in Native spiritual traditions. The public would still be allowed access to the area.

At the provincial level, a potential conflict is growing between recreationists and First Nations people over park access and use in BC. In late 2000, park officials closed part of popular Mt Robson Provincial Park so that local Aboriginal peoples could hunt. Local park users complained that they were not even informed of the closures, let alone consulted as affected stakeholders and suggested that 'there was one law for one group and one law for another' (*Edmonton Journal*, 25 Sept. 2000, A1).

At the landscape level, the BC government were hoping to enter into an election period in late 2000 by being able to claim that they were the first jurisdiction in Canada to achieve 12 per cent of the land base set aside in protected areas. The Mackenzie Land Resource Management Plan in Northern BC was to establish 12 new provincial parks totaling 668,006 ha, enough to raise the province from 11.6 per cent to over 12 per cent. They had not counted on the disapproval of the Tsay Keh Dene Band, however, who are in the middle of land claims negotiations with the BC government. Both the government and NGOs who had worked on developing the Plan were taken aback as they had thought they had First Nations approval ... but this approval was from different Bands. Even though the Plan has now been approved, it does not compromise any future land claims.

These three examples illustrate part of the wide range of specific issues that are arising as Canadian society tries to feel its way towards a future that respects social justice, historical inequity, and the cultural and conservation needs of the future.

tinuing significant impact on national park management in Canada. Parks Canada is evolving, albeit slowly, to meet the demands of this changing situation, but it must give greater attention to the question of how Aboriginal and treaty rights are to be incorporated with park management practices if it is to adequately manage our national parks.

Since the 1988 amendment to the National Parks Act, Parks Canada's mandate has focused more closely on the maintenance of ecological integrity. This reaffirmation of the Agency's conservation mandate was further underscored by the Panel on the Ecological Integrity of Canada's National Parks, which tabled recommendations to support Parks Canada's mandate to manage for ecological integrity (Parks Canada

Agency, 2000). The scientific definition and objectives related to managing parks for ecological integrity are new to many Aboriginal peoples, as they are to the general public. At first glance, ecological integrity objectives are perhaps in opposition to our perceptions about Aboriginal people's reasons for protecting lands in parks. Yet the Panel found widespread support for the concept of ecological integrity, provided that it encompass human use as part of the ecosystem. Some parks, such as Kluane, have already prepared Ecological Integrity Statements in co-operation with First Nations, where cultural landscapes and traditional activities are recognized and incorporated into ecological integrity considerations. Maintenance of ecological integrity appears to be consistent with the holistic world view of many Aboriginal peoples and may facilitate greater co-operation in the future management of national parks.

REFERENCES

Berger, T.R. 1977. *Northern Frontier, Northern Homeland*, 2 vols. Toronto: James Lorimer.

———. 1982. 'The Nishga Indians and Aboriginal Rights', in T.R. Berger, ed., *Fragile Freedoms: Human Rights and Dissent in Canada*. Toronto: Irwin Publishing, 219–54.

British Columbia. 1875, reprinted 1987. *Papers Connected With the Indian Land Question, 1850–1875*. Victoria, BC: Richard Wolfenden.

Calder v. Attorney General of British Columbia, 1969. 8 D.L.R. (3rd) 59, 71 W.W.R. 81 (Supreme Court of British Columbia).

Calder v. Attorney General of British Columbia, 1970. 13 D.L.R. (3rd) 64, 74 W.W.R. 481 (British Columbia Court of Appeal).

Calder v. Attorney General of British Columbia, 1973. S.C.R. 313, 34 D.L.R. (3rd) 145, [1973] 4 W.W.R. 1 (S.C.C.).

Canada. 1981. *In All Fairness: A Native Claims Policy*. Ottawa: Minister of Supply and Services.

———. 1984. *Inuvialuit Final Agreement*. Ottawa: Minister of Indian Affairs and Northern Development.

———. 1987. *Comprehensive Land Claims Policy*. Ottawa: Minister of Supply and Services.

———. 1990. Gwaii Haanas/South Moresby Agreement between the Government of Canada and the Council of the Haida Nation. Available from the Office of the Minister of Environment.

———.1993. *Vuntut Gwitchin First Nation Final Agreement*. Ottawa: Department of Indian Affairs and Northern Development.

———. 2000. Bill C-27, an Act respecting the National Parks of Canada.

Canadian Arctic Resources Committee. 1993. 'Nunavut Land Claim Agreement', *Northern Perspectives* 21: 3.

Cumming, P.A., and N.H. Mickenberg, eds. 1972. *Native Rights in Canada*, 2nd edn. Toronto: The Indian Eskimo Association of Canada in association with General Publishing.

Dasmann, R.F. 1976. 'National Parks, Nature Conservation and Future Primitive', *Ecologist* 6: 164–7.

Dearden, P., and L. Berg. 1993. 'Canadian National Parks: A Model of Administrative Penetration', *Canadian Geographer* 37: 194–211.

————, S. Chettamart, D. Emphandu, and N. Tanakanjana. 1996. 'National Parks and Hilltribes in Northern Thailand: A Case Study of Doi Inthanon', *Society and Natural Resources* 9: 125–41.

Delgum'uukw v. Auditor General of British Columbia, 1997.

Dewhirst, J. 1978. 'Nootka Sound: A 4,000 Year Perspective', *Sound Heritage* 7: 1–30. (On file at Public Archives of BC.)

Doering, R.L. 1983. *Nunavut: Options for a Public Lands Regime*. Working Paper No. 3. Ottawa: Nunavut Constitutional Forum.

Elias, P.D. 1989. 'Aboriginal Rights and Litigation: History and Future of Court Decisions in Canada', *Polar Record* 25: 1–8.

Fenge, T., I. Fox, B. Sadler, and S. Washington. 1986. 'A Proposed Port on the North Slope of Yukon', in Sadler, ed., *Environmental Protection and Resource Development: Convergence for Today*. Banff School of Management, Calgary: University of Calgary Press, 127–78.

Fisher, R. 1977. *Contact and Conflict: Indian-European Relations in British Columbia 1774–1890*. Vancouver: University of British Columbia Press.

Frideres, J.S. 1988. *Native People in Canada: Contemporary Conflicts*, 3rd edn. Scarborough, Ont.: Prentice-Hall.

Inglis, R.I., and J.C. Haggarty. 1986. 'Pacific Rim National Park Ethnographic History', unpublished manuscript on file at Royal British Columbia Museum.

Johnson, J. 1994. 'A Parks Canada Perspective on Vuntut National Park', in J. Peepre and B. Jickling, eds, *Northern Protected Areas and Wilderness*. Proceedings of a Forum, 1993, Canadian Parks and Wilderness Society and Yukon College. Whitehorse, Yukon.

Lothian, W.F. 1976. *A History of Canada's National Parks*, vol. 1. Ottawa: Parks Canada.

MacDonald, D., T. MacDonald, and L. McAvoy. 2000. 'Tribal Wilderness Research Needs and Issues in the United States and Canada', in S.F. McCool, D.N. Cole, W.T. Borrie, and J. O'loughlin, comps. *Wilderness Science in a Time of Change Conference*, vol. 2, *Wilderness Within the Context of Larger Systems*. Fort Collins: University of Colorado, 290–4.

McMillan, A.D. 1988. *Native Peoples and Cultures of Canada: An Anthropological Overview*. Vancouver: Douglas & McIntyre.

Mishra, H.R. 1982. 'Balancing Human Needs and Conservation in Nepal's Royal Chitwan Park', *Ambio* 11: 246–51.

Morrison, J. 1995. 'Aboriginal Interests', in M. Hummel, ed., *Protecting Canada's Endangered Spaces: An Owner's Manual*. Toronto: Key Porter Books.

Nash, R. 1970. 'The American Invention of National Parks', *American Quarterly* 22: 726–35.

Njootli, S. 1994. 'Two Perspectives—One Park: Vuntut National Park', in J. Peepre and B. Jickling, eds, *Northern Protected Areas and Wilderness*. Proceedings of a Forum, 1993, Canadian Parks and Wilderness Society and Yukon College. Whitehorse, Yukon.

Nowicki, P. 1985. 'Cultural Ecology and "Management" of Natural Resources or Knowing When Not to Meddle', in J.A. McNeely and D. Pitt, eds, *Culture And Conservation: The Human Dimension in Environmental Planning*. London: Croom Helm, 269–82.

Parks Canada. 1979. *Parks Canada Policy*. Ottawa: Department of Indian and Northern Affairs.

————. 1994. *Guiding Principles and Operational Policies*. Ottawa: Department of Canadian Heritage.

————. 1997. *State of the Parks 1997 Report*. Ottawa: Department of Canadian Heritage.

————. 1997. *National Parks System Plan*, 3rd edn. Ottawa: Department of Canadian Heritage.

————. 1999. 'Vuntut National Park: Interim Management Guidelines', unpublished.

————. 1999. Web site for individual national parks: <http://parkscanada.pch.gc.ca/parks/alphap2e.htm>.

Parks Canada Agency. 2000. *Unimpaired for Future Generations? Protecting Ecological Integrity with Canada's National Parks*, vol. 2, *Setting a New Direction for Canada's National Parks*. Report of the Panel on the Ecological Integrity of Canada's National Parks. Ottawa.

Peepre, J., and Jickling, B., eds. 1994. *Northern Protected Areas and Wilderness*. Proceedings of a Forum, 1993, Canadian Parks and Wilderness Society and Yukon College. Whitehorse, Yukon.

Raunet, D. 1984. *Without Surrender, Without Consent: A History of the Nishga Land Claims*. Vancouver: Douglas & McIntyre.

Sanders, D. 1973. 'The Nishga Case', *B.C. Studies* 19: 3–20.

Sanders, D. 1983. 'The Rights of the Aboriginal Peoples of Canada', *Canadian Bar Review* 61: 314–38.

Sewell, W.R.D., P. Dearden, and J. Dumbrell. 1989. 'Wilderness Decision-making and the Role of Environmental Interest Groups: A Comparison of the Franklin Dam, Tasmania and South Moresby, British Columbia Cases', *Natural Resources Journal* 29: 147–69.

Sparrow v. The Queen, 1986a. County Court, [1986] B.C.W.L.D. 599

Sparrow v. The Queen, 1986b. 9 B.C.L.R. (2nd) 300, 36 D.L.R. (4th) 246, [1987] 2 W.W.R. 577.

Sparrow v. The Queen et al., 1990. Supreme Court of Canada. Chief Justice Dickson, and Justices McIntyre, La Forest, Lamer, Wilson, L'Heureux-Dubé, and Sopinka. 31 May, *QuickLaw Reports*, file 20311.

Task Force to Review Comprehensive Claims Policy. 1985. *Living Treaties, Lasting Agreements: Report of the Task Force to Review Comprehensive Claims Policy*. Ottawa: Department of Indian Affairs and Northern Development.

Terborgh, J. 2000. 'The Fate of Tropical Forests: A Matter of Stewardship', *Conservation Biology* 14: 1358–61.

Tungavik Federation of Nunavut. 1990. Agreement-in-Principle Between the Inuit of the Nunavut Settlement Area and Her Majesty in Right of Canada. Unpublished mimeograph.

United States Department of Agriculture Forest Service (Fort Collins, Colorado). Rocky Mountain Research Station. *Proceedings* RMRS P15 VO14. Wilderness Science in a Time of Change Conference. Vol.4: *Wilderness Visitors, Experiences, and Visitor Management*. Missoula, Montana.

KEY WORDS/CONCEPTS

Catlin's view of national parks
Constitution Act (1982)
Indian
Innuit
Métis
First Nations
Robinson's 1850 Treaties
William's Treaties
Calder Case
Sparrow case
Delgum'uukw
Comprehensive Land Claim Policy
(1981)
Berger Inquiry
1979 Parks Canada Policy
joint management

Guiding Principles and Operational
Policies (1997)
local knowledge
National Park System Plan (1997)
Amendments to the National Parks Act
(1988, 2000)
National Park Reserve
ad hoc approach to Aboriginal
involvement in parks
Ecological Integrity Panel
Aboriginal Secretariat (1999)
Inuvialuit Final Agreement
Umbrella Final Agreement (1994)
Inuit land claims
Nunavut Agreement
Watchmen Program

STUDY QUESTIONS

1. Discuss how Catlin's view of national parks differs from more traditional perspectives.
2. Outline the significance of each of the following for Aboriginal involvement with parks in Canada: Calder Case, Constitution Act, Sparrow Case, Delgum'uukw, Comprehensive Land Claim Policy, Berger Inquiry.
3. Comment on the statement 'Adherence to the natural areas framework may have contributed to the estrangement of parks from Aboriginal people'.
4. Outline the significance of each of the following for Aboriginal involvement with parks in Canada: 1994 Parks Canada Policy; 1997 Systems Plan; 1988 Amended National Parks Act; 2000 Amended National Parks Act.
5. Comment on the significance of 'National Park Reserves'
6. Of what benefit are national parks to Aboriginal people?
7. Of what benefit are Aboriginal people to national parks?
8. Discuss the variability of Aboriginal involvement between Northern Canada and Southern Canada.
9. Discuss the variability of Aboriginal involvement across Southern Canada.
10. Examine a park management plan for evidence of Aboriginal involvement.

CHAPTER 14

Marine Parks

Philip Dearden

INTRODUCTION

The United Nations declared 1998 as the 'Year of the Oceans'. There was good reason to do so. As the global population continues to increase, the population is becoming increasingly littoral. More than half of the inhabitants of the world live within 200 km of a coast (Hinrichsen, 1998). More people means more waste products and more people depending on the ocean for their livelihood. The Food and Agricultural Organization (FAO) estimates that 70 per cent of the world's marine fisheries are over-exploited. In May 2001 the Fisheries Resource Conservation Council recommended that the annual catch of cod from the north and east coasts of Newfoundland be limited to 5,600 tonnes, down from 7,000 tonnes in 2000 and a far cry from the 800,000 tonnes of the 1960s. The stock is acknowledged to be at its lowest level in recorded history despite a 10-year moratorium. A similar crisis prevails in fisheries on the Pacific coast. We are also reaching further and further down the food chain in our efforts to feed ourselves (Pauly et al., 1998) and marine habitats are becoming increasingly degraded. The first major international survey of coral reefs found that 69 per cent of reefs were seriously degraded (Anon, 1998), and over half the world's salt marshes, mangroves and coastal wetlands have been destroyed.

The oceans and their well-being are integral to life on this planet, essential components in global cycles and energy flows. They are home to a vast array of organisms and display even greater diversity of taxonomic groups than their terrestrial counterparts. Not only do these organisms help feed us, they are also the source of many valuable medicinal products. We use the seas to dump our waste products and to carry most of our traded goods around the globe. The cultures of the world draw strength and inspiration from their historical and immediate associations with this enormous, vital medium.

Aware of increasing degradation, many nations are seeking to improve marine conservation activities. One approach has been to develop international regulatory agreements that cover a wide range of human interactions with the oceans, such as the London Dumping Convention, Marpol, the Montreal Guidelines, and the environmental sections of the Law of the Sea Convention. A second way, used mainly to address conservation of commercial species, has been through regulations to limit fisheries catches. The inadequacy of this approach by itself can be clearly seen on the Pacific and Atlantic coasts of Canada. A third way, and the focus of this chapter, is the protection of specific areas of the ocean through designation as marine parks or reserves. While each of these approaches is necessary in a comprehensive strategy to address marine conservation, the development of marine protected areas (MPAs) has received the least attention.

One reason for this neglect has been the difficulty in translating our well-established approaches for protection in terrestrial environments into the marine context. Setting a few boundaries will not prevent life nor wastes from flowing in and out of a marine sanctuary. However, it has become apparent gradually that these problems are not unique to the marine environment—that many of our terrestrial parks suffer from trans-boundary effects. Further knowledge of marine environments has also indicated the importance of designating specific areas for the protection of habitat and biodiversity both for their own value and also as a step towards maintaining viable fisheries.

For international purposes, marine protected areas are defined as 'Any area of intertidal or subtidal terrain, together with its overlying waters and associated flora, fauna, historical and cultural features, which has been reserved by legislation or other effective means to protect part or all of the enclosed environment.' (Kelleher and Rechia, 1998). The potential contributions of MPAs include:

- protection of marine biodiversity, representative ecosystems and special natural features (Sobel, 1993);
- support rebuilding of depleted fish stocks, particularly groundfish, by protecting spawning and nursery grounds (e.g., see Wallace et al., 1998);
- insurance against current inadequate management of marine resources;
- provision of benchmark sites against which to evaluate human impacts elsewhere and undertake scientific research;
- recognition of cultural links of coastal communities to biodiversity; and
- provision of opportunities for recreation and education.

Over 1,300 MPAs have been established in different countries throughout the world. The effectiveness of marine reserves in providing for the benefits mentioned above is largely conditional on size, the kinds of activities allowed within the borders, and the vulnerability to influences from outside, and ability to mitigate these.

THE CANADIAN CONTEXT

Canada has the longest coastline of any country in the world and the second-largest area of continental shelf. For at least 30 years Canada has sought to gradually extend its jurisdiction over these waters and was an enthusiastic and significant contributor to the UN Law of the Sea Convention between 1974 and 1982. Canada now has an exclusive economic zone (EEZ) that extends to 200 nautical miles (370.4 km) offshore in three oceans and covers over five million square kilometers, some 1.3 per cent of the world's oceans. This vast area with its diversity of habitats gives rise to a spectacular marine environment wherein all major groups of marine organisms are represented. There are some 1,100 species of fish and many globally important populations of marine mammals, including gray, bowhead, right, beluga, minke, humpback, and killer whales. Unfortunately several of these species are also on Canada's endangered lists (COSEWIC, 2000), including the beluga, bowhead, northern right, and Georgia Strait killer whales.

This biophysical diversity is paralleled by the jurisdictional complexity typical of Canada, with its multiple, overlapping obligations. The federal government, for example, is empowered to deal with navigation, fisheries, and general law-making and has generated a raft of legislation (e.g., the Fisheries Act, the Canada Shipping Act, the Canadian Environmental Protection Act, the Coastal Fisheries Protection Act) to enable it to do so. However, coastal provinces also have considerable influence and have jurisdiction over such activities as aquaculture, fish processing and marketing, and ocean-bed mining and drilling. In offshore areas the seabed falls under federal jurisdiction, but in 'internal' waters, under provincial. A 'federal' gray whale can enter a provincial marine park, and while still federal in the water column it may disturb the provincial substrate and eat a provincially protected amphipod that spent a short time as a free-swimming federally controlled larva, itself subsisting on federally supplied detritus from the water column. The gray whales can in subsequent years enter a biosphere reserve in Mexico, a port authority in California, cross federal and state marine protected areas, become a target for Makah traditional fisheries, or even become a member of the IWC sanctioned hunt in the Chuckchi Sea. Or wash up in a municipality on southern Vancouver Island and confound authorities as to who exactly is responsible for disposing of this once great and wonderful creature.

MPA PROGRAMS IN CANADA

The complexity is further compounded by the profusion of legislation at both federal and provincial levels for MPA establishment. At the federal level not one, but three agencies hold this mandate. Many of the 11 provinces having coastal waters also have multiple applicable legislation. Estimates suggest that Canada has some 155 protected areas with a marine component (Day and Roff, 2000).

Federal Initiatives

At the federal level three agencies have the power to establish some form of areal marine protection: Fisheries and Oceans Canada (DFO), Environment Canada, and Parks Canada. Table 14.1 summarizes the various agencies and the legislative tools at their disposal to designate protection. Fisheries and Oceans Canada through the Oceans Act (1997) is the lead agency in developing and implementing Canadian strategy for marine and coastal conservation, protection, and management (section 29). The Act also allocates powers of co-ordination to DFO to develop integrated coastal zone management plans in sections 31 and 32. A national steering committee co-ordinates the MPA programs of the three agencies.

TABLE 14.1 Federal Statutory Powers for Protecting Marine Areas

Agency	Legislative Tools	Designations	Mandate
Fisheries and Oceans Canada	Oceans Act	Marine Protected Areas	To protect and conserve: • fisheries resources, including marine mammals and their habitats; • endangered or threatened species and their habitats; • unique habitats; • areas of high biodiversity or biological productivity; and, • areas for scientific and research purposes.
	Fisheries Act	Fisheries Closures	Conservation mandate to manage and regulate fisheries, conserve and protect fish, protect fish habitat, and prevent pollution of waters frequented by fish.
Environment Canada	Canada Wildlife Act	National Wildlife Areas Marine Wildlife Areas	To protect and conserve marine areas that are nationally or internationally significant for all wildlife but focusing on migratory birds.
	Migratory Birds Convention Act	Migratory Bird Sanctuaries	To protect coastal and marine habitats that are heavily used by birds for breeding, feeding, migration, and overwintering.
Parks Canada	National Parks Act Proposed Marine Conservation Areas Act	National Park National Marine Conservation Areas	To protect and conserve for all time marine conservation areas of Canadian significance that are representative of the 29 Natural Marine Regions of Canada, and to encourage public understanding, appreciation, and enjoyment.

SOURCE: Government of Canada (1998).

Parks Canada

As can be seen from Table 14.1 the mandate of Parks Canada differs from that of the other federal agencies in its explicit statement regarding the encouragement of public understanding, appreciation, and enjoyment. DFO and Environment Canada are concerned particularly with conservation. Furthermore, Parks Canada has a specific

1 Beaufort Sea
2 Northern Arctic
3 Viscount Melville Sound
4 Queen Maud Gulf
5 Lancaster Sound
6 Eastern Baffin Island Shelf
7 Fox Basin
8 Davis and Hudson Straits
9 Hudson Bay
10 James Bay

Atlantic Ocean

21 North Labrador Shelf
22 South Labrador Shelf
23 Grand Banks
24 Laurentian Trough
25 Scotian Shelf
26 Bay of Fundy
27 Magdalene Shallows
28 North Gulf Shelf
29 St Lawrence River Estuary

Pacific Ocean

11 Hecate Strait
12 West Queen Charlotte Islands
13 Queen Charlotte Sound
14 West Vancouver Island Shelf
15 Strait of Georgia

Great Lakes

16 Lake Superior
17 Georgian Bay
18 Lake Huron
19 Lake Erie
20 Lake Ontario

FIGURE 14.1 Map of Parks Canada's marine natural regions.

goal of establishing a system of national marine conservation areas with each of the 29 defined marine natural regions (Figure 14.1) represented by one or more protected areas (Mercier and Mondor, 1995). In 1994 Parks Canada also produced a revised National Marine Conservation Areas Policy (Ministry of Supply and Services 1994) in which it is emphasized that, unlike their terrestrial counterparts, National Marine Conservation Areas (NMCAs) are managed for 'sustainable use' rather than for the strict protection of their ecological integrity. They will be managed on a partnership basis with local stakeholders, allowing most existing extractive uses to continue. Furthermore, unlike terrestrial parks, other agencies would have jurisdiction within the NMCAs for managing renewable marine resources and navigation and shipping, although the federal government possesses clear title to all coastal and submerged lands within an NMCA.

Within these multiple-use areas there will also be zones where higher levels of protection may be achieved. A three-tier zoning system has been proposed with a preservation zone where renewable resource harvesting and permanent facilities will not be allowed, nor will visitor use, under normal circumstances. Zone II will be a Natural Environment zone where renewable resource harvesting activities, including recreational hunting and fishing, will be prohibited. Research, public education, and low-intensity recreation will take place with minimal facility development. Zone III will see a wide variety of uses permitted consistent with maintaining ecosystem structure and function. Most traditional fisheries will be allowed to continue, although Parks Canada will negotiate fisheries management plans with DFO in and around NMCAs. Only ocean waste-disposal, seabed mining, and oil and gas extraction will be totally prohibited.

Zoning and other regulations will be specified in NMCA management plans, which are to be produced within five years of enactment and reviewed and tabled in Parliament every five years subsequently. These plans will specify provisions for ecosystem management, visitor use, protection, and zoning with ecosystem management and the precautionary principle being the main foundations. An Advisory Committee will be struck for each NMCA to advise the Minister on the management plan.

In June 1998 the Act to establish NMCAs was given its first reading in the House of Commons. but not passed into legislation before the general election in 2000. It has been brought forward again but still has not been enacted. Planning studies currently are underway to establish NMCAs in a number of locations including western Lake Superior, Gwaii Hanaas, and the southern Strait of Georgia in BC.

Although currently there are no legally established NMCAs, there is some marine representation within the national park system. Canada's first National Marine Park was established on 1 December 1987 through an agreement between Canada and the Province of Ontario. The site, Fathom Five, was formerly a provincial park that was transferred to federal jurisdiction when the Bruce Peninsula National Park was founded on adjacent lands. This site has long been recognized as important for its cultural significance in terms of shipwrecks and recreational diving. The Saguenay-St Lawrence Marine Park is an MPA with its own unique legislation, the Saguenay-St Lawrence Marine Park Act. Also, four marine protected areas contiguous with terrestrial parks have been designated: Kouchibouguac in New Brunswick, Pacific Rim in British Columbia, Forillon in Quebec, and Auyuittuq on Baffin Island in Canada's eastern Arctic (Figure 14.2). As marine park initiatives, these can be seen largely as add-ons to terrestrial park programs with minimal marine preservation mandates. Where regulation has been attempted, such as limiting smelt fishermen in Kouchibouguac, protests were successful in creating a 'business as usual' situation for commercial fishermen in the park (see, e.g., Delaney et al., 1992).

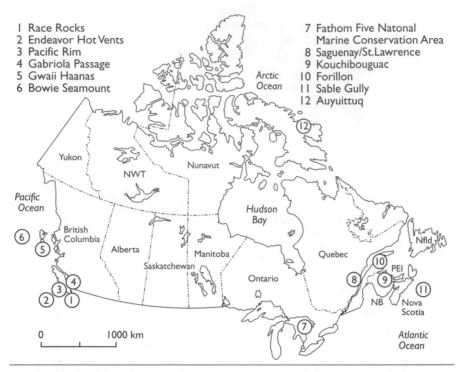

1 Race Rocks
2 Endeavor Hot Vents
3 Pacific Rim
4 Gabriola Passage
5 Gwaii Haanas
6 Bowie Seamount

7 Fathom Five Natonal
   Marine Conservation Area
8 Saguenay/St.Lawrence
9 Kouchibouguac
10 Forillon
11 Sable Gully
12 Auyuittuq

FIGURE 14.2 Marine sites mentioned in text.

FIGURE 14.3 Bonavista Bay, Newfoundland. Difficulties have been encountered in establishing national parks and implementing conservation measures wherever local communities have a strong fishing tradition. *Photo: P. Dearden.*

BOX 14.1 Proposed NMCA at Newfoundland's Bonavista-Notre Dame Bays

The Bonavista and Notre Dame Bays marine area was selected as the representative site of the Newfoundland Shelf region for consideration as a possible National Marine Conservation Area. In February 1997 the federal and provincial governments launched a feasibility study for a proposed NMCA of the two bays. An advisory committee comprised of professional fishermen, representatives of the aquaculture industry, fish processors, members of economic development boards, and residents of both bays was formed to assess the feasibility of the NMCA undertaking.

In March 1999, this committee expressed concerns on behalf of residents of the local communities, and voted against the establishment of the NMCA. The government made the decision to discontinue the feasibility study as there was not sufficient support to proceed.

The local communities felt that once the NMCA act is passed into legislation, fisheries might be curtailed by Parks Canada and this would negatively impact on their families and communities by threatening their livelihoods. Aquaculturists believed the NMCA to be incompatible with the objectives of their industry. The overall response was that the establishment of an NMCA in the region would pose a threat to the long-term sustainability of the aquaculture and fishery industries in Newfoundland. Local fishermen suggested that because they are already aware of the need for conservation and are involved in various conservation initiatives such as lobster enhancement and conservation harvesting practices, the creation of an NMCA in the area is not necessary.

The failure of the Bonnavista Bay initiative has been analyzed in more detail by Lien (1999). The analysis suggests that many factors concerned with the human dimensions of park establishment came together, acted in a synergistic way and made further development of the initiative difficult. This experience is not unique to Canada and emphasizes the need to have a well-resourced and designed consultative process if support is to be forthcoming from local communities (Kelleher, 1999).

Presently the Newfoundland Shelf area is not represented in the marine conservation area system. Following the failure of this project, Parks Canada reported that other options for representing this marine region will be investigated in due course.

SOURCE: Parks Canada:
<http://parkscanada.pch.gc.ca/marine/.ca/nature/who/nwa/coburg/ df07s03.en.html>
The Telegram (St John's), 11 March 1999 Final Edition p.4. Lien (1999).

Fisheries and Oceans Canada

Fisheries and Oceans has adopted many of the same approaches as Parks Canada, in that NMCAs will be oriented towards sustainable use and established through partnerships. They have also added the complete lexicon of approaches currently fashionable in resource management including 'adaptive management, precautionary approach, integrated management, ecosystem-based and regional flexibility' (Fisheries and Oceans, 1997). It remains to be seen quite how these approaches will be implemented.

FIGURE 14.4 Whale-watchers at Saguenay Fiord, Quebec. The area provides critical habitat for several whale species and supports a sizable regional income from whale-watching. It remains to be seen whether national park designation can be used effectively to prevent habitat deterioration through pollution in the area. *Photo: P. Dearden.*

There is a similar lack of certitude regarding NMCA location in that, unlike Parks Canada, there is no pre-determined goal of representing different regions. Instead areas will be established in terms of nominations that are forthcoming from regional groups, supplemented by regional overviews undertaken by technical interdisciplinary teams. An area identification list (AIL) will be produced of various nominees that have met—yet to be defined—criteria. These will then be subject to more intensive examination to choose between candidate areas. No timetable has been set for this process.

Similar to the Parks Canada approach, it is envisioned that there will be internal zoning within the protected area allowing various levels of resource extraction. The Oceans Act provides for regulations to manage NMCAs, but does not specify what these are, leaving wide latitude for interpretation and regional flexibility. Management plans for individual MPAs will provide details on protection standards, regulations, permissible activities, and enforcement. A management plan is required before an area can be designated under the Oceans Act. The lack of national standards raises the quintessentially Canadian debate about whether the program is in fact 'national' at all, or might just as well be left to provincial jurisdiction.

In line with DFO's emphasis on learning by doing, they established five pilot MPAs. These have no formal legal designation but were selected as promising sites where aspects of the national framework can be tested and refined. The only site on the Atlantic coast is Sable Gully (Box 14.2).

BOX 14.2 Sable Gully

Sable Gully is the largest underwater canyon in eastern Canada. The Gully is located approximately 200 km off the coast of Nova Scotia, at the edge of the Scotian Shelf where the sea floor suddenly drops to over two km in depth. Over 70 km long and 20 km wide, this area is home to many interesting and unusual species. The gully is a productive ecosystem that supports a diversity of marine organisms. The world's deepest diving whale, the bottlenose whale, is a 'vulnerable' species that lives in the gully year round (Fauchner and Whitehead, 1995). Fin whales and Northwest Atlantic blue whales, both also classified as 'vulnerable' by COSEWIC, make use of the gully throughout the year. Deep sea corals are a significant feature of the benthic fauna in the area, and nine species are confirmed to live in the gully. The occurrence of corals in such conditions provides exceptional opportunities for the study of these animals

Sable Gully is a unique ecological site that has attracted the attention of a wide range of government agencies, researchers, area resource industries, and conservationists. In December 1998, Sable Gully was announced as an area of interest under the Marine Protected Area program of DFO. Typically, MPAs in Canada and throughout the world have been located in coastal areas. Sable Gully is offshore, which presents unique challenges for management, research, and monitoring.

SOURCE: Sable Gully CD

Endorsement of Sable Gully Conservation Strategy, David Anderson, Halifax, NS. 3 Dec.1998, <www.ncr.dfo.ca/communic/speech/1998/dec3_e.htm>

On the west coast of Canada the sites are at Gabriola Passage off Nanaimo, Race Rocks off the southern tip of Vancouver Island, and two offshore sites, the Endeavour Hot Vents, 250 km southwest of Victoria, and the Bowie Seamount, 180 km west of the Queen Charlotte Islands. An announcement was made on 15 September 2000 that Race Rocks would be declared Canada's first MPA under the Oceans Act. However, a year later the formal designation had yet to be made. The hot vents are important sites for marine biodiversity. Of 236 species that have been collected at the vents, 223 were previously unknown to science, and represent at least 22 new families and 100 new genera. The food chains around the vents rely not on the sun for energy supply, as do most other species, but on bacteria that make carbon compounds from the sulphur-rich emissions. Seamounts are also important sites for marine biodiversity, rising more than 1,000 metres from the surrounding ocean floor and providing feeding sites of great importance to migratory seabirds and distinctive rockfish communities. Bowie Seamount rises to within 40 metres of the surface from depths of over 3300 m. In addition to these pilot sites two areas in the Maritimes have also been announced as Areas of Interest (MPAs), the first step in DFOs process to establish MPAs. The first of these is at Basin Head in PEI and the second is the Musquash Estuary in

New Brunswick. Planning Groups are now working at these sites with DFO officials to develop management plans and gather the information necessary for the areas to become formally designated under the Oceans Act.

Environment Canada

The main focus of the third federal component, Environment Canada, (Table 14.1) is wildlife, and particularly migratory bird species (Zurbrigg, 1996). The programs are administered by the Canadian Wildlife Service (CWS) and include designations for marine areas as National Wildlife Areas (NWAs) and Protected Marine Areas (PMAs)

BOX 14.3 Nirjutiqawik National Wildlife Area

Nirjutiqawik National Wildlife Area is located approximately 20 km off the south-eastern tip of Ellesmere Island. This NWA includes Coburg Island, the Princess Charlotte Monument, and all the water within a 10-km radius. The total area of Nirjutiqawik is 1650 sq. km, 78 per cent of which is marine based.

Approximately 65 per cent of Coburg Island is covered in glaciers and icefields, and the remaining terrain is rugged, mountainous highlands with peaks reaching more than 800 m above sea level. While extensive coastal glaciation has marked the western and northern sides of the island, the eastern and southern borders are covered in steep coastal cliffs. These cliffs, which range from 150 to 300 m, offer ideal habitat for the estimated 385,000 seabirds that nest in this NWA.

Local Inuit residents have long valued Coburg Island and the surrounding marine area because of its importance to their seal and polar bear hunts. The Canadian Wildlife Service began seabird research on Coburg Island in 1972, and recognized the biological importance of the region in 1975 when it was designated as an International Biological Program Site. Coburg Island was declared a Key Migratory Bird Habitat Site by the CWS in 1984.

The local residents wished to see some form of protection for the area's seabird colonies, marine mammal populations, and surrounding waters. It was suggested in 1989 that the CWS and local community work together to develop a strategy for protection, and subsequently, the local Hunters and Trappers Association recommended that Coburg Island and surrounding environment be protected as a National Wildlife Area. Regional and national Inuit associations, various government departments and the private sector have since supported the initiative, and the Nirjutiqawik NWS was officially created in 1995. A local management committee for the area has been formed, and negotiations with local Inuit on an Impacts and Benefits Agreement have taken place. To ensure effective management, a key component of the planning process for this NWA has involved the compilation of Inuit history of the area.

SOURCE: Environment Canada
<www.pnr-rpnec.gc.ca/nature/whp/nwa/coburg/df07s03.en.html>

under the Canada Wildlife Act, and migratory bird sanctuaries (MBSs) under the Migratory Birds Convention Act of 1917 and 1994. NWAs must be owned by, or leased to, the federal government and might include a wide range of habitat types from uplands through to marine areas up to 12 nautical miles (22.29 km) from shore. PMAs extend this jurisdiction to the 200-mile (370.4 km) limit, where the Minister may purchase, acquire or lease 'lands for wildlife research, conservation or interpretation of migratory birds or other bird species' (CWS, 1999). MBSs differ in that federal ownership is not required. Habitats are mainly coastal, including marine waters surrounding islands.

Although in the future these designations are not expected to play a major role in marine areal protection, they currently account for over 75 per cent of the marine habitats protected. There are 13 (out of 49) NWAs with marine components (see Box 14.3), and 56 (out of 98) MBSs—adding up to a total of over three million ha protected. Unfortunately over 95 per cent of this is concentrated in the Arctic, and as of yet no PMAs have been designated, although CWS is currently in the process of developing a set of national criteria to identify areas of interest. There is not even a minimum national set of regulations that apply to extractive activities, as regulations are developed on a site-by-site basis. Furthermore, despite the large areas involved, only one person a year is currently dedicated to MPAs (CWS, 1999).

Provincial Initiatives

In addition to this complex federal scene, provincial jurisdictions have been active in trying to create MPAs. Eleven of the 13 jurisdictions have coastal components, and all cannot be reviewed here. For the most part, provincial initiatives have tended to be fairly small and often attached to the coastal components of coastal provincial park systems. Table 14.2 shows the various provincial statutes that have been used for areal protection of the marine environment in BC. The Ecological Reserves Act and Parks Act are most significant. The Ecological Reserves program is oriented strictly towards a preservation mandate with no special orientation towards the marine environment. Nonetheless a substantial number of the Reserves (25) have a marine-oriented component and some also include subtidal components. They are, however, quite small. The provincial park system similarly has parks that include marine components (69), but no separate marine legislation exists at the provincial level for marine designations.

In 1994 an inter-governmental Marine Protected Areas Working Group and a senior Steering Committee were formed to develop a more integrated approach to protected area planning on the Pacific coast. In addition to Parks Canada, DFO and BC Parks, the BC Land Use Co-ordination Office (LUCO) and the BC Ministry of Agriculture, Fisheries, and Food were invited to join the Working Group. The Group organized a series of multi-stakeholder forums to gather input and feedback regarding key questions on the nature of MPAs and the process by which they should be established. The main output of the Working Group's deliberations is a paper (Government of Canada and Government of BC, 1998), which outlines the joint governmental approach to creating a system of MPAs by the year 2010. Three impor-

TABLE 14.2 Provincial Statutory Powers for Protecting Marine Areas in BC

Agency	Legislative Tools	Designations	Mandate
Ministry of Environment, Lands and Parks	Ecological Reserve Act	Ecological Reserves	To protect: • representative examples of BC's marine environment; • rare, endangered, or sensitive species or habitats; • unique, outstanding, or special features; and, • areas for scientific research and marine awareness.
	Parks Act	Provincial Parks	To protect: • representative examples of marine diversity, recreational, and cultural heritage; and • special natural, cultural heritage and recreational features. To serve a variety of outdoor recreation functions including: • enhancing major tourism travel routes; and • providing attractions for outdoor holiday destinations.
	Wildlife Act	Wildlife Management	To conserve and manage areas of of importance to fish and wildlife and to protect endangered or threatened species and their habitats, whether resident or migratory, of regional, national, or global significance.
	Environment and Land Use Act	'Protected Areas'	To protect: • representative examples of marine diversity, recreational and cultural heritage; and • special natural, cultural heritage, and recreational features.

SOURCE: Government of British Columbia, 1998.

tant elements provide the corner stone: a joint federal-provincial approach, shared decision-making with the public, and building a comprehensive system of Marine Protected Areas by 2010. The Marine Protected Areas so created would:

- be defined in law by one or more of the statutes shown in Tables 14.1 and 14.2;
- protect some, but not necessarily all, elements of the marine environment in the MPA;
- ensure minimum protection standards prohibiting ocean dumping, dredging, and exploration for the development of non-renewable resources. Above these minimums levels, protection would vary from area to area and also within areas.

The MPA system will be delivered as part of a comprehensive coastal planning process aimed at ensuring ecological, social, and economic sustainability. Six planning regions have been identified, and the first step in establishing MPAs would be the nomination of key areas within each planning region by stakeholders or technical committees for evaluation. The discussion paper solicits feedback and it is hoped that revisions occur before a final strategy is implemented. For example, there needs to be greater clarification of the relative priorities of the objectives that are listed above, emphasizing that the primary reason for the creation of Marine Protected Areas is to protect biodiversity and ecosystem processes. The minimum standards to ensure that this occurs are not very ambitious. There is clear evidence, for example, that bottom trawling is highly disruptive of marine ecosystems (see, for example, Watling and Norse, 1998), and yet it is not necessarily excluded. The same claim can be made for other activities, such as finfish aquaculture. The process for establishment also lacks clarity. There appears to be no coast-wide process that would assess the current status of protection and where there are gaps from the standpoint of conservation (see, for example, Ray and McCormick-Ray, 1995). The founding of protected areas is also tied to broader marine planning processes, which in theory is good, but in practice may lead to long delays in MPA establishment. There needs to be a separate process for the creation of MPAs that can proceed even in the absence of such broader processes.

It is intended that the marine protected area designations be embedded within a broader coastal zone planning process. At the moment such a process is underway within the so-called central coast area Land and Resources Management Plan (LRMP). Within this process the Land Use Co-ordination Office (LUCO) has the lead provincial role and Fisheries and Oceans Canada the lead federal role. The goal is to develop a consensus-based coastal nearshore planning process, which will meet the present and future needs of the area. LUCO will concentrate on the land and nearshore portions, while Fisheries and Oceans has started an Integrated Coastal Zone Management program (ICZM), which will address marine areas as well as the coastal zone. In both cases a common planning approach will be followed, including issue and value identification, general management objectives specification, determination of strategic-level zones and sub-zones, and specific management prescriptions will be followed. The MPA strategy discussed earlier will provide policy input to assist in making recommendations for coastal marine protected areas within this broader process, whereas the ICZM process will deal with the offshore component.

ISSUES

Speed of Establishment

Perhaps the most fundamental problem besetting MPAs in Canada is that we have so few, and of those we have perhaps only the Saguenay-St Lawrence really qualifies, and even here commercial and recreational fisheries and aquaculture continue (Dionne, 1995). Fathom Five is a nice dive site, but is not a major global repository for marine biodiversity. Gwaii Hanaas has yet to be declared. Most of the other sites held either provincially or by the CWS have little legal protection from destructive activities, and the DFO has only non-legislated pilot sites. Patient observers might comment that we are in a waiting period while new sites are designated. The less patient will point out that this waiting period is now almost 20 years long since the MPA initiative began at the federal level, and we are now no further ahead: meanwhile, the quality of the marine environment continues to deteriorate. It was almost a decade ago that the Canadian Council of Ministers of the Environment, Canadian Parks Ministers Council of Canada, and Wildlife Ministers' Council of Canada signed the Tri-Council statement of Commitment to 'accelerate the protection of areas representative of Canada's marine natural regions.' Nothing has been accomplished since in terms of actual increased protection on the ground. The political will to create effective MPAs will only materialize under strong and constant public pressure.

Level of Protection

Current levels of protection in existing MPAs are inadequate to ensure ecological integrity. Of the 106 MPAs in BC, for example, 90 per cent provide little or no ecosystem protection (MLSS, n.d.). Large-scale habitat disturbance such as that caused by dredging, mining, oil or gas drilling, dumping, bottom trawling, dragging, finfish aquaculture, or other large-scale extractive activities have to be excluded if MPAs are to achieve minimum protection standards. Watling and Norse (1998), for example, compare the impacts of bottom trawling with that of clear-cutting and conclude that it is both more destructive and more widespread. Yet bottom trawling is not prohibited from most existing nor planned MPAs in Canada. Few studies exist of the impacts on marine life of different kinds of protective designation. One study by Wallace (1999) on abalone populations within different reserve types on Vancouver Island showed a clear relationship between strict protection over longer time periods and size and abundance of animals.

Stakeholder Involvement

The level of protection is often a function of local wishes. Globally, protected area agencies are falling over backwards to 'include the local people'. It has become, and deservedly so, the mantra of the new century. Many parks were created in the days of Big Government, and local populations had little say in their establishment, and often contributed subsequently to making the park as ineffective as possible. Those times are gone. There is a difference, however, in paying due heed to local stakeholders and in compromising the fundamental goals of protected area establishment as a common resource for the good of all of society both now and in the future. In their efforts to appease local stakeholders, protected agencies are now reluctant to emphasize their responsibilities to a broader range of stakeholders. As a result, MPAs frequently are stymied, such as in the attempts by Parks Canada to establish them in the West Isles in New Brunswick and also in Bonavista/Notre Dame Bay in Newfoundland, due to objections from local resource extractors. It is doubtful whether scarcely a terrestrial park would have been created anywhere in the country had this been the basis for decision-making, as some segment of society is almost always involved with resource extraction in the area. Indeed, Yellowstone, the world's first national park would never have been established had the government of the US listened to the local stakeholders, who were there to slaughter the last of the mighty plains bison.

Even where MPA establishment might run the gauntlet of local opposition, all legislation allows such flexibility in terms of regulations, that what the park might actually at last manage to protect might be but a sad reminder of what could have been. When the Memorandum of Understanding was signed to establish Pacific Rim National Park Reserve, for example, crab fishing was allowed to continue, and has now grown to an extractive industry five times its original size. This kind of situation might in fact be more damaging than not having a park in the first place. When people see a green space on the map, they assume that the resources are protected from extraction. Their consciences are assuaged. With the compromises permissible under existing MPA legislation little such protection may be in place, but the public is misled into thinking that good conservation measures are in place.

The foregoing is not to argue against local input by resource extractors into MPA designation and management, but to point out that broader societal responsibilities of protected area agencies should not be uniformly sacrificed to the former as is currently the case. This situation is not unique to Canada (see Dearden, in press), nor to MPAs. As Ray and McCormick-Ray (1995: 37) point out by: 'Unfortunately, there is an expedient tendency to speak to the lowest common denominator in proposing MPAs (marine and estuarine protected areas) and their management, resulting from consensus-based participatory processes. This is self-defeating in the end, perhaps sooner than later.' However, it should be emphasized that the optimal situation is to establish MPAs that are ecologically viable and yet enjoy strong support from local communities. A case-sensitive approach is called for, but one that holds strong to conservation principles, one that invests in conservation education and actively tries to develop sustainable alternative futures for communities whose economic livelihoods are threatened.

System Plan

A key question for MPAs is site selection. This should hinge on the more fundamental question of what are we trying to protect and why. Parks Canada is the only agency to have adopted a system's framework to use regional representation as a main tool to guide site selection. There are, however, questions about whether this is the most effective classification system on which to base representation, with WWF proposing an alternative system (Day and Roff, 2000) and more detailed systems emerging at the provincial level (see, for example, Zacharias et al., 1998). The agency with the lead role in MPA establishment, DFO, has no such systems plan. This opens selection to many different kinds of influence that might favour, for example, sites about which more is known, or sites that might emphasize benefits to local fisheries rather than ecological criteria, sites that benefit commercial species rather than non-commercial species, or simply sites that are easy to establish rather than those that need to be established. A more explicit and comprehensive systems plan, based on sound ecological criteria is needed that all agencies with MPA interests can adopt.

Permeability

Although trans-boundary effects have become increasingly acknowledged in terrestrial parks, there is no doubt that the permeability of MPA boundaries is far higher. This creates great management challenges as species are more mobile and the reserves often cannot protect all life phases of any given organism (Allison et al., 1998). Indeed for highly migratory and mobile species, MPAs may afford little realistic protection (Duffus and Dearden, 1995, Clay, 1999). MPAs are also more vulnerable to trans-boundary flows from outside the reserve. When an oil spill occurred off the coast of the State of Washington the boundaries of Pacific Rim National Park Reserve did not prevent the 875,000 liters of oil killing 46,000 birds and soiling the beaches of the park. The Saguenay-St Lawrence MPA is downstream from some of the most polluted waters in North America. MPAs can only be as healthy as the surrounding waters to which they are connected.

The porous nature of MPA boundaries puts an even greater emphasis on ecosystem-based management (Chapter 12) than in terrestrial parks. In practice this means, for example, that attention must be devoted to establishing large, highly-protected areas and that these must be buffered by areas with less stringent protection. Sobel (1995) argues that one of the most common mistakes is to establish core areas that are too small and then to wonder why they are not effective in meeting their goals.

One well-known mechanism for provision of core and buffer zone components is the biosphere reserve. Both the new Clayoquot and Mt Arrowsmith Biosphere Reserves on Vancouver Island include marine areas, but are still too new to assess how effective management might be. There is also an active biosphere reserve proposal for the Scotian coastal plain on the Atlantic coast (Miller et al., 1999).

Connectivity

Thinking must progress beyond individual reserves to networks of reserves. Marine populations frequently have dispersive phases with little connection between reproduction and recruitment. It is therefore important to consider these kinds of movements and their temporal and spatial scale and the kinds of connectivity that are required to maintain links between different habitats. For this reason, marine park planners often favour several small over one large reserve, if a choice has to be made (Done, 1998).

Management Experience

Parks Canada is the oldest Parks Service in the world (Chapter 2). Despite recent criticisms (Chapter 9) they generally have a great deal of experience in managing terrestrial parks. Such is not the case in regard to the marine environment, nor is it the case with the other involved agencies. There is a greater wealth of experience available in other jurisdictions, such as Australia and New Zealand, and Canada can profitably draw on this experience.

One implication of this lack of management experience in the marine environment is the need to take an adaptive approach to management, as emphasized by the Ecological Integrity Panel (Parks Canada Agency, 2000) and discussed in more detail in Chapter 5. Adaptive management is particularly appropriate where levels of uncertainty are high. Management actions are undertaken as experiments from which we learn and modify our actions as a result of learning from them. Day (2000) has usefully summarized some of the learning experiences of the Great Barrier Reef Marine Authority over the last 25 years. They found that the original zoning system was inadequate to protect the range of biodiversity on the Reef and have had to devise more refined zoning systems, detailed management plans and a new Representative Areas Program (RAP), to adjust to these inadequacies. Canada can build on these experiences as we start our own adaptive management program with full attention to the Precautionary Principle (Lauck, et al., 1998).

Lack of Information and Monitoring Systems

MPAs suffer even more than their terrestrial counterparts from a lack of knowledge of their ecosystem functioning. Research needs to be promoted that can assist in greater understanding of these ecosystems as well as help guide management activities and implement an adaptive management approach. In particular, managers need to know (Kelleher, 1999):

- What is the state of the ecosystem, and particularly its dominant biota, rare and endangered species, ecological processes (such as sedimentation, absorption of nutrients, and toxic substances) and ecological states (such as water temperature and quality)?
- What are the pressures on the system, whether natural (such as, El Niño, severe storms) or human caused (such as, habitat destruction, pollution)?
- What is the range of management responses and what are the implications of each?
- Are management activities having the desired response and, if not, how should management be modified?
- Is management meeting objectives?

In order to answer these kinds of questions a mixture of monitoring, resource assessment and research activities is required (Table 14.3). Few agencies are equipped either in terms of knowledge base or infrastructure to answer all these questions, and this deficiency, of necessity, requires building links with the scientific community (Harding and Wilson, 1995). Again, this is a major thrust of the Ecological Integrity

TABLE 14.3 Resource Assessment, Applied Research, and Monitoring

Tools	Examples of use of the tool in Marine Park management
Monitoring	• A series of measurements that are repeated on the same site or individuals over a period of time. • Quantifying levels and types of activity in an area and changes in these (or the impacts of particular activities) over time. • Evaluating success and impacts of management strategies.
Resource assessment	• Finding out what is there and what is special about an area or resource. • Assessing the uses and values of an area, or the impacts for planning. • Assimilating the results of relevant research, monitoring, socio-economic, political, and other relevant information to assess trends and the need for adapting management strategies.
Research	• Assessing the specific causes of observed changes in areas or to resources. • Understanding the factors that control the distribution and abundance of animal and plant resources. • Establishing the existence of links between activities and impacts on an area or resource.

SOURCE: After Kenchington and Ch'ng (1994).

report (Parks Canada Agency, 2000), but needs particular development within the MPA sphere. Agencies should also not overlook the involvement of local community groups in these activities. Not only can they have valuable local knowledge to include (Neis, 1995), but often have resources they can make available. As communities are often affected by management regulations that emanate from research activities, understanding can be increased by inclusion at the earliest stages.

Lack of Resources

Despite Canada's pride regarding the extent of our coastline and continental shelf, despite Parks Canada's global reputation as the oldest and one of the best national park services in the world, despite public awareness of the plight of our fisheries on both coasts and the need for more effective conservation, the level of resources accorded to MPA programs is minimal. With the best intentions in the world, agencies concerned with the establishment and management of MPAs cannot perform the task satisfactorily if they are chronically under-financed. Only public pressure on political masters is likely to solve this problem.

CONCLUSIONS

The fundamental conclusion from the foregoing is that we are not doing very well. Protection of the marine environment is one of the weakest, if not the weakest, aspect of Canada's protected area programs. In British Columbia, for example, Zacharias and

BOX 14.4 Connected Thinking: The 'Baja to Bering' Initiative

The high connectivity of the marine environment requires that conservation initiatives occur over large spaces through linked initiatives. This is the converse of what has happened in the past, where MPAs have been small, isolated, and designated with no consideration for the links between them. One of the most ambitious of connectivity schemes has been suggested by the Canadian Parks and Wilderness Society (CPAWS), which is promoting the concept of a series of linked marine reserves extending from Mexico to the Arctic, the so-called 'Baja to Bering' initiative (Jessen and Lerch, 1999). This distance, over 20,000 km, includes some of the most productive and diverse marine habitats in the world and is also the home range of the Pacific Gray whale that migrates along this route every year. The initiative seeks to:

- establish a representative network of large core MPAs, with the highest level of protection possible, including substantial no-take areas;
- ensure the maintenance of ecological linkages and functional habitat connections between these core protected areas; and
- identify and protect the habitat requirements of keystone species in the marine environment.

FIGURE 14.5 A Gray whale migrating through Pacific Rim National Park Reserve.

FIGURE 14.6 Killer whale (A38) at Robson Bight Ecological Reserve, BC. Can marine protected areas help fulfill conservation goals for wide-ranging species such as whales?

Howes (1998) calculated that a grand total of 1.25 per cent of the marine area was in some form of protective designation (Tables 14.1 and 14.2), and many would dispute whether even these are afforded any real protection. Furthermore, in 20 years of trying to establish a national MPA program we have established really only one such park, the Saguenay-St Lawrence. Even here, the level of protection is minimal, as it is in the proposed and established programs of the major agencies. They plead that such flexibility is necessary in such a diverse country. Indeed, it might well be. But it also raises the spectre that even when new areas are designated they will be mere 'paper' parks rather than performing their fundamental role in the protection of marine biodiversity. The failure to pass the Marine Conservation Areas Act before Parliament dissolved in 2000 may not be a bad thing in some people's eyes. Parks Canada still has a mandate to establish marine conservation areas under both the Parks Canada Agency Act and the Department of Canadian Heritage Act, and could proceed under the National Parks Act or site-specific legislation, such as occurred in the Saguenay.

Public apathy, stemming from the still mistaken perception of the vastness of the oceans, is at least partially responsible for this lack of progress. As Rachel Carson (1961: xi) stated almost 40 years ago in the preface of her classic work, *The Sea Around Us:*

> Although man's record as a steward of the natural resources of the earth has been
> a discouraging one, there has long been a certain comfort in the belief that the sea,
> at least, was inviolate, beyond man's ability to change and despoil. But, this belief,
> unfortunately, has proved to be naive. (Carson, 1961: xi)

Not only do we need to establish MPAs and ensure that they have strong protection, but we also need to ensure that they play a major educational role in raising public awareness of the complexities of the seas and our dependence upon their environmental processes. Given the publicity accorded to the Parks Canada Ecological Integrity Panel and its report (Parks Canada Agency, 2000), it may well be that a marine equivalent is required to provide some much-needed stimulus to the development of Canada's MPA program.

REFERENCES

Agardy, T., ed. 1995. *The Science of Conservation in the Coastal Zone*. Gland: IUCN.

Allison, G.W., J. Lubchenco, and M.H. Carr. 1998. 'Marine Reserves are Necessary but not Sufficient for Marine Conservation', *Ecological Applications* 8: S79–S92.

Anon. 1998. 'Reef Check', *People and the Planet* 7: 5.

Canadian Wildlife Service. 1999. 'Marine Protected Areas—Opportunities and Options for the Canadian Wildlife Service', discussion paper prepared for the Marine Protected Areas Working Group. Ottawa: Environment Canada, Jan.

Carson, R. 1961. *The Sea Around Us*. Oxford: Oxford University Press.

Clay, D. 1999. 'Marine Protected Areas in Canada: An Inadequate Strategy for Bluefin Tuna (*Thunnus thynnus thynnus* L)', in *Protected Areas and the Bottom Line*. Proceedings of the 1997 Conference of the Canadian Council on Ecological Areas, Fredericton, NB. Information report MX 205E/F. Ottawa: Natural Resources Canada, 198–208.

Committee on the Status of Endangered Species in Canada (COSEWIC). 2000. *Canadian Species at Risk*. Ottawa.

Day, J.C. 2000. 'Marine Park Management and Monitoring—Lessons for Adaptive Management from the Great Barrier Reef', paper presented at SAMPAA IV Conference, Waterloo, Ont.

―――― and J.C. Roff. 2000. *Planning for Representative Marine Protected Areas: A Framework for Canada's Oceans*. Toronto: WWF.

Dearden, P. (Forthcoming). '"Dern Sai Klang": Walking the Middle Path to Biodiversity Conservation in Thailand', in Dearden, ed., *Environmental Protection and Rural Development in Thailand: Challenge and Opportunity*. Bangkok: White Lotus Press.

Delaney, G., H. Beach, M. Savoie, and F. Leblanc. 1992. 'Commercial Fishery Studies in Kouchibouguac National Park, New Brunswick, Canada', in J.H.M. Willison et al., eds, *Science and the Management of Protected Areas*. New York: Elsevier, 283–6.

Dionne, S. 1995. 'Creating the Saguenay Marine Park—A Case Study', in Shackell and Willison (1995: 189–96).

Done, T. 1998. 'Science for Management of the Great Barrier Reef', *Nature and Resources* 34: 16–29.

Duffus, D., and P. Dearden. 1995. 'Whales, Science and Protected Area Management in British Columbia, Canada', in Agardy (1995: 54–64).

Faucher, A. and H. Whitehead. 1995. 'Importance of habitat protection for the Northern Bottlenose Whale in the Gully, Nova Scotia', in N.L. Shackell and J.H.M Willison, eds, *Marine Protected Areas and Sustainable Fisheries*. Wolfville, Nova Scotia, 99–102.

Fisheries and Oceans. 1997. *An Approach to the Establishment and Management of Marine Protected Areas under the Oceans Act*. Ottawa: DFO.

Government of Canada and Government of BC. 1998. *Marine Protected Areas, A Strategy for Canada's Pacific Coast*.

Hinrichsen, D. 1998. *Coastal Waters of the World: Trends, Threats and Strategies*. Washington: Island Press.

Harding, L.E., and R.C.H. Wilson. 1995. 'Integrated Marine Ecosystem Monitoring: The Pacific Marine Ecozone Trial', in Shackell and Willison (1995: 13–20).

Jessen, S., and N. Lerch. 1999. 'Baja to the Bering Sea—A North American Marine Conservation Initiative', *Environments* 27: 67–89.

Kelleher, G. 1999. *Guidelines for Marine Protected Areas*. Gland: IUCN.

——— and C. Rechia. 1998. 'Lessons From Marine Protected Areas Around the World', *Parks* 8: 1–4.

Kenchington, R.A., and K.L. Ch'ng, eds. 1994. *Staff Training Materials for the Management of Marine Protected Areas*. East Asian Seas Action Plan. RCU/EAS Technical Report Series No 4. Bangkok: UNEP.

Lauck T., C.W. Clark, M. Mangel, and G.R Munro. 1998. 'Implementing the Precautionary Principle in Fisheries Management Through Marine Reserves', *Ecological Applications* 8: S72–S78.

Lien, J. 1999. When marine conservation efforts sink: What can be learned from the abandoned effort to examine the feasibility of a National Marine Conservation Area on the NE Coast of Newfoundland? Paper presented at the Canadian Council on Ecological Areas 16th Conference, Ottawa, 4–6 Oct.

Marine Life Sanctuaries Society (n.d.) *Deepen Your Understanding—Marine Protected Areas, A Guide to Establishing a Marine Protected Area in Your Community*.

Miller, C.A., M.M. Ravindra, and J.H. Willison. 1999. 'Towards a Scotian Coastal Plain Biosphere Reserve for Southwestern Nova Scotia', in *Protected Areas and the Bottom Line*. Proceedings of the 1997 Conference of the Canadian Council on Ecological Areas, Fredericton, NB. Information report MX 205E/F, Ottawa: Natural Resources Canada, 177–97.

Mercier, F., and C. Mondor. 1995. *Sea to Sea: Canada's National Marine Conservation System Plan*. Ottawa: Parks Canada.

Ministry of Supply and Services. 1994. *Guiding Principles and Operational Policies*. Ottawa: Parks Canada.

Neis, B. 1995. 'Fishers' Ecological Knowledge and Marine Protected Areas', in Shackell and Willison (1995: 265–72).

Parks Canada Agency. 2000. *Unimpaired for Future Generations? Protecting Ecological Integrity with Canada's National Parks*, vol. 2, *Setting a New Direction for Canada's National Parks*. Ottawa: Report of the Panel on the Ecological Integrity of Canada's National Parks.

Pauly, D., V. Christensen, J. Dalsgaard, R. Froese, and F. Torres Jr. 1998. 'Fishing Down Marine Food Webs', *Science* 279: 860–3.

Ray, C.G., and M.G. McCormick-Ray. 1995. 'Critical Habitats and Representative Systems in Marine Environments: Concepts and Procedures', in Agardy (1995: 23–40).

Shackell, N.L., and J.H.M Willison, eds. 1995. *Marine Protected Areas and Sustainable Fisheries.* Proceedings of the Third International Conference on Science and Management of Protected Areas, Wolfville, NS.

Sobel, J. 1993 'Conserving Biodiversity Through Marine Protected Areas: A Global Challenge', *Oceanus* 36: 19–26.

———. 1995. 'Application of Core and Buffer Zone Approach to Marine Protected Areas', in Agardy (1995: 47–52).

Wallace, S.S. 1999. 'Evaluating the Effects of Three Forms of Marine Reserve on Northern Abalone Populations in British Columbia, Canada', *Conservation Biology* 13: 882–7.

———, J.B. Marliave, and S.J.M. Martell. 1998. 'The Role of Marine Protected Areas in the Conservation of Rocky Reef Fishes in British Columbia: The Use of Lingcod (*Ophiodon elongatus*) as an Indicator', in N.W.P. Munro and J.H.M. Willison, eds, *Linking Protected Areas with Working Landscapes.* Proceedings of the Third International Conference on Science and Management of Protected Areas. Wolfville, NS, 206–13.

Watling, L., and E.A. Norse. 1998. 'Disturbance of the Seabed by Mobile Fishing Gear: A Comparison to Forest Clearcutting', *Conservation Biology* 12: 1180–97.

Zacharias, M., and D. Howes. 1998. 'An Analysis of Marine Protected Areas in British Columbia, Canada, Using a Marine Ecological Classification', *Natural Areas Journal* 18: 4–13.

———, ———, J.R. Harper, and P. Wainwright. 1998. 'The British Columbia Marine Ecosystem Classification: Rationale, Development and Verification', *Coastal Management* 26: 105–24.

Zurbrigg, E. 1996. *Towards an Environment Canada Strategy for Coastal and Marine Protected Areas.* Hull, Que.: Canadian Wildlife Service.

Web sites

DFO: <www.oceansconservation.com>

Parks Canada:
<http://parkscanada.pch.gc.ca/marine/.ca/nature/whp/nwa/coburg/df07s03.en.html>

Great Barrier Reef Marine Park Authority: <http://www.gbrmpa.gov.au>

Race Rocks.com <http://www.racerocks.com>

KEY WORDS/CONCEPTS

international agreements
fisheries management
UN Law of the Sea Convention
Exclusive Economic Zone (EEZ)
jurisdictional complexity
Department of Fisheries and
  Oceans Canada
Environment Canada
Parks Canada
Oceans Act (1994)
sustainable use
strict protection
stakeholders
multiple use areas
zoning system
ecosystem management
precautionary principle
adaptive management
integrated management
regional flexibility
National Wildlife Areas (NWA)

Protected Marine Areas (PMA)
Migratory Bird Sanctuary
Ecological Reserves Act
gap analysis
Land and Resources Management Plan
Tri-Council Statement of Commitment
bottom trawling
aquaculture
fish farms
speed of establishment
level of protection
stakeholder involvement
systems plan
permeability
connectivity
management experience
lack of information
monitoring
lack of funding (resources)
biosphere reserve

STUDY QUESTIONS

1. What values or benefits flow to humans from marine environments?
2. Provide reasons to account for the slow progress in creating marine parks.
3. Outline the major threats to the viability of marine protected areas.
4. Compare 'sustainable use' with 'strict protection'.
5. Compare the marine protection strategies for each of the following agencies: Parks Canada; Fisheries and Oceans Canada; and Environment Canada.
6. Comment on the failure of the proposed Bona Vista and Notre Dame Bay National Marine Conservation Area.
7. What is significant about each of the following marine protected areas: Sable Gully; Race Rocks; Nirjutiqawik?
8. Discuss the challenges of stakeholder involvement in MPA planning.
9. List major issues involved in the management of marine protected areas.
10. Why is the 'Baja to Berring' initiative so important?
11. Review the Parks Canada systems plan for marine protected areas. Identify any one natural area, and conduct research to determine what efforts have been made to establish an MPA. What obstacles have been encountered? What suggestions can you make?

CHAPTER 15

Stewardship: Expanding Ecosystem Protection

Jessica Dempsey, Philip Dearden, & J. Gordon Nelson

There is as yet no ethic dealing with man's relation to land and to the animals and plants which grow upon it . . . The land relation is still strictly economic, entailing privileges but not obligations. The extension of ethics to this third element in human environment is, if I read the evidence correctly, an evolutionary possibility and an ecological necessity . . . The land ethic simply enlarges the boundaries of the community to include soils, waters, plants, and animals, or collectively: the land.

Aldo Leopold, 1949

INTRODUCTION

Historically, Canadian protected areas have been located in the public domain, established and controlled by federal, provincial, and local governments. This approach has worked to secure large pieces of public land, like Banff and the Tatshenshini-Alsek Provincial Park, for conservation. However, in the last few decades, it has become obvious that governments are unable or unwilling to protect all desired or necessary areas with their limited resources. For example, Parks Canada has shouldered a 25 per cent budgetary reduction from 1994–5 levels (Parks Canada Agency, 2000: 13–2), with 14 terrestrial regions still requiring representation and an entire system of marine conservation areas yet to be established. In addition, as the Panel on the Ecological Integrity of Canada's National Parks (Parks Canada Agency, 2000) clearly indicated, many national parks are having difficulty maintaining ecosystems in established areas. Shifts in park theory, based largely on ecosystem science, as emphasized in Chapters 4, 5, and 12, have altered traditional preservation practices, which largely concentrated on activities inside park boundaries. In the 1960s to 1980s, areas outside the park were mapped as blank and generally ignored in the planning documents. New ecosystem-based theory clearly

FIGURE 15.1 Parks such as Waterton Lakes depend heavily on co-operation from surrounding landowners to sustain wildlife populations. *Photo: P Dearden.*

shows that isolated, 'island' parks in a sea of un-sustainable land use fail to protect ecosystems even within individual parks.

Expanding protected areas through land acquisition and reducing external impacts on established protected areas are important tasks for protecting ecological integrity. Thus, private or private-public approaches to conservation, often called stewardship, are becoming increasingly vital. This chapter defines what stewardship is and explores its emerging importance and dominance on the Canadian protected areas landscape. It discusses the 'why' of stewardship broadly and within the Canadian context. It surveys a 'steward's toolbox' to determine how it can be achieved, and looks at the major players involved in stewardship. Finally, the chapter examines the challenges and limitations of stewardship in the Canadian landscape.

STEWARDSHIP

Stewardship can be described as 'people taking care of the earth' (Brown and Mitchell, 1998: 8). This definition can encompass actions such as recycling, composting, or land donation to a trust. However, this chapter focuses on a narrower definition of stewardship—actions contributing directly to ecosystem protection—hence, as 'collective responsibility for common property, actions taken by private individuals to protect ecosystems. . . . The concept encompasses a range of private and public/ private approaches to create, nurture and enable responsibility in users and owners to manage and protect land and natural resources' (Brown and Mitchell, 1998: 8).

In practice, stewardship takes many forms. It includes landowners voluntarily restricting damaging land use, planting native species over exotic, placing protective covenants on their land. It includes community members contributing to wildlife monitoring programs, doing passive education for tourists and visitors, and participating in collective restoration. Stewardship is also park visitors voluntarily choosing not to hike a sensitive trail, or to participate in park host programs. Corporations can also practice stewardship through sustainable land practices that reduce damage to wildlife habitat.

From these examples, it is obvious that stewardship deviates from regulated protection as found in most park legislation. In many cases stewardship restricts or reduces destructive activities, while still maintaining a working landscape. In addition, stewardship should not be confused as an activity solely for private parties, as Brown and Mitchell (1998: 9) succinctly note, it also requires ' . . . government control, which provides a framework in the form of tax and other incentives, land-use planning and a supportive climate for private organizations'.

EMERGING IMPORTANCE OF STEWARDSHIP

Scope
Stewardship is claiming more space in the geography of protected areas. The Nature Conservancy of Canada (NCC) alone, one of many conservation organizations, has protected approximately 1.6 million ha since 1962 (Nature Conservancy Canada, Ont. Web site). In 1999, Ducks Unlimited Canada (DUC) secured almost 80 000 ha of wetland, and enhanced over 80 000 ha. In total, DUC is responsible for protecting over seven million ha of wetlands since 1938 (Ducks Unlimited Canada, Web site, 2001). For a benchmark, Parks Canada, established in 1885, is responsible for over 22 million ha. While this is not a direct comparison of conservation value (national parks offer stronger ecological protection, and there are many other stewardship organizations protecting land than DUC and NCC), it does demonstrate the significance of stewardship as a force for conservation.

Smaller, provincially based and local land trusts are also increasing in number. In the Southern Vancouver Island-Gulf Islands area, where natural heritage is fading quickly and land prices are increasing, there are at least eight land trusts operating to protect endangered spaces, most established in the last five years. Government agencies, such as Environment Canada, and various provincial ministries also are embracing stewardship. For example, numerous funding programs exist for community stewardship, and some ministries publish guides or Web sites (for example, Environment Canada's 'A Guide to Conservation Programs and Funding Sources for Agro-Manitoba'), which educate and support local initiatives. Legislative changes amenable to stewardship have also recently been passed, resulting in incentives and encouragement for ecological gifts and donations.

Rationale for Increase

Challenges facing protected areas in the 21st century demand new approaches to conservation. As Dudley et al. (1999: 4,5) write:

> . . . *in the future protected areas will have to be linked more effectively to sustainable development*. Protected areas—and the people responsible for protected areas— will have to be more flexible, more responsive and more adaptable than has some- times been the case in the past. Protected areas need to expand both physically and philosophically, and to connect with each other, the wider landscape and more generally with society and the economy (emphasis added).

Stewardship enables and advances many of these necessary shifts. It has emerged as a tool for sustainability by encouraging private landowners and public land leases to manage beyond harvest, for ecosystem protection. Working landscapes are often conserved, along with biodiversity 'bridging the perceived dichotomy of natural and cultural heritage' (Brown, 1998: 5). Private landowners and corporations become responsible for 'taking care of the land' while harvesting resources and

FIGURE 15.2 Creston Valley Wildlife Centre nestled between the Selkirk and the Purcell Mountains in southeastern British Columbia is a stewardship initiative with a substantial inter- pretive component. Although created originally with government funding, the Centre now relies extensively on private contributions to maintain this important wildlife area. *Photo: P. Dearden.*

BOX 15.1. Stewardship: Acting Quickly to Protect Rare Ecosystems

The Southern Vancouver Island and Gulf Islands region is currently subject to development on many fronts. When areas of significance or rare habitats become threatened, conservation organizations and environmental activists often campaign and protest for protection. Conservancies and land trusts are becoming involved with these campaigns with money and support to purchase all or part of the land. These organizations often succeed in bringing together the developer, the government, and conservation organizations/advocates to negotiate a deal and the purchase arrangements quickly and creatively.

A campaign by The Land Conservancy (TLC) entitled 'Save the Sooke Hills', aims to protect a 1375-ha (3400-acre) property in the Sooke Hills outside of Victoria, BC from subdivision and development. The land is crucial habitat for completing the 'Sea to Sea Green Blue Belt', a linking of existing parks and marine areas from Saltspring Island all the way to East Sooke Park. In addition, it is home to two salmon-bearing streams, and many of Vancouver Island's most threatened native plants and animals. In 1999, TLC began a campaign to raise the 5.3 million dollars needed to acquire the land. Advertisements and notices in the newspaper read 'You Can Make the Difference: Let's Buy This Together and Give it to our Grandchildren'. At present, TLC are very close to that goal. In the past, unless the government chose to purchase the property, the area would be divided and developed without option. However, TLC is able to garner public support and funds to act in a timely fashion, where governments are not. For more information on this project see: www. conservancy.bc.ca/Projects/CRD/SOOKEHILLS.htm.

---

maintaining livelihoods. Conservation thus 'connects with society and the economy', and also expands notions of 'protected areas' philosophically, beyond state-regulated entities (Dudley et al., 1999).

Since stewardship depends on local people/community support and desire, the commitment of even a few to its values fosters collective responsibility for the land. It: 'puts conservation in the hands of the people most affected by it' (Brown, 1998: 1). The spread of a Leopoldian 'land ethic' (Leopold, 1949) not only protects land previously subjected to destructive uses, but also garners support for state-driven protected areas and conservation activities. The funding, legislation, and fate of national parks and conservation initiatives is still largely political, and public will for their establishment and care is crucial. These comments bring to mind the UNESCO Biosphere Reserves Program, which was launched in the 1960s to provide for various kinds and levels of parks and protected areas as part of a framework for maintenance of 'harmonious' landscapes and monitoring, research, education, and sustainable use of the land.

Expanding protected areas physically and connecting them to one another and the rest of the landscape are also facilitated by stewardship. New 'bioregional' approaches (McGinnis, 1999) broaden thinking and planning from individual protected areas to surrounding lands and waters or greater park ecosystems. At higher or larger scales, these new approaches require planning for connected networks of government and private protected areas, in addition to regional or landscape conservation planning, management, and decision-making. This broader thinking and planning has been enabled not so much through governments as through public-private interaction and stewardship. 'The stewardship approach . . . offers a means of extending conservation practices beyond boundaries of conventional protected areas, to address needs on the "land between"' (Brown and Mitchell, 1998: 8). An outstanding example is the Yellowstone-to-Yukon corridor or bioregion led by the Canadian Parks and Wilderness Society (Locke, 1997) (Chapter 1).

The stewardship approach allows for increased flexibility, responsiveness, and adaptability. Where public protected areas require acquisition of funds that are often difficult to get, public consultations that take time, and intergovernmental negotiations that can take decades, conservation easements and stewardship approaches '. . . can often react more quickly, flexibly and cost efficiently than government agencies to land conservation opportunities' (Brown and Mitchell, 1998: 14). When sensitive ecosystems become available for acquisition or are under threat, private organizations can act and build support quickly (Box 15.1).

Canadian Context

In Canada, stewardship plays an important part in ecosystem conservation. In areas of high private ownership and landscape modification—for example, near urban areas—private or smaller conservation initiatives may actually be the only viable tools. For example, in Ontario, parks and protected areas are concentrated in the North, where population and settlement is low. In the south, it is more difficult to protect significantly large areas. In response, regional governments (Waterloo and Halton, for example) have created systems of small Environmentally Sensitive Policy Areas (ESPAs) to protect small sensitive and significant natural features. The Ontario government is also promoting the creation of Areas of Natural or Scientific Interest (ANSIs) on private land (Nelson, 1993). A similar situation exists in the Georgia Basin on the west coast of the country where less than 5 per cent of the Garry Oak range remains on the Saanich Peninsula of Vancouver Island and on the Gulf Islands, and where the loss of marsh habitat has been dramatic: 54 per cent in the Nanaimo Estuary, 53 per cent in the Cowichan Estuary, 93 per cent in Burrard Inlet. In the Fraser Estuary 82 per cent of the historic area of salt marsh habitat has been lost (Georgia Basin Ecosystem Initiative, Web site). The Georgia Basin Ecosystem Initiative jointly funded by Environment Canada and the BC provincial government is using a combination of public-private approaches to deal with this problem.

A considerable amount of critical endangered species habitat lies in private hands. Due to weaknesses in provincial endangered species legislation (where it exists), and to the current lack of federal legislation, stewardship is necessary to ensure habitat is maintained, and in some cases restored. To encourage private landowners to protect endangered species habitat, provincial governments are using a variety of techniques. In Alberta, Operation Burrowing Owl encourages rural landowners to voluntarily protect endangered owl nesting sites, protecting 26,371 ha of grassland habitat in Alberta (Dearden, 2000).

BOX 15.2. Southern Interior British Columbia Grasslands: One of Canada's Most Endangered Spaces

Grasslands make up a significant portion of native ecosystems in Canada. However, they constitute only 2.5 per cent of BC's native ecosystems, of which only 50 per cent is natural, making it the most significant ecological zone in BC. The southern interior and central interior grasslands are home to 55 endangered or threatened wildlife species, more than any other ecological zone (see CPAWS BC and Fast et al., 1996). Regardless of these problems, less than 1 per cent of the remaining natural grasslands are protected in BC. A gap analysis conducted by the BC Land Use Co-ordination Office (LUCO) shows that grasslands within the Central Interior and the Southern Interior Ecoprovinces are internationally significant, have major gaps in their representation, and urgently warrant protection (Fast et al., 1996). In addition, both the federal and provincial governments have identified the South Okanagan and Similikameen valleys as one of Canada's most endangered natural systems. The area is one of the remaining 14 regions requiring representation in Canada's national park system. Current threats to grasslands include urban development, livestock overgrazing, and cultivation of alien species.

There are many challenges hindering action on this issue. Much of the land in this area is locked up in private hands, or private ranching leases on public lands. Many conservation organizations are working on protecting more grasslands, co-ordinated through the Grasslands Conservation Council. Stewardship is playing an important role in progress. For example, The Nature Trust of BC runs the 'Ranch Lands Conservation Project' in the South Okanagan, which consists of land acquisition, co-operative management, and scientific monitoring in the area. The primarily goal of the 'Ranch Lands Conservation Project' is to increase biological diversity conservation in this endangered habitat, while at the same time, allowing the continuation of sustainable ranching on 'biodiversity ranches', currently declining as multi-generational family ranches are subdivided into suburban 'ranchettes' for a growing urban population.

The Land Conservancy (TLC) has similar goals for grasslands, and is acquiring critical grasslands like Harper's and Reynold's Ranches. Reynold's Ranch connects Churn Creek and Big Bar Badlands provincial parks, securing an important network of protected grasslands. TLC intends to continue operating the ranch as an example of how ranching can be a sustainable, environmentally compatible endeavour, protecting large continuous spaces and species. Maintaining working landscapes is an important part of the conservation strategy for the grasslands, demonstrating links between stewardship and sustainability.

Maintaining ecological integrity in current parks also requires the extension of stewardship to neighbouring and connecting lands. As the Panel for the Ecological Integrity of Canada's National Parks states: 'Achieving the goal of maintaining ecological integrity will require dedication, co-operation, learning, and agreement from all Canadians, politician to park manager, park visitor to park neighbour' (Parks Canada Agency, 2000: 1-2). Even large parks like Banff cannot survive on their own; they must be embedded in a greater park ecosystem that conserves connecting habi-

---

BOX 15.3 Georgian Bay Ecosystem Conservation Plan

The Georgian Bay Islands National Park (GBINP), established in 1929, encompasses only 2500 ha, and compromises 59 islands strung along the southeastern coast of Georgian Bay. In the 1997 State of the Parks Report, it reported major impairment to ecological integrity (Parks Canada, 1998). To reduce the undesirable impacts and effects of human activities around this highly fragmented park, an Ecosystem Conservation Plan (ECP) for the Greater Park Ecosystem (GPE) was prepared (Nelson and Skibicki, 1997).

The ECP is based on a map that identifies ecologically significant areas (nodes) and corridors within the region . The GBINP, Ontario Parks, the Ontario Ministry of Natural Resources, local governments, and private organizations are co-operatively implementing the ECP, which consists of a Core Area, a Near-Core Area, and an Area of Co-operation and Communication. These broad zones are similar to those advocated for UNESCO Biosphere Reserves, an arrangement that is now being considered for the region around Georgian Bay Islands National Park. Many of the protection strategies are stewardship-related. For example, recreation users (inside and outside park) are having significant impacts on the ecological integrity of the park. The plan recommends the development of educative materials and methods to inform users about significant species/habitats and their sensitivities to disturbances. In addition, to encourage local involvement and responsibility for ecosystem health, the ECP recommends a Greater Park Ecosystem Forum be created to engage the public.

Since the plan's conception, the local District of Muskoka is considering protecting the nodes and corridors around the national park by designating them as Environmentally Sensitive Areas (ESAs in its Official Plan, which will limit harmful development. Private trusts such as the Muskoka Lakes Heritage Foundation and Georgian Bay Trust Foundation are also acquiring appropriate lands around Georgian Bay Islands National Park. In the recent provincial Lands for Life planning program for northern Ontario, the National Park has been linked to nearby Massassauga Provincial Park and other public and private lands in the broad context of a plan for an eastern Georgian Bay Heritage Coast. The ECP seems to be encouraging the type of management and connectivity that the Panel for the Ecological Integrity of Canada's National Parks is suggesting (Parks Canada Agency, 2000).

tats and practices sustainable land management. Smaller parks rely on surrounding lands to an even greater extent (Box 15.3).

STEWARD'S TOOLBOX

Many tools and methods facilitate stewardship. 'Specific tools vary according to social, legal, ecological, and institutional constraints, but all operate to encourage, enable, or formalize responsible management' (Brown, 1998: 10). The following description draws largely from Brown and Mitchell (1997,1998), who provide an organized and concise description of tools and techniques for stewardship. Although the tools are separated below, they are often used in combination to build stronger and longer-term land conservation.

TABLE 15.1 Toolbox Summary

Cost	Attainability	Degree of Commitment/ Formality	Tool
↓ Increasing	↓ More Difficult	↓ More Formal	Education Recognition Verbal Agreement Creative Development Technical Assistance Management Incentives Management Agreement Easement Private Land Acquisition

SOURCE: After Brown and Mitchell (1997: 105).

Education

Often landowners, whether private, community, or corporate, are unaware of existing important or sensitive habitats on their property, and thus are unable to take precautionary measures to protect them. Education and communication of these features is one of the most powerful of stewardship tools. Education formats are limitless and can be attuned to the subject, area, and audience. For example, on the west coast a joint initiative by the provincial government and the federal government identified sensitive ecosystems for the southern Gulf Islands and Eastern Vancouver Island. Efforts have been made to educate people who participate in land-use and planning decisions (local government staff, councillors and committee members; conservation organization representatives; staff from federal and provincial agencies; First Nations) about these sensitive ecosystems and management needs. One-day workshops were organized, which included field trips to sensitive areas. Passive education methods, including informative pamphlets and Web sites, are also used to convey information.

Recognition

Education can be very effective in reaching landowners and changing land-use practices and a reward system can reinforce the education effort. Public recognition of out-standing work is one type of 'reward' for being a land steward. This can be done in different ways—from formal awards ceremonies to plaques or signs showing participation. For example, the Alberta Cattle Commission gives an 'Environmental Stewardship Award' to one Alberta cattle producer per year who demonstrates excellent livestock management and environmental practices on his/her land. The Habitat Steward Program in central Alberta provides landowners (of greater than 2 ha) who conserve habitat with a large sign proclaiming: 'This landowner conserves habitat for native plants and animals.' To date, 128 landowners have participated in the program, representing over 5600 ha (14,000 acres). Going this little step further encourages people to continue their stewardship practices and generates interest for others to join in.

Verbal Agreement

For those landowners unwilling to go to a written, legally binding agreement, but who still want to participate in 'taking care of the land', often a verbal agreement will be accepted. Although this technique depends on the goodwill of the landowner to carry-out the agreement, it can be highly effective in creating a sense of responsibility and sustained stewardship. For example, in the southern Ontario Carolinian zone, the Ontario Heritage Foundation has facilitated over 1,000 verbal agreements with private landowners who now conserve over 6,000 ha of rare and threatened ecosystems. Awards were also given to participating landowners to recognize their efforts (Ontario Heritage Foundation—Carolinian Canada Web site).

Technical Assistance

Often a landowner may wish to participate in stewardship restorative activities but lack the technical skills and equipment. Thus, a stewardship organization or the government might provide assistance for restoring habitat on the land, in exchange for a verbal agreement or perhaps even something more formal. For example, the Ontario Wetland Habitat Fund provides financial and technical assistance to landowners who undertake projects to improve the ecological integrity of wetland habitats on their property. Landowners must have a conservation plan with clear objectives for their property in order to be eligible to receive funding for up to 50 per cent of the project cost, to a maximum of $5,000. NGOs, like the Habitat Acquisition Trust Foundation in Southern Vancouver Island, also provide advice and assistance to citizens in the area about their stewardship options.

Creative and Eco-friendly Development

In many parts of Canada, development is one of the greatest risks to sensitive or rare ecosystems. Creative development encourages careful planning of site location and building design to maintain all or some habitat. For example, urban developers might choose to save important trees, by changing development plans and building layout.

'Smart Growth', urban development that restricts low-density suburban sprawl from expanding into important surrounding ecosystems, also protects habitat and is a form of stewardship practised by local governments and developers alike.

Management Incentives

Landowners who chose to become stewards by maintaining or changing land practices/management are sometimes eligible for financial incentives offered by a stewardship organization, or more likely, by the government. These might include incentives for keeping land forested or for changing sewage treatment practices to protect marine ecosystems. For example, in Ontario the Conservation Land Tax Incentive Program encourages and supports long-term stewardship on private lands by providing tax relief to those who participate (Dearden, 2000). Lands classified as 'conservation lands', which include the most environmentally important habitats, are completely exempt from property tax. Managed forests (with approved management plan) and farmlands are assessed at 25 per cent of residential property tax rates.

Management Agreement

While management incentives work for more passive land management, sometimes active management is required to maintain declining ecosystems. Management agreements are used when the landowner is willing to let another organization manage parts or all of their land actively for conservation purposes, while retaining ownership. This technique is being used heavily in Prince Edward Island where the provincial government has negotiated over 300 voluntary agreements allowing active wetland conservation (Brown and Mitchell, 1998). Incentives, rent payments, or formal leases (providing income to the landowner), might be added to this agreement to encourage and sustain stewardship over the long term. Management agreements are not binding on a new owner, but a lease or rental agreement is usually followed through for the entire contract (Coalition on the Niagara Escarpment, 1998).

Conservation Easement

While the above tools and techniques are subject to the goodwill of landowners and the renegotiation of agreements, verbal or written, a conservation easement is a far-reaching agreement between a landowner and an organization that restricts or limits certain land uses and management. These restrictions are built into the land deed in perpetuity, protecting the land indefinitely. Easements can take many forms, and can be made flexible to suit the landowners and the organizations needs and desires. For example, easements can apply to all or only a portion of the property, can set management restrictions in sensitive forest areas, or allow for trail access across private land.

In Canada, most provinces and territories have some kind of easement legislation, but exact names for this tool varies throughout Canada: in BC they are called conservation covenants and in Manitoba they are conservation agreements. Sometimes the provincial legislation includes modest incentives, like tax relief, to encourage landowners to participate and to ensure long-term land protection. Some organizations 'buy'

BOX 15.4. Coastal Island Acquisition

In the last decade, the west coast has been experiencing increasing conservation activity, especially through private land acquisition. One larger acquisition occurred in 1995, when Jedediah Island, a beautiful 258-ha (640-acre) piece of land was purchased through extensive private fund-raising activities, in addition to generous donations ($1.1 million) from the late Daniel Culver and the provincial government. Saving the island from impending development, Jedediah Island is now a Class A provincial park. For more information on the park, see <www.env.gov. bc.ca/bcparks/explore/parkpgs/jedediah.htm>.

While Jedediah became a provincial park, other island acquisitions come with strings attached. Kirkland and Rose Islands, located just off the Vancouver megalopolis, were purchased by the Nature Trust of BC in 1989 to protect sensitive bird habitat. The islands were sold to the Nature Trust at market value for about $3 million by a group of wealthy hunters. The hunters then donated $1.5 million back to the Nature Trust, with a provision that the group continue to have exclusive hunting rights on the islands from 1 September to 31 January each year. In addition, the hunters pay the property taxes, take out liability insurance, and finance management of the property for the benefit of waterfowl habitat, costs ranging into the tens of thousands each year. (Vancouver Sun 27 November 2000). As this example demonstrates, land acquisitions by private NGOs are flexible arrangements, catering to the needs of current owner as well as meeting some conservation goals.

easements, providing the landowner with some financial compensation. In most cases though, the easement is a voluntary donation. Conservation easements are becoming commonplace all over the country, in part due to changes in legislation and to the boom in land trust establishment as well to as to a growing ecological consciousness.

Private Land Acquisition

The strictest form of protection is complete land acquisition, where a conservation organization acquires all rights to the property by donation or purchase. This is a very costly stewardship technique due to land expense (see Box 15.1), and on-going land management costs. However, creative arrangements reduce some of these barriers. For example, a landowner might donate land to a conservation organization for a one-time tax receipt (an ecological gift), he or she might sell land at full price but then donate some back for management, or donate property as part of their will. Citizens may also donate funds to the conservation organization for land acquisition. Some land trusts work out mortgage agreements with lending institutions to spread payments over a longer term, or collaborate with government agencies to reduce management costs. For example, a piece of land might be owned by a land trust, but managed by the government. This way, land organizations can reduce their on-going costs, and free up resources for further land acquisition.

STEWARDSHIP PLAYERS

Although stewardship is often associated with private, individual actions 'caring for the land', there are many different actors who contribute to, and encourage stewardship. Non-governmental organizations (NGOs) are very active participants. National organizations like the Nature Conservancy and Ducks Unlimited play important roles, as do a plethora of local land trusts and conservation organizations. These private organizations acquire land and negotiate conservation easements (Brown and Mitchell, 1998), and act as monitors over these protected areas (see Box 15.5). Some organizations provide technical assistance to landowners who wish to improve wildlife habitat, or at least direct them to the people and resources. Other conservation organizations play an educative role, informing the public about endangered species and spaces. For example, the Canadian Nature Federation does not own land, but rather educates Canadians about important spaces and species, giving them the opportunity to volunteer on conservation projects and programs.

BOX 15.5 Case Study The Islands Nature Trust—Prince Edward Island

Who are they?

The Island Nature Trust is a not-for-profit organization dedicated to protection and management of natural heritage on Prince Edward Island. Incorporated in 1979, they were the first of many private, provincially-based nature trusts in Canada. Because Prince Edward Island is over 90 per cent privately owned, private landowners have a critical role to play in land conservation. The Islands Nature trust has an extensive private stewardship program.

Who runs it?

The trust is governed by a Board of Directors which includes:
- 12 members of the Trust; and
- one representative from each of our four founding organizations: PEI Museum & Heritage Foundation, PEI Wildlife Federation, Natural History Society of PEI, and the Biology Department of the University of PEI.
- They also employ staff to run programs, fund-raise, and carry out day-to-day tasks, as well as direct a large volunteer base to help on all fronts.

What do they do?

- Acquire lands for conservation purposes;
- Manage lands as an example of appropriate and sustained use;

- Help private owners voluntarily protect their lands;
- Work with government and private landowners to create a true natural areas network on Prince Edward Island, consisting of core protected areas connected by corridors;
- Employ staff and carry out any research that is deemed necessary in identifying and protecting representative and/or exceptional natural features, communities, and systems; and
- Educate the public to recognize the value of and the need for protecting habitat and wildlife.

Supporting Funds?

Currently on a year-to-year and project-by-project basis;

- Solicit funds annually from a variety of foundations, businesses, and corporations, as well as hosting several annual fund-raising events; and
- Have recently established an Endowment Fund in an effort to secure some longer-term funding. Once the Fund reaches a reasonable size, half of the annual interest income may be used to support ongoing conservation work.

Tangible Accomplishments?

- Own over 2,300 acres of forest, marsh, sand dune, offshore island, river frontage and pond.
- Have helped private landowners voluntarily protect over 2,000 acres of their own lands under legal agreements, and
- Have worked with the Government of Prince Edward Island to legally protect more than 10,000 acres of provincially-owned land.
- Run Conservation Guardians where over 40 volunteers monitor protected and other areas across the province.
- Piping Plover Protection: Throughout the April to August breeding and nesting season, Trust staff and volunteers visit nest sites to monitor this endangered species, encouraging visitors to stay away from critical areas.
  Information taken from: http://www.peisland.com/nature

In Canada, the public sector also contributes to the success of stewardship in a number of ways. By sponsoring education programs, governments disseminate important information about harmful activities and positive changes. For example, some government ministries sponsor stewardship Web sites that act as clearinghouses and one-stop information centres for interested citizens (see Alberta's at www.landstewardship.org). Through funding programs like EcoAction 2000, the federal government provides resources for community organizations to participate in environmental stewardship.

Legislative changes and incentive programs (as discussed above) also enable and encourage stewardship. At the federal level, changes to the income tax act in 1996 allowed NGOs and government agencies to issue tax receipts for donations of a covenant or full title of important habitat. Changes to the federal Income Tax Act and the Quebec Income Tax Act announced in their 2000 budgets reduced the income inclusion rate on capital gains arising from 'ecological gifts' (donations of ecologically sensitive lands and easements), from two-thirds to one-third. The federal government has estimated that this reduction will add $5 million to the annual cost of tax assistance for donations of ecologically sensitive land. To encourage the continued protection of these lands, lands taken out of protection are subject to a substantial tax penalty equal to 50 per cent of the value of the land at the time of disposition (as opposed to the time of acquisition). Information on these changes can be found at <www.cws-scf.ec.gc.ca/ecogifts/>.

However, regardless of these incentives, it is important to recognize that individuals, communities, and corporations are still the final arbiters of successful initiatives. The willingness of private landowners and individuals to 'care for the land' is the essence of stewardship. The responsibility does not only lie with those who own or directly manage habitat, because all citizens can act as stewards by participating in restoration activities, such as exotic plant pulls, or by donating money to conservation organizations, or by staying on the trail in an existing park. Although financial 'carrots' are important, much of the incentive for participation in these activities comes from personal satisfaction and a 'conviction of individual responsibility for the health of the land' (Leopold, 1949: 240).

BOX 15.6: What can I do?

There are many ways individuals can become stewards for the earth, for example by:

- Donating your time or money to a conservation organization (see Appendix for examples);
- Writing letters to the government advocating for protected areas on public and private lands;
- Planting native plant species in your backyard;
- Educating friends and family about their options for stewardship; and
- Protecting rare spaces on your own property.

However, most stewardship occurs when the players act together for conservation goals in partnerships. For example, Ontario Parks invests yearly in the Nature Conservancy, which they in turn invest in land acquisitions and protection. The Conservancy delivers many times the amount of protected areas with these funds than the government could have with the same amount (Parks Canada Agency, 2000:

BOX 15.7. Niagara Escarpment Biosphere Reserve

The Niagara Escarpment, a green corridor stretching 725 km long from Queenstown near Niagara Falls on the Niagara River up to the tip of the Bruce Peninsula, is an excellent example of partnership building and co-operation between government, conservation organizations, and private landowners (see Figure 15.3). A strong regulatory and policy framework guides and limits development in the area. In 1973, the Niagara Escarpment Planning and Development Act was passed, limiting inappropriate development in the area and in 1985, after significant public consultation, the government adopted the Niagara Escarpment Plan, which now guides development and management. In 1990, the area was declared a UNESCO Biosphere Reserve (see Ch 14).

Regardless of these important tools, private, voluntary actions also play a large part in fulfilling ecosystem integrity and health in the Escarpment. The Coalition on the Niagara Escarpment (CONE) published Protecting the Niagara Escarpment: A Citizen's Guide in 1998 to 'help people help' protect the escarpment. This guide gives background information on the area, and more importantly demonstrates how local landowners and citizens can get involved using the entire range of stewardship tools.

Even with declining government funds for protected areas, protected areas in the Escarpment area continue to grow with successful stewardship. Organizations like the Escarpment Biosphere Conservancy have acquired over 160 ha (400 acres) of rare or endangered landscapes (easements and purchase). CONE provides information to landowners so they can conserve biodiversity and increase property values. They continue to oppose inappropriate development that counters the Niagara Plan and the Biosphere Reserve designation. Given the pressures on the land— seven million people reside within 100 km of the Escarpment—conservation is still moving ahead. Private stewardship is playing a large role, aided tremendously by the strong legal, government-sponsored Niagara plan and legislation.

For more information: CONE Web site at www.interlog.com/~cone/; and the Escarpment Biosphere Conservancy www.escarpment.ca/

9–12). A recent initiative funded by Canada's Millennium Foundation, brings four conservation organizations together for 'Natural Legacy 2000', a nationwide initiative to conserve Canada's wildlife and habitats on private and public lands. In Victoria, BC the Land Conservancy (TLC) is close to acquiring significant amounts of Garry Oak, in part due to a landmark arrangement where the local municipality has agreed to advance TLC a three-year interest-free loan of almost $400,000 to acquire the property. On a smaller scale, a single conservation easement is usually the result of many different players co-operating: the individual who owns the land, the local land trust with the advice and expertise, the government providing the legislation and financial incentive, and science (government and research institutions) providing direction and inventory of critical habitat.

CHALLENGES AND LIMITATIONS OF STEWARDSHIP

Stewardship is playing a larger role in Canadian protected areas every year, and is helping sustain ecosystems within and outside of existing parks. However, it cannot replace continued investment in strong federal and provincial protected areas, which have powerful legislated mandates for ecological integrity. In addition, there is still a vital need for endangered species legislation to protect critical habitats on a systematic, networked basis.

Although Canada is making headway legally for stewardship incentives, there is still a need to improve the current legal framework (Brown and Mitchell, 1997), expand conservation easement legislation into those jurisdictions currently without it, and improve tax incentives for land donations and easements.

Lands restored or protected via stewardship are also subject to many of the same challenges facing national and provincial parks. As the Panel for the Ecological Integrity of Canada's National Parks clearly states, protecting ecological integrity is a difficult task, which needs active management. Like the national parks, private organizations may lack the science and training necessary to manage lands, or to gauge priorities for land acquisition. There is a need for partnerships between land conservation organizations and research institutions, as well as government agencies.

Partnerships and relationships between conservation organizations and government agencies are often combative, rather than co-operative. It is a real challenge to create a 'climate for productive, enduring partnerships among sectors' (Brown and Mitchell, 1997: 112) and to 'develop both the methods and the willingness to bring together different government and non-government groups to practice co-ordinated management in appropriately identified areas' (Nelson, 1993: 54). While this chapter has described several examples of good co-operation, there is still need to cultivate better relationships across boundaries among federal, provincial, and municipal bodies as well as non-governmental groups.

A disadvantage to a stewardship approach is that although conservation organizations are able to respond quickly to development pressures or opportunities (see Box 1), acting fast and quickly also can lead to downfalls—many resources are

BOX 15.8 Small Pieces of the Puzzle Fit into a Larger Picture

The North American Waterfowl Management Plan (NAWMP), an international conservation program involving Canada, the United States, and Mexico, was established in 1986 (Mexico signed on in 1994) to restore waterfowl populations to 1970 levels. Under the Plan, waterfowl population goals were established and the key habitats that would require restoration and protection to reach those goals were identified. Both government and NGOs carry out specific programming and implementation of the plan, through joint ventures, and private-public partnerships across the continent. Ducks Unlimited, a major player in private stewardship of wetlands is significantly involved in each habitat joint venture, working with community organizations and local land trusts in Canada to deliver habitat programs. The program has been very successful, and demonstrates how small-scale stewardship initiatives can fit into a continental-scale conservation program.

Box 15.9 Some Ingredients for Successful Stewardship

The recipe for successful stewardship is flexible, contextual, and contingent. Specific ingredients vary depending on the time and place. In general though, stewardship requires increased business or political acumen in addition to traditional ecological, science-based knowledge. The following list summarizes some of the more important aspects involved in organizing for stewardship. The stewardship organization must be able to:
- Acquire and maintain local support for the organization and its actions. This means both in-kind (volunteer), land donations, and monetary support.
- Maintain relatively stable staff and core funding to organize long-term campaigns, to make mortgage payments, and demonstrate accountability. A strong board of directors and advisory group is also important.
- Make deals and partnerships with other organizations, private landowners and donors, and the government (from federal to local).
- Strategically position themselves politically to create and seize new stewardship opportunities. The staff of the organization is crucial in this regard.
- Remain flexible and creative to achieve goals.
- Utilize the media and communications to promote their organization.
- Access research and science to prioritize land acquisitions and guide management.
- Enforce conservation on protected lands for perpetuity.

required to generate support, and the area may not fit into an overall plan that protects biodiversity. As Brown (1998: 6) notes, 'There is an essential tension between responding to opportunities that arise and taking a strategic approach', and thus a real need to 'strike a balance between opportunism and strategy'. Conservation, government, and community sectors must work together to create a unified strategy for protecting landscapes based on ecosystem science. Co-ordinating various stakeholders for a unified protected area strategy is a challenge, but there are signs that this is happening more often and on larger or broader scales (see Box 15.8). For example, acquisition of the Sooke Hills by TLC (Box 15.1) would help complete the large-scale regional Sea to Sea Green Blue Belt protected areas strategy.

CONCLUSION

Notions of 'protected areas' in Canada are expanding from predominately top-down, centralized, and government-lead approaches to more wide-ranging efforts by governments, NGOs, corporations, and individuals at the local, regional, provincial, national, and international levels. National parks and other agencies, both private and public, are paying much more attention to the development of conservation strategies and networks, building frameworks for improved ecosystem protection and human well-being. Success from these efforts requires a mix of top-down and bottom-up approaches, specialized tools and techniques, and co-operation across traditional boundaries. Stewardship is quickly proving to be an important part of this emerging protected areas paradigm because it is flexible, responsive, partnership-based, and cultivates conservation values outside park boundaries and within society at large. By itself, stewardship provides inadequate ecosystem protection. However, united with other approaches, and in the context of an overall protected areas plan, it complements and enhances Canadian conservation efforts, helping to maintain protected area values in the landscape.

ACKNOWLEDGEMENTS

J.G. Nelson would like to thank Parks Canada and Ontario Parks for their continued support of parks and protected areas research. All authors would like to thank the Social Sciences and Humanities Research Council (SSHRC) for funding protected areas research upon which this paper draws.

REFERENCES

Brown, J.L. 1998. 'Stewardship: An International Perspective', *Environments* 26, 1: 1–7.

――― and B. Mitchell. 1997. 'Extending the Reach of National Parks and Protected Areas: Local Stewardship Initiatives', in Nelson and Serafin, (1997: 103–16).

――― and ―――. 1998. 'Stewardship: A Working Definition', *Environments* 26, 1: 8–17.

Coalition on the Niagara Escarpment. 1998. *Protecting the Niagara Escarpment: A Citizen's Guide.* Coalition on the Niagara Escarpment, Ontario.

CPAWS BC. Grasslands Homepage: <mypage.direct.ca/c/cpawsbc/grasslands.html>. Accessed 11 Jan. 2001.

Ducks Unlimited Canada. Facts: <www.ducks.ca/aboutdu/facts.html>. Accessed 11 Jan. 2000.

Dearden, P. 2000. 'Endangered Species and Terrestrial Protected Areas', in R. Boardman and K. Beazley, eds, *Politics of the Wild: Canada and Endangered Species.* Toronto: Oxford University Press, 75–93.

Dudley, N., et al. 1999. 'Challenges for Protected Areas in the 21st Century', in S. Stolton and Dudley, eds, *Partnerships for Protection: New Strategies for Planning and Management for Protected Areas.* London: Earthscan, 3–12.

Fast, A., S. Jessen, and D. Lloyd. 1996. 'B.C.'s Precious Grasslands Facing Extinction', *BC Environmental Report* 7, 3: 10–11. Available at: <www.bcen.bc.ca/bcerart/Vol7/bcspreci.htm>.

Georgia Basin Ecosystem Initiative. Habitat and Species Page. <http://www.pyr.ec.gc.ca/GeorgiaBasin/ehabitat.htm>. Accessed 11 Jan. 2001.

Leopold, A. 1949. *Sand County Almanac.* New York: Oxford University Press.

Locke, H. 1997. 'The Role of Banff National Park as a Protected Area in the Yellowstone to Yukon Mountain Corridor of Western North America', in Nelson and Serafin (1997: 117–24).

McGinnis, M.V., ed. 1999. *Bioregionalism.* New York: Routledge.

Parks Canada. 1998. *State of the Parks 1997 Report.* Catalogue no. R64-184/1997E. Ottawa: Canadian Government Publishing Centre.

Nature Conservancy Canada. <www.natureconservancy.ca>. Accessed 11 Jan. 2001.

Nelson, J.G. 1993. 'Beyond Parks and Protected Areas', in P. Dearden and R. Rollins, eds, *Parks and Protected Areas in Canada: Planning and Management.* Toronto: Oxford University Press, 45–56.

――― and A.J. Skibicki. 1997. *Georgian Bay Islands National Park Ecosystem Conservation Plan: Planning for Nature Conservation in the Georgian Bay Islands National Park Region.* Heritage Resources Centre, University of Waterloo with Parks Canada, Department of Canadian Heritage. Waterloo, Ont.

――― and R. Serafin, eds. 1997. *National Parks and Protected Areas.* New York: Springer.

Ontario Heritage Foundation—Carolinian Canada. <www.heritagefdn.on.ca/Heritage/natu-ral-carolinian.htm>. Accessed 11 Jan. 2001.

Parks Canada Agency. 2000. *Unimpaired for Future Generations? Protecting Ecological Integrity with Canada's National Parks*, vol. 2, *Setting a New Direction for Canada's National Parks.* Report of the Panel on the Ecological Integrity of Canada's National Parks. Ottawa.

Vancouver Sun. 2000. 'Hunters stalk waterfowl preserve: Four islands off Ladner are the play-ground of an exclusive club of affluent wildfowlers', 27 Nov.

Further Web sites:

Alberta Land Stewardship: <www.landstewardship.org>.

Canadian Nature Federation: <www.cnf.ca/>.

Ducks Unlimited Canada: <www.ducks.ca>.

Environment Canada's EcoAction 2000: <www.ec.gc.ca/ecoaction/index_e.htm>.

Environment Canada's 'A Guide to Conservation Programs and Funding Sources for Agro-Manitoba': <www.mb.ec.gc.ca/nature/whp/lsd/df08s00.en.html>.

Escarpment Biosphere Reserve Foundation: <www.escarpment.ca/>.

Georgian Bay Trust Foundation: <www.gblt.org/>.

Habitat Acquisition Trust Foundation (BC): <www.hat.bc.ca>.

The Land Conservancy of BC: <www.conservancy.bc.ca>.

Muskoka Lakes Heritage Foundation: <www.muskoka.com/jack/muskheritage.html>.

Natural Legacy 2000: <www.naturallegacy2000.com/>.

Nature Trust of BC: <www.mybc.com/groups-naturetrust>.

Ontario Heritage Foundation—Carolinian Canada: <www.heritagefdn.on.ca/Heritage/natural-carolinian.htm>.

Ontario Nature Trust Alliance: <www.ontarionature.org/enviroandcons/onta.html>.

The Ontario Wetland Habitat Fund: <www.wetlandfund.com/>.

Sensitive Ecosystems Inventory—Vancouver Island and Southern Gulf Islands: <www.pyr.ec.gc.ca/wildlife/sei>.

Smart Growth: <www.smartgrowth.bc.ca/; www.smartgrowth.org>.

KEY WORDS/CONCEPTS

stewardship
Nature Conservancy of Canada
Ducks Unlimited
bioregional
Sea to Sea Green Blue Belt
education
recognition
verbal agreement
creative development
technical assistance
management incentive
management agreement
easement
private land acquisition
non-governmental organization (NGO)
Canadian Nature Federation

STUDY QUESTIONS

1. Why is stewardship needed in Canada?
2. List some examples of stewardship.
3. How does stewardship differ from the management of parks and protected areas?
4. What can government do to promote stewardship?
5. What can individuals do to promote stewardship?
6. Select any NGO, and research the recent activities of the organization? Discuss the extent to which these activities compliment the role of existing parks and protected areas.

PART VI

Conclusion

The idea of wilderness needs no defense.
It only needs more defenders.

Edward Abbey, *The Journey Home*

The final section comprises just one chapter as we attempt to bring together some of the key challenges for the future. Much has been achieved in the past 10 years, through the creation of new protected areas, and the development of new management approaches, but it is evident that much remains to be done. Some of the issues that come to mind include the completion of systems plans for park designation, improvement of visitor management in some parks, the resolution of issues around existing town sites in parks, the implementation of ecosystem approaches to management, and the development of marine protected areas. All this needs to proceed in a time of declining public resources for parks. These issues and challenges are summarized in Chapter 16.

CHAPTER 16

Challenges for the Future

Rick Rollins & Philip Dearden

Canadians value nature, and attach special importance to parks and protected areas—places where nature is least altered by human structures or activity. Public opinion polls, measuring the sentiments of Canadians, attest to this fact. Such feelings have been expressed poignantly in the reflections of such prominent Canadians as Pierre Elliot Trudeau, who wrote in his memoirs (1993: 253) 'I think a lot of people want to go back to the basics sometimes, to find their bearings. For me a good way to do that is to get into nature by canoe—to take myself as far away as possible from everyday life, from its complications and from the artificial wants created by civilization'. Other Canadian leaders in politics, literature, arts, and entertainment have spoken of their attachment to nature: Emily Carr, the Group of Seven, Robert Service, Neil Young, Robert Bateman, and Jean Chrétien, to name a few.

Of interest to us has been how this valuing of nature has been translated into the idea of parks and protected areas. Banff, our first national park, was created largely as a tourist attraction, to help finance the cost of building the Canadian Pacific Railway in the late 1800s. In those days, undeveloped natural areas were not in short supply. National parks were seen as part of a national economic policy to develop Western Canada through farming, ranching, and tourism.

Of course this view of the role of parks has changed over the years. During the twentieth century we became aware of the tremendous changes in the natural landscape wrought by human activity throughout the world. In Canada, parks were no longer viewed just as tourist attractions, but as 'cathedrals' or 'benchmarks', as described in Chapter 1. We emphasized that parks were special places where nature would be allowed to run her course, where humans would not interfere with natural forces, where visitors would have to accept limitations on the types of activities and the types of facilities or services found in parks. In many famous parks in the US, such as the Grand Canyon, Yellowstone, and Yosemite, this philosophy has led to the reduction of public facilities in those parks. In Canada, this has occurred in Point Pelee, and 'growth' has been limited in Banff, and elsewhere.

At one time, park managers were charged with a 'dual mandate' to protect parks and to provide appropriate visitor experiences. In practice, it was often very difficult for park managers to manage these dual purposes. To allow for high levels of protection often resulted in opposition from visitors or from the tourist industry. To manage for greater use and enjoyment led to concerns from the environmental community. The concept of ecological integrity emerged as a way of providing a clear direction to park mangers that the protection of natural values would be the first priority in national parks; visitor services and tourism would be the second priority. The adoption of ecological integrity represents a major shift in the way national parks are to be managed in Canada. Many provincial park agencies are adopting this perspective as well. Yet we remain concerned about the ability of individual park managers to carry out their obligation to support ecological integrity.

In 1989 the Endangered Spaces campaign was launched in an effort to apply public pressure to politicians and bureaucrats and complete a system of parks that would adequately represent the diversity of ecosystems and life forms that characterize the Canadian landscape—and to do this by the year 2000. It was estimated that this would require at least 12 per cent of Canada to be set aside, as suggested by international practice, but the 12 per cent figure was not to be a ceiling for protected area establishment. However, as evident in the analysis presented in Chapter 4, this goal has not been achieved in most jurisdictions. Although great progress has been made, more remains to be done. One of the most significant challenges for the future will be to complete this national system of protected areas before opportunity to do so no longer exists.

The 12 per cent target was derived from estimates provided by the IUCN as a minimum but achievable goal. It needs to be stressed that 12 per cent is a low estimate, contingent upon factors such as park size, the location of park boundaries, the connectivity between parks, and the nature of land use in adjacent territories, as outlined in Chapter 5. These factors present a host of concerns for future park managers. Although the number of parks in Canada has increased, and the number of natural regions protected has been increased, the size, boundaries, and isolation of most parks have created a challenge for managers to maintain viable populations of many species. Wide-ranging species such as wolves, coyotes, caribou, and grizzly bears drift in and out of park boundaries. It is apparent that even in the largest parks, a true conservation strategy will require attention that extends beyond park boundaries.

The emergence of ecosystem management, as discussed in Chapter 12, addresses the notion that parks, no matter how large, are influenced by human activity beyond park boundaries. This dramatically impacts the work of park employees whose purview ended at park boundaries. Park managers are now challenged to work with jurisdictions, individuals, and communities surrounding park boundaries—a task for which most park managers lack training and experience.

One aspect of this connection between parks and outside communities is the opportunity to work with First Nations groups, many of whom have traditional territories or existing land claims within park lands. The collaboration between First Nations and park agencies has been critical in the establishment of many new parks, such as Gwaii Haanas in the Queen Charlotte Islands (Chapter 3, Chapter 13). The opportunities for developing co-management agreements, and other management initiatives, are significant, yet may prove challenging to put into practice. Types of concerns include the controversy over hunting by First Nations groups in Algonquin and other parks, the establishment of a burger stand on the West Coast Trail by the Nu-Chah-Nuulth band, or even the stance taken by several First Nations groups against park establishment in some areas.

Though the number of parks has increased, funding for parks has decreased dramatically. Parks are under-resourced, and park managers are stressed and often demoralized by the inability to attend properly to their stewardship responsibilities. Since park agencies are unlikely to experience adequate government funding in the near future, alternative revenue sources will need to be examined, including foundations, user fees, and the like. This resourcing issue will have a profound effect on park management in the future. Some parks may need to be closed entirely to visitors for a period of time. Some parks may become inaccessible to some visitors as new fees are introduced, such as the $110 fee now in place on the West Coast Trail. If corporate sponsors are recruited will parks be forced to accept the type of branding now used in sport arenas in Canada—will there be a G.M. National Park?

Determining appropriate visitor use in parks remains a substantial issue, even after 30 years of soul-searching around this issue. For example, BC Parks has made a commitment in policy to ecological integrity, yet allows hunting in many parks. Most park agencies have moved to a policy of non-motorized travel within parks, yet this has not entirely resolved use issues. Conflicts between use types remain, such as backpackers versus horseback riders, or canoeists versus anglers. Other concerns relate to the impact of visitor use on park resources. For example, in Jasper National Park, river rafting has been strongly curtailed to protect waterfowl. In the recent past new recreational activities such as mountain biking, windsurfing, and hangliding have been introduced in some parks. The impacts of these and new activities will need to be monitored and assessed.

One aspect of park use that has received considerable attention in recent years is ecotourism, described in Chapter 8 as a form of nature tourism activity that respects the integrity of local ecosystems and local cultures while contributing to the economic viability of sustaining protected areas. At first blush, ecotourism appears ideally positioned to contribute in a positive way to the management of parks and protected areas. Proponents have argued that ecotourism will result in a new ethical approach to nature-based tourism. Well-informed ecotourism guides can do much to provide appropriate low-impact visitor experiences, perhaps managing visitors more effectively than possible with existing approaches. However, critics have suggested that ecotourism is merely a more sophisticated commercial exploitation of natural places. For example, some critics are concerned that ecotourism companies, once established within a park, over time will begin to assert demands on park managers for greater access or the development of new facilities to make their operations more profitable. Ecotourism offers much promise but will need to be watched carefully in the future.

Marine parks, as described in Chapter 14, remain obscure in the Canadian context. Bill C-8 was lost with the dissolution of Parliament in the fall of 2000, dealing a severe blow to any momentum in this area. In the first edition of this book, published in

1993, we identified Marine Parks as a significant need considering the tremendous amount of marine biodiversity, virtually none of which is protected in Canada. Marine areas are significant recreational venues for activities such as sailing, scuba diving, sport fishing, and kayaking. Commercial fishing and other industrial activities also depend on the marine environment. Obviously many issues remain to be resolved in the marine parks context. How can marine biodiversity be protected when marine life freely moves in and out of protected areas? How can marine parks be protected from industrial use from adjacent water and lands? What kinds of recreational use are appropriate; what conflicts might occur? For example, conflicts occur in Gwaii Haanas between motorboaters and kayakers. What guidelines will be developed for new types of activities, such as whale-watching?

Parks are important to Canadians, so it is somewhat paradoxical that Canadians are generally unaware of the many threats to our parks. Very few parks have retained the same level of biodiversity as when they were first protected. Some spectacular species such as woodland caribou, lynx, martin, wolves, and grizzly have all but disappeared from some parks, but Canadians just don't seem to notice. Apparently, the occasional visits we make to our parks from time to time are not sufficient for most people to become aware of the changes that are taking place. Managers, on the other hand, have been charged with the responsibility of monitoring change, and reporting when danger signs begin to emerge. Monitoring indicators of ecological health, as well as indicators of public use and enjoyment, are at the heart of ecosystem management, Limits of Acceptable Change, and other management frameworks discussed in this book. However, we are concerned that parks may lack the scientific infrastructure or financial resources to carry out this monitoring in a rigorous and systematic fashion. Without adequate monitoring, management actions are not defensible, and we will have made little progress in protecting the values we cherish in our parks.

It is unlikely that the progress described over the past 10 years would have occurred without the sustained public pressure engineered by a variety of environmental groups, including: Canadian Parks and Wilderness Society; Sierra Club; Sierra Legal Defence Fund; World Wildlife Fund Canada; Canadian Nature Federation; and, the Western Canada Wilderness Committee. Other grass roots organizations, such as the Friends of Clayoquot Sound, have been extremely effective advocates for protected areas. While the academic community has provided much of the theory and research needed to support the creation and management of parks and protected areas, the implementation has required public support, usually mustered by environmental activists. Ongoing public support for the environmental groups involved with the protection of wild spaces will be essential over the next decade to ensure continued political commitment.

Since 1990, we have seen much progress in Canada and in other countries regarding a number of environmental issues, yet huge concerns remain around, for example, the loss of old-growth forests, the collapse of the east coast cod industry, the collapse of the west coast salmon industry, controversies surrounding fish farming, and the hunting of grizzly bears. On a global scale, species extinctions continue, global warming is a reality, ozone depletion continues, and attempts to improve air quality through international negotiations such as the Kyoto Summit have not translated into significant actions internationally.

These global-scale changes and the ensuing ecological dislocations that occur will be a challenge to protected area managers all over the world. Parks and protected areas play a role in addressing these major environmental issues, but it is apparent that stewardship outside of parks is equally significant (Chapter 15).

The issues voiced above, however, should not be allowed to obscure the positive changes that have occurred in the protected area system in Canada in the last decade of the millennium, as summarized in Chapter 1. The last 10 years have set a platform of legislative, policy, and institutional change that should provide a sound basis for facing the challenges of the future. Nor is Canada alone in these concerns. The US National Parks Service after years of chronic under-funding has been pledged a further $5 billion over the next five years to renew its infrastructure. And, borrowing a leaf from Parks Canada's book, the system will now be subject to a state of the parks report, that (in the US) will be required on an annual basis.

The need for additional funding is also paramount in Canada. However, other resources also remain critical. Among the most important will be knowledge. We will need new knowledge to understand the social and ecological systems of our parks and surrounding areas. We will need to use this knowledge effectively in management decision-making. And we will need to pass on this knowledge to create an informed and supportive public. Knowledge is also the essence of our university, college, and school systems, and one of the greatest challenges over the next decade will be building synergistic relationships between the parks and these educational systems.

REFERENCE

Trudeau, P.E. 1993. *Memoirs*. Toronto: McClelland & Stewart.

KEY WORDS/CONCEPTS

public opinion polls
national economic policy
park values
dual mandate
ecological integrity
Endangered Spaces Campaign
12 per cent protected area target
viable populations
wide-ranging species

ecosystem management
First Nations
resourcing (funding) for parks
appropriate visitor use
recreation conflict
ecotourism
marine parks
stewardship
limits of acceptable change

STUDY QUESTIONS

1. Interview a park manager, to solicit her/his views regarding ecological integrity and ecosystem management. Ask for concrete examples of how these concepts are being implemented. Do these measures seem adequate?

2. Examine the protected area systems plan for the province in which you live. Conduct research to determine how complete/ incomplete the systems plan appears to be. Conduct interviews with park officials to determine what impediments exist. Discuss possible solutions.

3. Interview a representative from any environmental organization, such as the Canadian Parks and Wilderness Society, or the World Wildlife Fund Canada. Discuss what are the outstanding current issues in parks in your region and elsewhere. Discuss what actions or strategies might be effective in resolving some of these issues.

4. Look for recent articles about park issues appearing in newspapers, magazines, television, or radio. Outline the issue presented in the article, and prepare a response to the issue, drawing upon specific concepts found in this text.

Index